Cooper's Leather-Stocking Novels

Strange order of things! Oh, Nature where art thou?

– J. Hector St. John de Crèvecoeur

Cooper's Leather-Stocking

Novels * A Secular Reading

* by Geoffrey Rans

The University of North Carolina Press * Chapel Hill and London

© 1991 The University of North Carolina Press

All rights reserved

Manufactured in the United States of America

95 94 93 92 91   5 4 3 2 1

Library of Congress Cataloging-in-Publication Data
Rans, Geoffrey.
  Cooper's Leather-stocking novels : a secular reading / by
Geoffrey Rans.
      p.   cm.
  Includes bibliographical references and index.
  ISBN 0-8078-1975-1 (alk. paper)
  1. Cooper, James Fenimore, 1789–1851.   Leatherstocking
tales.   2. Historical fiction, American—History and
criticism.   3. Frontier and pioneer life in literature.   I. Title.
PS1438.R3   1991
813'.2—dc20   91-10607
                    CIP

To the life and work of James Franklin Beard

CONTENTS

*A person looks at my Emanuel and says, Hey! he's not altogether from
the white race, what's going on? I'll tell you what: life is going on. You
have an opinion. I have an opinion. Life don't have no opinion.*
– *Grace Paley, "Zagrowsky Tells," in* Later the Same Day

In American literary history Cooper's place is secure. Few have denied,
from his own day to ours, that he was America's first novelist of importance or, whatever reservations critics have had about the prodigious
volume of his oeuvre over the thirty years of his artistic life, that his
reputation rests upon the achievement of the Leather-Stocking novels. It is
a commonplace to speak of the series' enduring appeal and the hold it has
retained on the American imagination. Certainly, the stories Cooper told
about Natty Bumppo have had an extended afterlife in our century's
popular media: movies, television series, and comic books. Influential
critics affirm their significance, and constant allusion suggests a widely
shared familiarity. They certainly must form part of our cultural literacy;
they are always in print and are always, at least singly, prescribed. And
yet, for all the testifying, it is difficult to escape the feeling that Cooper is
not really well known, that—despite a substantial body of responsive and
careful criticism, a cadre of scholars and critics who have dedicated a
lifetime to the study of his work, and James Franklin Beard's masterful
edition of Cooper's *Letters* and his ongoing scholarly edition of Cooper's
works—he is not yet thoroughly *read*, and that, except in the most general
commonplaces, it is not easy in literary terms to persuade students of
Cooper's claim to their attention. One recent critic who has written
brilliantly of *The Last of the Mohicans* confesses to not having read it until
it became necessary to teach it; another, whose book on the New England

Renaissance has been deservedly acclaimed, uses the Modern Library condensation of Cooper's five novels, *The Leather-Stocking Saga*. An American colleague in his middle years, of high qualifications in romantic literature, had to ask me which Leather-Stocking novel he should read first. Those who know Cooper are familiar with the glazed look of incomprehension, ignorance, or disbelief that greets the introduction of his name and that I detected when I declared six years ago that I intended to write this book, and that it would fill a gap, for there was then no single critical work devoted to this indispensable masterpiece. Since then we have had *Plotting America's Past* by William Kelly, whose critical procedures and agenda are, as my notes indicate, quite different from mine. It remains puzzling to me that mine is only the second book on these novels.

Cooper was often attacked viciously during his own lifetime, not always, as Dorothy Waples's still-interesting book demonstrates, from disinterested motives; Twain's celebrated assault on Cooper's literary offenses has left its mark and continues to validate the condescending smile. Although Cooper has had in this century far more supporters than detractors, often even his strongest advocates have been on the defensive, maintaining his seriousness in spite of artistic shortcomings. Those who have made powerful claims for his artistic merit have occasionally seemed strained, as if they were making a special plea. Also, despite the high quality of the work of many of Cooper's critics, especially over the last thirty-five years, it hardly seems that the large claims for his canonical significance have been valorized by a confident body of criticism, as have the claims for, say, Melville, Hawthorne, James, and Faulkner. Recently, this picture has shown signs of changing with the work of Tompkins, Fisher, Motley, and Wallace, among others, partly in response to new attitudes toward criticism that value aesthetic criteria less exclusively than did their predecessors, or, rather, value history more and are willing to allow artistic interest to inhere in texts that fail the strictest tests of completeness or even to find merit in the absence of completeness.

To a generation (still thriving) nourished in a critical tradition that valued textural complexity, irony, implication, and—at all costs—unity of artistic effect and structure, Cooper did not offer the instant gratification and challenge offered by Melville, Hawthorne, James, and Faulkner. Such a generation was disarmed and even embarrassed by Cooper's apparent structural shambles, his failure to resolve (a frequently recurring phrase), his seemingly awkward use of well-established fictional forms.

Taught to think that economy and authorial reticence were necessary components of fiction worthy of critical acclaim, they felt comfortable in dismissing Cooper's more expressly didactic fictions but uneasy in accommodating the Leather-Stocking novels. Neither allegory nor the historical romance enjoyed high favor, and certainly Cooper's didactic authorial interventions seemed to them a sign of weakness. The intellectual and historical conflicts and contradictions that absorbed Cooper were often seen as *artistic* flaws. Certainly, the Leather-Stocking novels, which so transparently display these features, discomfited the sophistication of the most respected critical techniques. Some critics there were—more resourceful perhaps—who used a strategy of critical overflight and drew attention to Cooper's capacity to heal the discursive rifts that continually open up in his text by a romance reconciliation,[1] as in *The Pioneers*, or by the embodiment of America's history in tragic—or comic—mythic narratives of epic dimension as in *Mohicans* or *The Prairie*. We need neither deny that Cooper's work has such a dimension nor affirm that such an approach is invariably reductive (no serious reader of Slotkin could think that he skirts complexity or fails to understand the evident dangers of a mythical approach); in that context, *The Deerslayer* is an imposing achievement, combining as it does elements of *Bildungsroman*, epic, and an allegory which is fully achieved and canceled in the same moment. Such positions, as Slotkin concedes in his most recent volume, are fully secure only if—as has too often been the case—we allow their disregard of what is only too apparent at the ground level of the texts: that they leave untouched what was before unresolved; they only transcend.

When Vernon Parrington in 1927 drew attention to the complexity and difficulty of Cooper, he was clearly not intending an aesthetic judgment.[2] We should not be too anxious to excuse Cooper's structural transgressions—if they preoccupy us—by ascribing them to a highly conflicted view of a highly conflicted history from a standpoint in Cooper's highly conflicted present. Nor should we wish to strip Cooper of his greatest fictional gift by resituating these conflicts in his personality rather than finding them in the very life of his novels. History is not structurally sound, however much thematics or narrative may be deployed to make it seem so; to invite closure is to invite misrepresentations. If there is a personality issue for readers of Cooper it is to understand how profoundly that invitation would offend so honest and frank a man. His instincts were, I believe, always toward realism, however romantic the surface might appear. Even the ultimate "failure," as McWilliams finds it, of *The Crater* and *The Redskins*, the novels most clearly determined by Cooper's own political views, must be ascribed to honesty before the facts.

The range of Cooper criticism, which I treat more fully in chapter 1, is wide and varied. His work has been subjected to examination by critics of most persuasions: new critical formalistic, generic, psychological, biographical, symbolic, historical, phenomenological. Some pay special attention in full-length studies to Cooper's attitudes toward landscape and pictorialism and to his sea fiction, while others examine Cooper in the context of larger cultural and historical considerations: the frontier, the American Adam, or, more recently, the American Abraham. This range itself testifies to the intrinsic interest of the author. To most critics, if not all, Cooper is unavoidable.[3] However, there can hardly be any question that the reigning tendencies in the last sixty years have been first the sociopolitical and then the mythological. Although the two strains might seem at odds, this is not always so: while McWilliams is clearly the most accomplished of those who lay emphasis on Cooper's political beliefs— bringing the issues opened by Parrington, Spiller, Waples, and Ross to a new level of sophistication—he clearly is very responsive to aesthetic considerations, as he is to the operation of myth. Indeed, I—and others— would see McWilliams as most deeply concerned with political myths. Slotkin, the most convincing of all the myth-oriented critics, is also among the most sensitive of Cooper's commentators to political and historical dimensions. And it is useful to the student that this is so, for if the American imagination has always been willing to inflate the balloon of myth, political or otherwise, it has always been ready to puncture it as well: in the most distinctively American works both elements are present at the same time. In this, the Leather-Stocking series is kissing cousin to Faulkner's Yoknapatawpha novels, Natty kin to Ike McCaslin: in both, mythic constructions are submitted to the censure of historical reality. But, rather than to affirm either position or both, my aim is to suggest that such irreconcilable conflicts impose on the writer another imperative different from resolution, and that Cooper recognized it. Without sacrificing continuity or ignoring generic models, he nonetheless declines the preemption of the reader that closure effects. Specific intention aside, it seems clear to me that he constantly frustrates simple programs of solution and coerces the attentive reader into judgment—and possibly conclusions beyond the control of his own well-understood desires.

The wide array of critical directions that have been followed in the criticism of Cooper's novels argues if nothing else a textual richness with which he is not always readily credited. That richness inheres not primarily in complexities of style, depth of psychological and philosophical insight, or the embroidered indeterminacy of Hawthorne, Melville, and James, but rather in the honest mental stresses of a frank republican mind contemplating the contradictory operation in history of basic intellectual positions that turn out in practice to be anything but simple. That seems to me to be undeniable, and it is not surprising that, in this century, the first dominant wave of Cooper criticism was political, social, and historical in its focus: Parrington, Spiller, Ross, Outland, and Waples all, in their different ways, draw attention to Cooper's own political beliefs as the underpinning of his fiction. Wisely, few critics since have felt the need or desire to expel the political element from this most political of novelists, even when, like Bewley, Henry Nash Smith, and McWilliams, their agenda includes sophisticated examination of and carefully argued claims for Cooper's art. Axelrad is clearly right when, in his too little read *History and Utopia*, he points to the dominance of this tradition in the twentieth-century critical reception of Cooper; he also, with illuminating results, questions the dominance in Cooper's political theory of republican, optimistic, agrarian assumptions and reinstates in our consideration another, more conservative, pessimistic eighteenth-century viewpoint, which he centers on Volney and finds most fully expressed in America in the allegorical paintings of Thomas Cole and in Cooper, who, he argues, encodes in his fiction a cycle of decline. It is a useful corrective and complement, at least, to see Cooper as from the beginning more consistently conservative than most have felt comfortable in allowing. It is, perhaps, worth remembering that, while Jeffersonian agrarianism sounds to present ears liberal, it is so basic, so infrequently questioned, as to be as reasonably called conservative; certainly Cooper's profound outrage at the aberrations of what should be both his gentlemen and his agrarian yeomen is the anger of a conservative whose most deeply held pieties are blasphemed.

It would be fair to say that earlier sociopolitical critics see Cooper's novels in the context of the eloquently expressed political views in his letters, nonfiction writing, and authorial intervention in the novels themselves; sometimes the stress has been on the interplay between Cooper's ideas, his career, and the specific political history that was played out around him. Most often, a quasi-biographical narrative is constructed that represents Cooper's struggle to sustain his political ideals—the process by which they underwent modification at one stage or another of his life and how they are expressed in various ways in the fiction. Some see a major change in the later 1830s with the "Home" novels and the Three Mile Point controversy;[4] others might set the major change at the Littlepage novels. McWilliams, in what is by far the most thoroughly argued treatment, sees the long-resisted change, the move from conservative to reactionary, in which Cooper sounds comically like James's Basil Ransom, as coming only at the very end of his life.[5] Axelrad too, although he is not primarily interested in biography or politics, sees Cooper's work as expressive of and determined by an external, really theological, cyclical framework. McWilliams and Axelrad should be read together; if, as I do, one finds merit in both the former's insistence on Cooper's optimism (doubts and reservations notwithstanding) before the very end of his career and the latter's insistence on Cooper's pessimistic view of human social potential, then one is bound to question the total validity of any single-minded view.

And yet a univocal reading is precisely what most critics have sought, either of Cooper's life and work as a whole, or of individual novels. Even though most critics have seen the deep contradictions that fissure Cooper's work, most have sought to resolve these in biographical, often psychological, terms—Cooper working out a personally borne dilemma, which sometimes has been seen as familial and inherited, sometimes political or circumstantial.[6]

What McWilliams shares with Axelrad, and they with others—including cultural critics who see Cooper in the context of large recurring historical or figurative concepts such as the frontier, the machine in the garden, the American Adam, and critics who wish to see Cooper as part of a continuing literary tradition involving concerns with genre, symbol, structural patterns, myth making, cycle, and legend—is this: while each way of proceeding has produced convincing readings from which all readers can profit, those readings all seem to me fundamentally illustrative. Each has a sort of love affair with closure, with resolution, in various registers; each produces powerful versions of the text, McWilliams's as persuasive in its service of its master narrative as Axelrad's in the service of his. No one, including me, can be immune from this hazard of literary history and criticism, but this book says something else.

In a broad way, I offer a political reading of Cooper, but its point of departure, notwithstanding my obvious indebtedness to certain kinds of Marxist thinking about literature, as will appear in chapter 1, is rather a personal one: why do I find Cooper so rewarding, especially in the novels I deal with here, when my view of the desirable republic is so diametrically opposed to his? Obviously, this precluded departing, as previous "political" commentators on his work did, from Cooper's own views. In any case, McWilliams has done that so well that to repeat that process is unnecessary.[7] And it should be added here that, given the strength of Cooper's convictions, directly and implicitly offered in his texts, given the lack of embarrassment on Cooper's part about didactic fiction, the temptation is always strong in favor of Cooper's intended meanings.[8]

While I could see that there were ways of seeing Cooper's texts aesthetically, in some novels as unified wholes, as satisfying expressions of Cooper's underlying views[9]—and in numerous specific passages I am as responsive to the power of Cooper's prose as others have been—the appeal for me did not seem to lie only there. Nor did it lie with biography, psychology, or, least of all, with myth, loud as the chorus in favor of it has been. I could detect the presence of mythic structure and intent—it is almost impossible to miss—but I could not equate mythic structure with literary merit; and, even if I could, I knew that the appeal did not for me lie there, either. All these approaches share a failing: they make a similar base-superstructure assumption that makes "vulgar" Marxism so unappealing. I discovered that in the end what made Cooper for me so truthful a novelist was, in spite of his attempts to resolve his plots and in spite of his strongly articulated sense of his own beliefs, the absence of resolution. And I do not, in saying that, imply at all that Cooper was inventing the modernist text in the 1820s. What interested me was not the conflicted Cooper or the contradictions involved in his and America's political position, but the conflicted text. Cooper's text was, clearly, American history, and his reading of it is registered for us in the novels; this is as true of *The Monikins, Miles Wallingford, The Crater,* and the Littlepage novels as it is of the Leather-Stocking series. Looked at in this way, even aesthetic failures to resolve the issues raised in a novel become testimony to the honesty of his texts.[10] For us, his readers for whom he wrote the novels, the text need be only the novels. Addressing a history that had written itself no conclusion and that could not be represented by Cooper as complying with his deeply cherished expectations of it, he affords texts that do not read consistently through to closure because they cannot. That he sometimes provided conventional endings of a sort that would satisfy his readers is incontestable; it is equally true that the endings, like so much else in the texts that has been taken to be definitive, lie open to question. The questioning is so open and so frequent that one is faced with an embarrassing choice: either Cooper was consistently dumb and lucky, or he knew what he was doing. I incline to the latter view. Unable to resolve, he could only, being honest, present the reader with representative facts and authoritative positions in all their contradiction. If, instead of privileging Marmaduke Temple, we attend to *all* that is written in *The Pioneers*, Templeton is likely to sound more like the tower of Babel or *McCabe and Mrs. Miller* than the peaceable kingdom in the making that the novel's opening pages seem to promise. As McWilliams has pointed out, fulfillment of Cooper's social hopes is always withheld—it could hardly be otherwise. The contending voices in the text are told to shut up only at the end; after so many pages, "peace" is too short a word. The obligation is left firmly upon the readers to make sense if we can; and, it must be added, to be enabled to recognize conflict, contradiction, and even confusion where they exist is also to make sense. What I try to present for the next reader is Cooper's text in all its unresolved plainness and breathtaking honesty. That is not to say, however, that the reader is to expect an uncomplicated text.

Although I share much with and am deeply indebted to all those who have gone before, occupy common ground with those today who more and more accept a materialist grounding for fiction, and distrust the canon and the implications and consequences of prior aesthetic categories, I carry no party card. If I subscribe to Tocqueville's view, I also share his uncertainty: "I should say more than I mean if I were to assert that the literature of a nation is always subordinate to its social state and political constitution. I am aware that, independently of these causes, there are several others which confer certain characteristics on literary productions; but these appear to me to be the chief" (*Democracy* 2:63). Certainly, to affirm the priority as he does is not at all to simplify the matter at hand. My procedure was, I thought, to be simple, and was not to use the novels to illustrate a thesis, or a theory, or any determining notion, but to read and see what happened. That too, of course, is a theory, if a somewhat down-market one. And I was not innocent; I already knew that the texts I was to read again were full of contradiction. What the reading produced only intensified that awareness; and, since, as a working principle, I would see Cooper's views as an element in the novels, equal among others, not a determinant despite their authoritative delivery, what emerged was a problematic text, critical of itself at all points. As the five principal chapters proceed, I do assume the determining presence of the novels preceding the one presently under discussion. I assume a reader of *Mohicans* who has read *The Pioneers*; for Cooper's contemporary readers and reviewers that was a reasonable assumption, as a reading of Dekker and McWilliams's *Critical Heritage* volume indicates. For Cooper's readers today I believe the order of publication to be the best one,[11] in that it highlights and extends the critique that develops within each novel beyond its particular limits, not merely into other novels but in the strangely disjointed movement it compels, as the reader contemplates—ever more critically—the broad expanse of historical time the novels together encompass.

I do believe that the constructive conflicts that arise derive primarily from Cooper's unsparing honesty about events, historical and fictional, and ideas, his own and others'. One is constantly forced, often even against Cooper's own cherished ideas, into a critical position; if Cooper is an extremely severe critic of the ideas and actions of others, he is also his own severest critic, subjecting his own most dearly held beliefs to the least flattering of tests. This is manifest from the beginning. If, as most agree, Marmaduke Temple embodies in part Cooper's own political and social convictions, he is submitted to a virtual fire storm of implicit and explicit criticism. If it is partly true that Natty and Chingachgook are idealized, legendary, near-mythical, epic figures, they are much else too: as men they grow old and die, victims—as we first encounter them—of a specific history; and, if they embody first and last certain ideals, that indicates not simply an elegiac exercise in nostalgia, but also a profound notation of civilization's incapacity to accommodate its own ideals. That performance at least is not casual. Similarly, while Heyward is Cooper's notion of the promising American gentleman hero, he is also unmistakably made to embody racial values that reflect no credit upon him, to embrace chivalrous virtues that are relentlessly exposed as empty, and to exemplify the very attitudes that have dispossessed indigenous peoples and, incidentally, valorize the complaints that unite Magua, Tamenund, and Chingachgook. At the end of *The Prairie* Cooper presents his most comprehensive class-ridden view of the future of American society, with Middleton, his by-now-familiar middle-class gentleman, at its political apex; just before this, however, the epic exchanges between Mahtoree and Hard-Heart make clear that such a view renders the Indian at best a petitioner, almost certainly preterite, and Middleton's mediation doomed. One needs no theory, no master narrative, to understand this—one needs only to attend closely to the entire text.

And yet, when all is said against it, to stress Cooper's own views is not unreasonable; he was never reticent about his opinions, and, especially after his return from Europe, he became ever more insistently polemical and didactic. In the light of that, while Leather-Stocking has never lacked attention, it is not surprising that more and more careful attention has been given to Cooper's more explicitly didactic works. To take only a pair of instances, both McWilliams and Motley offer distinguished readings of *The Wept of Wish-Ton-Wish* (1829) and *The Crater* (1847); the unmistakably determinate nature of these works encourages these critics to read the Leather-Stocking novels in the same way, without eliminating their contradictions. Cooper's—and his critics'—vital exploration of the dynamics of social decline in even these two transparently didactic novels cannot, in the end, find a resolution in either artistic or conceptual terms. This, it seems to me, is not a failure in the ordinary sense; rather, it was inevitable, given Cooper's rootedness in history. His stance is prophetic in both senses of the word, and the fulfillment of either progress or decline could be the subject only of fear or desire.

The political critique that is concentrated in the deliberate literary formations of meaning in *Wept* and *The Crater*—as in the Littlepage manuscripts, *The Sea Lions*, *The Two Admirals*, the Miles Wallingford novels, the European novels, and the Home novels—is, of course, also present in the Leather-Stocking novels, but in a less contained, less determined, less allegorical manner. They are more diffuse: the critique in them is more pervasive, if less conclusive, but they are not for that less persuasive. It is this characteristic that I insist makes the series different and that, when fully grasped, tends to make irrelevant—or, at least, prejudicial—qualifications based upon failure to resolve problems of genre, political meaning, or artistic wholeness.[12]

I present the Leather-Stocking tales, Cooper's most durable work, not as an integrated whole, either as a series or in its individual components, either artistically or politically, but rather as a text which faithfully reproduces the conflicts Cooper faced in his present and in the history his novels contemplate, in which his own principles, ideals, and desires form only part of a complex text which unrelentingly forces the reader into a critical rather than a convinced posture. That, be it the intended result or not, produces a reader who, faced by constant contradiction, voices in combat, is compelled to think, to become critical about history. In this, Cooper is not so far in spirit from Faulkner as might be thought.[13]

Cooper always knew the difference between word and deed, desire and outcome, and always allowed them to act upon one another. He never withdrew from the deed and the human will, individual or institutional, that issues in deeds. The deeds may be unalterable, but they are not immune from judgment; the capacity to judge, Cooper's or ours, however, alters nothing, explains nothing. The explanations—mythic, political, aesthetic—help,[14] but the greatest work is that which brings us face to face with reality in all its intractable complexity. Cooper is as good at that as anyone else.[15]

I begin this preface with Grace Paley's Zagrowsky, and I return to him before turning to some brief explanations of my own. He says—the circumstance does not matter here—"Why? why? The answer: To remind us. That's the purpose of most things." It is as simple—and as difficult—as that. Nothing goes away; everything gets in. Cooper's Leather-Stocking novels comprehensively reminded his generation. They continue to re-mind ours.

In the subtitle to this book I employ the term "a secular reading," which deserves some explanation. It has gained some currency of late largely in association with the theory and criticism of Edward Said, who has had a large impact on my thinking and whose visits to my home institution have been so influential. It might also suggest affiliation with the so-called New Historicists who are transforming American studies today. However, my use of the term is not meant to define such connections; anyone can see that it lacks the insistent and consistent theory of Said or Carolyn Porter, and it certainly does not carry the weight of historical investigation that characterizes the work of Cathy Davidson or Walter Benn Michaels. Nonetheless, the term has a descriptive function for this book. What I mean to convey, primarily, is that the "reading" contained between its covers focuses on the novels and their interpretation of a real history, and that it rejects all transcendent views of the matter. The informed reader would know at once that this book would be opposed to mythological interpretations, to symbolic or formalist readings, to worlds elsewhere or by themselves; as my reader already knows, I would include also those readings that privilege Cooper's own views as transcendent of the world of the text.

Yet, it could be objected with some force, as Axelrad has affirmed in stressing a divine history, that Cooper criticism has been very largely secular and political. It has been asserted by Beard and many others that the patriot Cooper sought to embody in his fiction the "Revolutionary Mythos"; but that, as Beard saw, is no simple matter—and not merely because of the contradictions which rapidly manifested themselves. While I concede the merit of this view, it seems both limiting and a mystification; as Brook Thomas suggests, it was clear to many that the function of romance in part was not to reveal realities but to affirm the dominant national ethos, "to engrain in the public imagination the truly sacred nature of America's political institutions" (*Cross-Examinations*, 2). David Simpson has observed, "The history of colonialism, whether within or outside a nation state, is not a history of the uncontested superimposition of a coherently unitary metaphysic upon an opposition inevitably perceived as inarticulate. It only looks that way when the winners have time to relax and write their histories" ("Literary Critics," 729–30). What this book adds is that, dedicated as he was to his understanding of founding American republican principles, Cooper is no writer of winners' fictions, nor is he an unthinking celebrant at the new republic's altar. Conventions of fiction making might endorse marriage as a suitable denouement, but the opposed claims of settler and aboriginal, landowner and leaseholder, were not so easily settled. The conflicts of high principle and allegiance had their correlatives in real wars that were not merely the convenient site for a romance, in real struggles for ownership and power. McWilliams demonstrates with irresistible clarity that Cooper's distrust of a property-owning aristocracy with political power was a matter not merely of principle but confirmable in the political realities of the world about him. If I provide less of the "actual" history than might be expected, that is because his biographers and, in their different ways, critics and historians like McWilliams, Thomas, Axelrad, Slotkin, Waples, and Beard have done that much better than I could. Also I have proceeded on the assumption that the novels themselves contain all that is necessary for present purposes. If, as I suggest, Cooper forces his readers into their own readings of history, he affords them the materials with which to do it.[16]

James Wallace has recently qualified the wide consensus that Cooper deliberately entered the world of epic-romance by drawing attention to his more homely intent to address and educate a reader less elevated than the chorus of critics who were calling for a truly American romance (*Early Cooper*, 121). If, as I think, Wallace is right, then we should pay as close attention as he does to such "comic" interludes as those in the Bold Dragoon. When Natty grumbles over the association of Right and Law with Might and Property, we should take it as more than a character note; if we give it full weight it might make us read the ending somewhat differently. When Elizabeth discusses law with her father, it is far more important to attend to both contending arguments than to determine who wins. In the same spirit, we should in the same scene accept the directly expressed authorial view of Elizabeth's excess of female emotion only in the context of the contradiction fashioned by the shape of the entire scene, as I shall more fully explain in chapter 2.

Wallace's strictures against the hegemony of the myth approach in Cooper criticism, which I share and deal with in chapter 1, should also be extended, as I have suggested, to those critics who privilege Cooper's own views, and *his* dilemmas. It makes far more sense to me to suggest with Wallace that the Leather-Stocking series as a whole educates its readers in a far more taxing way than do Cooper's less diffuse, less equivocal didactic novels.[17]

While this book offers, mainly, readings of each of the five Leather-Stocking novels, its first chapter is a somewhat Hydra-headed introduction intended to give various kinds of context: to suggest the abiding interest Cooper retains for us in our time, to survey and argue with the prevailing critical attitudes a present day reader is most likely to encounter,[18] and to speculate about why Cooper's critics shied away for so long from radical materialist readings of his texts. I have included also in the introduction a section on Crèvecoeur, written after the rest of the book, as a sort of prolegomenon for Cooper. Crèvecoeur, like Cooper, seemed to me to have suffered misrepresentation and oversimplification. To generations of students he was merely the author of "What is an American?" just as Cooper had been the creator of a "significant myth," Natty Bumppo. He was taken account of but not attended to, known but not known. Even Slotkin in 1985 was able to write, "Crèvecoeur's geopolitical map is an allegorical tableau, stable, and relatively free of catastrophic change" (*The Fatal Environment*, 88). In fact, it seems to me, Crèvecoeur is as deeply aware of catastrophe as Cooper, explores as deeply as he the threats to and betrayal of the agrarian political myth he shares with Cooper. At the same time, Crèvecoeur's *Letters* raise some crucial issues about the nature of narrative that are helpful in reading Cooper. Also, his treatment of the Indian presence raises interesting contrasts to Cooper's quite different disposition of that issue; for neither, however, can the marginalization with which they begin be sustained. For these and other reasons it seemed appropriate to include him; to place him at the beginning as I do is also to suggest that my reading of Cooper is not as eccentric as it might at first appear and that Cooper—seen as darkly critical as I see him—is not without precedent.

My aim has been modest if, in execution, attended by the usual difficulties. I wanted to justify the Leather-Stocking series as a masterpiece on its own terms, or at least on terms different from those prevailing when I began the work. As far as possible, I wished to isolate myself as I wrote from the community of Cooper scholars so as not to write the sort of book that at every corner turned acknowledges shared concerns, differences of opinion. This was not out of contempt for that community or out of fear of combat; as to that, some of my readers will find me too respectful, whereas others will detect a few remaining traces of animus. While this isolation facilitated the development of my own viewpoint, it also seemed—and still seems—appropriate for a book that says above all that these novels are sufficient unto themselves. I wished, too, less to insist upon my own conclusions than to offer my readers an example of how to reach their own, and to present the novels as a site for disputation that allows the reader to reach valid conclusions that might be quite different from my own.

The underlying vanity of my procedure emerged when I had completed writing my readings and turned to see what had been going on while I was away. Not merely did I find points of correspondence between what I had to say and what I had inconsiderately put out of mind, but also I found that new voices were to be heard with whom I found much in common and from which I received much encouragement and illumination. This caused me considerable discomfort in the writing of the introduction and offered a lesson in humility. One never works in isolation. It was a salutary experience to have the feeling of isolation, even embattlement, converted into a sense of community—to find that one was not out of step but in a new mainstream.

I respectfully dedicate this book to the memory of one who never needed to learn so basic a lesson.

ACKNOWLEDGMENTS

Over the years my work has received financial support from the Social Science and Humanities Research Council of Canada and from the University of Western Ontario. I have worked at the Huntington Library and at the libraries of Yale University and the University of Toronto, as well as at my home library, the D. B. Weldon Library of the University of Western Ontario. My thanks to all.

Friends and colleagues have read all or parts of the manuscript at various stages: Ernest Redekop, Kristin Brady, Jean Matthews, Annette Kolodny, Sherry Sullivan, Russell Reising, Jane Tompkins, Ian Steele, Jane Millgate, and Elaine Hedges. Thanks are offered to all these for praise, blame, encouragement, excoriation, and even for tactful silence, with the customary immunities.

My manuscript was read by two referees, then anonymous to me. To Everett Emerson, I am grateful for enthusiastic affirmation and encouragement, and to William Kelly, I owe an immense and unpayable debt for an extraordinary analysis of the manuscript's faults that has helped me enormously.

A special word of thanks goes to the incomparable Launa Fuller who typed this manuscript for me twice. Teresa MacDonald was of the greatest assistance in the final stages, as was Peter Georgelos.

Iris Tillman Hill, Kate Torrey, Ron Maner, and Stephanie Sugioka at the University of North Carolina Press represent for me a model of what editing should be and too often is not. I count myself fortunate indeed to have benefited from the frankness, firmness, knowledge, and sensibility of Ms. Sugioka, who copyedited the manuscript.

No words of thanks can be adequate for the patience of my wife, Goldie.

June 1989

The militant struggles of the Mohawks of Kanesatake and other places in Quebec during the summer of 1990, as well as the voices of men and women who spoke for them and the voices of those who attacked them, helped me to keep thinking that what I have to say about Cooper remains worth saying.

December 1990

PRINCIPAL WORKS OF COOPER CITED

I have used the fine new edition of Cooper's works published under the general editorship of James Franklin Beard by the State University of New York Press. In each chapter dedicated to a single novel, all quotations from the novel discussed are identified by page number in the Beard edition; where other novels are cited, and in chapter 1, the name of the novel is also included.

Cooper, James Fenimore. *The Pioneers: or The Sources of the Susquehanna: A Descriptive Tale*. Albany: State University of New York Press, 1980. (Text established by Lance Schachterle and Kenneth M. Anderson, Jr.)

———. *The Last of the Mohicans: A Narrative of 1757*. Albany: State University of New York Press, 1983. (Text established by James A. Sappenfield and E. N. Feltskog.)

———. *The Prairie: A Tale*. Albany: State University of New York Press, 1985. (Edited by James P. Elliott.)

———. *The Pathfinder: or The Inland Sea*. Albany: State University of New York Press, 1981. (Edited by Richard Dilworth Rust.)

———. *The Deerslayer: or The First War-Path*. Albany: State University of New York Press, 1986. (Edited by Lance Schachterle, Kent P. Ljungquist, and James A. Kilby.)

ONE ∗ Introduction

No portion of this Earth
To nurture Hell's infernal grisly brood,
Was by its holy Maker e'er design'd;
Or to remain a dark and frightful waste,
When wisely furnish'd for the residence
Of rational, humane and polish'd Man.
– Daniel Bryan, Mountain Muse *(1813)*

On Lyell Island off the West Coast of Canada in 1985, a band of Haida
Indians attempted, by passive resistance, to prevent a logging company
from working over their ancestral lands. They prevailed for a time. The
logging company, whose rights were of long standing, sought and received
court orders from British Columbia judges; the Haidas continued to resist.
The Royal Canadian Mounted Police removed the lawbreakers, whose
faces were smudged black and who bore rattles as their only arms. They
were charged, bound over, and urged to keep the peace and obey the law.
Predictably, the environmentalists were involved in demonstrations, and
the matter is presently under review at the federal level. This event made
for dramatic television; it occupied every Canadian talk show for several
days—Indians were interviewed free on location, and suited experts were
engaged to talk for a fee in the studio. Three months later we had, mostly,
silence. Several years earlier, British Columbia had led the fight to include
property rights in the Canadian Charter of Rights.

Although an uneasy truce prevailed on Lyell Island in 1989, provincial
and national authorities had clashed with, among others, the Lubicon of
Alberta, the Innu of Labrador, and most recently, in a conflict involving
both Canadian and United States authorities, the Mohawk. The disputes

involve such matters as political autonomy, land and mineral rights, wildlife conservation, and the poverty of aboriginal people. For the Innu, the confrontation is both with the Canadian government and NATO, who deploy low-level training flights over their tribal territory. The confrontation of white invader and the first peoples of this continent is not over, not at least on my side of the forty-ninth parallel. Five hundred bands have land claims; fewer than 8 percent have been settled. Were he living, Cooper would be startled by supersonic bangs, but the confrontations of white and red would seem dismayingly familiar.

John P. McWilliams, in the peroration to his book on Cooper, predicted that the problems of political justice Cooper addressed are "likely to remain crucial and unresolved." Cooper, had he been able to experience the open operation of political action committees and the normalization of political lobbying by the rich and powerful, had he watched with us the Watergate, Iran Contra, or HUD hearings, would have agreed. Cooper, perhaps, has more to say to us today than ever before—and not only to North Americans. Each new television image of an aboriginal people displaced, scattered, or destroyed, in Borneo, Brazil or elsewhere, in the name of civilization, commerce, and progress—each should remind us of Cooper, who first felt such actions important enough to inscribe and interrogate in his fiction. Each time we hear of yet another forest put to the torch or clear-cut with dire predictions for the ozone layer; yet another plant or animal species rendered extinct; yet another tract of arable land or wilderness worked to exhaustion or paved for development (Cooper would have used the ironical "improvement"); yet more pollution of air and water and unmanageable waste; still more accidental coastal oil spills from sea to oil-slicked sea; or another factory ship strip-mining the ocean of fish—at such times Cooper should be in our minds to admonish us, to remind us of two centuries of indifference. To focus too exclusively on his luminous creation of myth is to endanger our consciousness of his relentless inscription of the historical reality that makes the myth exotic. Alice Walker's tragicomic displacement of the history of American—perhaps all—colonization to Liberia in *The Color Purple* is only the latest version of the tale first treated extensively in fiction by Cooper.

As this book was being written, steel mills were closed down in Ohio and whole communities were ruined. Family farms were bankrupted and sold off; Dan Rather and Charles Kuralt wept, but the banks had to be paid, and agricultural business experts coldly analyzed the situation. In the cities, vast unemployment, poverty, hunger, urban blight, and violence provided media images of problems for which no solutions were in sight. The agrarian vision of Jefferson and the industrial dreams of Judge Temple seemed to be dying an agonizing and ugly death.

All this has, in my view, a great deal to do with Cooper and how we read him. I am not, of course, the first to propose a political and historical reading of Cooper, as my preface indicates, but it is certainly true that such a view has not, perhaps until recently, commanded assent. But surely, today Cooper can hardly be denied relevance: the racial history that he so memorably inscribed reinscribes itself today in the Americas and elsewhere, and contemporary evidence for the sorry tale he told is easy to find. The consequences of slavery, the nightmare of the Enlightenment conscience, in which Cooper shared, remain with us. The enlightened dreams of civilization, progress, and prosperity—agrarian and industrial—that justified colonization, dispossession, and expansion have failed or have produced results that Marmaduke Temple, Crèvecoeur, Franklin, and Jefferson could not have imagined. "Many ages will not see the shores of our great lakes replenished with inland nations, nor the unknown bounds entirely peopled. Who can tell how far it extends? Who can tell the millions of men whom it will feed and contain?" (Crèvecoeur, *Letters*, 67–68). Cooper, oddly echoing Crèvecoeur, strikes a more cautious note: "Within the short period we have mentioned, the population has spread itself over five degrees of latitude and seven of longitude, and has swelled to a million and a half of inhabitants, who are maintained in abundance, and can look forward to ages before the evil day must arrive, when their possessions shall become unequal to their wants" (*Pioneers*, 16).[1] Franklin and the rest did not live to see America reproduce the conditions from which they invited impoverished Europeans to escape: landlessness, the poverty line, unemployment, stifling cities, and demeaning labor in dehumanizing factories.

In the academy, where he is usually—apologetically—studied, the aesthetic-formal criteria of the New Criticism that dominated for four decades have not worked well with Cooper, largely because of the implicit or explicit banishment of political, historical, and social factors as irrelevant to critical judgment.[2] The result has been that, to account for Cooper's enduring power and notwithstanding his confused fictional surfaces, we come to rest on the eternally reiterated "figure of significant myth," by this point a mere consensus phrase. Alternatively we have tried to show that, usually in places only, Cooper is as profound a symbolist as those who follow him in the canon,[3] or sometimes that Cooper's ambiguities and conflicts are unsuspected aspects of his artistic practice and to be valued for their art. Both these positions have merit, but the priority accorded them has masked and preempted other issues. Daniel Peck's supercilious dismissal of politics and history as a literary consideration in Cooper, the most clearly political novelist of his time in America, has been typical of the prevailing academic categories; his easy assumption that "historical" is opposed to "literary significance" (*A World by Itself*, ix) has been widely shared.[4] Against that I argue that Cooper's Leather-Stocking novels (and not only those) produce in a peculiarly honest form the contradictions of American life and consciousness of history in his time, and the failure of history and politics to resolve or eliminate them—so that they continue *as issues* beyond his time and even into the present day—and that these considerations, not eternal but merely durable, account for the abiding interest we have in the series. One of the great puzzles in any rigorous reading is how it could ever have stirred the patriotic sense, how the pride taken in the emergence of an American voice could have so completely obscured what that voice was saying, the criticism the series embodies.

When I first contemplated writing this book, I did not think I had a thesis beyond a general dissatisfaction with the tendency of criticism on Cooper and the lack, then, of a full study of all five Leather-Stocking novels. The detailed—perhaps overdetailed—reading I proposed to carry out contained, I see now, its own theoretical bias: that only by attention to all the details, as they cohere and conflict, within and across the novels' boundaries, as the reader assembles his accumulating memories through the series, mounting novel over novel, allowing incident and phrase to recall other incidents and phrases—only thus can the novels' meanings emerge. The perennially repeated arguments for their mythic appeal elide too much, forcing us to ignore the conflicting unresolved details that constitute their meaning. Of course, the mythical dimension has considerable force, and Cooper quite deliberately constructs and emphasizes it in *The Prairie* and *The Deerslayer*, and explicitly lays claim to part of it in his 1850 "Preface to the Leather-Stocking Tales"; but the approach this book embraces—I hope in a plain enough manner—suggests that excessive attention to the idealized construction of the mythic Natty and his red-skinned companions sacrifices the way in which the books unfailingly yield political and historical messages—messages that reveal not only the myth of Natty in both his romantic and cultural dimensions, the exemplar of Christian behavior, but also the enlightened, rational, agrarian, revolutionary myth as _only_ myths, subverted by the chaos of unresolved historical detail that surrounds them.

That this interpretation may not be Cooper's intended meaning is not the issue confronted here; nor is it part of my argument that Cooper has constructed a more complex and devious form than he is usually credited with, thereby to absorb him into the canon at its highest level along with Melville, Hawthorne, and James. Rather I suggest that Cooper's artistic resolve to embody the truth is at odds with the truth he would have liked to express. The artistic resolve prevails over the ideological desire; it is hard to see that the criteria of the romance aesthetic available to Cooper,[5] more economically followed, would have produced a more striking result. As Engels remarked in a well-known letter to Minna Kautsky, "A socialist-based novel fully achieves its purpose . . . if by conscientiously describing the real mutual relations, breaking down conventional illusions about them, it shatters the optimism of the bourgeois world, although the author does not offer any definite solution or does not even line up openly on any one particular side" (Becker, _Documents_, 483). Cooper was obviously no socialist, but in every other respect he satisfies Engels's criteria; and that, given the firmness and vehemence of Cooper's own views, seems to me an extraordinary thing to have done. What Engels does not take into account is the force of bourgeois deafness. Since the problems Cooper addressed remain with us, unresolved for us as for him, the novels retain their disconsoling significance. In this light we may be able to discern connections between early and late nineteenth-century fiction, between romanticism and naturalism, other than yet another variation played upon the theme—by now too familiar—of innocence and experience.[6]

The Importance of Crèvecoeur: Breaking the Tablets, Destroying the Text

However, although Cooper, in this respect, seems to have reached forward to touch Frank Norris, Hamlin Garland, Sherwood Anderson, and John Steinbeck, he found his roots in the eighteenth century.[7] The trenchant republicanism of the opening of _The Pioneers_ catches—and exactly—the tone and meaning of so much of Franklin and Jefferson. It poetically echoes the confidence of Crèvecoeur's third letter, so widely shared in America's sense of itself: "By the literal account hereunto annexed, you will easily be made acquainted with the happy effects which constantly flow, in this country, from sobriety and industry, when united with good land and freedom" (*Letters*, 104–5). That founding conviction makes our contemporary rural tribulations so poignant. It is perhaps Henry Adams who, making the ironical pretense of not knowing in 1891 what Jefferson and Madison could not know in 1817, most comprehensively puts the issue:

> The traits of American character were fixed; the rate of physical and economical growth was established; and history, certain that at a given distance of time the Union would contain so many millions of people, with wealth valued at so many millions of dollars, became thenceforward chiefly concerned to know what kind of people these millions were to be. They were intelligent, but what paths would their intelligence select? They were quick, but what solution of insoluble problems would quickness hurry? They were scientific, and what control would their science exercise over their destiny? They were mild, but what corruptions would their relaxations bring? They were peaceful, but by what machinery were their corruptions to be purged? What interests were to vivify a society so vast and uniform? What ideals were to ennoble it? What object, besides physical content, must a democratic continent aspire to attain? For the treatment of such questions, history required another century of experience. [*A History* 2:1345]

Cooper certainly raises those questions in the Leather-Stocking novels, but he does not attempt the answers Adams ironically implies (although perhaps he did so in *The Crater*).

But the connection between Crèvecoeur and Cooper seems to me to be a revealing one, not merely in some shared political and historical assumptions but also in the experience they share of the developing conflict between ideal and practice in revolutionary America.[8] One need not seek long to find Cooper in Crèvecoeur's *Letters from an American Farmer* at the most superficial level of interests held in common: the delight in and reverence for nature; the importance each placed upon liberty under rational laws; the emphasis placed on family, continuity, and inheritance and on the ownership of land. Crèvecoeur's industrious "congregation of respectable farmers and their wives, all clad in neat homespun, well mounted, or riding in their own humble waggons" (67) are cast in the same mold as the rural citizens who assemble for Judge Temple's court. For both there is no question about the origin in Christian Europe of our notions of virtue; both feel the threat to civilization of frontier barbarism, the betrayal of reason and law, of whiteness. Both are uneasy about slavery: for Crèvecoeur, his encounter with it is little short of traumatic; for Cooper, the issue appears only three times, problematically distributed among Munro, Heyward (a Southerner), Temple, Jones, and Magua. Both agree that it is associated with degenerate luxury rather than with the yeoman virtues of the northern states—though, characteristically, Temple's slaveholding at one remove complicates the issue in Cooper. Agamemnon, like Melville's Babo, does not offer testimony.

The most important common ground of the two men lies in that nexus of eighteenth-century belief they shared with so many others. Crèvecoeur repeatedly stresses the point; a single example will suffice: "We are a people of cultivators, scattered over an immense territory, communicating with each other by means of good roads and navigable rivers, united by the silken bands of mild government, all respecting the laws, without dreading their power, because they are equitable. We are all animated with the spirit of an industry which is unfettered and unrestrained, because each person works for himself" (*Letters*, 67). No reader of the opening paragraph of *The Pioneers* will miss its virtual identity with the famous Letter III, "What is an American?" That Crèvecoeur spoke both as loyal subject and citizen, and Cooper only as a republican, does not impair the agreement that allows us to see a continuity between colony and republic which is important to the meaning of the Leather-Stocking novels. The bitter disappointment of their secular piety animates both *Letters* and Leather-Stocking: in Crèvecoeur it comes as a series of unlooked for explosions in Letters IX and XII; in Cooper it is from the beginning pervasive. In both it problematizes the texts and raises issues in acute forms about the nature of narrative and reading. Thematically, the ruin noted in the epigraph to chapter 3 of *The Pioneers* by the lines, "Yet man can mar such works with his rude taste, / Like some sad spoiler of a virgin's fame," is not confined to "nature's handy work" but is extended to man himself as cause and victim.

However, Crèvecoeur's most famous words give no hint of that; *vox dei*
or Crèvecoeur's own voice, it is *vox Americana*:

"Welcome to my shores, distressed European; bless the hour in which
thou didst see my verdant fields, my fair navigable rivers, and my
green mountains!—If thou wilt work, I have bread for thee; if thou
wilt be honest, sober, and industrious, I have greater rewards to
confer on thee—ease and independence. I will give thee fields to feed
and clothe thee; a comfortable fireside to sit by, and tell thy children
by what means thou hast prospered; and a decent bed to repose on. I
shall endow thee beside with the immunities of a freeman. If thou wilt
carefully educate thy children, teach them gratitude to God, and
reverence to that government, that philanthropic government, which
has collected here so many men and made them happy. I will also
provide for thy progeny; and to every good man this ought to be the
most holy, the most powerful, the most earnest wish he can possibly
form, as well as the most consolatory prospect when he dies. Go thou
and work and till; thou shalt prosper, provided thou be just, grateful,
and industrious." [*Letters*, 89–90]

A deistic theology, a physiocratic philosophy, a political system, and a
rational economics seemed to go hand in hand. Views such as these are as
effective in conferring a moral and spiritual dimension on daily life as is
Jonathan Edwards's or Ann Bradstreet's intense piety; each bushel har-
vested confirmed a view of the nature of divine will, national destiny,
individual moral virtue, practical subsistence, personal and family prosperity, and commercial opportunity. At this point, it is Nathaniel Ames's
hero who prevails: "The Man, who, cloath'd in the Manufacture of his
own House, comes to the City on his lofty Steed, loaded with the Fat of the
Land, in Sacks as white as Snow, true Emblem of Neatness and Delicacy"
(*Almanacks*, 392).

In Cooper, such sentiments immediately yield, at the end of the first
paragraph of *The Pioneers*, a simple, progressive theory of history:

In short, the whole district is hourly exhibiting how much can be
done, in even a rugged country, and with a severe climate, under the
dominion of mild laws, and where every man feels a direct interest in
the prosperity of a commonwealth, of which he knows himself to
form a part. The expedients of the pioneers who first broke ground in

the settlement of this country, are succeeded by the permanent improvements of the yeoman, who intends to leave his remains to
moulder under the sod which he tills, or, perhaps, of the son, who,
born in the land, piously wishes to linger around the grave of his
father.—Only forty years have passed since this territory was a wilderness. [15–16]

Crèvecoeur offers a precisely similar view of history; the match is so close
that one almost suspects that Cooper had the *Letters* before him as he
wrote the opening of *The Pioneers*. Crèvecoeur's development of his view
of history is of the greatest interest, for he very quickly registers its
inherent complexity.

As Crèvecoeur moves, in Letter III, from the coast and developed
settlement inland to "more modern settlements" (*Letters*, 42)—in effect,
from ideology to history—he recognizes instantly that in America to move
forward in time, outward in geographical space, is to move backward in
time to a more primitive stage of society—a place of risk, violence,
wildness, and disorder "where men are wholly left dependent on their
native tempers, and on the spur of uncertain industry, which often fails
when not sanctified by the efficacy of a few moral rules. There, remote
from the power of example and check of shame, many families exhibit the
most hideous parts of our society" (72). From that frontier point, at "the
great woods," one can only read the future by reading the past. The
violent forester pioneer is superseded explicitly by the past, "the most
respectable army of veterans" (43). The structure is inexorable, each
phase irresistibly replacing the last; it is also reciprocal—to move into the
future is to move into the past and vice versa. Crèvecoeur concedes
without embarrassment that "the lawless" are responsible for disgraceful
acts of dispossession and racial slaughter, soberly deplores their actions,
and accepts the benefits the slaughter and fraud bestowed on his "freeholders." Crèvecoeur's discovery of his own inclusion in the process is the
story the *Letters* tell. The achronological order of Cooper's series adven-
titiously serves Crèvecoeur's nonlinear view of American history.[9] Although Crèvecoeur does not discuss narrative in such terms as I have used,
he does openly address the available narrative forms (90), and the deliberate strangeness of his final passages must raise the possibility of an unexpected fictional innovation.

The most familiar of his narratives is set immediately after the words of "our great parent" quoted earlier; the "History of Andrew, the Hebridean" has the clear fictional purpose simply of illustrating by an example, in a story fully equipped with moral and narrative closure, the composite philosophical proposition that precedes it. He clearly distances himself from both the historian and the maker of high romance in his "History"; the story he tells, though, is advanced as true, a history. At the same time, he immediately affirms its structure, "the progressive steps of a poor man, advancing from indigence to ease; from oppression to freedom; from obscurity and contumely to some degree of consequence—not by virtue of any freaks of fortune, but by the gradual operation of sobriety, honesty, and emigration" (*Letters*, 90). The embrace of the didactic is total. The story is presented not only as a series of events in an intended structure but as a confident anticipation based on previous experience and driven by its familiar meaning. And its meaning is authorized by "actual" history—his grandfather's experience (purely invented) and an apostrophe to William Penn. Andrew's history, fully decked out in the trappings of sentimental fiction, does not disappoint us. It is brought to a full closure with a house-raising that embraces a whole community and an accounting that is at once ideological and financial. The story entertains and fulfills every republican hope given above.

"Andrew" is merely the most extensive fable *Letters* contains. While Crèvecoeur often observes nature for its own sake, for the pleasure observation affords, he just as often produces small beast fables from his observation: man, birds, bees, and their interrelationships generate meaning. But the distinction between history and fictional narrative does not arise for Crèvecoeur in a critical way, for "Andrew" *is* history in that it would make no sense if it could not in essence be verified against actual histories (his fictitious grandfather!) of American freeholders. Such discussion, though his text inexorably raises it today, would probably surprise Crèvecoeur, for his assumptions were so resolutely and explicitly Aristotelian ("entertaining and instructive," 91) that didactic fiction and history were as readily assumed by him as by Cooper. Modern reluctance to accept didacticism was not shared by Cooper and Crèvecoeur; for Cooper the step into transparent allegory was not so long or so innovative a move as it might appear to us.[10]

Letters IV–VIII, with their descriptive, historical, economic, and sociological studies of Nantucket and Martha's Vineyard, exactly repeat the fully closed scenario and meaning of "Andrew." "My simple wish is to trace them throughout their progressive steps, from their arrival here to this present hour; to inquire by what means they have raised themselves from the most humble, the most insignificant beginnings, to the ease and the wealth they now possess; and to give you some idea of their customs, religion, manners, policy, and mode of living" (108).

It is in these chapters too that Crèvecoeur speaks again of the fate of the Indians, this time more coolly than in Letter III, accepting their "doom" and the convenience for our European forefathers of the providential sicknesses that decimated them. The survivors—"meek and harmless" and few in number—assimilate, Christianize, and prosper (122). After a doleful listing of the disappeared tribes of the Massachusetts coast, he notes, "nothing remains of them all, but one extraordinary monument, and even this they owe to the industry and religious zeal of the Europeans, I mean the Bible translated into the Nattick tongue" (122–23). The surviving tribes withdrew, but "in a few years their territories were surrounded by the improvements of the Europeans; in consequence of which they grew lazy, inactive, unwilling, and unapt to imitate, or to follow any of our trades, and in a few generations, either totally perished or else came over to the Vineyard, or to this island, to re-unite themselves with such societies of their countrymen as would receive them" (123). Crèvecoeur's view is clear. He may regret the violent excesses of the frontiersman, but he entertains no doubt of the superiority of the European; if the Indian is doomed, the white European is destined. The only possibility for the Indian is to assimilate, "to follow . . . our trades" or perish. Cooper never renders the matter so unambiguously. It is not until the final letter that Crèvecoeur releases the potential energy of these passages—and, even then, it is left to the reader to make the dismaying connection. In Cooper, we read Middleton's promise to Hard-Heart in *The Prairie* in the light of our reading of *Mohicans*, which we have read remembering *The Pioneers*.

Letter IX, which shifts the locale to Carolina, totally transforms the text—this letter is not a simple addition to reveal a darker side or provide a balanced view. The South is a world in which, for the white European, luxury has replaced labor, acquisitiveness and litigation thrive, and lawyers rather than the law rule. Here, instead of the rational communities of New England, heartless greed and human exploitation prevail; the seamless garment of reason, morality, religion, and action given in the preceding letters is rent in Charles-Town. To say that is not to interpret but merely to take notice; Crèvecoeur says it:

Is there then no superintending power who conducts the moral oper-
ations of the world, as well as the physical? The same sublime hand
which guides the planets round the sun with so much exactness,
which preserves the arrangement of the whole with such exalted
wisdom and paternal care, and prevents the vast system from falling
into confusion; doth it abandon mankind to all the errors, the follies,
and the miseries, which their most frantic rage, and their most dangerous vices and passions can produce? [173]

The South's premature aging, a debilitated physical life, and early death
are set against the North's mature enjoyment and healthful life, "dissipa-
tion and pleasure" against "labour and prudence." If the contrast developed were only an affirmation of the moral superiority of the northern
states as, in Franklin's phrase, "the land of labour," it would not detain us
long, but Crèvecoeur does much more.

The founding categories of law, land, labor, and freedom are deformed
into perversion. The cupidity of lawyers and the venality and acquisitiveness of landowners have converted land into property and money; the
tutelary law is transformed into "mazes of the law" in which a "whole
patrimony" becomes forfeit to the now parasitic lawyer.[11] The sacred
relationship among land, labor, and man is fractured by slavery. Human-
kind is split into elite and preterite. For the slave, labor produces not
prosperity but misery. The simplest of human responses, "kindness and
affection," are denied. Sex and procreation, sentiment and family, for the
slave become an affliction: "harmless joys" produce a "double misery."[12]
Commerce becomes the mere accumulation of gold; land is only commodity. In the context of the total inversion he has fashioned, so detailed
in its negative matching with the virtues extolled in the preceding chapters, his outburst is not merely formal: "Strange order of things! Oh,
Nature, where art thou?" (169).

Crèvecoeur's outrage is never merely abstract; he fully imagines the
"fraud" and "barbarous treatment" of the taking and transportation of
slaves; in Carolina, the freeholders become planters and then "whippers."
The "obduracy contracted by habit" has overcome the most basic humanity. The humanity of Quaker emancipation, his affirmation of African
human potential, serves only to intensify his outrage. A clergyman's remonstrance is greeted thus by one of his hearers: "Sir, we pay you a genteel

salary to read to us the prayers of the liturgy, and to explain to us such parts of the Gospel as the rule of the church directs; but we do not want you to teach us what we are to do with our blacks" (*Letters*, 172). Crèvecoeur calls the planter's assumption "this astonishing right," "this barbarous custom"; the word "right" is shrewdly chosen as travesty of and memorial to a code betrayed. But this is not a mere observer's commentary: it registers his deeply involved sense not merely that Charles-Town or Carolina or the South has gone wrong, but rather that the whole world, and his confident assumptions about it, have been grotesquely perverted.[13]

The doleful tale of slavery, plunder, and "the cruel right of war, and . . . lawless force" (161) in Africa is reproduced in America. The violence, then, that characterized life before the arrival at the frontier of his veteran freeholders is not simply superseded; a twentieth-century reader might wonder if violence—and all that attends it—is not the freeholders' future and if Crèvecoeur did not dimly see it. The tone is no longer that of Nathaniel Ames but that of his fire-eating Federalist son, Fisher Ames. The attitude is distinctly Hobbesian: "Everything is submitted to the power of the strongest; men, like the elements, are always at war; the weakest yield to the most potent; force, subtlety, and malice, always triumph over unguarded honesty and simplicity" (*Letters*, 174). For Crèvecoeur this is the destruction of the political fabric, man's moral being, and nature itself: "So irresistible is power, that it often thwarts the tendency of the most forcible causes, and prevents their subsequent salutary effects, though ordained for the good of man by the Governor of the universe. Such is the perverseness of human nature; who can describe it in all its latitude?" (*Letters*, 174). The underlying tale here is that we say this, we think this, but we enact something quite different. Such a view does not exempt Crèvecoeur: it reflects precisely the movement and structure of the *Letters*. The relevance of all this to Cooper is that processes, attitudes, and judgments, brutally exposed in Crèvecoeur, in Cooper are embedded in a fictional fabric. Crèvecoeur offers a "general review of human nature"; "what is called civilized society" is judged more severely than the savage state. How often that note is struck in Cooper!

The final episode of Letter IX is, once more, a narrative. Crèvecoeur walks through "a pleasant wood" only to be drawn to the hideous spectacle of a slave suspended in a cage in a tree to be pecked to death by birds of prey. He gives him water; the slave asks for poison. The obscene parody of the crucifixion is unmistakable. The episode acts in precisely the way "The History of Andrew" does in Letter III; the narrative serves only to illustrate the position advanced in the rest of the chapter. As in Cooper, narrative is always seen as a vehicle of meaning.

I have spent so long with this letter because it seems to me important to correct the way in which Crèvecoeur has been traditionally viewed and because, in the conflict it so relentlessly insists on, it allows us to see Cooper as less exceptional in the bleaker aspect in which I present him. It is beyond question that Crèvecoeur repeatedly repudiates in great detail the views held to be most characteristic of him; in doing so, he follows the expressive pattern adopted earlier. Just as it is a misrepresentation to isolate Letter III as "Crèvecoeur's view," Letter IX cannot be evaded as merely inconsistent or an aberration; together they constitute a problematic narrative. Letter IX totally transfigures the work and imposes over the previous ideologized narratives a master narrative, in which "Nature and Nature's Laws"—now the first phase, merely, of the new narrative—are revealed as socially ineffective. Cooper's practice, while involving similar elements, is significantly different in that the dialectic of reality with ideality is made to pervade the entire five-novel, achronological text.

The onset of the Revolution, to which Crèvecoeur reacts in "Distresses of a Frontier Man," Letter XII, attacks his agrarian assumptions from another direction. It is easy to forget, seeing so much that unites Crèvecoeur to Franklin, Paine, and Jefferson, that he firmly declares his loyalty to the crown and affirms the continuity of American experience with the European, especially the British.[14] The Revolution is, of course, utterly devastating to that conviction in that it enforces discontinuity; he is unable to resolve his conflicting loyalties. Cooper in *The Spy*, *The Pioneers*, and *Wyandotté* renders his tribute to the importance of this aspect of American history, but he is not himself in conflict in his loyalties and is therefore able to fashion the appearance of reconciliation. Crèvecoeur's sense of himself and the freeholders as European has already been referred to: the Indians, like the slaves freed by Quakers, are accepted only on European terms. Now uniform moral action has become inconceivable, the simplicities fractured. In the crucial exchange on Mount Vision between Elizabeth Temple and John Mohegan there occurs a similar demolition of European values, "fear God and live in peace" (401); it is just as telling, but it merely embarrasses Elizabeth whereas it paralyzes Crèvecoeur:

Some have asked, whether it was a crime to resist; to repel some parts of this evil. Others have asserted, that a resistance so general makes pardon unattainable, and repentance useless; and dividing the crime among so many, renders it imperceptible. What one party calls meritorious, the other denominates flagitious. These opinions vary, contract, or expand, like the events of the war on which they are founded. What can an insignificant man do in the midst of these jarring contradictory parties, equally hostile to persons situated as I am? And after all who will be the really guilty?—Those most certainly who fail of success. Our fate, the fate of thousands, is then necessarily involved in the dark wheel of fortune. Why then so many useless reasonings; we are the sport of fate.[15] [*Letters*, 205]

History has overtaken his confident, philosophically determined, primary narrative and overturns him for a moment into cynicism. Not merely are whites fighting whites, as Mohegan reminds Elizabeth on Mount Vision that they did, but the Indians whose elimination he had so elaborately registered earlier seem to have been revived to compound his torment and terror.

Crèvecoeur's declared resolve to retire to an Indian village, location unspecified, is not of course what he did in his life, though one can think of certain poets who might have thought it a rational solution. Crèvecoeur *chose* his conclusion, and it strikes me as a singularly appropriate one. As a practical proposition, it is untrue; as a fictional gesture, it takes up so much that precedes it, raises significant questions, and so fully expresses the futility of the experience he registers in the *Letters*, as well as in itself being transparently futile, that I prefer to presume intent. Only if one allows a monolithic authority to Letter III and believes that the prayer of the book's penultimate paragraph has been answered is another conclusion preferable.

As Crèvecoeur contemplates life in an Indian village far from "the accursed neighbourhood of Europeans," where "its inhabitants live with more ease, decency, and peace, than you imagine: where, though governed by no laws, yet find, in uncontaminated simple manners all that laws can afford," we catch a familiar romantic note; he now envisions a reversion "into a state approaching nearer that of nature, unencumbered either with voluminous laws, or contradictory codes, often galling the very necks of those whom they protect" (*Letters*, 211). The rejection is complete; enter

Natty Bumppo. He will go to the Indians, but he will not assimilate to them, though they are, presumably, free to assimilate to him. But, given that Crèvecoeur has so fully inscribed the elimination of the Indians, the reader might wonder where he will find them. Is Crèvecoeur as lost as they are? It seems to me that he is, seeking vainly what his like have destroyed. It is the great merit of *Letters from an American Farmer* that it inscribes this sense of loss so indelibly. In doing so, Crèvecoeur fathers Cooper.

If *Letters* had been written by a certified ironist, one might suspect the author of satirical intent. Indeed, one might learn more from it by reading it in a comic spirit, but, however constructive, this would be a kind of misreading. Most often, what students have been offered of Crèvecoeur is "What is an American?" (Letter III)—at least as far as "The History of Andrew"; if one is also given Letters IX and XII, one might infer reasonably that Crèvecoeur is an example of the endless oscillation of hope and disappointment often held to characterize American literature. The danger of making such an assumption is that the particular significance of a thorough reading of Crèvecoeur is swallowed up in a literary historical myth of balance, compensation, and reciprocation in which the presence of a pattern allows us to overlook the intense experience of particular instances.

Read in the way I suggest, *Letters* is a work that destroys its own "text"—that is, the eighteenth-century pieties that constitute Letter III and the examples, fictional and actual, that illustrate them. The "text" is, however, not merely ideological; it animates an America that is presented as a haven. When it disintegrates under the impact of human depravity and the civil strife of the Revolution, the only haven Crèvecoeur can imagine has already been destroyed imaginatively within the destroyed "text." There is nowhere even to imagine with conviction. What he does imagine explicitly destroys the meaning of his "text"; and, if the village were to exist and he were to go there, it must be at risk from his very presence, as his destroyed but remembered "text" makes clear. Cooper, I shall maintain, inhabits and inherits the same dismayingly problematic world and produces in his five novels an equally problematic text.

Cooper among the Critics

As Nicolaus Mills has pointed out (*American and English Fiction*, 11), the dominant trend in the criticism of American fiction, which has preferred the romance/myth tradition, begins with Lionel Trilling's *The Liberal Imagination* (1950) and the attack there on Parrington's *Main Currents in American Thought*. If in 1973 Mills's counterattack seemed rather labored, it must be understood that by that time Trilling's progeny were thick upon the ground. It is only relatively recently that other voices have been heard in any number insisting that, perhaps, membership in the American pantheon has been rather artificially and unhistorically restricted. These voices also suggest that the sophisticated techniques of analysis that, with reciprocal reassurance, established Hawthorne, Melville, and James on the highest step of the dais might themselves be limited in their capacity fully to reveal the authors they best serve, and limiting of what books are actually read in the academy (thus preserving both the integrity of the canon and certain ways of viewing it). This new emphasis comes not primarily from within literary studies but rather from the feminist movement, from black studies, from interdisciplinary studies, and from theoreticians.[16]

Michael Davitt Bell's recent *The Development of American Romance* is an interesting case in point. Working backward from James's preface to *The American*, Bell manages to reduce Cooper to the merest mention, and, perhaps more important, he virtually ignores a whole dominant version of romance that had received no serious challenge for thirty years.[17] Whatever merits the readings of particular authors might have, the book's claims as literary history are seriously impaired by this; it is literary history that lacks a sense of history—no Indians, no politics, certainly none of the works for whose inclusion Jane Tompkins has argued so persuasively, and no awareness of the sort of considerations raised by Nina Baym's *Novelists, Readers, and Reviewers*. This failure has been costly to the comprehensive reading of Cooper.

There is also a critical practice that attempts to rescue Cooper the artist from those who would make him something less and from Cooper's own error in thinking he had something to say. Daniel Peck's formulation is merely the most frank: "Studies of Cooper's pictorialism, then, are as unsatisfactory as examinations of his social thought and historical consciousness. All of these tend to hold his fiction at a distance, to place it rather than engage its imaginative qualities directly" (*A World by Itself*, xi). Peck casually assumes that "social thought" and "historical consciousness" are unconnected with "imaginative qualities" and that to say so is in some way above politics. He renders "the dynamics of Cooper's space *as* space" (xi) but does not see that Cooper saturates his spaces with politics and history. Speaking of *The Crater*, Peck remarks,

> Cooper uses *The Crater* to attack every contemporary abuse he can think of—the irresponsibility of newspapers, political and religious factionalism, mob rule, and social and educational experimentation. Because the novelist's anger is so close to the surface, and because the urge to rebuke is so strong, Cooper's island experience is irreparably damaged. The writer, failing to respect the world he has made, becomes the most intrusive and destructive "outsider" in the novel. Far more than any of his fictional plunderers, Cooper himself robs this paradise of its integrity. [158][18]

For Peck, only "Cooper's island experience," his "Adamic" dimension, is authentic; the rest—the novel's entire dynamic—is "a mere vehicle for ideas." Pastoral has no political or ideological dimension for him. *The Deerslayer*'s setting is in "a time *before* history" (159). Hutter is reduced to "one of the archetypal despoilers of [Cooper's] imagination," Harry March a "moral copy" of him; nothing they can do can "violate the pastoral" (160); but it is equally necessary to see Natty's characterization here as ideologically saturated. It is not true that at any level the pastoral is unviolated (pastoral can exist, it is arguable, only in the context of or under threat of violation): Natty's first word is of the settlements; Harry March's coarse and destructive racism is not a matter of words merely but of catastrophic and callous action—his enthusiastic voice is heard above the din of the final indiscriminate slaughter; the scalping is endorsed and rewarded by the colony. The reader knows that Peck's "self-contained world of the imagination, a 'cosmos' produced by reverie" (159–60) is *already* destroyed and is of as little effect as Hetty herself. It is no more timeless than Natty himself.

Although Trilling would not "go . . . gladly" to "the dark and bloody crossroads where literature and politics meet" (*The Liberal Imagination*, 11), he would certainly have seen what Harry March means within the novel, within the series, and in history: that force of racial prejudice and violence, legitimized by society, and hardly insignificant in later history and literature. What Harry means disqualifies the existence of Peck's "world by itself." Cooper always knew that the blood was real.

The ubiquitous view that the Leather-Stocking novels constitute for the reader "a significant myth" seems to me, in part, a salvage operation, a critical flight on the part of those who find Cooper's means unacceptable in some way: he is too repetitive, his plots lack credibility even within the parameters of the kind of romance he wrote, he does not satisfy the demand for texts and textures that reward the quest for complexity. However, Natty's irresistible power and appeal can be ascribed to myth. In order to realize it fully we must constitute the trajectory of Natty's history chronologically. Such an ordering produces at its furthest point such aberrations as Allan Nevins's Modern Library volume *The Leatherstocking Saga*, but it does have the merit of offering Natty as a witness to history in the order of its occurrence. This version offers us Natty first as an almost perfect example of human conduct, fully idealized; then as a mature warrior and the would-be lover of Mabel Dunham; and finally as the aged forester, dispossessed of his freedom in nature and exiled to the site of his final mythical incarnation as father of the nation at his death in *The Prairie*. Even at its best, in William Goetzmann's "out of time, out of space," "ever so much more historical than history itself" ("James Fenimore Cooper," 86), the effect is to marginalize history, to cancel the effect—also a historical one—produced by the novels read in the order of their appearance. For the modern reader—as for Cooper's original readers—the order of composition enforces the reader's making of the text.

Few readers of *The Deerslayer* could be unaware in 1842 of Natty's fate in *The Pioneers* of 1822, so that, whatever Cooper's intentions, the mythic/romance dimension of the rites of passage could not be taken unqualified. The achronological order forces the reader constantly to assess fictional presence against the story already told in previous fictions of the character's and the nation's historical future—the obvious exception being *The Prairie*. But even there the habit of overlaying, achronological reading should enable the reader to accumulate into Mahtoree's appeal to Hard-Heart before their final combat the memory of Mohegan's conversation with Elizabeth on Mount Vision, Tamenund's vast historical oration, and Magua's sad state—and to understand Hard-Heart's near fatal distraction and hesitation. For Mahtoree to prevail would embody the threat to white civilization that Hard-Heart's hesitation implies; if Cooper intimates an America in all its classes "fathered" and hieratically blessed by Natty, then Hard-Heart's trust in the great white father preserves the nation emblematically. At the same time we are made to doubt that his trust will be reciprocated. Goetzmann has no doubt: "But alas, the reader realizes sadly that Leather-Stocking and his Indian friends are destined, like Uncas the last Mohican, to vanish before the march of empire—however good that empire may be" ("James Fenimore Cooper," 84). "Alas" and "sadly" combine with "destined" and "vanish" to convey a magical inevitability. The effect is quite different if we replace "vanish" with "be destroyed" or "be vanquished."

Goetzmann comes to rest here on the central issue: the irreducible conflict between the world as it was, or is imagined to have been, and the world as it is becoming and will be, or perhaps has already become. Most critics have seen this—one would have to be blind not to. Cooper worked with two irreconcilable myths: the romantic myth of the Leather-Stocking—in effect, the pastoral vision—and the superseding republican agrarian myth. A recent simplified version of the Natty myth, under the heading "Mythic Individualism," testifies to its durability: "A deep and continuing theme in American literature is the hero who must leave society, alone or with one or a few others, in order to realize the moral good in the wilderness, at sea, or on the margins of settled society. Sometimes, the withdrawal involves a contribution to society, as in James Fenimore Cooper's *The Deerslayer*."[19] Neither myth, from the outset, went unthreatened: Harry March, Ishmael Bush, and Tom Hutter have as sound a title to the name of frontiersman as Natty has; Judge Temple's agrarian future vision is under threat from Dickon Jones and Hiram Doolittle. Cooper and Crèvecoeur are not alone in this: even H. H. Brackenridge and his classmate Philip Freneau, joint authors of the Miltonic *The Rising Glory of America*, were to express their misgivings along with many others at the century's turn.

Marius Bewley's formulation of all this in terms of a double dialectic for Cooper among attitudes typified by Adams, Jefferson, and Hamilton usefully insists on historical context, at least in terms of ideas;[20] it releases Cooper from an isolation in which he must be read in purely aesthetic terms, strictly as a novelist facing problems of composition. In Bewley's version, Adams, the aristocrat, is set against Jefferson, the agrarian; then, conceiving an alliance beneath the skin between those two, Bewley places that against Hamilton's capitalist spirit. However, this valuable clarification cannot reduce Cooper to easily manageable terms. These novels are huge in their dimensions: their historical scope ranges over the century that spans Natty's first appearance and Cooper's composition of it, and far beyond that in Tamenund's memory and lore; its geographical scope too is as large as the exploration of America in his time allowed; and the work teems with an almost bewildering array of invented and historical detail. Rarely is any statement allowed to stand uncontested, any episode tending in one conceptual direction unchallenged by another leading elsewhere. If Cooper fashions no fictional or conceptual resolving schema, he enables his reader to see. As Barthes observes of Charlie Chaplin, "To see someone who does not see is the best way to be intensely aware of *what* he does not see" (*Mythologies*, 40).

Bewley substitutes his own myth of liberal balance:

> The greatness of Adams and Jefferson lies in this: that while each was stubbornly what he was, each was endowed with a flexibility of mind and sensibility that carried with it the wonderful creative power of organically reshaping itself to meet the exigencies of change. This is not the shiftiness of expediency, but the expression of a disinterested intelligence and integrity that is animated by the processes of life. It is the faculty of reconciling opposites, of discovering new unities and new harmonies that are not discontinuous with the old. In short, it is the mark of creative intelligence, whether it is exercised in politics, in science, or in art. [*The Eccentric Design*, 42]

He knows that "the new industrial philosophy would soon threaten" "selfhood and personal dignity" (44), but he prefers to find the genius of American politics in "reconciling opposites." And he imposes this on Natty: "If there is a poetry of tolerance, Deerslayer is its expression" (97). I can find little in Cooper so Olympian as this; for Cooper, there was no myth capable of erasing or consoling for the ineluctible contraries, the truth of genocide, the threat to the forest. Cooper does not resolve; the more closely one regards the details the truer the account becomes, but it is not the higher truth of resolved opposites but the more homely truth of recognizable confusions unresolved.

In the novels, voices come at the reader from all directions to disallow oversimplified interpretations. The case of Magua illustrates the point; as Terence Martin makes clear, he is a peculiarly intensified incarnation of one half of a generically determined romance polarity, his satanic majesty opposed to the idealized Apollonian characterization of Uncas; he is also the stereotype of the Indian brave, ruined by rum and punished or scolded for the addiction—and that alters the generic registration somewhat in offering a comprehensible motive for his actions. His complaints align him with almost every other Indian in the series, including, in this novel,

Tamenund; more specifically, the reader, remembering *The Pioneers*, underlays Magua's words with Mohegan's eloquent complaints after his drunkenness at the Bold Dragoon and when he is close to death and only too sober at Mount Vision. As a result, it is impossible fully to gratify the romance polarity; Magua is aligned with his virtuous antagonist Chingachgook as well.

The search for a resolution of conflict in Cooper's work, sometimes almost desperate, is the most typical shared characteristic of his critics. Thomas Philbrick sees that ideas drive events in Cooper, but he cannot accept that the book's tone and meaning are dominated by Natty and his exile. He argues for a cyclical evolution and for Oliver as the final focus for the reader's mind, combining as he does elements of Natty, Chingachgook, and his own loyalist bloodlines to colonial times with the republicanism of the Temples by his marriage to Elizabeth:

> The stability and validity of the Indian possession of the land have been passed on intact to the representative of white civilization.
>
> In this transfer of rightful authority, the human world of the novel completes the cycle of change which the seasonal progression in its natural world has echoed and reinforced. ["Cooper's *The Pioneers*," 593]

The suggestion is closer to Cooper's desire than the conclusions I offer. Although Philbrick argues for a cyclical process, his underlying logic is linear and leads forward "toward the full union of its diverse materials" to a new "stability." I contend that we are meant to see that succession coexisting with what preceded it; Doolittle may leave but Cooper is careful to let us know that he is not disabled, that he lives on, capable of menacing other Templetons. If *The Pioneers* is part of the Leather-Stocking series, it is also the first in the Effingham trilogy, and a Stedfast Dodge and Aristabalus Bragg reincarnate Jones and Doolittle. Too much in *The Pioneers* resists absorption for Philbrick's view to prevail: Mohegan does not just die—he explicitly resists peaceful reconciliation; Natty eludes both Temple's fruitless pursuit and Elizabeth's charitable Christian accommodation. In the same way, the union of Chingachgook and Natty on the last page of *The Last of the Mohicans* cannot constitute within the fiction a resolution which defies verification in history. The final tableau is moving precisely because it can be of no avail. To see it otherwise is to relieve the reader's memory of its obligation. It is not necessary to share

Lukács's political bias to find Gorky's analysis of Cooper "truer" than the liberal hopes of Philbrick and Bewley: "[Gorky's] analysis shows the divided attitude of the classics of the historical novel clearly. They have to affirm the downfall of the humanly noble Indian, the straightforwardly decent, straightforwardly heroic 'leather stocking', treating it as a necessary step of progress, and yet cannot help seeing and depicting the human inferiority of the victors. This is the necessary fate of every primitive culture with which capitalism comes into contact" (Lukács, *The Historical Novel*, 346).

Such views as Philbrick's and Goetzmann's transcendentalize history in ways that are foreign to Cooper. While it is true that one cannot at will summon up herds of buffalo, woods teeming with game, and the presence of the disappeared Indian nations, it is quite another matter to suggest that what happened was inevitable because it happened. However realistic we must be, reason does not require arguments that eliminate so much: human motive and error and the larger political determinants of empire, trade, possession, and power. In short, the notion of inevitability makes reasons unnecessary to give and makes irrelevant the circumstances, conveyed by the immense wealth of detail in Cooper, in which the great movements of history take place.

For example, the opening episode of *The Pioneers*, quite apart from its agrarian assumptions, which I have already indicated, is crammed with historical circumstance. Elizabeth's dominant eye on the scene, since she is returning, is acutely sensitive to the change that is taking/has taken place, the transitional stage of history in which she is set; in that transition she is not merely witness but also actor—she will replace Remarkable Pettibone as mistress of the domestic realm. The confrontation of Natty and Temple involves important questions of property, power, and the change wrought in the natural habitat by a radically invasive new agricultural technology. The first face we meet is black, the slave Aggy (in the light of Jones's treatment of him, we might remember Crèvecoeur); and if Temple's strange behavior in this scene is not enough, his shifty possession of a slave (he is a Quaker too) suggests that all is not well in this agrarian peaceable kingdom over which he presides. While Cooper often smiles over the professions of law, medicine, and architecture on the frontier, he always carefully renders them as part of a stage of history, capable of explanation—Todd's initiation may be irregular but he will become a reasonable practitioner, even though in Oliver's case a younger Natty with a steadier hand and Chingachgook's Indian knowledge would suffice. Temple himself contains not merely the agrarian proposition but a vision of future progress, innocently projected as unambiguously beneficent; yet it is he who unleashes the commercial and exploitative spirit, embodied by Doolittle and Jones, which must be as dangerous to his ambitions as it is fatal to Natty's way of life. Nor is the agrarian position itself innocent, as the opening of *Mohicans* will, soon after *The Pioneers*, establish: the ground is already bloodstained, as Cooper insists—that is also, by the way, the final/initial gesture of *The Deerslayer*. The land, the basic agrarian assumption, is never virgin. It is won and fought over and possessed in ways that clearly betray the principles upon which the republic founds itself.

Another critical evasion is to make the conflict that we come to know in the novels ultimately reside with Cooper himself as a personal dilemma, which with some is relentlessly psychologized. Edwin Fussell, who certainly cannot be accused of excluding the historical, nonetheless is able to conceive "a morally and aesthetically estimable America, as first embodied in his own personality, and then in the personalities of Leatherstocking and his friends the Noble Savages" (*Frontier*, 28–29). However true this is, the problem to be faced by all critics of Cooper is that while the imagination could control and validate Natty as an idealized figure and there could be found external verification for the destruction of what Natty represents—and of the Indian whose eradication so intensifies his pathos and idealization—there was no historical confirmation for the fulfillment of the desire and hope that Cooper cherished for American civilization, as McWilliams too points out. To make the issue rest in Cooper's dilemma is to elide the only solution Cooper found: to represent both sides, unreconciled. He is disconsolate, but he does not fashion for himself delusive consolations. To find, as Fussell does, Cooper's "alienation from his country . . . more significantly psychic and ethical than sociological" (29) merely confuses the issue; Cooper never separates the ethical reactions from the sociological, political, and historical causes that give rise to them. Why inspect the absent and unverifiable psychic component when the undeniably present conflicts in the text invite more profitable scrutiny?

On the level of moral esteem, civilization offers no parallel to Bush's transformation or Natty's self-sacrifice; Fussell rightly insists upon an underlying affinity between Natty and Bush but does not quite grasp how deeply his shrewd insistence on Temple's ineffectiveness wounds the *idea* of the Revolution. The idea is rendered ineffectual against the powers of acquisition, demagoguery, and destruction; the words alone will not avail and find too little expression in action. In short, the text condemns the very principle it most wishes to endorse, in a fashion very similar to Crèvecoeur's. To see that is to learn how to read the entire series, to fathom the despair that a century and a half have done little to dispel.

Focusing on Cooper's dilemma, the critic is often led, predictably, into the realm of psychology; the absence of the patient makes the practice luxuriously easy. Daniel Peck and Richard Slotkin, and even such political and historical realists as Robert Clark and Wayne Franklin, are tempted into these muddy waters. Eric Sundquist's suggestion that the "incestuous" marriage of Effingham with Effingham in *Home as Found* offers a defeated fictive solution of a problem that Cooper could not resolve in actuality is illuminating as a trope. However, it also contrives to ignore any serious treatment of the issues of political justice that Cooper raises in so conflicted a form in the Effingham trilogy, of which *The Pioneers* is the first volume (*Home as Found* is also the sixth volume in the Leather-Stocking series, if only in the sense that, for a brief yearning moment, he is remembered there). Sundquist's ingenuity as a critic is undeniable, but in hot pursuit of his perception, he is led to accept oversimplifications: "David Noble has convincingly argued that in the long run Judge Temple . . . is Cooper's truly intended archetypal hero and that the aim of the Leatherstocking series is finally to depict the collapse and passage of the nostalgic Adamic myth represented by Natty" (*Home as Found*, 2). Sundquist goes on to stress the "near failure" of the Temple myth in *Home as Found* and to suggest the centrality of Cooper's interest in the question of authority in America.[21] One can readily agree that Temple was intended as Cooper's "archetypal hero," but it is not true that Cooper allowed himself to fulfill that intention. How "civically responsible" is Temple? How "just" is his leadership? How "just" can it be? Is "resolute" quite the word for him? And, if it is, what in the circumstances can "resolution" accomplish? These questions—and many more—are *openly* addressed in the novel. The "middle-ground represented by Judge Temple" seems to me more like a battleground on which the complex skirmishing of American political history is carried out. Sundquist's overcomplicated instrument produces an oversimplified text.

Henry Nash Smith simplifies in a different way. He charts with such a rich sense of historical, political, social, and economic circumstance the stages by which the agrarian ideals were betrayed that it seems grudging to complain. Smith's acute and informed sense of the contesting claims of "civilization" and "cultural primitivism" allows him to raise the literary problem of grafting the most available genre onto the changing historical situation. He finds that Cooper fails artistically. Cooper's inability to "solve" the social and historical problems he raises leads to "a compromise statement that represents his unwillingness or inability to accept the full implications of the conflict he has stated" (*Virgin Land*, 69). The conflict that Smith and R. H. Pearce firmly established for Cooper criticism is beyond question. However, the "compromise statement" is Temple's, not Cooper's. While Cooper may have endorsed the feelings Temple expresses, Smith's insistence that Cooper solve problems and share views with his characters distracts us from seeing that Cooper is *inscribing* the conflict and uneasy compromise. While Smith's focus on the generic problem serves to reveal the social and class problems the novels face, his insistence on Cooper's *artistic* failure not only begs the question but also deflects from the presence of the failure as an element *within* the text. The complete, resolved social theory and aesthetic form called for would preclude the complete registration of irresolution the series offers; what for Smith is a failure, for me largely defines the work's merit.

If Smith's judgment on aesthetic grounds is misleading, the mythic approach is much more so. D. H. Lawrence began myth criticism of Cooper in 1923 with a memorable phrase; Cooper composed "a wish-fulfillment vision, a kind of yearning myth" (*Studies*, 60). As usual, myth and arbitrarily invoked psychology go hand in hand. Lawrence, unfailingly condescending, denies Cooper the capacity to make fiction. His inattention to the text is typical of what mythic schemata especially do: they, like Smith's aesthetic one, distract us from the text.[22] I shall touch upon only two examples of a widespread critical practice, those of Edwin Fussell and Richard Slotkin.

Fussell points incisively to the processes with which he deals:

The simple truth is that the American West was neither more nor less interesting than any other place, except in mythology or in the swollen egos of Westerners, until by interpretation the great American writers—all of whom happened to be Eastern—made it seem so . . . by conceiving its physical aspects . . . and its social aspects . . . as expressive emblems for the invention and development of a new national civilization, and not as things in themselves. [*Frontier*, 13]

He tellingly draws attention to the "temporal paradox," whereby to deal with the West, so powerful a locus for the future, was to deal with the past; he cites James Hall's *Tales of the Border* (1835) to this effect. Turning to Cooper, he makes the routine gestures of aesthetic embarrassment toward his "protracted and fumbling epic" but finds his best subject in "the Western frontier where American society might be conceived as passing from one set of principles to another in two directions at once" (28).

Fussell's desire to find Cooper the person in the text rather than its author makes Tamenund's final words the author's own "moral antipathy to the Westward movement" (*Frontier*, 42), which defines Cooper as a major American writer. The claim made on our attention is what he is said to have believed, not the remarkably cross-grained achievement evident in the alignment of Magua, Chingachgook, and Tamenund, complicated by the persistent issue of miscegenation.[23] Against the realized presence of Tamenund, Fussell offers a substitute myth in which Cooper enjoys equal status with his characters: "At the end of the novel, Hawkeye alienates himself from his people, transcends the limits of American civilization (as understood by Parkman and such types), and becomes the true hero of the new American civilization hopefully coming into existence through his renunciation and transcendence. The nobility of Uncas passes to him, and the nobility of Uncas's races passes to Cooper" (45). The evident circularity of this apart, Chingachgook and Natty are left isolated and unwitnessed at the end of *Mohicans* (except of course by the narrator and his reader). Natty can *only* be transcendent, can *only* renounce. He is, as the reader already knows, even actively and willingly involved in the creation of the conditions that will superannuate him; and, if he embodies many of the moral ideals of the civilization, he embodies them alone, and civilization expresses itself repeatedly in ways that cancel his virtues. If Natty is mythic-heroic, he is *only* that.

Fussell is fully aware of the complex ironies registered in Cooper, but, like Smith on different grounds, he wants the united resolving image too much; it strains credulity to have Natty "atone for the sins of civilization" (*Frontier*, 59). If the wilderness is the city of God, it is only fair to add that the city of man—however suited it may be to Jasper, Paul, Middleton,

Heyward, Effingham, and Temple—is deaf to the voice in the wilderness. The pervasive irony of Cooper's series is that each evocation of Natty as the idealized wilderness figure—including that in *Home as Found*—serves only to emphasize civilization's indifference to him and what he means.

Fussell attempts to construct the myth of Natty on ethical grounds embodying "both the civilized and the natural virtues." Fully aware of the aberrations of civilization, he so presents them that some sort of moral renewal within the system might amend matters. In such a schema, "Leatherstocking was purely and simply that new man, the generic American, the metaphor of the Western frontier fleshed out as a human being" (*Frontier*, 67–68). Now, Natty may have been isolated, but he exists in, bears witness to, and is victim of a historically identifiable social context. That context renders Natty possible only as metaphor, only as a hybrid who does not reproduce himself.

The ethical dimension is vitally important in Cooper but is neither symbolic nor metaphorical; rather it is symptomatic. The moral hypertrophy in Cooper's series, whether in Hetty, Elizabeth, or Natty, is so important because it is ineffectual. If it transcends American civilization, it is because it can find no accommodation there; however "ethical and religious" (64) the situations are, they are also pathetically marginal. To stress the issue as Fussell does is to deflect the impossibility Cooper recorded and to annul the defeated tone of the series' final paragraph. To transcendentalize the events of frontier warfare into "the eternal warfare of opposing principles" (66) is to deprive them of a geography and a history, to make events determined by human will and political power bloodless illustrations of eternal principles, to deny what the books tell, and to mystify "civilization" as Cooper's novels do not. It is, perhaps, one of Barthes's "degraded forms" of "Neither-Norism": "They are always predicted in a prudently compensatory perspective: a final equilibrium immobilizes values, life, destiny, etc.: one no longer needs to choose, but only to endorse" (*Mythologies*, 153).

Richard Slotkin offers the most thorough treatment of Cooper, and his forebears in writing of the American frontier, along mythological lines. No one else gives so full an account of the construction of the myth of the frontiersman—its local refractions and its transformations of historical and economic determinants. One of Slotkin's most important achievements for the student of American literature lies in his demystification of the canon. He establishes the *central* significance of "minor genres" for the experience they encompass and the patterns they reveal. "Minor" works are examined with the care usually reserved for the "major works."

There is, however, a heavy price to pay in the establishment of a new mystification, the formation of an American mythology founded on Jungian assumptions that draws the American experience, individual and national, into a shared psychology.[24] The basis of it is so well founded in historical actuality that it need not be contested. After all, how could the encounter of Christianity and paganism, civilization and wilderness, not produce internal and external conflict? How could a nation set itself the task of evangelization that ends in bloody extermination, of colonization that ends in expropriation, of improvement that ends in spoliation, without suffering psychological wounds? However, while Slotkin is fully aware of the political, economic, and historical forces at work, he rarely does more than mention them before returning to his relentlessly mythographical readings of his texts. Commenting on the roasted Indians in Benjamin Tompson's "New-Englands Crisis," Slotkin remarks, "In one sense they did wish to cannibalize the Indian—to take into themselves the Indian's strength or prowess, his ability to live within the environmental laws of the wilderness" (*Regeneration through Violence*, 90–91). It may be so, and Slotkin rarely speaks lightly, but the subjection of the Indian is psychologized, becomes part of a white myth, and the material expression of the will to conquest and land acquisition is marginalized.

Addressing the history of the books' publication, Slotkin produces the mythic pattern of death and rebirth; if we accept that, we elide the value of that order in raising issues, just as Lawrence did with his well-known crescendo of beauty; the reader's dialogue with the text and his own developing memory of the text are diminished. To stress the deer ritual loses Doolittle's instrumentality in the episode. To insist on the ritual of Mohegan's death on Mount Vision sacrifices what Elizabeth and Chingachgook have to say to one another there. The insistence on the pursuit of myth requires that Natty be threatened by Judith Hutter or be tempted to evade the conditions of his furlough—he is not; Judith's imposture in the Indian encampment is not, as Slotkin maintains, that of a "goddess" (*Regeneration through Violence*, 502) but, quite explicitly, in her intention as in the succeeding action, that of an embodiment of imperial white power. Warley and the Redcoats mysteriously disappear from the text.

I do not deny the power of myth in societies, both "civilized" and "savage," but I cannot accept the effect it has as an instrument of literary or historical interpretation in censoring whatever does not fit and in conferring literary merit wherever its presence is discerned. It is one thing to observe the patterns of mythic accommodation in societies, to observe that a pattern may be shared among societies—pre-Christian, Christian, and post-Christian; preindustrial, industrial, and postindustrial. It is quite another to assume that those patterns are determinant rather than resultant, and to ignore significant differences between the adaptations and the "original" and in the motivations and circumstances of their uses. It is a kind of magic in which hindsight is transfigured into foresight and human responsibility disappears in a puff of smoke. The inevitability conferred by myth formulation is very comforting; who can—or needs—prevent or correct the inevitable? It is Lawrence who explicitly—and by example—gives a mandate to banish the public, political, historical consciousness from art (*Studies*, 35).

Arthur K. Moore's *The Frontier Mind* brings to the entire issue a tonic realism:

> It scarcely needs saying that during the western expansion in America material benefits fell not to the Indian fighters, although they often claimed great tracts of land, but to the executives, the Marmaduke Temples. . . . As the executors only, they had to share the rewards with the conceivers, whose foresight and capital made conquest possible. The cultural structure erected in the wilderness was actually not of the pioneers' devising but of the capitalists', and it was intended to perpetuate the values of the ruling class of the East. [158]

The acidity of passages like this may mislead the reader; Moore is actually somewhat conservative in his preferences, but as a historian he exercises a predisposition to tell an unvarnished truth that tallies with Cooper's fictional Temple and with Crèvecoeur's account of frontier expansion. Moore, amplifying Smith, points shrewdly to the unsuitability of the romance form, with its insistence on chivalry, to American circumstances and white-Indian warfare.[25] The most vexing problem is the fashioning of an appropriate hero; Natty and Oliver "between them possess the important qualities united in the knight of medieval romance, but neither is a complete hero for lacking in some part the character which distinguishes the other in his proper sphere—the court or the forest" (169–70). This is true enough if we can accept the priority Moore gives to the generic issue, but Cooper makes the unsuitability work for him in surprising ways: war at the outset of *Mohicans* is seen antiromantically, antiheroically, and those who might satisfy the romantic role—Heyward, Munro, Montcalm—are startlingly ineffective; the tragic-heroic dimension is shifted onto the Indians. The conventional romance possibility is consistently undermined, just as Natty's deracinated presence in Temple's court shreds the legal simplifications Cooper would like to prevail.

Moore certainly knows that the "fair products of the Enlightenment who marched safely in the rear of the emigration displayed more avarice than benevolence"; he observes that "popular literature after all is scarcely the vehicle for scrutinizing the myth of progress" (*The Frontier Mind*, 182). However, that is precisely what it becomes in the hands of Cooper. It is simply not true that Cooper "winked at inequities" in the interests of "the ideal consequences of progress" (183). We cannot doubt that Cooper's sympathies lay with the civilizers, but he lays bare the contradictions and futilities of their liberal virtues. The impossibility of Natty's situation is no greater than that of Elizabeth Temple, except that she has power. If Natty, unlike the heroes of romance and epic, received no rewards, it is not because Cooper failed to offer them but because civilization had no rewards to offer—only compensations that had, by Natty as ideologue, to be refused.

It is true that Cooper "could not establish control" (*The Frontier Mind*, 197) over Natty, and he does not attempt to; to "control" Natty would misrepresent the issues. Moore, implying an artistic failure, says that Natty shows "a lack of substantiality when placed on intimate terms with personages of specific quality" (197); that Natty is ambiguous does not make him unspecific—his and Chingachgook's anomalous presence in Temple's domain poses a substantial question to the developing society. The question and their presence has such "substantiality" that Natty's legal problems come to dominate the romance narrative, and the elements of romance are made to serve what is really the subplot, which contains a subtext at variance with that of the main plot. Rather than making Natty fit progressive ideology, romantic reaction, or frontier realities—or reconcile all three—Cooper allows full play to the incongruities; Natty becomes the focal point at which a transitional society reveals itself. The effect upon the modern reader is to command attention to the internal contradictions of the society as it develops.

Robert Clark's response reveals myth's dehistoricizing tendency, its removal of ideology's inadequacy, and its resistance to rational denial. American writers "try to affirm the nation's moral superiority and give expression to an ideology which was scarcely capable of explaining the contradictory facts of territorial expansion. When the writer remarked these contradictions he was not able to find an alternative system of belief and could only repress his awareness of historical experience and move to myth" ("History," 22). Clark's insight applies less well to American authors than to American critics and historians. He is a psychological determinist and finds the resort to myth inevitable: Cooper is unaware, the servant of the myth that serves his inadequacy. Surely, all the insupportable elements of received idealism, itself a social myth, are constantly exploding into fragments in the novels, which again and again reveal—as Clark is often quick to see—the myths' inadequacy, or civilization's refusal of an ideal of behavior, or the very contradictions Clark insists on. I do not see how it can make critical sense to maintain "repression" when so much is revealed.

If it is largely true that in mythical constructions, as in factualist ones, there is "no-one to accept responsibility for the attribution of values, and in neither can humanity be represented as the responsible agent for its own history" (Clark, "History," 38), it remains impossible to convict Cooper of moral indifference. It is simply not the case that Cooper survived the ideological contradictions by moving "to suspend the rational, objective and critical faculties" (50). In fact, he constantly calls these into play and forces the reader to judge conduct and human history and society's ideology. Cooper does not buy the myths, but I fear that Clark has bought the view of American criticism that Cooper did so. Clark in fact offers an excellent formulation of Cooper's art: "The discourse of the romance will thus oscillate between an urgent inscription of myth and an equally urgent attempt to deconstruct it. The latter move, of course, only lends strength to the former, for if deconstruction were to succeed it would manifest the incompatibility of the text and the world" (60). Clark's reluctance to allow Cooper awareness and critical insight, his insistence that Cooper is *forced* against his will to make myth and *forced* to attempt deconstruction, belies Cooper's always alert critical judgment and the possibility that Cooper's strength lies in *allowing* "the incompatibility of text [myth?] and the world." Cooper, of course, could not use Clark's critical vocabulary, but possession of a vocabulary is not a precondition of insight.

Clark is determined to construct an unverifiable Freudian account of

Cooper's repressions: "[Natty as mythic construction] denies what white men are in reality by abolishing history, economy and political belief. He is thus able to resolve the contradiction between white men's possession of stolen land and their desire to believe themselves morally redeemed" ("History," 79). In fact, his interesting conclusion is enabled only by a text that ruthlessly exposes Temple and his ideology, rests its plot explicitly on protection of property, and exiles its mythologized moral voice. The myth does not pacify a troublesome issue but rather exacerbates it. Cooper surely cannot be convicted of "abolishing history, economy and political belief"; how do we then explain the presence of sanctioned violence and venality in Hutter and the amoral presence of empire in Warley in the novel that most extensively mythicizes Natty? And Natty is not invariably idealized—when he leaves Mabel free to wed Jasper, he steps back into history and at once expresses the lie in which the expropriated and expropriators reverse roles.

Philip Fisher argues convincingly the political dimension of Cooper's fiction. His attempt critically to recover *popular* forms that achieve "the self-terminating work of the imagination" (*Hard Facts*, 7)—that crystal-lize an issue or experience in such a way that it is, so to speak, played out—deserves to be followed up by others. It allows him not to follow the canon and to examine novels by Harriet Beecher Stowe and Theodore Dreiser. His approach to such things as "the first murderous act" rather than to literary forms offers the basis for a reach into the past every bit as valid as the pursuit of a continuous interest in symbolism. By abandoning the formulaic approach to romance and by stressing the exemplary, didac-tic, synecdochic, and allegorical effects of fictional action, he not merely reestablishes a critical strain for some time unfashionable but constructs a means of viewing American fiction that allows us to see Stowe and natu-ralism (a hardy plant in modern American fiction) as developments, not mere aberrations.[26] This approach also allows a natural entry for a range of meaning in which the moral forms only a part, along with the historical, political, economic, materialistic, and social.

Fisher is admirably clear on the "therapeutic" value (hegemonic func-tion) of the historical novel, which "trains resignation and gives an ele-vated moral tone to stoic regret. It pictures forces as beyond control, already underway, and creates central figures who embody processes they do not control" (*Hard Facts*, 18). Part of the value of Fisher's insight is that it clearly enunciates the political function that literature may have through its literary effects.[27] It might be added that the more fully the matter is exposed, the less we need to share such feelings; they become a part of the object we contemplate, as well as part of our subjective feelings on the matter. Cooper seems often actively to enable this by making those feelings part of the text's matter: for example, in Natty and Chingachgook's indeterminate opening conversation in *Mohicans* or Elizabeth and Oliver's discussion on property in *The Pioneers*.

Fisher's greatest merit is the subtle realism with which he reads the text of *The Deerslayer* in all its detail. He draws us away from the isolation of narrative incident or the reduction to a simple rite of passage; he is able to see, as Cooper does, that acts have consequences—Natty kills, a wigwam loses it provider, a wife is widowed; Hetty and an Indian maiden are pointless victims of stray bullets. Because of this, he is able to assemble the small or isolated actions into the larger actions of history; often they are unwilled—the massacre is not the willed outcome of Cooper's plot. But, even so, Fisher will not accept the inviting, mystifying argument of the inevitability of history, "self-serving history told by the winners" (*Hard Facts*, 72–73). Instead, he argues, "The great central hard facts occur in this way: they are incidental to thousands of other transactions that seem to have nothing to do with them and, as secondary results to whatever primary result is intended, they again and again, as if by accident, resume the configuration of their historical solution. . . . At a saturated moment of history every intention . . . will again and again register the same individual outcome" (73). Marriage, migration, settling a farm—all issue in massacre. I have given only his conclusion, but Fisher's argument is fully supported by a detailed response to the text.

However, by isolating *The Deerslayer*, Fisher misses an opportunity he is especially well equipped to meet: to study the five-novel Leather-Stocking text, which by its seemingly random order of composition invites the fullest achronological exploration of several of the issues he raises. Taking *The Deerslayer* in isolation, Fisher sees the coexistence of the overt goal, to rescue Hist, and the latent goal, to kill the Indian, and his account works well: Judith's "masquerade of civilization fails" (*Hard Facts*, 61), Hist and Chingachgook's armed attempt fails, the entire group is threatened, and they are freed by a massacre of the Indians. However, the reader already knows of Uncas's death and of the success of empire (Judith's failure is momentary only) from the novels that precede this one, so that while an element of irony may be involved, we can hardly be surprised or concede Fisher's notion of latency: the outcome is predictable in plot terms and imperative if the truth already told is not to be betrayed. Harry's "stupid greed" is not primitive; it has been institutionalized by Sheriff Jones. Warley's brutality has already had its consequences. The *incident* is new to the reader; it is the climax of *this* novel, but it at once exists together with what Cooper's contemporary reader already knows. It is confirmation of what has already happened, even if in this novel's time it is yet to be.

Cooper does, in Fisher's striking formulation, show "society's conscience" and "society's fist" operating independently, but he constantly reminds us that this is the case and, if he cannot change history, enforces judgment. Civilization cannot be treated as inevitability's infant son claiming to be a first offender, that he didn't mean it and won't do it again (the order of the novels' appearance makes of that "he always will because he always already has"). The moral force of Cooper's text lies precisely in his insistence on accountability, in his always taking us beyond the revelation of historical pattern into human judgment and responsibility, but a step short—which the reader may take—of the systematic condemnation the case requires.

In writing this section, I have had two purposes in mind: to remind the reader of various critical approaches that have been taken to Cooper and to offer, by my commentary on them and differences from them, a developing presentation of my own view, which has governed the five plain readings of the Leather-Stocking novels that follow.[28] In Jane Tompkins I find a critic with whom I am in virtually total agreement: she "sees literary texts not as works of art embodying enduring themes in complex forms, but as attempts to redefine the social order. . . . novels and stories should be studied not because they manage to escape the limitations of their particular time and place, but because they offer powerful examples of the way a culture thinks about itself, articulating and proposing solutions for the problems that shape a particular historical moment" (*Sensational Designs*, xi). She argues against those who take "work that affects people's lives, or tries to, as merely sensational or propagandistic." Her determination to examine texts "in relation to the religious beliefs, social practices, and economic and political circumstances that produced them" (xiii) produces irresistible readings of Susan Warner, Charles Brockden Brown, and Harriet Beecher Stowe; and, in doing so, she raises vital questions about how we read (or have been taught to read) and how we form canons. It must be said—and fully recognized—that the reinstatements she argues for are a part of the feminist enterprise[29] that is capable of a far more radical effect upon criticism, history, scholarship, and cultural studies than the more exclusively theoretical movement that, generally speaking, has had no effect whatsoever upon the canon. I believe this to be largely because the feminist impulse is generated outside the academy, in the world, and is capable of thinking that what takes place in that world affects and may be affected by literature. Therefore, the effect it has, in works like those of Tompkins, Baym, Kolodny, and many others, is not only that attention is paid to the women writers filleted out of the canon but that male writers too are read in a new way—not for the universal values of which they speak or the literary standards they are said to set but for the account they render of the world they address. In this, feminist criticism shares many of the same impulses as the worldly political criticism of Edward Said, Raymond Williams, Frederic Jameson, and Terry Eagleton.

It is therefore not surprising that Tompkins should include Cooper among the writers she studies and for whom she offers a new way of reading. For one thing, what she has to say about Warner and Stowe must alter the way we see Cooper's heroines, in particular Elizabeth Temple or Inez in her strange appearance on the rock in *The Prairie*. However, Tompkins's approach is not only polemically founded; it is based on a clear understanding of the way in which contemporary criteria legitimized and reinforced the sociopolitical function of literature (*Sensational Designs*, 44–45). She is concerned to argue that the reality of American facts did not bear out optimistic revolutionary ideologies—and that is not difficult to substantiate both from many historical accounts and from postrevolutionary writers like Brackenridge and Freneau, as well as in Cooper, Irving, and others. But she does not offer yet another set of time-transcending American themes; she insists rather that in order to understand we attend less to formal transformation and more to the forming power of political issues and historical circumstance.

Tompkins's devastating attack on certain tendencies in Cooper criticism is one of the great satisfactions of recent criticism; I shall not summarize it—it should be read in full by everyone seriously interested in how engaged criticism may proceed. Suffice it to say that she makes brilliant sense of the detail that mythicizers evade and dispense with; she distinguishes "social criticism written in allegorical mode" (103) from the eternalization that reduces Cooper to an illustrative footnote to "Jung, Freud, Joseph Campbell, or Mircea Eliade" (102). Cooper was, she maintains, "a profound thinker . . . obsessively preoccupied not with the subtle workings of individual consciousness, but with the way the social world is organized" (99), and that leads her—and us—to enquire on what grounds the latter concern is inferior to the former.

Her treatment of *Mohicans* shows a remarkable capacity to reduce an exacting study of detail to a generalizing statement that remains insistently specific: "Conjunctions of opposed terms . . . are not coincidental. . . . Rather an obsessive preoccupation with systems of classification—the insignia by which race is distinguished from race, nation from nation, tribe from tribe, human from animal, male from female—dominates every aspect of the novel" (*Sensational Designs*, 105). The "irreconcilable conflicts" draw forth the stereotypes (or are served by them) rather than genre's exerting the determining force.

Since her position opens up the complete field of the novel, it is possible to differ with her on detail while respecting the overall tendency of her views. While her major purpose in the chapter is to suggest a new way of reading Cooper, I do not feel that she pushes it far enough. We know what she means when she says that the novel denies the possibility of racial union; she finds that the rejection is "explicitly" made, that in fact its meaning is limited by an allegory based on simple Anglo-Saxon assumptions of cultural superiority. But the novel, it seems to me, offers more than that single determinant of meaning. Natty certainly embraces those assumptions; Cooper's plot faithfully traces Anglo-Saxon fear of miscegenation. It also offers Munro's defiant miscegenation, of which Cora, Cooper's most admirable woman, is the present evidence, as well as his pious hope of racial equality before God, Heyward's embarrassed racism, and Tamenund's dignified espousal of racial intermarriage as desirable. In short, the novel renders the issue far more problematically than Tompkins allows. Similarly, I feel—as I do with Fisher—that the treatment of one novel, isolated from the entire series, closes off a vital area of the reader's activity in constituting the text; that, at its simplest level, *Mohicans* is successor to *The Pioneers*; and that the opening conversation of Natty and Chingachgook occurs with the reader's knowledge of its irrelevance.

Whatever exception one might take is far outweighed by the quality of her readings and the stimulation offered by the stand she takes: "[Cooper's] characters are elements of thought, things to think with; and the convolutions of the plots, the captures, rescues and pursuits of the narrative, are stages in a thought process, phases in a meditation that is just as rigorous and complicated in its way as the meditations of Strether by the river" (*Sensational Designs*, 119). And, we might add, just as resistant to solution.

It's Not Just an Academic Question

A separation between man and nature is not simply the product of modern industry or urbanism; it is a characteristic of many earlier kinds of organized labor, including rural labor. Nor can we look with advantage to that other kind of reaction, which, correctly identifying one part of the problem in the idea of nature as a mechanism, would have us return to a traditional teleology, in which men's unity with nature is established through their common relation to a creator. That sense of an end and a purpose is in important ways even more alienated than the cold world of mechanism. Indeed the singular abstraction which it implies has much in common with that kind of abstract materialism. It directs our attention away from real and variable relations, and can be said to ratify the separation by making one of its forms permanent and fixed.
– Raymond Williams, Problems in Materialism *[82–83]*

When early nineteenth-century critics prescribed the terms on which an American romance could be undertaken, the native peoples of North America were seen as offering two opportunities—one historically based, the other merely literary: historically, they would be antagonists in the stirring events of colonization, participants in the military action considered needful to romance on the Scott pattern; in their literary function, they—and their legends—would provide part of the necessary apparatus of the mysterious.

It was not long before voices were heard protesting that—whether accurately rendered or not—Indians were not "interesting" enough to sustain protracted fictional treatment. Thus is mirrored and revealed, in literary historical terms, the reification of those we set out to destroy. Cooper, however, is never so crass, even though in the later works of the series the Indian presence is less marked. His Indians are unfailingly seen as the victims they were; the romance polarization of good and bad Indian vanishes before the relentless power of empire; they are complicit in their own destruction, and aware of and eloquent about both the character of their conquerors and the history of their own degradation.[30] Elements of this kind go far toward demystifying, implicitly, the myth of the American Revolution and its Declaration.

However interesting prescriptive criticism may be, the critic's constant dance with the notion of perfection, of failures and successes, can perhaps operate only on the level of rhetoric and form; at another level, it is a symptom rather of the impossibility of the perfect novel as an enterprise. No novel can fully register reality—its conditions of production prescribe that impossibility. The more convincing a character is made, the more life*like* (thus noting an ineffaceable difference) it is, by that much it exists beyond the printed texts, raising questions the author can neither control nor answer, nor—if we are wise—should we be other than grateful that this is so. All terminations, conceptual or narrative, are unrealistic; narrative lines and structures may end, but the life they offer to imitate obviously does not.[31]

The inclination to address critically the political, ideological, economic, and social portent of novels brings with it perils that, properly understood, reveal certain limits of critical propriety and fictional possibility and representation. It has to be said at once that even critics who regard themselves as objective, purely judicial, and resolutely unpolitical, rarely—if ever—are. When they observe with satisfaction that Darcy and Elizabeth learn from the experience Jane Austen bestows on them and that their marriage is not only the consummation of their love but also a celebration of the restoration of order, that marriage—advantageous marriage to a landed gentleman—is an appropriate ambition, perhaps the only appropriate one, for a young woman. Critics have sometimes found a similar satisfaction in the ending of *The Pioneers*. Such a finding, surely a not uncommon one, is as political as Igor Webb's dissatisfaction with the marriages that end *Dombey and Son*, *Our Mutual Friend*, and *Shirley*, as a sort of betrayal of what the novels reveal, as a revelation of the novelists' "inability to draw us away from things gone dead that we may most fruitfully participate in the active human creation of human society" (*From Custom*, 213). Webb here forgets the hazards of his occupation. The courtship-marriage pattern is not only "conventional"; for all the perspicacity of Shirley's critical reflections on the realities of marriage, spinsterhood, the desire for meaningful occupation, and dominant and insensitive males, marriage to a masterful male in Victorian England is a *realistic* resolution. Commending order and deploring a lack of political correctness seem equally to impair the novelist's obligation to register a truth fully enough for the reader to respond to it.

The nature of the case must be clearly understood. The novelist cannot escape history or the political implications of the situations he or she imagines; if the novel embodies or develops contradictions in the relationships of male and female as they exist in the society outside the novel, it does not follow that the artist has the obligation within the novel to resolve the problem in a way that the society has not yet accomplished—if it ever will. Most novels exist because that is the case. It suffices that the account rendered is full, true, and vital enough for the reader to be moved into consciousness. If the conventional marriage ending is at odds with what precedes it, so much the better for *our* consciousness. What can it mean when such fictional marriages are called artistic failures? Surely, only that the critic places some unarticulated notion of artistic success above verisimilitude; surely it is not "a sign of failed comprehensiveness" in the novel, whatever it may be in the author (and whatever unreasonable demand the critic may make for it). Is inconsistency any less convincing, less comprehensive, than consistency? Is it impossible to think that anything else might look like fantasy—or allegory, where alone, I suspect, that perfect conjunction of conceptual and narrative correctness can exist? It is not, by the way, that Webb does not know all this, but he is prone at the end of the day to find lack of *political* resolve in the author an *artistic* fault in the work.

The canon of fiction as studied in the traditional syllabus is hardly a hotbed of revolutionary sentiment and intention; however critical of society, mores, and class it may be—however pitying of the exploited, oppressed, and starving classes—it rarely moves in the direction of radical social change. At the most, usually, a novel will implicitly call for reform within the existing structures. If we require of it—to obtain critical assent—that it manifest a correct political analysis of the conditions it describes and dramatizes, we are asking not for illumination but for confirmation of what we already have decided upon—a pointless pursuit. The "failure" aesthetically to resolve contradictions that politically and historically were unresolved is not only a fictional strength in realistic terms but a political strength as well, for it more thoroughly reveals the situation that must be understood before change can take place.

Cooper was hardly original in his handling of conventional romantic elements or unconservative in his social views, but the marriages in all but one of his novels are not merely conventional; they carry a large freight of social and political meaning. They invariably support the established society and are determined by class, property, opportunity, education, social standing, and the law that expresses and protects all of these factors. The civilization envisioned in the opening paragraphs of *The Pioneers*—and embraced throughout the series—reaches its point of highest promise in the Temple-Effingham nuptials: in them, Loyalist and revolutionary are reconciled; property—a source of potential discord—is stabilized and reconfirmed (even, one might argue, sacramentalized); and class standards are upheld. Oliver and Elizabeth are gentle, pious, virtuous, and appropriately educated—and in Oliver's experience with Natty and Chingachgook, and Elizabeth's sensitivity to the historical displacement of forester and Indian that her proprietorship entails, it may be argued that another sort of reconciliation takes place, on the symbolic level if not on a historical one. While Cooper thus endorses the civilized values—they *are* what he wants—his novels reveal ruthlessly the irreconcilable contradictions that undermine their reliability; even the most fundamental and mystified concept, the law, is shown to be woefully inadequate in both principle and practice. Even its chief spokesman Marmaduke Temple is not simply allowed naively to witness how imperfect his absolutes are but is rendered as a character who in practice chooses, whimsically, to ignore his responsibilities.

We need not question that Cooper would have liked to resolve the historical and ideological contradictions, nor is it relevant—*if* true—that artistic means were lacking; rather such a resolution was not possible and would have been patently absurd; the lack of resolution represents not a failure but a refusal. The refusal to reconcile what cannot be reconciled, to eliminate what is inconvenient (his critics' failing rather than his), constitutes the highest fictional value Cooper possesses—and his greatest political utility in that it reveals fully the price that was exacted for the establishment of "civilization" and demystifies its most prized virtues. Cooper's concurrence with his reader—or his incomplete consciousness—is irrelevant; it does not impair the opportunity his work offers the

reader to reach full consciousness. His problem must become our problem, or he is merely a pathetic case of futile irresolution. It is not merely
ingenious to suggest that Temple's law, Cooper's "march of civilization,"
is as much a myth, as deficient in actuality, as is the *beau idéal* of Chingachgook and Natty; each, in Cooper's fiction, is subjected to the shock of
reality and is either destroyed or has its integrity shattered.

To make Cooper's irresolution the issue, to psychologize the impasse he
presents between the twinned idealizations of Natty and civilization, is to
render the matter merely anecdotal. To see him in his work as typical,
exemplary, and unable to elude the historical and social contradictions of
the rational, progressive, humane society he and revolutionary America
endorsed is to become aware of how radical the novels are. Life, liberty,
and the pursuit of happiness, equality and democracy—all have quite
different meanings for Temple and Oliver from what they have for Natty
and Chingachgook. The logic of capitalism is such that it must render its
published guiding political principles idealistically, since they do not appear in its social and economic practice—eternal verities impervious to
what happens in the material world. As Herbert Marcuse observes:

> It took a centuries-long education to help make bearable the daily
> reproduced shock that arises from the contradiction between the
> constant sermon of the inalienable freedom, majesty and dignity of
> the person, the magnificence and autonomy of reason, the goodness
> of humanity and of impartial justice, on the one hand, and the general
> degradation of mankind, the irrationality of the social life process,
> the victory of the labor market over humanity, and of profit over
> charity, on the other. [*Negations*, 121–122]

Cooper allows us to see this, if we choose to—which is not to say that he
would draw from it the conclusions I have. Cooper is one of the instruments of our awareness, as Balzac was for Marx and Engels, and for the
same reasons.

Natty is certainly an idealized fiction, but in the historical situation the
novels give us, he and Chingachgook are as much victims as industrial and
agricultural workers were to become. It should be obvious that the inhu-
manity of the system cannot be eliminated on the idealistic level; indeed,
idealism is a cushion, a cordon sanitaire, between society and criticism of
it. If the ideals rest unexamined and constitute absolutes in an unchange-
able region apart from material conditions, they act more to inhibit

practice than to inspire it.[32] In fact, as contemporary political discourse shows (I write during the Nicaraguan Contra crisis of 1985–86), the notions of freedom and democracy remain thoroughly mystified and are rarely examined. As Marcuse sarcastically remarked years ago, "The soul can understand what the mind must condemn" (*Negations*, 112).

If Cooper's Leather-Stocking series is as potentially inflammatory as I suggest it is, why was so disconcerting a work so popular in so proud and patriotic a postrevolutionary place and time? One reason suggests itself: responsibility confronted as a fait accompli, and on so highly idealized a plane, becomes a kind of luxury; it is safely in the past, beyond remedy; it is even elevating, and will permit an undisturbing sigh of regret that things were not otherwise than the accomplished fact inevitably confirms them to be. His contemporaries found in him what they wanted to find.

Cooper did write as if the abstract principles of the Declaration were, if not yet fully realized, at least imminent and realizable; the envisioned society was for him embryonically there in Templeton. At the same time he relentlessly reveals it taking its origin in the very qualities of greed and preemptive acquisitiveness that its highest values forbid. The idealization is thus manifested as illusory and transitory, leaving the reality that exposes it untouched. The idealization at no point comes into effective action within a social reality.

When Cooper's criticism of society was more directly expressed, in the novels and other writings of the 1830s and 1840s, he was branded an aristocrat, and his patriotism was impugned.[33] But the criticism was always there, and his readers chose to miss it. What is more, the criticism emerged not simply from pique or personal disappointment but from his sense of what the duties of a patriotic American citizen were—to say honestly what he saw and to express fearlessly what he thought. American ideals of freedom of speech and thought were not mere ideals for him but guides to action. He pretended neither not to have seen what he did see, nor to find merit in silence. He would have seen anthropologist Clifford Geertz's point:

> As in more familiar exercises in close reading, one can start anywhere in a culture's repertoire of forms and end up anywhere else. One can stay, as I have here, within a single, more or less bounded form, and circle steadily within it. One can move between forms in search of broader unities or informing contrasts. One can even compare forms

from different cultures to define their character in reciprocal relief. But whatever the level at which one operates, and however intricately, the guiding principle is the same: societies, like lives, contain their own interpretations. One has only to learn how to gain access to them. [*Interpretation of Cultures*, 453]

Cooper offers us a close reading of his own society; deeply described, attentively scrutinized, it interprets itself to us.

Georg Lukács, in *Theory of the Novel*, envisions an ideal modernist work in which "all the fissures and rents inherent in the historical situation [will] be drawn into the form-giving process" (60). We note that Lukács does not call upon such an artist to offer a solution, to mend the tears. He or she need not even prophesy the solution. Indeed, the form giving clearly does not depend on some abstracted idea of form but must be limited or altered by the subject matter. It is clear also that the search for solutions may in effect betray realism and prevent the full enactment fictionally of the situation in all its aspects.

I have been puzzled by the impulse, in so many justly esteemed critics of Cooper, toward deflective conclusions—that is, these critics sheer off toward conclusions that release tensions and dissolve conflicts which are the unresolvable heart of the matter and which on the whole they are perfectly conscious of. It is surprising in part because, from Charles Brockden Brown to the present, most major American novels do not reach a confident and resolved sense of closure; also, even before contemporary theory had made us so sensitive to indeterminacy, the old New Criticism had developed analytical techniques that were revelatory of many of the indeterminate texts that are so central in the established canon—Poe, Hawthorne, Melville, Thoreau, Emerson, and James. These techniques also satisfied the desire to look at these texts as insulated from the populous, public, historical, political world in which they were made. Needless to say, some texts suited that assumption more readily than others. Even those that did often suffered from the privation; those that did not suffered—like Cooper's—misrepresentation. As I have indicated, that situation is changing.

The difficulty with Cooper in particular has been that the problems his novels address have remained with us in North America, and almost all the critics I have here touched upon are American, so that the problems found in the novels, Cooper's problems as it were, are also the critics' own problems—American problems that await solutions in our own times just as urgently as they ever did. If that is true, it may be suggested that the various forms of liberal solution imposed upon Cooper's work are displacements of the critics' uneasy accommodations to the conflicts that so durably abide. The exclusions that result obscure Cooper's willingness to view the complete picture. Other voices are now being heard that forbid the exclusions we have casually practiced—of black writers, of women writers, of political writers—that question the restrictive aesthetic categories through which the exclusions have been enforced. To those voices I add my own. To collude with the genteel "unpolitical" withdrawal by academic criticism from an ugly history, from the world, is to take an attitude that these novels implicitly scorn. The formal ingenuity that fails to see may comfort itself with the notion of political detachment, but it is merely naive to suggest that telling generations of students that politics and history do not matter is without political consequences.

What follows is an attempt to read closely, as fully as I can, the five novels of the Leather-Stocking sequence in the order in which they were published, in order to allow, as Geertz might say, "access" to the interpretations they contain.

TWO * *The Pioneers* (1823)

INTERRUPTED PRELUDE

The author has no better apology for interrupting the interest of a work of fiction by these desultory dialogues, than that they have reference to facts.
– *James Fenimore Cooper,* The Pioneers

The commentary on the Leather-Stocking novels that follows suggests that Cooper, in the work for which received literary history most values him, delivers a criticism of American society and history and of its most deeply held values that is far removed from a celebration of America and the poetic evocation of a figure of significant myth. In this, his tone resembles less the radiant prophecies of the Revolution or of Nathaniel Ames's Almanacks than it does the anxious postrevolutionary warnings of Freneau and Brackenridge—and, not infrequently, of Irving. Even though he lacks Crèvecoeur's note of hysterical panic, Cooper's demolition of the republican hope is as thorough as Crèvecoeur's bitter denunciation of America's betrayal of its guiding ideas.

Cooper's patriotism is not in question here; that he loved his country and fully shared the exalted hopes of the Revolution is beyond argument, as is his firm conservative democratic understanding of the principles that he felt must animate a new republic.[1] His patriotism had another dimension—a determination to tell the truth about, and to, his country, that had dire consequences for his popularity with his audience. This course of action amounted to much more than pointing with melancholy regret to the price paid by the likes of Natty and Chingachgook for the rising glory of America; nor did he merely indicate local instances in which something went wrong and some Americans fell short of the highest goals and principles of the Revolution; instead Cooper offered, in what he did rather

46

than in what he might be thought to have intended, a radical criticism of both practice and principle. Even though he endorsed the enlightened conservative principles of Marmaduke Temple, the novels demonstrate, without the possibility of error, the nature of power in the developing Euro-American imperium and the manner in which "the humane laws of this compassionate country" (4) served power and property. Cooper did not expose this practice with any subversive or counterrevolutionary intent, and he would not find my terms or political bias to his liking. For him, it was partly a matter of character: Cooper, conservative by disposition, was constitutionally incapable of suppressing the truth—or inconvenient facts—in the interests of theory. It is precisely this completeness of the picture that allows the matter to be put as I have put it, without damage or insult to the text. It is also one of the marks of a great novelist.

Even in the Littlepage manuscripts (1844–46), his most partial conservative texts, there is clear evidence in the treatment of Susquesus, of Indian rights, and of Aaron Thousandacres of his incapacity to ignore, of his willingness to give full voice to what was inconvenient to his own views of private property (the discussion between Corny and Dirck in chapter 4 of *Satanstoe* is a case in point). Indeed, this pattern is present as early as *The Spy* (1821), in which the desired ending of the Revolution and the contrived reconciliations of opposing factions are not allowed to mask how the war that generated the new republic also spawned the opportunistic and predatory Cowboys and Skinners, and rendered marginal its self-sacrificing republican hero, Harvey Birch, the spy of the novel's title and a clear predecessor of Natty Bumppo. *The Pioneers* itself faithfully inscribes its deconstructive pattern in its initial pages: the confident ideology enshrined in its highly abstracted opening landscape is qualified by the muted fear of an "evil day that must arrive" and by an episode dominated not by Christmas, good cheer, and joy at Elizabeth's return home but by the mumbled complaints of Natty, unheard by Temple but given to the reader.[2]

The sort of argument that I wish to make is possible only by close attention to the details of texts that are widely read and written about. While those readers most familiar with them may find my procedure too leisurely in pace and condescending to a reader's presumed lack of knowledge, I hope that they will agree that an approach demanding a rereading of the texts must itself manifest, in its attention to detail, a response to the task it has set them.

For the time being, one example will serve as emblem both of the kind of conclusion I reach and of the sort of detail I find significant. On the morning of Natty's trial, Cooper fashions a description of the pioneers and yeoman citizen-farmers converging on the courthouse (which serves also as church and academy); none is identified by name, and the tendency of the passage is toward typicality—it is clearly a set piece:

> Ever since the dawn of day, the highways and wood-paths that, issuing from the forests, and winding along the sides of the mountains, centered in Templeton, had been thronged with equestrians and footmen, bound to the haven of justice. There was to be seen a well-clad yeoman, mounted on a sleek, switch-tailed steed, ambling along the highway, with his red face elevated in a manner that said, "I have paid for my land, and fear no man," while his bosom was swelling with the pride of being one of the grand inquest for the county. At his side rode a companion, his equal in independence of feeling, perhaps, but his inferior in thrift, as in property and consideration. This was a professed dealer in lawsuits,—a man whose name appeared in every calendar; whose substance, gained in the multifarious expedients of a settler's changeable habits, was wasted in feeding the harpies of the courts. He was endeavouring to impress the mind of the grand juror with the merits of a cause now at issue. Along with these was a pedestrian, who, having thrown a rifle frock over his shirt, and placed his best wool hat above his sunburnt visage, had issued from his retreat in the woods by a footpath, and was striving to keep company with the others, on his way to hear and to decide the disputes of his neighbours as a petit juror. Fifty similar little knots of countrymen might have been seen, on that morning, journeying towards the shire-town on the same errand. [358]

Cooper is offering an exemplary picture that precisely fulfills the expectations of the novel's opening paragraph; that "well-clad yeoman" and the "fifty similar knots of countrymen" would appeal to the Crèvecoeur of Letter III—they labor, they prosper, they have property, and they enjoy the privileges and responsibilities of a nation governed by rational law. But within the prevailing benignity there is a sour note; as with Crèvecoeur, it has to do with the law. If one of the most solemn responsibilities of the citizen is to serve as a juryman for his fellow citizens in a court of law, the yeoman's "pride" is justified; he is a kind of proof of the existence of a true democracy. The process in court is the further practical proving ground of the law. The yeoman's companion, however, "a professed dealer in lawsuits . . . whose name appeared in every calendar" (as jurymen's do not), is clearly engaged in jury tampering. At the very moment, then, at which the highest claim is registered, it is subverted in no uncertain terms. Nothing could be more deliberate, nor is it isolated, a cautionary grace note. Indeed, I shall argue that so conflicted an observation indicates the driving force of the preceding plot and its meaning, which have often been found full of conflict and uncertain in aim.

There has been a tendency in the criticism of Cooper to see him as an awkward narrative craftsman and a man in deep, personal conflict in the principles he embraced. Some critics see him as caught between his belief in opposed principles of aristocracy and democracy[3]—and he is; others, like Stephen Railton, find a psychological basis for his divided loyalty to "civilization" and to the wilderness, to Temple and to Natty and Chingachgook—or, like Slotkin in *Regeneration through Violence*, a large psychohistorical one. Some would have us see Cooper as a prime example of a basic thematic pattern in American literature, hope followed by disappointment. Others again, like Ringe, would find in the passage cited an example of Cooper's unswerving moral attention, his consciousness of the threat vice poses to virtue. The fault in all these views is that they distract from the written text, what is verifiably there, and from Cooper as a writer capable of objectively seeing and presenting a view of a present or historical situation as full of conflict and unresolved tension, whether he himself was in conflict about it or not.[4]

In the example I have given, there is really no need to go outside the text—it contains its own explanation. In this, I believe it to be entirely typical. Moreover, if the plot is looked at in this way and assumed to convey meaning, it will be seen to respond to the requirements of whatever it is that Cooper discerns and of what that means.[5]

The approach to a critical reading of *The Pioneers* is encumbered by obstacles. There had been—and continued to be in Cooper's time—extended consideration of the nature of an appropriate American fiction,[6] most often discussed under, and resulting in prescriptions based on, the assumptions pervading the most popular model of the time, Scott's Waverley romances. While *The Pioneers* displays some elements of such a romance—an imposing scene, stirring incidents, an often elevated rhet-

oric and sentiment, moral idealization, and a sense of the historical significance of the events recounted—it would be difficult to maintain that in
this novel Cooper satisfies those criteria or to think that he intended to.
"The Sources of the Susquehanna: A Descriptive Tale," the dual subtitle,
alone indicates an uncertainty about the novel's generic nature, which
distances Cooper from romance criteria without offering a satisfactory
alternative for the novel and which constantly intrudes upon any romance
expectations that may be aroused.

Nor does Cooper's preface of 1823 offer a reassuring sense of certainty.
Not merely does he play the time-honored games of pretense that surround prefaces, even ending a letter called a "preface" with an invitation
to the publisher to ask for a preface if he wants one, but he also quite
specifically disclaims the romance and embraces "reality"; his use of the
term "novel" is not casual. Even so, a certain witty disingenousness apart,
Cooper conveys a sense of discomfort—as if he is conceding the categories
on which he must be judged ("interest," beauty of scene) and defending
against them[7]—a kind of good-humored truculence about criticism that
masks a reticence, in part protecting his privacy, in part recognizing that
the descriptions that follow are not quite as advertised—only pleasant
sketches and vignettes, dear to memory, in which Cooper is pleasing
himself. They are there, and they are often pleasing, but the tale that is told
in the novel can hardly have been for him a source of unqualified pleasure.
He even concedes that criteria of "interest," which have all to do with
plot, are less well met than they might be. Cooper does not justify his plot,
but it may be open to the critic to do so. At the least, it can be argued that
Cooper's narrative awkwardness answers well to other concerns he has.

This is immediately apparent in chapter 1, as a dialogue is established
between an idealized agrarian "present" (1823) of peaceful achievement
and an actual past that has produced the present—a dialogue that must
make the reader wonder about the security of that idealization. The
historical questions raised by the opening episode dominate the entire
novel and, more immediately, produce an enormous delay of the plot as
the historical problems assert their priority. History relentlessly deforms
and problematizes the forms Cooper puts to use. Even if we accept the
insistence of Wayne Franklin and others on the personal, biographical
drive of Cooper's art—the importance of his loss of property and patrimony—it is equally true that those personal experiences are the product
of historical forces that Cooper objectifies from the outset.

A formidable obstacle too is the accumulated critical weight of the connection of the Leather-Stocking novels to epic, romance, and especially myth. Whatever epic or romance virtues Natty, Chingachgook, Oliver, and Elizabeth may possess, they hardly achieve their full and unqualified potential in this novel. Whatever mythical weight Natty and Chingachgook carry here resides in what they are given in *The Pioneers* to remember in idealized terms of their past unspoiled life in an undefiled terrain. In their present circumstances in the work, they are presented as the superannuated victims of historical processes, of changing technologies, of alien cultural assumptions, and of the imperialistic movements that had dominated European action in American history for more than two centuries and would dominate it for two centuries more.

In fact, for a series of works whose major claim on our attention has so often been urged to be Natty as a figure of significant myth, Natty is rarely free to exemplify the "*beau idéal*" Cooper was to claim as justifying his idealizations in his 1850 preface to the Leather-Stocking Tales, now arranged in the chronological order of Natty's life. In *The Pioneers* of 1823, Natty is conceived in much more homely realistic terms: an irascible, disappointed, threatened old man who does not like what is happening to him. And in that mode he is quite credible. As James Franklin Beard indicates, quoting Richard H. Dana, Sr.'s letter to Cooper in 1823, Natty was appealing as more than a victim:

> Grand & elevated as he is, making him so is no departure from truth. He read in a book filled with inspiration, look on it where we [will]. But, alas, too few feel the inspiration there—or scarcely in that [other] Book which God has given us. Natty's uneducated mind [shown?] us in his pronunciation & use of words belonging to low life, mingled with his inborn eloquence—his solitary life, his old age, his simplicity, & delicate feelings, create a grateful & very peculiar emotion made up of admiration & pity & concern. So highly is his character wrought that I was fearful lest he would not hold out to the end. But he does grow upon us to the very close of the last scene, which is, perhaps, the finest, certainly the most touching in the book.—A friend of mine said at Natty's departure, "I longed to go with him." [Introduction to *The Pioneers*, xlviii]

Beard is right to note the response to "pathos" and the "finer, tragic note," but the fantasy of Dana's friend of joining Natty in exile implies a deeper recognition of the betrayal that exile draws our attention to. Where Natty may be is in some way preferable to the civilization that exiles him. In Dana's comment we might hear a melancholy echo of Crèvecoeur's distresses and his exile.

Perhaps the most significant question the critic and the reader must address is this: In what order must I think of these novels? The order of composition? The chronological order of Natty's life? Once the whole series has been read, in order of composition, neither order can prevail exclusively over the other, but the mythical view is sustainable only by reading back into *The Pioneers* the elevations of *The Prairie* and *The Deerslayer*, and, perhaps, *The Last of the Mohicans*.[8] Should Mohegan's speech on Mount Vision be seen as prelude or sequel to *Mohicans*? Either way, *Mohicans* confirms that speech, but it is, for me, a more powerful version if the reader views Chingachgook with the knowledge that he became Mohegan; Cooper's first readers had no choice but to take the richer proposition that all the heroism of *Mohicans*, however much it may raise the level of pathos we feel for Chingachgook's decline, goes for so little, raising only regret. The later-written novels have always to cope with the earlier ones—above all *The Pioneers*. While it is tempting—and possibly true—to imagine that Cooper uses *Mohicans* to equip Natty for the mythic status he will confer on him in *The Prairie* and that it was simply necessary for him to do so, it is impossible to erase the knowledge of *The Pioneers* as we read all its successors.

However we view the matter, we cannot contend that myth, legend, or epic dominates this novel; the central action of the work, the Temple-Effingham tale, has little to do with projecting a fictional narrative that stands in for something that cannot otherwise be explained. If epic projects national ideals and desires, they certainly are expressed in the novel, but they are not fulfilled; the focus is rather on memory, regret, and remorse for what is known. The treatment too is surprisingly realistic, even naturalistic; Natty must lose, because history says he does. Here as elsewhere, history places constraints on desire: Temple's attempt to re-write Natty into the tale is forbidden as a lie, a sentimental desire—and yet a desperate one.[9] Natty may be unreal, too good to be true, but the tale he inhabits is only too clear. Given the assured ironic tone of the 1823 preface, we may feel at liberty—at least as a critical option—to take Cooper's assurance of "the humane laws of this compassionate country" as equivocal.

Even if we argue for a kind of elegiac romance, a fictionalized *compleynte* for a lost perfection, with Natty and Mohegan as figures of lost innocence, too much is missing. They are not to a significant degree responsible for their own fall, and no redemption is offered them. In fact, it is their lack of effective agency (though not of complicity) in their own loss that allows the sentimental honoring of their memory and example that will later figure so centrally in *The Prairie*. Over the whole series, Cooper insists that if their lives' meaning may be sentimentally cherished, their actual existence is not to be tolerated; he never alters the terms of history in the service of literary sensibility. Even Oliver and Elizabeth, those most attached to Natty and Chingachgook, are political realists in their central discussion of the issue in chapter 25.

In his own time—and frequently thereafter—Cooper's capacities as a maker of plots were called in question. It is not difficult to see why. It should not be assumed that Cooper's readers and critics shared the disdain of Hawthorne, Melville, and James for closure. One fancies that Cooper would not have written at all under the exacting requirements of Melville's *Pierre* (198–99) or of James's "The Art of Fiction." In any event, Nina Baym has fully established the overriding importance of plot and dénouement for nineteenth-century American novelists. By such criteria Cooper is obviously lacking, and his early reviewers were quick to see it; whatever his virtues in description, character, and liveliness of episode, they cannot excuse his failure in narrative coherence. From a modern standpoint, his plot making is, on its surface, embarrassing. Even granting the immunities allowed by a genre that legitimized the romance of young love beset by stirring physical dangers and rescues, and the conventional narrative hazards of coincidence, concealed identity, and mysteries dissolved into happy endings, Cooper hardly measures up. Even Cooper seems to recognize it, as more than halfway through the novel the epigraph goads the narrator, "Come! to thy tale" (275). The plot depends on the withholding of two pieces of information: what Temple learned in the letter (chapter 25), and what Natty, Mohegan, and Oliver have to conceal in the hut. All the mystification surrounding Oliver rapidly becomes merely repetitive in the absence of any apparent progress toward revelation and dénouement. This impairs Oliver's credibility and makes his softening of attitude through love and his retained resentment merely distracting.

The central plot line is not only undeveloped but also so ill articulated that it is easy to miss for most of the book's duration. It can progress only through Temple or Oliver, and since their motives and actions are kept out of view, no coherent development of the plot is possible. The descriptive set pieces and other matter seem to lead nowhere. We cannot claim that Cooper did not consider questions of plot coherence and suspense, for he is evidently concerned to plant Temple's puzzled sense of familiarity with Oliver's features and to register Oliver's overstressed hostility and suspicion from the outset. The progress of the romance of Oliver and Elizabeth does little to advance the main plot. When the main plot is finally resolved, it is done with such neat dispatch that we could almost accuse Cooper of impudence from which no claim to the "Descriptive Tale" could exculpate him. One could perhaps develop a more persuasive argument for Cooper's procedure by resorting to a comparison with Shakespeare's late romances— the similarities are often quite striking. One might even develop a position that would place Cooper, in his attempt to accommodate material too various and complex for conventionally closed narrative, in a line that leads to the indeterminate romances of Melville, Hawthorne, and James.

It is undeniable, however, that the dénouement is brought about not by the deliberate action of Oliver's mission nor by Temple's action but by the action of the much more memorable subplot that has little necessary relation, as a plot, with the main tale. As a result, the outcome seems almost accidental. It is as if the primacy of the Effingham-Temple plot is challenged by the subplot; the main plot deals exclusively with land possession and is subject to resolution, while the subplot whose action provides the occasion for it deals with an absolute and irreversible dispossession. The central concern is not feudalism, aristocracy, or democracy but property. This subversion of the main plot's interest, moreover, by the subplot is wholly typical, as will become apparent, of the entire work: no ostensibly dominant interest is permitted unmodified play. Even the descriptive elements are rarely merely descriptive; most are heavily didactic and thematically centered, just as are many episodes in the romantic subplot. For example, the encounter with the panther and the fire on Mount Vision illuminate the extent to which Temple has failed to tame the wilderness and to eliminate Natty from civilization's consciousness. As a result of all this, conceding Cooper's failure to satisfy criteria of plot while maintaining that this failure does not impair his ability to make sense, we might be better advised to consult what Cooper does rather than what he does not do.

The attempt, then, to make Cooper's text fit and serve criteria outside itself must fail, or achieve only partial success. However justified and historical such attempts may be, they do no justice to the novel we have before us and the novels that are to be determined by it. The best that such an attempt can produce is a drawing of accounts that is bound to fragment the work (more than it already is) in showing which bits satisfy which criteria; in such a process what the text itself is and does and means loses priority to categories external to it.[10] Cooper claimed in *The Pioneers* to "please himself"; not to do so would place him between the competing claims of opposed critics: "There I am, left like an ass between two locks of hay; so that I have determined to relinquish my animate nature, and remain stationary, like a lock of hay between two asses" (3). We might allow, then, the work to exist in its own way, nourishing to all.

How carefully we read *The Pioneers* is of the highest critical importance, since that becomes the determining factor in our reading of the novels that follow it. Whatever attraction the sequence read in chronological order possesses, *The Pioneers* is the controlling determinant simply because as the first written it prescribes certain unalterable conditions: the circumstances of Natty's old age and his exile, unalterable and known at the outset, must affect the way we receive not only the account of his death but also the accounts of his youth and maturity. The knowledge gained from *The Pioneers* confers a kind of freedom from mere narrative sequence upon the reader and imposes an intensified obligation upon his interpretative attention; narrative sequence solves nothing—everything is already known, but very little is resolved unambiguously as to its meaning.

Also, it is in *The Pioneers* that Natty becomes interesting, less for what he does than for what is done to him, less for what he says than for what he means. The interest in him arises from the impossibility of his position, which is the result of society's incapacity to act according to the beliefs it states. The instability of the ideology that is revealed inheres not so much in Cooper's personality as in the historical circumstances he addresses.[11] There is nothing in the later works to undercut this, and all of them are deepened and animated by the reader's memory of their future or past.

The Pioneers is bracketed at its opening and closing by two passages— the first is three paragraphs long, while the second is more extended; both are ideologically loaded and appear to be intended to control our interpretation of the fiction. Whatever the intention, it is plain that the purport of both passages is severely compromised by the text whose physical limits they form.

The text seems to plant its ideological feet firmly. Its initial tone is formal, confident, abstract, almost Augustan. Although a locale is given, "near the centre of the state of New York," the topography offered is typical, not, until after the first three paragraphs, specific. Nor are we at once given a time of year; the hibernal epigraph must wait for its confirmation in an actual scene of winter. The landscape projected is agricultural with elements of the picturesque, but no furrows are visible, and the scene is unpeopled; "vales" are "narrow," "streams" "wind," and all is uniformly plural and unspecific. The flowing together of tributaries into greater rivers gives a general geographic description that seems emblematic of the cohesion of the state rather than specific to Lake Otsego, Cooperstown/Templeton, or this particular source of the Susquehanna. It does not resemble Natty's lambent descriptions of scenes remembered, Mohegan's rhapsodic idealization of an Edenic land before the whites came, Elizabeth's sensitive responses to particular scenes at particular seasons, or even Cooper's own evocations of the changes of the seasons or his grand set scenes.[12]

In fact, the landscape is highly ideologized. Those plural "villages," "roads," "farms," "academies," and "places for worship" are seen by no corporeal eye but announce the achievement of the goals of the American Revolution. By 1823, Cooper seems to be saying from a historically privileged viewpoint, hopes have been achieved as realities: education, religion, human industry, law, and polity are achieving what the founding fathers had envisaged for them. The vocabulary suggests an already accomplished rational, agrarian, progressive, prosperous postrevolutionary standpoint: "rich," "cultivated," "thriving," "neat," "comfortable," "moral and reflecting," "manufacturing," "wealth," "liberty" are some of the terms used to set the scene. Cooper's terms would have gratified Franklin, Jefferson, and Crèvecoeur, and they echo the aspirations and language of Timothy Dwight, Nathaniel Ames, and the Freneau and Brackenridge of *The Rising Glory of America*. A similar passage is superimposed upon Elizabeth's view of the movement of the settlers as spring breaks:

> In short, the whole country was exhibiting the bustle of a thriving
> settlement, where the highways were thronged with sleighs, bearing

piles of rough household furniture, studded, here and there, with the smiling faces of women and children, happy in the excitement of novelty; or with loads of produce, hastening to the common market at Albany, that served as so many snares, to induce the emigrants into those wild mountains in search of competence and happiness. [216]

I suspect we are not intended to believe that "bustle" and thronging were actually seeable by Elizabeth. At the outset, the issue is given a clear ideological summary: "In short, the whole district is hourly exhibiting how much can be done, in even a rugged country, and with a severe climate, under the dominion of mild laws, and where every man feels a direct interest in the prosperity of a commonwealth, of which he knows himself to form a part" (15–16). The issue is presented in both ideological and practical terms: the existence of these ideas in these conditions produces these results.

He closes what is really a momentous paragraph with a diagrammatic summary of American history from the agrarian viewpoint: "The expedients of the pioneers who first broke ground in the settlement of this country, are succeeded by the permanent improvements of the yeoman, who intends to leave his remains to moulder under the sod which he tills, or, perhaps, of the son, who, born in the land, piously wishes to linger around the grave of his father.—Only forty years have passed since this territory was a wilderness" (16). In actual time the period is brief, "only forty years"—well might the changes seem "miraculous"; but, for Cooper as for Crèvecoeur, whom Cooper precisely repeats, what is inscribed here has the force of an inevitable pattern. Both men had as strong a sense of human destiny and divine will as any Puritan's;[13] but the form they perceived gratified human reason, promised to satisfy human desire, and dignified human effort. Here for the first time we are given the title word "pioneers," with a time placing that suggests that this tale is set at a point some way into the second stage, that of the yeoman. But however idealized the historical conception might be, it is at once given a realistic historical location in a sovereign state whose power and dominion had to be fought for, and in which states possess territory and exercise power. If "independence" suggests political separation, the motives of property, power, development, and enterprise are shared with the displaced ruler. If all three stages—pioneer, yeoman, and the rooted son—are included in Cooper's tale, their limits are exceeded in that Natty and Mohegan are given their story, which is clearly at odds with the radiant fulfillment of this passage, and in that Cooper clearly indicates a future that will place the prophecy at risk.

It might also seem at this point that Cooper advances for the reader the kind of model of moral and social stability for which Scott was so much admired throughout the nineteenth century, ever more so as the latter decades of the century tried to cope with a radical realism and naturalism bent on revealing the forces that control human existence. Even though Natty is to find no place in Temple's civilization and submits it to question, he does not subvert stable moral values; rather he affirms them from a standpoint of a radical conservative idealism in deploring their absence or deformation. It is this, rather than any nostalgia he may represent, that makes his presence in every sense so critical. The hero of Cooper's ideological preamble is Marmaduke Temple, whose views and language clearly enforce this ideology—as does his characterization, whatever his weaknesses (he may be, as heroes often are, symptomatic in every aspect). The better we come to know him, the more apparent it becomes that he speaks for the ideology of 1823 (the time of the opening paragraphs)—as do Elizabeth and Oliver, whatever their differences with Temple. He is consistent in this too; his earlier life, as given in chapter 2, offers him as the ideal product of the course of American history: his industry, his sense of the future, his opportunism, his altruism, his sense of community, his feelings for liberty and tolerance, his support of the revolutionary cause—all fit him for his heroic role. If this is so, then it must be asked why it is that Natty occupies our attention far more than Temple does. Natty here is actor-antagonist, victim, and witness, but he exercises no control. His power is limited to certain kinds of action. His power is never unqualified; it is circumstantial and episodic at best because history forbids that it be more—and Natty and Cooper's readers always know this. If he or they should forget, narrative consequences, embodying history, will quickly admonish them. However, powerless as he is, Natty's presence reveals—and Temple's experience and actions exemplify—how vulnerable Cooper's apparently seamless gesture really is.[14]

Fixing his action at a particular point in history is not a straightforward matter for Cooper. The time at which his tale takes place, 1793—ten years after the peace of 1783 and seven years after the first settlement of the area—is thirty years before 1823, the "now" of the opening paragraph. And the historical coordinates are seen to involve two generations and,

shortly, in the account of Temple's personal history, two generations still
further back, culminating in the conflicting loyalties of the revolutionary
war. Natty's discontented ruminations add a further, less time-fixed dimension of historical change and instability. If Cooper is unable to allow
his central statements of belief to go unchallenged, it is equally true that he
finds it difficult to disentangle a merely present incident from its antece-
dents and its consequences. That difficulty is as central to Cooper's consciousness as it is to Faulkner's. Not merely does this help to explain the
deformations of plot in *The Pioneers*, but it also makes the achronological
composition of the Leather-Stocking novels coherently expressive of the
mind behind them, and the constant revision imposed by it on the reader is
thereby rendered not a distraction but a central part of the activity of
reading. Instead of proceeding with his tale, Cooper relates in chapter 2
not merely the previous history of the Temple-Effingham association but
also its intimate involvement with the Revolution and with a theory that
accounts for the alternating fortunes, as generations pass, of rich and poor
immigrants and for the antagonism of commercial and gentlemanly instincts. Temple is seen as one who breaks with the past but remains
attached to traditional values. The progressive materialism is set ironically
against pretended piety. Education is extolled, but so is the acquisition of
property.

Cooper's reaching back into the past is not confined to a single ground-
clearing chapter. It is a constantly reiterated feature of the novel: it begins
with Elizabeth's registration of the present measured against the past and
includes repeated evocations of the past by Temple, Natty, and Mohegan,
of hazards and satisfactions of settlement, of the battles of midcentury and
the Revolution, and of the Europeans' dispossession of the Indians. Miquon (Penn) is referred to. Hollister's expedition against Natty's hut to the
accompaniment of "Yankee Doodle" is made ironically to recall the Revolution. The dénouement with its production of the senile Major Effingham
may thus seem to be less a magical means of resolving narrative entangle-
ments than the emergence in material form of the specter of history that
has stalked every other page of the novel. The release of Oliver and
Elizabeth from their narrative prison is possible only after the resolution
of the past. But Natty's and Mohegan's past cannot be resolved; one must
die, the other go into exile.

Cooper, then, may seem to have opened his novel with an end; we might
well expect that what follows—"our tale"—will justify it, showing us

how an earlier stage has led to this present "end" of 1823, and that these benign consequences may justify certain means or excuse certain primitive aberrations as stages of growth toward our present blessed state, as Crèvecoeur does in Letter III. This is *not* what happens in *The Pioneers*, nor is it particularly typical of Cooper even at his most ideologically determined. If we dispose of preconception and deal only with what is given in the novel, it is reasonable to suppose that Cooper acts to expose the simplification the passage represents without, of course, abandoning the moral and political view it embodies: to reveal the prices paid, the turbulent and violent passions involved and forces at work, the raw motives of acquisition, the destructive improvidence of the settlers, the weakness of Temple as a defender of the revolutionary faith, the inherent contradictions of the "mild laws" that underpin the social edifice, the perversion of those laws to serve personal ends, the unreliability of human morality in the presence of republican opportunity—all this must lead to a questioning of the validity of Cooper's grand opening statement, which reflects the very basis of the Declaration of Independence, the culmination of the dominant ideology of the eighteenth century from the revolutionary standpoint. In effect, then, *The Pioneers* deconstructs the affirmative gesture with which it begins and calls in question all that Cooper and the nation piously cherished. Cooper does not do this out of perverseness or out of a love for the problematic but rather out of a true sense of history and the imperatives thus placed upon him. The result is more interesting than a fictional illustration of a national piety could be. And, however long we have to wait for the emergence of the tale proper, the process of deconstruction and rendering problematic begins at once with the confrontation of Natty and Temple over the deer. It is surely not out of keeping that this episode anticipates—without legal consequence for Temple—the later deer episode, which makes final the issues Natty so early raises.

There is, in this opening phase, one note of warning: the population of New York State "has spread itself over five degrees of latitude and seven of longitude, and has swelled to a million and a half of inhabitants, who are maintained in abundance, and can look forward to ages before the evil day must arrive, when their possessions shall become unequal to their wants" (16). The "evil day" is projected as a certainty but placed in a future inconceivably distant (Cooper again echoes Franklin and Crèvecoeur—it is a virtual commonplace). However, so many actions in the tale will hasten that day. It is no exaggeration to say that Temple conceives a large part of his responsibility as the staving off of that day—hence his game laws.[15] The willing but weak-willed governor seems powerless against it, reduced often to mere compliance or witness—yet he invariably speaks in the spirit of the opening paragraph. Far from being mere crudities and errors of early frontier development, the predations of Doolittle, Jones,[16] and Riddel on republican probity show—and Temple's anxiety confirms it—a real flaw, a real and present threat to America's destiny. The past (1793) tends to confirm the threat projected into some dim future beyond 1823.

One might guess that this passage, so clearly separate from what immediately follows, was written after the novel's completion; if not, it was certainly subject to careful revision in 1832. It is difficult to concede that Cooper, who was so fully aware of the issues, was not aware of the effect this opening must have. I do not suggest that Cooper had some subtle aesthetic or formal purpose in this but, rather, that throughout this novel—and almost everywhere else—he did not shirk awkward inconsistencies that threatened his own ideological positions. Whatever formal or interpretative issues arise derive from the reality addressed rather than from aesthetic considerations—and they are not the less substantial for that. In fact, Cooper always permits his sense of the realities of the case to override the attractions of comforting conclusions and closures. This in part stems from an awareness—especially available to one who deals in historical time—that convincing beginnings and endings are difficult to sustain (life clearly does go on) and that historical assessments are nothing if not provisional and, while necessary, necessarily artificial. The indeterminacy of so many of his American texts is driven not by theory but by history.[17] Cooper knew that even death is an end only for the person who dies and that freedom from the burden of past history is a futile desire for him or Temple or America, as it would be later for Hester Prynne and Ike McCaslin.

If the problematic nature of Cooper's opening is fully exposed only in the light of what follows it, the conflicting forces at play in the book's final two chapters confirm the tendency of his tale. As we have already seen, Dana, contemplating the end of *The Pioneers* in 1823, recognized Natty's great virtues and their exceptional nature. The melancholy of Dana's friend implies that something is amiss in the world Natty left behind. Certainly it is not exactly the world evoked on the novel's first page. Natty

is exiled, but the departure of one who embodies so many of the civilization's pieties indicates a dislocation in the world he leaves behind far
greater than in the lonely figure of Natty. The long-standing idealization
of Natty as a figure of myth arises from his separation, and while Cooper
does promote it—especially in *The Prairie* and, briefly, in *Home as
Found*,—it is equally true that the separation is enforced by historical
processes and that Cooper does not permit unrestricted play to the self-
consolation that mythicization carries with it. Dana's letter locates the
alienation where it belongs, within society itself. This mythical figure can
carry its full force only if the ruthless facts of history are allowed theirs.
Cooper's concern about accuracy of fact is evident in the frequent footnotes and the precision with which he offers his time coordinates, and it is
borne out in a more general way by the fidelity with which he adheres to
the actual, rather than merely mythical, loss that Natty's exile represents—both for Natty and for the society he abandons. If the loss can be
reduced to myth, then nothing is really lost, or the loss need never be
confronted as the result of human action and will in history. Cooper will
not allow that evasion.

Not surprisingly, the life of Templeton in 1793 does not reflect the
fulfilled revolutionary wish of the opening paragraph; more significantly,
it does not offer much evidence to support hope for its fulfillment in the
future—and this is true, as will be more fully shown later, in all the
specifics given for a civilized society: husbandry, economy, law, morality,
and religion are all in disarray.

Nowhere is this disarray more apparent than it is in chapter 39, as *The
Pioneers* approaches its climax and dénouement: Natty's privacy is again
threatened by Hollister's parody of a revolutionary army at the instigation
of the stupid and venal Jones and Doolittle, both officers of the law, but
also with Temple's weak-willed compliance. It is not that Temple would
have endorsed this particular escapade (he is conveniently out of the way)
but that his history of compliance with and indulgence of Jones allows
Jones, under the impact of confused and ludicrous rumor, to assume he
would. Jones's willingness in this, in any case, makes us yet again doubt
Temple's judgment in the nepotistic appointment. Small as the scale of the
action is, Cooper's writing here is very pointed: apart from Jones's own
inclinations, he has the support of "the busy fancies of the populace" and
its "feverish state" of mind, in which those, "who, by their own heedless-
ness had caused the evil [of the fire]" (426) carry the loudest voice in

casting blame on Oliver and Natty. It is a very deliberate picture of chaos that pervades the entire small social fabric; the chief participants are those who have already brought Natty to the bar of legal process; only Judge Temple's last-minute exercise of authority prevents a true calamity; as he says, it is a "posse of demons" rather than a "posse comitatus." If the posse does not proceed from a well and evenly established system of law, nor does Temple's "I command the peace" inspire confidence in an even and predictable exercise of authority through the law. He is not the hero of the situation but merely the voice of his society's last resort.[18]

Temple's intervention is immediately preceded by Doolittle's vulgar and profane invocation of the law: "Gawl darn ye! this shan't be settled so easy; I'll follow it up from the 'common pleas' to the 'court of errors'" (435). Temple's first words recognize the breakdown of the law: "Silence and peace! why do I see murder and bloodshed attempted! is not the law sufficient to protect itself, that armed bands must be gathered, as in rebellion and war, to see justice performed!" (435). Temple's "command" follows the sheriff's attempted resistance of Temple. Oliver's voice from atop the Vision is unequivocal; its concession to the law is in the name of the Almighty and is entirely in harmony with Temple's elevated rhetoric: "Hold! shed not blood!" cries a voice from the top of the Vision—"Hold! for the sake of Heaven, fire no more! all shall be yielded! you shall enter the cave!" (435). This collaboration in the face of imminent social collapse brings a halt to the episode and prepares for the dénouement. Natty's composure at this point is total. "Amazement," not the law or its silent authority ("the law sufficient to protect itself"), "produced the desired effect." When the judge a little later, now in full command, orders the return to the village of the militia, he publicly rebukes his sheriff and, with the peremptory authority of his office and his class, clears the scene of those who have no business there. Cooper observes that "the habitual respect with which all the commands of the Judge were received induced a prompt compliance" (439). Far from affirming merely the return of peace and justice, this draws attention to how infrequently the Judge issues his commands and how little he has controlled—or seemed willing to control—his community.

In chapter 40 Cooper contrives a highly ceremonious pageantlike episode in which the dénouement of the main plot can be played out. All is formal and carefully delivered; the picture is elaborately composed—Effingham, his attendants about him, Natty, Hartmann, and Oliver. For all his senility, the old man speaks with the pathetic dignity of a broken Lear—not "insanity" but, in Oliver's words, "the decay of nature." When the true identity of Oliver and the major is revealed, the story is completed by Temple—at this moment, Oliver and Temple are again in unison. As Temple reveals his story, and Oliver his, the process is twice repeated. Temple's honesty, industry, high sentiment, decency, and honor in principle and action are revealed; Oliver's proud familial dedication and the purity of his Caucasian blood line are displayed (though not without severe if brief criticism of white ways versus Indian ones). The reading of Temple's will reconciles the two men and prepares the way for the inevitable wedding.[19] All tensions now are released, and the dispatch of Cooper's proceeding renders the preceding mystifications still less satisfying as a narrative substructure. However, the episode itself has great lucidity of purpose: the peerless virtues, if occasionally misguided, are here clearly manifest—they are the virtues upon which a civilized society must rest. Their presence here can only highlight their absence and ineffectuality elsewhere. At the same time, Cooper has revealed—of course, with no condemnation or irony intended—that the resolution is entirely in terms of property.

However strongly earlier scenes have engaged our sympathy for Natty and despite Natty's recent deliberate criminal act, the Temple-Effingham issue involves, we are told, "heavier interests" than his. Cooper intends no irony here, but the words and the dénouement are unavoidable; for all the engraved and spoken pieties of the final chapter, what counts historically is property. Cooper does not say so explicitly, but his book speaks for itself; Jones's coarse view of property is endorsed by the action. Natty stands over against those interests, complains consistently about them, and knows that they spell his doom. Natty in chapter 40 and as remembered on Major Effingham's headstone is a faithful "servant," not the idealized woodsman Dana responded to, the intimate with nature's book. Natty's complicity in the downfall of his way of life is thus memorialized on the inscription, as it is in the last line of the book—he is "the foremost in that band of Pioneers, who are opening the way for the march of the nation across the continent" (456). As in Crèvecoeur, the foresters prepare the way for, but then must be absorbed or displaced by, those who come later. The intention is clearly to honor Natty and to endorse the march of empire at the same time. The book's final line reaffirms the civilization of the opening paragraph, but the receding figure of Natty is exiled, defeated in the pioneer mission affirmed for him. The irony is compounded by the fact that Doolittle has preceded him "further west, scattering his professional science and legal learning through the land; vestiges of both of which are to be discovered there even to the present hour" (446–47). Natty will not then be able to put the past behind him; it is out there already to meet him. The movement to the future that involves the repetition of the past is similar to that already noted in Crèvecoeur—but the focus here is on the displaced rather than on those who prevail. The "present hour" also reflects on the present hour so elaborately depicted in the opening paragraph. If the outlook for Natty is unpromising, so it is for Temple and what he represents. Thus 1793 and 1823 glide together.

No legal or moral question about the Temple-Effingham title is entertained: the Indians granted the land to the Fire-eater, Major Effingham. Mohegan's laments before the turkey shoot and on the Vision are not for expropriation but for the massive changes wrought by European technology—plow, axe, gunpowder, and rum. It is given to Elizabeth, on grounds of sentiment rather than law, to feel a lack of right to possess the land the Indian previously owned. Although Cooper's narrative voice notes European dispossession (84), that is a matter of history, not of law. However, whatever sentiments may attach to Natty and the Indians, they are, as the book insists, of lesser weight. The critical point here is not that the reader accept that they are, endorse Cooper's well-known views on property, or reject both, but rather that Cooper offers a full and complex view of the matter which permits various analytical responses and disdains to mask the prevailing consideration.[20]

There are certain striking parallels: Natty's care for old Effingham matches his hospitality to Temple, but the society that is the beneficiary of his acts will honor them only verbally—Natty must change (take a house from Oliver and Elizabeth) or be ridden over. There are no exceptions, and gratitude, that bourgeois Christian virtue, has its limits. The act can earn little against acquisitive European history. A more important parallel is to be found in the revelation that Natty and Temple are protecting the identical interest—Effingham's. Cooper lays no special emphasis on the irony of this, but we must not miss what he has placed before us: Natty's vulnerability is of a very different order from Temple's, and the identity of purpose does not equalize the immunities of their respective social rank and class. And it is precisely Natty's protective agency that leads to his demise; he and it are exposed to the coarsest and meanest intrusions, and

Temple's rule of law helps him little. Natty's early "might often makes right here" (22) and his later "and justice [in heaven, before God] shall be the law, and not power" (455) reflect an uncomfortable truth in this agrarian peaceable kingdom. Natty states the issue clearly, even amidst the profuse piety, kindness, and sentiment of the final chapter. Whatever Natty may represent idealistically, the price he pays for an act whose motivation is identical to Temple's is far greater. The injustice is apparent. The possessors and inheritors are as helpless as their unintended victim, Natty, but they are better off because aligned with the trajectory of history. That is not quite how they would put it, but that is the truth of it.

Nowhere is that helplessness more apparent than in the final chapter, where Christian virtue has its final chance. Earlier we have seen the law brought to bear on Natty; Temple, sensitive to the conflicting loyalties involved, moves to correct the effect of the law by paying Natty's fine. Again we see that the conflict between law and justice can be resolved only if there is a Temple to see the point and act upon it. The much more serious crime now facing Temple is that Natty—as he has several times threatened—has actually discharged his rifle; Temple's wounding of Oliver provokes no such dilemma, we might note. Cooper's summary treatment of the affair—a posthaste pardon from Albany—is curiously rendered: the pardon is sought "to reconcile the even conduct of a magistrate, with the course that his feelings dictated to the criminals" (446). Temple acts for himself, for the integrity of the institution, and only then for Natty and Ben. "Pardons" are issued by those who cannot be accused of wrong to those who have done no wrong at all, or none that is inexcusable or unprovoked by illegitimate excesses in the name of the law, or by law officers. The freedom of action of Doolittle, Jones, and Riddel—"demons" on the loose in this rational Eden—validates Oliver's remark, as he disclaims Indian blood: "I have seen the hour, Judge Temple, when I could wish that such had been my lineage and education" (441). Temple does not respond. In view of the sheer energy of Jones's disruptions it is difficult to swallow that he is tamed by the word "visionary" (447); it is precisely the kind of good-humored, compliant evasion that too often appeals to Temple. And, as we have seen, Doolittle leaves but is hardly rendered impotent.

Cooper does not suggest that as the spirit of enterprise spreads through the land the abuses will cease, that the wastefulness and acquisitiveness of the European settler will diminish, that society, its institutions and officers, and its ruling pieties will be any more effective in controlling them. But Doolittle does represent what democracy will have to control. In his later work—the Littlepage manuscripts, the Home novels, *The Crater*, *Ways of the Hour*—there is no reason to think that the lapse of the twenty-seven years after *The Pioneers* offered any better comfort. It is entirely characteristic of Cooper that desire is qualified by reality.

The major business of the final chapter, after the tying of loose ends, is the conversation of Oliver, Elizabeth, and Natty at the graves of Effingham and Chingachgook, now restored to his Indian name, safely dead. As they make for the spot, the site of Natty's hut, Elizabeth tells Oliver of the arrangements she has made to improve the prospects of Reverend Grant and Louisa; her management, as benign and charitable mistress of the territory, is complete and can be so because it concerns two people so clearly ensconced within the European power structure. It is a telling prelude to their imminent failure on a comparable mission to Natty.

The episode is awash with Christian piety and high sentiment, held by all parties with unimpeachable sincerity. But it is all supererogatory. Much earlier, in chapter 25, Elizabeth has expressed her own misgivings in an at first playful context: "I grieve when I see old Mohegan walking about these lands, like the ghost of one of their ancient possessors, and feel how small is my own right to possess them" (280). Her sentiments are worthy, but they do not override her sense of reality; history cannot be reversed, and compensation is impossible. What she here observes of Mohegan includes Natty in its sphere: "But what can I do? what can my father do? Should we offer the old man a home and a maintenance, his habits would compel him to refuse us. Neither, were we so silly as to wish such a thing, could we convert these clearings and farms, again, into hunting-grounds, as the Leather-stocking would wish to see them" (280). Oliver shows his true allegiance as he accepts her view and expresses and endorses her Christian virtues: "But there is one thing that I am certain you can and will do, when you become the mistress of these beautiful valleys—use your wealth with indulgence to the poor and charity to the needy;—indeed, you can do no more" (280). We shall see her do what she can for Louisa and encounter with Natty the limits she has already expounded in this passage. One can share her grief and regret without failing to see that Christian piety is as compromised in its power as the law is. Oliver's "you can do no more" is an intended compliment; it also marks a limit, even if it is not one endorsed by the Gospels.

They commiserate over the graves and console themselves with future meeting in the hereafter—a vision of a union that has proved unachievable in the here and now. Natty, confronting a death that cannot be too far off, asks what these flocking settlers shall read on the headstones. Natty's elevated tone is echoed by the inscription that Oliver reads to him. Effingham's virtues are celebrated, the misfortunes of his history regretted, and the "tender care of his old, faithful, upright friend and attendant, Nathaniel Bumppo" memorialized (451). Natty is pleased at what the reader notes as Natty's own premature epitaph. And it is strangely put: Effingham's "descendants rear this stone to the virtues of the master, and to the enduring gratitude of the servant"—not their enduring gratitude to the servant. The gratitude of Oliver and Elizabeth is patent; it is spoken but not inscribed. Natty recognizes the kindness of the thought.

Natty's announcement of his departure is met with tears and dismay, and offers of a "tender care" that will reciprocate his own toward Effingham, the "home and a maintenance" they have already agreed he will refuse (which is not to suggest that their offer is unmeant). Natty is relentless, however; Oliver can forgive the judge, for his resentment was misplaced and restitution of property is possible; but for Natty, Temple is fatal, forgiveness is beside the point, and property is not the issue. Natty, unlike Louisa or Oliver, cannot be absorbed, nor is any meaningful indemnity possible. All three know it: only Natty fully accepts the knowledge—and Oliver, only when he sees their earlier insight confirmed. Their magnanimity is without effect. The offers are made and Natty must reject them; he is not simply obstinate—he *cannot* be reconciled. Obviously, this is the familiar polarity of nature against civilization: "Why, lad, they tell me, that on the Big-lakes, there's the best of hunting, and a great range, without a white man on it, unless it may be one like myself. I'm weary of living in clearings, and where the hammer is sounding in my ears from sun-rise to sun-down. And though I'm much bound to ye both, children; I wouldn't say it if it wasn't true; I crave to go into the woods ag'in, I do" (453–54). The woods, however, for all their comfort, are also a place of exile; nor shall the plains be immune. European civilization is not merely polar to Natty's way of life but destructive of it—and the destruction will continue. But it also destroys its own past and betrays or renders ineffective its own ideals—those of Oliver, Elizabeth, and Temple and of Cooper in the work's opening paragraph.

Oliver has urged the intransigence and necessity of Natty's intention

(454)—we can't "dispossess" Natty of his "habits" (he does not add, "whatever else we may have dispossessed him of"; he does not need to). But he continues lamely to offer the "hut on one of the distant hills, where we can sometimes see you." Elizabeth does not give up easily; she even contrives to forget her earlier conversation with Oliver: "This is so new! so unexpected!" said Elizabeth, in almost breathless excitement; "I had thought you meant to live with us, and die with us, Natty" (454). *Her own* indebtedness, *her own* fear for him, makes her finally put it plainly: "For my sake, if not for your own, stay" (455).[21] Natty pacifies her fears but is unrelenting. His final vision of an afterlife is less than consoling: "The whites shall meet the red-skins in judgment, and justice shall be the law, not power." Natty is able to concede their genuine kindness of intent; the reader is privileged to read its self-interest, as he is in the matter of the pardon. Temple's final pursuit of Natty is futile but necessary *for him.*

In the light of all this, then, the final sentence of the novel is not an idle commendatory gesture to Natty; it recognizes his complex implication in a movement of imperial history that can only destroy him. This is not to deny the mythical dimension that grows within the book and will yield richly in the works that follow it but rather to affirm that it is after all only a myth, the product of a reality whose destructive power it is meant to mitigate with the thought that the fate is transcendently inscribed. A larger providence may be at work. *The Pioneers* in its own time and since has moved generations of Americans, but one must wonder whether the patriotic gratitude of Cooper's first readers grasped how radical Cooper's criticism of America and its values was. Cooper may have preferred to say something else, but what he actually writes is pessimistic in the highest degree. If Cooper's Miranda and Ferdinand suggest the dawn of a new day, one might be inclined to address Prospero's words to Elizabeth and Oliver, "'Tis new to thee."

What I have attempted to show in this section is that, in its opening and closing, *The Pioneers* projects not a single vision of America in 1793 or 1823 reflecting Cooper's social criticism and America's pathetic dilemma, but rather a profoundly dialectical view that relentlessly confronts ideology with reality and enforces the attentive reader's constant revisionary activity. What remains is to demonstrate that this is equally true of what lies between. In the course of doing so, I will pay close attention to Cooper's much-maligned plot in order to show how well it serves the novel's dialectical dimension. This will necessitate close attention to detail and some repetition, which will, I hope, justify themselves by what they reveal.

The novel's action opens with the confrontation of Temple and Natty over a deer and Temple's wounding of Oliver. Six chapters pass before the bullet drops harmlessly into Elnathan Todd's hand, and a seventh before Oliver's wound is dressed. The first day occupies fifteen of the novel's forty-one chapters. It is hardly a model of economy: this opening episode is constantly delayed, interrupted, and put to other than narrative uses, while not in itself seeming potentially to lead us very far. It seems very much like a false start.

However, Cooper responds to the "descriptive" part of his subtitle even though his novel does not yet much resemble a "tale." Largely through Elizabeth's eyes (and Cooper's over her shoulder), we respond to the terrain, the domestic and public architecture, and the interior furnishing. Through them we become as aware of change as we do in the contributions to historical theory made by Cooper in chapters 1 and 2. In addition, Cooper populates his village with a cast of characters—immigrant and native, aboriginal, European, and African, professionals and journeymen—with a complete range of classes, excluding, of course, a hereditary nobility. It is evident that Cooper wished to furnish his tiny community with a populace representative of the various strands that constituted the American population at large. In doing so, however, he drafts into service a very large tract of history all placed against the background of his reflections on immigration in chapter 2: apart from the Temples and the history of Marmaduke's rise to prosperity, we are given a German immigrant, a refugee from the French Revolution, a veteran of the American Revolution, a slave menaced by his bullying surrogate owner, a lawyer, a magistrate, a doctor, an Indian degenerated into drunkenness, an aged declining backwoodsman, and an indecipherable young man who belongs nowhere and everywhere. Although there is no plot development, Cooper's cast teems with implicit historical narrative. In one sense, the absence of a single developing plot line conveys, under these circumstances, the presence of another plot, America's, a compendium of histories.

However, the question of social and political coherence is always arising. It is not insignificant—and may once more recall Crèvecoeur—that Aggy the slave, surely inessential to any plot in the work, is so grossly bullied by Jones. If Oliver and Elizabeth meet in this phase of the book and find some common ground in gentility and piety, suspicion of Oliver's racial purity inhibits romantic involvement. Mohegan may seem superfluous—a mere exotic adornment; he is certainly not absolutely necessary to the major narratives in the novel, and yet he too is there to bear meaning. It is not left to the reader to infer this, for Cooper several times directly addresses the issue of dispossession of native peoples by European immigrants. In addition, the return of Elizabeth as an educated lady, prepared to be the mistress of the manor, is relieved of its neutrality by the displacement of Remarkable Pettibone and the ensuing class antagonism, which is carried a significant stage further in the discussion, before Temple's arrival, in the Bold Dragoon.

Even Natty in the early stages may seem incidental, merely intrusive. He also brings to the conversation a rich dimension of the martial colonial past of America. His major role—as in the opening scene—is exactly to intrude. He is rendered marginal by the passage of history, the presence of Temple; it would be convenient if he would allow himself to be forgotten, but he insists on being taken account of. He, like Mohegan, is essential not merely to America's sense of its history but also to the resolution of the major plots. In contriving it so, Cooper makes it impossible for the reader to pass him over, even as, in the implication of the dénouement, civilization moves to its third stage. This intrusive function of Natty's disallows free passage to the dominant ideology of the plot.[22]

If the opening episode is in itself of no great consequence for the plot, it is proleptic of Natty's later killing of a deer out of season. The later action sets in train the series of events that brings all the narrative elements to their conclusion; it is also the most complex and interesting action in the novel, and since it too brings Temple and Natty face to face in an altered relationship of power, it is bound to draw the reader into a comparison of the two men's conduct—at the simplest level it will be seen that the judge is as much a prey to his own impulses as Natty is, rather than simply a defender of law or honor.

Given the importance of "mild laws" in the formation of the new communities, the "humane laws of this compassionate country," it is notable that no legal issues are brought to trial as a result of the opening episode. Oliver's killing of a deer is overlooked by the potential plaintiff; when Oliver appeals to right and law, Temple concedes the deer. This is appropriate when so much of the country remains wild; the right to hunt is granted precedence over property rights.[23] Between the two killings there intervene the new game laws, which, though not directed at those like Natty who know better than to kill a nursing doe, will bring Natty to his trial. Natty's dissent from those laws asserts his own prior right and affirms that the scarcity of deer is brought on, not by hunting, but by settlement; he sees it, correctly, as an expression of power. Temple sees the new law as ultimately serving private property: "Armed with the dignity of the law, Mr. Bumppo," returned the Judge, gravely, "a vigilant magistrate can prevent much of the evil that has hitherto prevailed, and which is already rendering the game scarce. I hope to live to see the day, when a man's rights in his game shall be as much respected as his title to his farm" (160). Major Hartmann observes that the land is not for deer but for Christians; chapter 7 has already bluntly named Christians as dispossessors. If the game laws have the protection of private property as their motive, then the judge has a personal interest in the case he will try. It must always be remembered, of course, that Cooper regarded property as a prime bulwark of civilization.[24]

Temple's argument is removed only in tone from Jones's earlier commentary:

> "Well, 'duke, you are your own master, but I would have tried law for the saddle, before I would have given it to the fellow. Do you not own the mountains, as well as the valleys? are not the woods your own? what right has this chap, or the Leather-stocking, to shoot in your woods, without your permission? Now, I have known a farmer, in Pennsylvania, order a sportsman off his farm, with as little ceremony as I would order Benjamin to put a log in the stove. By-the-by, Benjamin, see how the thermometer stands. Now, if a man has a right to do this, on a farm of a hundred acres, what power must a landlord have, who owns sixty thousand—ay! for the matter of that, including the late purchases, a hundred thousand?" [93]

Not merely does Jones see rights as increasing with the holding of property, but significantly he sees nothing wrong with the judge's enjoying a personal advantage from his office. "A'nt Marmaduke a Judge?" says Richard indignantly; "Where is the use of being a Judge or having a Judge, if there is no law?" (93). The remark is outrageous, but it draws no remonstrance from Temple.

The concern for property strangely takes precedence in discussion over the more serious issue, the wounding of Oliver. The judge's offense remains untried. His immunities are stressed by their being ignored. He needs no pardon: his offense is unintended, if careless; Natty's is intended and justified by laws relating to self-defense, privacy, unreasonable search and seizure, and prior restraint.[25] And the appointment of Jones as sheriff will ensure Temple's continued immunity, not by Temple's design but by Jones's stated intention.

There is, however, a trial of sorts at the Bold Dragoon. Given the cast of caricatures that participate in it, it is easy to disregard it or to see it as light relief. In fact, the disputants at the Bold Dragoon seem more aware than those at the judge's manor that wounding a man is a criminal offense. Doctor Todd's common sense in this scene is echoed later by Billy Kirby when Natty gives up the evidence to the sheriff's party. Lippet—is he the "dealer in suits" we see later tampering with a juryman?—speaks Temple's constant refrain: "The law, gentlemen, is no respecter of persons, in a free country. . . . Though some may get property . . . they are not privileged to transgress the laws" (152). Whatever we may think of Lippet's motives, Cooper would agree with him. Mrs. Hollister, not the most coherent of thinkers, endorses Jones's previous hints about the advantage the judge's money gives him, but she also allows his character to excuse him from the consequences of his action. "He's a good man is Joodge Temple, and a kind one, and one who will be no the likelier to do the pratty thing, bekaase ye would wish to tarrify him wid the law" (153–54). Her argument is sensible but is based on men, not laws—like Elizabeth's arguments later; it is also the precise argument later advanced for Natty and rejected—by Temple, on whose behalf it is here submitted. He later will make Lippet's point in order to condemn Natty and claim for himself a disinterestedness that we have seen is at least questionable. Dignity aside, it seems to me that the observations made at the Bold Dragoon are more serious and sensible than those of Temple. In retrospect, it is a strange scene indeed, enacted in the presence of Doolittle who will pervert all versions of the law.

In the absence of any revelation of the true plots there can be little formal legal argument. The particular issue of the ownership of the Temple lands is deflected onto what is repeatedly presented, by Cooper's narrative reticence, as Indian rights and historical change. Cooper, by his development of Mohegan in chapter 7 and later, seems willing to allow the misapprehension to generate its own crucial interest, only in the end to be displaced—but not eliminated—by property. In any event, such narrative as there is in the early part of the novel exists as a framework upon which issues of discussion are spread that are of great significance both to the plot and its meaning.[26]

The treatment of Mohegan in this novel is typical of Cooper's procedure: he is never primarily interested in the advancement of the plot; rather, he loads the characters and the insignificant episodes they are involved in with complexities of meaning and significance that cannot be eliminated, thus making impossible the reduction of the novel to a single preferred meaning favorable to those who prevail.

Mohegan first enters to treat Oliver's wound and dress it; but before he does so, we are offered a brief discussion of Indian history "before the Europeans, or, to use a more significant term, the Christians, dispossessed the original owners of the soil" (83). The issue is not fudged or avoided. "Europeans" is deliberately revised to "Christians"; by peace or war, Penn's means or the Puritans', the "object" of "dispossession" is effected. Above all, it is evident that none of this is necessary to the plot, and we must conclude that, in *The Pioneers* at least, Cooper had higher priorities than narrative. Not merely does he gratuitously insist on dispossession, but also he evokes it emotionally with an intensified rhetoric. Mohegan is the sole representative of a "nation in ruins" after "wartime, disease, and want" had laid it low; his long hair, it is imagined, is grown to "hide the shame of a noble soul, mourning for a glory once known" (86). However literary the language is, it is not merely conventional, for it represents the consequence of dispossession. The property on which the novel's outcome turns and which in part causes the great breach between Effingham and Temple—and, later, Oliver and Temple—is what "the original owners" were dispossessed of and continued (and continue) to be dispossessed of. The whole issue of dispossession that attends Mohegan's entrance is, by the end of chapter 7, coarsened by Jones's alignment of the rights of power, ownership, and the law. However fastidious we may be about this brutal realism, he sees the truth of the situation. Hartmann is quite close to the mark when he observes (93) that Jones is using the law to overprotect property as the hunter will use his rifle to protect his rights. Temple does not protest. Once more, the law is demystified.

Mohegan, then, carries the burden of his race's fate into the novel and is not a merely exotic decoration of the text, possessed of arcane healing powers (narrowly observed, Cooper notes, by Dr. Todd); he is also given a history more complex than mere stereotype would permit. He lays no claim to the land, whose transformation he so lyrically bewails, but is concerned only that it remain in the hands of him to whom his tribe gave it as a gift. His generosity has carried an enormous price for him. He bears around his neck "a silver medallion of Washington," the token of the race which he has served and which has dispossessed him and his kind. Like Natty, he is complicit in his own downfall. He has surrendered his native religion and language to those of his conquerors and has taken (been given) a name that they will recognize.[27] Just as his generosity and service earn contempt rather than Christian reward, the name that combines European and Indian is a lie—such a union is possible only in a name. And yet, stripped and dislocated as he is, he remains an intrusive and disturbing presence, and he shows a tactless critical spirit not entirely in keeping with his cowed demeanor. He accuses Temple of betraying his Quaker upbringing in wounding Oliver; Temple passionately denies intent. Mohegan responds: "The evil spirit sometimes lives in the best heart, . . . but my brother speaks the truth; his hand has never taken life, when awake; no! not even when the children of the great English Father, were making the waters red with the blood of his people." This is an exceedingly complex statement; its first clause suggests hidden harmful motives behind good intentions; its third implies that Temple might have taken life when he was asleep (or closed his eyes or averted his face—later, in *Mohicans*, we should recall this in judging Montcalm at the massacre at Fort William Henry); the fourth implies cowardice and the bloodiness of the English— Mohegan will return to this note during the fire on Mount Vision. Pondered as we always do Hawthorne, Melville, and James, this passage reflects profoundly and comprehensively on European attitudes. Mr. Grant's Christian injunction, "Judge not, lest ye be judged," sounds hollow and evasive; the point, however, is that the judgment is made. That John declares Temple "innocent" cannot erase the validity of the earlier judgment; it means only that Temple meant no harm, not that he did none. The child's cry, "I didn't mean it," is intended to evade consequences; since Temple is who he is, the squire and judge, his appeal is indulged. Again, as with Mrs. Hollister, Temple is excused on grounds similar to those he will deny Natty.

Chapter 7, then, which opens with the revision of "European" to read "Christian," has for its benediction the Reverend Grant's affirmation of the equality of all before God: "The Great Spirit overlooks none of his children; and the man of the woods, is as much an object of his care, as he who dwells in a palace. I wish you a good night, and pray God to bless you" (95). Grant later reveals to Oliver (143) his own uncertain earthly grasp of this divine principle, and, if we take the entire chapter into account, the principles to which he here and later appeals must ring hollow. Oliver and Mohegan must show patience, even though those dispossessors, as Grant in chapter 12 is ready to admit them to be, need make no earthly recompense. It is a hypocritical position that serves only might. If, as several of Cooper's Indians point out, the principle is on every Christian's lips and is so easy to understand, why is it that the principle is so rarely acted upon? Immediately, in chapter 8, it is evident that Le Quoi, another displaced person, finds a more secure berth in the revolutionary republic than Mohegan or Natty. He is, of course, white and civilized.

The critical spirit of the broken Mohegan has its finest moment on Mount Vision with Elizabeth, the most sympathetic to his claims; she is also fully aware of her incapacity to alter the course of history or to make effectual restitution, as we have seen. She may offer a calico shirt for a basket, and *her* fine sense of morality concedes his "natural right to order what you will from us" (400), and she praises his conversion to the Christian way, "to fear God and to live at peace" (401). Mohegan's retort utterly demolishes white moral pretensions:[28]

> "Stand here, daughter, where you can see the great spring, the wig-wams of your father, and the land on the crooked-river. John was young, when his tribe gave away the country, in council, from where the blue mountain stands above the water, to where the Susquehan-nah is hid by the trees. All this, and all that grew in it, and all that walked over it, and all that fed there, they gave to the Fire-eater—for they loved him. He was strong, and they were women, and he helped them. No Delaware would kill a deer that run in his woods, nor stop a bird that flew over his land; for it was his. Has John lived in peace! Daughter, since John was young, he has seen the white man from Frontinac come down on his white brothers at Albany, and fight. Did they fear God! He has seen his English and his American Fathers burying their tomahawks in each other's brains, for this very land. Did they fear God, and live in peace! He has seen the land pass away from the Fire-eater, and his children, and the child of his child, and a new chief set over the country. Did they live in peace who did this! did they fear God!" [401]

"Such is the custom of the whites, John," she replies. John scornfully rejects such custom as violence and theft:

> "Where are the blankets and merchandise that bought the right of the Fire-eater?" he replied, in a more animated voice; "are they with him in his wigwam? Did they say to him, brother, sell us your land, and take this gold, this silver, these blankets, these rifles, or even this rum? No, they tore it from him, as a scalp is torn from an enemy; and they that did it looked not behind them, to see whether he lived or died. Do such men live in peace, and fear the Great Spirit?" [401]

Mohegan here speaks in ignorance of Temple's clandestine honest dealing with the Fire-eater. The point is not his ignorance but the conclusion he feels entitled to express. It is for Mohegan as if Effingham, in acquiring an Indian name, in being adopted by an Indian tribe, inherits treatment habitually reserved for Indians. That Effingham is not, in fact, deprived ironically marks a racial difference that no name, John or the Fire-eater, and no religion, Christian or pagan, can erase. Surely, we cannot sustain the notion that Cooper composed such passages absentmindedly; such passages command recognition that the sigh of regret over the sad consequences of white, European, Christian empire exists alongside a clear-sighted condemnation. In this context, Grant's invocation to Oliver and Mohegan, meant as a moral injunction, a religious commonplace, takes on quite a different cast when we remember who the "enemies," cursers, haters must be: "But I say unto you, love your enemies, bless them that curse you; do good to them that hate you; pray for them that despitefully use you and persecute you" (139). An extension like the one I here present suggests a degree of coherence, not at once apparent if we consult narrative only. In short, then, the entrance of Mohegan far transcends his function in the plot and leads to an extraordinary efflorescence of problematic issues—historical, religious, and legal. Not only that—Mohegan's speech refers not only to the Effingham-Temple situation but contains also the germ of the *in propria voce* opening of Cooper's next Leather-Stocking novel, *Mohicans*.

What is true of the religious principles of the new republic is apparent also in the secular sphere—most particularly in the economy. As spring approaches, the enterprise, movement, energy, and industry that are to produce the vision of the opening paragraph are evident:[29]

Elizabeth saw many large openings appear in the sides of the mountains, during the three succeeding months, where different settlers
had, in the language of the country, "made their pitch"; while the
numberless sleighs that passed through the village, loaded with wheat
and barrels of pot-ashes, afforded a clear demonstration that all these
labours were not undertaken in vain. In short, the whole country was
exhibiting the bustle of a thriving settlement, where the highways
were thronged with sleighs, bearing piles of rough household furniture, studded, here and there, with the smiling faces of women and
children, happy in the excitement of novelty; or with loads of produce, hastening to the common market at Albany, that served as so
many snares, to induce the emigrants to enter into those wild mountains in search of competence and happiness. [215–16]

As we shall see, an earlier, less sunny vision will shortly be remembered by
Temple; the question will remain, in the light of the whole text, how
confidently we can trust this generation's providence over that of the last.

Before the weather breaks, we have been made privy to Natty's discontent about the effects of agriculture and settlement upon his way of life, to
Oliver's and Mohegan's dramatic outbursts on dispossession and the consequences for the Indian of white Christian European empire, and to the
discussions between Jones and Temple on the use of natural resources,
waste, and the duty to the future—conversations in which the depth of
their difference and the thoroughness of Jones's commitment to the plun-
dering of nature are first revealed. However, as spring advances, the discussion moves out of doors, and in a series of descriptive episodes, Cooper
offers further development and exemplification of the economy in action.

The first of these episodes occupies chapters 20 and 21; it opens with a
formal elevated evocation of early spring, which is alternated with the
utilitarian signs of agrarian industry, "to enkindle the hopes of the hus-
bandman" (220), and simple pleasure, as Oliver, Elizabeth, Louisa, Le
Quoi, Temple, and Jones set out to visit Billy Kirby's sugar bush. Earlier
discussions of the prodigal and provident consumption of wood for fuel
are continued in relation to the production of sugar; Jones's concern is
with technique for quantity production, whereas Temple's is with the
entire process: production, development, and conservation—wholesale
waste and destruction for instant gain have no appeal for Temple. Their
first view of Kirby's enterprise affords an image of waste: "A deep and

careless incision had been made into each tree, near its root, into which little spouts, formed of the bark of the alder, or of the sumach, were fastened; and a trough, roughly dug out of the linden, or bass-wood, was lying at the root of each tree, to catch the sap that flowed from this extremely wasteful and inartificial arrangement" (224). Kirby's hymn to plenty is a coarsened version of the national agrarian hope; it is sung to the tune of Yankee Doodle. Jones joins in and keeps time with his whip. (The tune is heard again as Hollister's militia set out to take Natty.) It is, of course, a plenty that is threatened by this Yankee waste. Temple makes "frequent expressions of dissatisfaction" (226):

> "It grieves me to witness the extravagance that pervades this coun-
> try," said the Judge, "where the settlers trifle with the blessings they
> might enjoy, with the prodigality of successful adventurers. You are
> not exempt from the censure yourself, Kirby, for you make dreadful
> wounds in these trees, where a small incision would effect the same
> object. I earnestly beg you will remember, that they are the growth of
> centuries, and when once gone, none living will see their loss rem-
> edied." [228]

Kirby's response is identical to Jones's; he cannot imaging the abundance ever ceasing and consults only today's commercial opportunity. Temple's sense of responsibility to the future is based on how long trees take to grow. Cooper inscribes not merely a criticism of human character but of the commercial basis on which the kind of economic growth Temple can imagine depends. Temple expresses his enlightened rationalism convinc-ingly, but he speaks and rides away—and that is the pattern of his behavior throughout. What he leaves behind is an image of "human life in its first stages of civilization," but there is little promise in it, or in Temple's actions, for the future stages. "Perhaps," Cooper observes, no damage is done to the "romantic character" by Billy's ballad of heedless destruction:

> "And when the proud forest is falling,
> To my oxen cheerfully calling,
> From morn until night I am bawling,
>   Woe, back there and hoy and gee;
> Till our labour is mutually ended,
> By my strength and cattle befriended,
> And against the musquitoes defended,
>   By the bark of the walnut tree.—

"Away! then, you lads who would buy land,
Choose the oak that grows on the high land,
Or the silvery pine on the dry land,
    It matters but little to me." [230]

However the reader, Cooper, or Elizabeth composes the view, Billy's song celebrates himself as a mere function in historical and social change. It is a hymn to alienation. Although Temple issues a veiled threat of laws to conserve the forest, there is no decisive action or will in evidence. In fact, the "first stages" distinctly put the later ones at risk.

Temple is the ruler and ideologue of the views of the novel's opening paragraph and the one who—by moral force, by office, and by wealth—can facilitate and form the ambitions of the smiling migrants of spring. But we are never allowed to overlook the presence and force of Jones and Kirby. As the outing proceeds in chapter 21, Temple juxtaposes the dangers of the rough transitional paths they are traveling with the dangers of too hasty change. His didactic emphasis exactly matches Cooper's. "If thou hadst seen this district of country, as I did, when it lay in the sleep of nature, and had witnessed its rapid changes, as it awoke to supply the wants of man, thou wouldst curb thy impatience for a little time, though thou shouldst not check thy steed" (232). The passage aligns the present scene with the one just past, leads to Temple's narrative of his arrival in the territory, and provides a motivation in his personal experience for the views he has been expressing. His tale of the "starving time" five years earlier (which may remind some readers of William Bradford) oddly rewrites the spring migration passages and reinscribes the waste of Billy Kirby. The migrant families "in search of competence and happiness" (216) are translated into "a swarm of locusts" (234), "adventurers" prey to "speculation" and "the restless spirit of emigration." And "famine" threatens. Evidently, the "evil day" (16) is not ages away but soon produced, in this brief account, prophetically. The possibility of eventual scarcity, scoffed at by Jones and Kirby, needs no imagination—it has the authority of recent fact. The spirit that produced the "starving time" abides in Kirby and Jones. At that time, the settlers had to revert to the wild for sustenance; now, according to Natty, their very settlement has put that recourse in jeopardy. However, for Temple the "loads of produce" that succeed settlement compensate for the suffering. In fact, for him, "pain, famine, and disease" are privations to be endured "in order to accumulate wealth" (232). The implicit question, left to the reader to put, is this: "What will happen if the starving time returns?"

Temple's difference from Jones and Kirby is not just theoretical; his concern and providence, his rejection of the merely commercial motives of the speculators, saves his people: there is "no grinding of the poor"; his rational and humane use of his wealth provides the loaves, and nature provides the fishes. He provides the perfect exemplum of agrarian virtue in action; "All this," Cooper adds in his 1832 footnote, "was literally true." Temple's narrative provides not merely his reasons for his views but offers a historical context in which the previous scene and the two following this "desultory dialogue" may be viewed.

Temple also conjures a vision of the terrain before settlement: picturesque, sublime, unspoiled, unimproved—its structure matches that of the opening paragraph. In this context, he recounts his first meeting with Natty and their immediate estrangement, but a bond is forged here, which, though he must disregard it later (but Natty will not allow him to forget it), is identical with those bonds that Elizabeth, Louisa, and Pump refuse to deny. Oliver injects into what is largely an interrupted monologue by Temple the issue of possession and Indian land rights. It is not revealed at this point why Oliver behaves so coldly, but it is perfectly clear that what started out as merely descriptive has generated issues having to do with the economic development of the society—law, property, right, equity, and indebtedness—that all both affect the health of the state and constitute the central issues that will animate the tale which has still not properly begun. The episode of the falling tree neatly illustrates Temple's warning at the beginning of the chapter and forges yet another bond between Oliver and Louisa, Elizabeth and Temple, that matches Temple's to Natty.

These bonds warrant a digression; they are important on the human and narrative level and afford a rich vein of complication that leads to conflicts of allegiance and morality, and they place in question simple views of both history and the claims Temple makes for the force of law. The bonds are tied in the face of the hazards of nature. While Natty's role in *The Pioneers* is not heroic and little of the mythic clings to him, victim and witness as he is, the transitional stage Cooper chooses to depict confers upon him a necessary role, shared with Oliver, that complicates Temple's insistence upon a nation of laws. However marked the signs of change may be, the terrain remains dangerous. Oliver twice in the earlier episodes comes to the rescue of settlers at the mercy of natural hazard and human folly. Temple twice warns Elizabeth of the dangers of the country. Bear come to "view the progress of the invader." Other dangers exist that require Natty's knowledge of the countryside, his skill with the rifle, and his domicile in the wild—dangers evoked by Pump's early reference to a roaming wild cat, Natty's mention of wolves, and the discussion of Louisa and Elizabeth about wolves. Elizabeth's response to Louisa's terror makes a central claim that endorses the vision of the opening paragraph; it should be noted that this discussion occurs immediately before the spring expedition:

> "The enterprise of Judge Temple is taming the very forests!" exclaimed Elizabeth, throwing off the covering, and partly rising in the bed. "How rapidly is civilization treading on the footsteps of nature!" she continued, as her eye glanced over not only the comforts, but the luxuries of her apartment, and her ear again listened to the distant, but often repeated howls from the lake. Finding, however, that the timidity of her companion rendered the sounds painful to her, Elizabeth resumed her place, and soon forgot the changes in the country, with those in her own condition, in a deep sleep. [212][30]

The testing of Elizabeth's confident claim is made central in one aspect of the major plot that follows; by inscribing Natty's necessity in the actual circumstances, Cooper imposes upon himself and the reader a questioning of the simple authority of the law.

Natty also is instrumental in saving Elizabeth in the fire on Mount Vision from the consequences of a careless civilization, the "swarm of locusts" at their destructive work. Temple is given to allowing Natty as an exception to the general rule, as in some sense not requiring the restraints of law. It is worth noting that when Temple does act to "save" his civilization, insisting on the spirit and the letter of the law, he is as exceptional in his way as Natty is in his, and equally threatened. Part of the intent of his discourses on history in chapter 21 is clearly to establish the behavior that should characterize the agrarian nation against the wastefulness that surrounds the chapter on both sides; however, the negative social forces far outweigh Temple's example and teaching, rendering him *merely* exceptional and, in the worst account, a man merely of words. I do believe that Cooper meant us to consider the worst account as well.

The bond so early established between Natty and Temple is based upon Natty's hospitality. Temple confesses to Oliver his failure to understand Natty's coldness and resentment when he learns Temple's "name and object." It is over the issues of rights, justice, and legality of tenure that the final dramas will be worked out. Oliver's "cold" and sardonic "Doubtless, sir, your title is both legal and equitable" reinstates Natty's hostility in the text. Temple's mission "to accumulate wealth" has consequences of impoverishment and displacement for others that Temple's altruism and faith in legality cannot indemnify. It must be added that it casts a shadow over the established virtue and prosperity the opening announces. All this is fully registered once more in the exchanges between the two men in the succeeding well-known episodes of the pigeon shoot and the netting of the bass. In both episodes the opposition between Temple and Jones on issues of humanity and economy is reiterated; in both Temple attempts a rapprochement with Natty under the banner of a shared disdain for waste; Natty rejects Temple's overtures by word and symbolic deed—as he must, for to him waste is characteristic of settlement, not, as it is for Temple, an aberration from the standards of civilized settlements. Natty has recognized from their first encounter the price he will pay for Temple's settlements, which represent a technology that must destroy Natty's life and willfully does so. The destruction is not unintended.

The settlers have a reasonable motive for deterring the pigeons, as Kirby points out, but their slaughter turns the stomach. Temple's sense of regret (always with Cooper a sign of decent humanity) is disdained by Jones—and it is he who commands the exploit, raising the shout of "Victory!" over what Temple sees as "innocent sufferers" (250): "I see nothing but eyes, in every direction, as the innocent sufferers turn their heads in terror. Full one half of those that have fallen are yet alive: and I think it is time to end the sport; if sport it be" (250). Cooper quite deliberately—as he will so often later do—sickens the reader. The best that can be said of Temple is that he knows his folly, as the rest do not: "Judge Temple retired toward his dwelling with that kind of feeling, that many a man has experienced before him, who discovers, after the excitement of the moment has passed, that he has purchased pleasure at the price of misery to others" (250). What is true of pigeons in this episode is true also of the consequences of Temple's larger actions on men. But Cooper has composed the episode with great care; Temple is persuaded by Natty, after the first fusillade, of the "wasty ways" of the proceeding but still participates in the second:

"Even Marmaduke forgot the morality of the Leather-stocking as [the flock of pigeons] approached, and, in common with the rest, brought his musket to a poise" (249). Temple can only regret—not command, not alter; he, in effect, once more rides away. The passenger pigeon is extinct. It should be noted too that Temple's impulsive participation in a destructive act has, as its sole consequence, a troubled conscience; Natty's impulses have more serious consequences for him.

The netting of the fish produces essentially the same patterns: unresisted impulses of enthusiasm and excitement, regret, Temple's rejected attempt at an unwelcomed alliance with Natty, his difference with and submission to Jones, who once more presides over a scene of insensate waste—this time without the excuse of the pigeons' predations on the crops. And, once more, Temple turns away: "Marmaduke appeared to understand that all opposition to the Sheriff's will would be useless, and he strolled from the fire, to the place where the canoe of the hunters lay" (266). The alliance of Natty and Temple is scornfully noted by Jones: "A very pretty confederacy, indeed! Judge Temple, the landlord and owner of a township, with Nathaniel Bumppo, a lawless squatter, and professed deer-killer, in order to preserve the game of the county! But, 'duke, when I fish, I fish; so, away, boys, for another haul, and we'll send out wagons and carts, in the morning, to bring in our prizes!" (266). The suggestion embedded in this is that Temple, for all his authority, is as powerless as Natty.

Temple's conservation laws do not ensure, once the fish is in season, respect for their spirit; only their letter is consulted—and exploited. Even so, Temple might have prevented the second, utterly pointless haul. Natty comments not merely by his careful, concentrated spearing of a single fish; he also uses the same spear to save Ben Pump's life, which is almost lost in the careless, greedy action. This "miraculous draught" (253) furnishes a cruel parody of the first draught of loaves and fishes during the "starving time." Jones's contempt for Temple's views is manifest in a summary comment:

> "Disappear, 'duke! disappear!" exclaimed the Sheriff; "if you don't call this appearing, I know not what you will. Here are a good thousand of the shiners, some hundreds of suckers, and a powerful quantity of other fry. But this is always the way with you, Marmaduke; first, it's the trees, then it's the deer, after that it's the maple sugar, and so on to the end of the chapter. One day, you talk of canals,

through a country where there's a river or a lake every half-mile, just because the water won't run the way you wish it to go; and the next, you say something about mines of coal, though any man who has good eyes, like myself—I say with good eyes—can see more wood than would keep the city of London in fuel for fifty years." [260]

The allusion to mines leads to the first movement toward the development of the plot that is fatal to Natty. Jones's comments stir only laughter in Temple. However, the second haul constitutes a dismissal of Temple and all he stands for. Temple, for all his high rational principle and refined sensibility, cedes power to Jones. The act is potentially fatal to Templeton and, by extension, to America and actually fatal to Natty's way of life, which Temple would always wish to accommodate. However reluctantly, we must admit that Jones has a more accurate sense of how this world will work. Cooper incessantly draws attention to Jones in such specific and deliberate terms that it is hard to imagine that Cooper did not know what he was doing.

These spring scenes, then, in which the sap rises, the fish teem, and the birds fly overhead, opening with a conventional evocation of life awakening and agrarian hope fulfilling itself, are characterized by an orgy of destruction. The "locusts" of the starving time have reinstated themselves and must qualify the orderly historical prophecy of the book's opening sentences. The "evil day," the disappearances feared by Temple, are not so far off, and their presiding spirit is Jones. The fire that almost destroys Oliver and Elizabeth is the result in part of actions initiated by Jones, Doolittle, and Riddel—and in part by the poor husbandry of the settlers themselves.

If Jones declares victory over the pigeons, he has equally vanquished Temple, whose "cheerful" avoidance of the challenge he represents is entirely inadequate to cope with Jones's energy. Temple may be the patriarch-founder of Templeton and the hero-ideologue of the agrarian prophecy, but he does not control or lead his community; he has abdicated those functions to Jones, who certainly dominates the first half of the book and, arguably, perhaps the whole work. His energetic will to prevail is evident from the beginning. He intrudes noisily on the most contemplative of moments; his ever-present whip suggests his brutality; he coarsens the law into mere self-interest; he is ill mannered, ignorant, and arrogant, and his violence is moderated only by his cowardice and mendacity. He is completely insensitive to, or simply bigoted and self-interested about, all the crosscurrents—historical, social, and racial—that touch on the presence of Oliver, Natty, and Mohegan. Several dialogues seem concerned mainly to place Jones's crude energy and ignorance against Temple's and Elizabeth's more rational attitudes.

Although Temple can tell Pump to ignore rumors, he cannot prevent Jones's starting of them and—at the final stage—acting upon them with nearly catastrophic results. Jones also resists Temple's principled view if a society "in which all are equal who know how to conduct themselves with propriety" (205). He dismisses with contempt Temple's most provident considerations; he is insensitive to the past, wasteful in the present, and unresponsive to the needs of the future. In religion, he is willing to subvert the sensible compromises of Grant and Temple; his spirit always tends to self-interested factionalism.

In spite of all this, in full knowledge of cousin Dickon Jones's faults, Temple consigns the design and building of his house and the public building to Jones and Doolittle; ignorance, incompetence, and an undiscriminating taste prevail and are the object of Cooper's satirical wit—but Jones's pretentious criteria spread through the as yet sparsely inhabited valley. The emblematic value of this process, relatively early in the novel, should not go unmarked.

For Temple personally, and for the new society he leads, law and morality are the most important issues. He is always careful of his own moral position and the evasions of others, and resists the presentation of rumor as fact; he is also capable of self-correction. In such matters, Jones invariably falls short. And yet, when it comes to the appointment of his sheriff, Temple prefers Jones. The security of principle that guides his insistence, as he welcomes the young man into his "family" (205),[31] that Oliver be treated as a gentleman until shown to be otherwise is quite absent here; he has every reason to know Jones's faults as well as the reader does but appoints him to "the executive chair of the county." At once, Jones's prejudice against Oliver is so evident that it draws from Temple the mild admonition, "Surely, Dickon, you will not execute till I condemn!" (205). Jones's response to the appointment is instructive: he finds with characteristic vanity that Temple is "a judicious man, and knows human nature thoroughly" (182), but he also sees it as a favor—Temple "never forgets his friends." It is, in fact, an act of unadorned nepotism—they are, as Jones cheerfully points out, "sisters' children" (200). Moreover, Jones is willing to reciprocate the favor—"I am wholly yours," he assures Temple. Cooper makes sure that no attentive reader can miss the point. Unlike Temple and Todd, who grow to be worthy of respect in their judicial and medical functions, Jones is unqualified now and will remain so. Nor is the appointment a single aberration in Temple: in architecture as in law, in small matters as in large, he licenses the destructive spirit of Jones, evident in the fishing and pigeon episodes, with almost catastrophic results for his community and deadly ones for Natty; Jones is the executor (he fancies himself as an executioner [182]) of European civilization's sentence on Natty.

Jones's first action in office, overriding Elizabeth's reservations about invasion of privacy, is to eavesdrop on the conversation of Natty, Oliver, and Mohegan. The moment is a complex one; not merely does Jones—without cause—violate his victims' rights, but he also quite fails to understand what he hears. This is the juncture at which Cooper introduces Mohegan's trenchant lament for the past: " 'The white man brings old age with him—rum is his tomahawk!' "

> "The smokes were once few in these hills. The deer would lick the hand of a white man, and the birds rest on his head. They were strangers to him. My fathers came from the shores of the salt lake. They fled before rum. They came to their grandfather, and they lived in peace; or when they did raise the hatchet, it was to strike it into the brain of a Mingo. They gathered around the council-fire, and what they said was done. Then John was the man. But warriors and traders with light eyes followed them. One brought the long knife, and one brought rum. They were more than the pines on the mountains; and they broke up the councils, and took the lands. The evil spirit was in their jugs, and they let him loose.—Yes, yes—you say no lie, Young Eagle, John is a Christian beast." [185]

This passage concentrates idealization of an Edenic past with the reality of historical process. It draws from Oliver his condemnation of "the cupidity that has destroyed such a race" (186). The accusation is never withdrawn or qualified; it reiterates Cooper's own commentary (83), and Grant later repeats it, as will Mohegan on Mount Vision. Not least, Elizabeth hears and understands, and it informs her conversation with Oliver and Louisa in chapter 25. Jones is impervious to the appeal of all this. Throughout this passage and the ensuing turkey shoot, Jones evinces a ludicrous officiousness that amounts to a parody of judiciousness;

Cooper lets us see not only that but also Temple's "smiling" whimsical deference and his overly easy deflection of Jones's misdirected racial prejudice and spiteful intentions toward Oliver.

The ascendancy which Temple allows Jones is not merely a grace note of the narrative or of character; it relates directly to the possibility of fulfilling the book's opening prophecy. Temple in fact cedes not merely his own authority and control but, with them, his principles to Jones. It is Jones's alliance with Doolittle and Riddel, for both of whom Temple has only contempt, that drives the tale told in the second half of the work. The driving force of the text, as of the developing civilization, is not Temple's rational agrarianism—of which, be it added, he is the material beneficiary—but rather the rapacious "cupidity" denounced by Oliver and incarnated by Jones and his cohorts. Temple may, like a *deus ex machina*, command Jones's withdrawal, Elizabeth and Oliver may propose the remedy of Christian charity (refused), and Grant, like Natty, may insist that God in his time shall put matters right—in another life, not this one. But the power of Jones is more immediate and imposing, and Cooper arranges no narrative elimination of him, as he does of Riddel and Doolittle; Jones thrives—and Temple indulges him. Doolittle is removed from this scene to thrive in another. He reminds one of the sour ending of Irving's "Sleepy Hollow"; the valley is cleansed of Ichabod Crane but the intelligence is that "he had changed his quarters . . . had kept school and studied law at the same time, had been admitted to the bar, turned politician, electioneered, written for the newspapers, and finally had been made a justice of the Ten Pound Court" (*Sketchbook*, 358).

"Come! to thy tale," urges the epigraph to chapter 25; and while, like the footnote to chapter 21, it signals Cooper's awareness of his dereliction of narrative responsibility and his readiness to return to it, the reader will find little explicit prosecution of the tale in it. The plot's incessant delays impose an obligation to ask what sort of work it is that we are reading, in which such delays and "desultory dialogues" occupy more attention than any other factor. If what I have been arguing is that Cooper consistently forces upon the reader the obligation to assess the nature of American history, I shall now—as the plot begins to unfold—attempt to argue that the shape of the plot itself merely continues that process in another way.

The mysterious letter that so disturbs Temple is surely a key element in the plot, but the reader is no more enlightened about it than Oliver is. The remainder of chapter 25 serves to draw Elizabeth and Oliver closer together, but not yet romantically. The degree of Oliver's domestication, always fragile until the end, is discernible in the urbane drawing-room exchange on his identity and lineage, which like the letter are kept obscure.[32] We see him easily share—in proleptic irony—Elizabeth's class assumptions about marriage and display the established church piety that first aligns them at the Christmas service. The signs of Oliver's growing approximation to Temple are not absent before: his unfailing gentlemanly behavior, his language, his shock of envy and pleasure at the interior of Temple's house, his familiar hand on the piano, his gallantry, and now his genuine concern for Temple's anxiety—all serve to establish a thread of development that will figure more importantly as the tale develops. Even his confident and amused condescension to the young ladies' racial ignorance helps qualify him as Elizabeth's eventual gentleman consort. The drawing-room banter becomes suddenly serious as Elizabeth doubts her "own right to possess" these lands.[33] As she confesses the futility of her feelings, she draws from Oliver agreement both on that and on the obligation of Christian charity; "You can do no more," he says, striking a somewhat defeated note. Even Christian virtue is of no effect against Christian depredation, as the ineffectual appeals of Elizabeth to Natty and Mohegan at the end repeatedly enforce. Here then—as in the "descriptive" part of the text—the unresolvable issues raised fire the engine of the plot that will now develop. This chapter's final gesture sets against this impasse Jones's active spirit, unrestrained by thoughtful reservations, that will dominate the action of the plot—and of history, as he dominates Temple and Templeton. If the dialogue of Oliver and Elizabeth confers meaning upon history, Jones and his like make that history; the virtue that in the young lovers seeks to moderate the effects of depredation is rendered void by the activity of Jones and the absence of Temple.

The economy of Cooper's plotting when it finally does begin stands as a remarkable contrast to the awkward concealments of the twenty-five chapters that precede it. Oliver, Temple and Jones, and Louisa and Elizabeth set out on three separate trails—Oliver to discover Doolittle near Natty's hut, Temple and Jones to investigate the rumors of the mine, and Louisa and Elizabeth merely to take the air. Cooper here develops a complex of neatly related actions that involve all the characters in a double climax, but the action takes place not merely for the sake of narrative "interest."

Oliver's discovery of the prying Doolittle around Natty's hut clearly serves to privilege the reader; the consequences of Doolittle's cutting the dogs loose are dire, and the reader is forced by his knowledge to assess them more fully than Temple can. Doolittle is a magistrate in confederacy with a sheriff. Any assertions in the name of the law by these two—and by Temple—are subverted by the reader's knowledge of this action. High principles of the law cannot comfort or compensate the victims of its corrupt officers. Magistrate Doolittle is cast as that most odious of legal tools, the agent provocateur, who provokes the crime to which he bears witness, here complicated by a venal motive and the absence of a warrant. This detail of plot then is anything but the gratuitous complication it at first sight may seem.

Natty greets Oliver's news with a promise of violence, which Doolittle will ultimately provoke him to fulfill. Oliver reminds Natty—as he will throughout the episode—of the law, again reminding us of where Oliver is ideologically situated. Like Jones's violent interruptions elsewhere, Doolittle's action violates a moment of tranquil reflection as Natty—after his routine, but here sharply pointed, complaint against "the money of Marmaduke Temple, and the twisty ways of the law" (291)—evokes, in a passage of transcendent beauty, an idealized past and a ravishing, unspoiled landscape of memory, a unity of creation (292–93) (although even that is interwoven with a reminder of the violence of the revolutionary war). Natty's reminiscence is intruded upon by the cry of the hounds, cut free by Doolittle, driving a buck toward their master, as they had at the outset driven the game within reach of Temple's gun.

Although Natty eventually hunts on impulse—like Temple in the opening scene—he does not act as an innocent; he knows the law, in part shares at least its ostensible motive, and is repeatedly warned by Oliver. Natty's warning off of Hector, here as elsewhere, is an icon of rational command and obedience that Natty cannot emulate. The deer is killed, and Doolittle's ends are well served, but, for the moment, the only consequence Cooper allows is a sense of regeneration for the two old men. Their discovery that Hector's tether has been cut alerts them to their danger and sends them off on different paths—freeing Natty to save Elizabeth and Louisa from the panther. Dramatic as the ensuing scene is, fully establishing for us Elizabeth's piety, loyalty, and fortitude, its importance lies in the dilemma it creates for Temple. Natty's rescue renews the bond already joining Temple and Natty, whom Temple must judge for killing the deer.

This is the very crux and meaning of the narrative, whose mainspring is the Jones-Doolittle confederacy. The simple action of Doolittle, not strictly required for the plot, yields richly in the complication of significance it produces.

The third strand in the plot—the "mine"—is developed in the conversation of Temple and Jones. Temple notes, "We seem to differ so materially, and so often" (316), only to be abruptly cut off by Jones—a sign of his confident power and of Temple's weakness. Temple's contempt for Jones's confederates, Riddel and Doolittle, is a plain exception to his usual good nature. Temple has no difficulty in rejecting idle speculation and rumor; he is strictly rational about it, and, although he is not at all taken in by what he sees and what Jones says, he is drawn by two things: that the excavation is on his "own land" (323) and that the mine fits into his vision of the future. "To his eye, where others saw nothing but a wilderness, towns, manufactories, bridges, canals, mines, and all the other resources of an old country, were constantly presenting themselves, though his good sense suppressed, in some degree, the exhibition of these expectations" (321).[34] Even so, he will resolve the matter not on the basis of suspicion or vision but by open and direct enquiry: "There may be more in this than I at first supposed. I have suffered my feeling to blind my reason, in admitting an unknown youth in this manner to my dwelling;—yet this is not the land of suspicion. I will have the Leather-stocking before me, and, by a few direct questions, extract the truth from the simple old man" (325). The words conjure up Natty's presence, but the questioning does not ensue. Temple, at the very moment when all considerations are to be overwhelmed by the feelings of a grateful parent, is placed in his openness didactically against the furtive Jones and Doolittle.

Much as we admire him for his upright, frank reason, we are left with a question that defies coherent answer: Why, given his differences with Jones and his contempt for Doolittle, does he allow them to occupy the offices they hold? He fails to see—or to act upon—their obvious disqualifications. This is not really mild reason at all but feeble tolerance; it leads to the incarceration of Natty and the frustration of his own rational, kindly, Christian inclination to have it both ways: to insist on the letter of the law and to pay the fine he imposes. Nor does Temple's attitude restrain Jones's inclination to act, in the name of the law, on preposterous rumors.

As the three-pronged episode ends, Elizabeth's narrow escape prevails in Temple's consciousness: "All thought of mines, vested rights, and examinations, were absorbed in emotion; and when the image of Natty again crossed his recollection, it was not as a lawless and depredating squatter, but as the preserver of his child" (325). We note again how Cooper returns to the issue of property ("vested rights," "lawless depredating squatter") even as he notes how feelings supervene over such legal considerations. Temple will, in his capacity as judge, be called upon by Oliver, Elizabeth, and Natty himself to allow his feelings to prevail, and he will be unable to do so, for good reasons. Although a private sense of virtue and the demands of a mild law should go hand in hand, they do not. The fault is not in Temple but in the society and the law that restrains it. What it amounts to is that Cooper's plot consistently disallows an effective sub-stitution of one feeling for another. The need for law is constantly affirmed from the outset, but the text repeatedly denies the oversimplification by the contrivances of plot. Natty kills a deer and a panther, and all of civilization's assumptions about the law are in calamitous disarray.

The plot also reveals that Jones's false suspicions do ironically lead to the revelation of truth, but in themselves they are destructive of the law and at variance with the Constitution in very obvious ways. The truth revealed is not what Jones anticipates or intends, nor is it merely the revelation of the true Temple-Effingham story; those rumors are moti-vated by the very cupidity which Oliver and Grant deplore, the crude impulse to acquisition of which the law becomes the enforcer. That force destroys Natty and Chingachgook, and menaces Temple's society too. Far from being expelled, those feelings of "vested rights" are central, and, for all his many virtues, Temple represents them too. It is this that confers an especially deep sense of futility on his final pursuit of Natty. It deserves only the single sentence Cooper bestows upon it.

Although, as we approach the trial, Temple is made to concede the limits of his wilderness taming and hence his abiding need for Natty, and Pump firmly establishes the bond that ties him to Elizabeth and Natty and attempts to resist Doolittle's mission—a warrant for Natty's arrest—Temple is rendered powerless by Doolittle's shrewd appeals to law and the man behind the law. Although Temple tries to have Doolittle himself issue the warrant, Doolittle insists that Temple discharge his responsibility. And Temple must allow Doolittle and, among others, Riddel to execute it. Cooper again allows Temple no escape, even though Doolittle is recog-nized as a venal "harpy." His remedy—let the law work, and Elizabeth will pay the fine—consoles him, and Elizabeth and Oliver; but, apart from the fact that the design will be frustrated, the intent, though kind, suggests that laws will not alone suffice without the actions of men. The shape of Temple's circumvention claims for himself the exemption that Oliver will claim for Natty and that Temple will refuse.

Natty's impassioned protection of his right to privacy is seconded by the reader's prior knowledge of Doolittle's prying ulterior motive. Although Natty's armed resistance to Doolittle's demands (made "in the name of the people" from his safe position under the bank) makes Natty subject to more serious charges, it is also true that Natty and Billy have resolved by common sense the original issue covered by the warrant. But reason does not prevail. Once more, Cooper's plot incorporates the defeat not merely of Temple's Christian charity but also of the spirit of reasonable compromise. The reader, aware of Doolittle's complicity as the cause of the entire process, is forced to question the law; how can we, knowing all this, not side with Pump and Elizabeth? Not share a sense of satisfaction that Pump's vengeance is completely justified? What the law cannot do, Pump will. If Cooper allows the evidence that might have led to a directed dismissal to go unmentioned in court, his motive can only be that he aims at the historically necessary exile of Natty and wishes the law to be as severely questioned as it is. Cooper's motives for scorning happy endings, wish-fulfilling closures, are as compelling as James's or Melville's, if differently based.

Cooper does not leave it merely to an interpreting reader to infer the deficiencies of the law. He makes them the central issue of what remains of the narrative. Temple's insistence on the rule of law, not of men, is a deeply laid American principle—and he is right; but so are Elizabeth and Pump, given the forces at work that are protected by the law, and they could justify themselves by referring to the Declaration of Independence itself. As the plot advances, it is clear that it is driven not by Oliver and Natty's mission, though that is Natty's motive for resistance, but by the will of Jones and Doolittle.

Temple and Oliver, up to the point of their bitter quarrel in chapter 31, have been drawing ever closer together, where they ideologically belong. Just before the quarrel, Elizabeth and Oliver are drawn into a closer and more romantic relationship. Pump once more emphasizes the bond they all share with Natty, and Elizabeth and Oliver express it with feeling. The entry of Temple, informed of Natty's "obstinacy" (neither knows the other's hidden motives), breaks that bond in an exchange of great power on both sides. The law has proved to generate its own energies, and it is Doolittle, Riddel, and Jones who have set the machine in motion. What they threaten is not merely a set of personal relationships but bonds that cement a new society together, revolutionary with Loyalist, forester with settler, class with class.

Temple's confident legal commonplace—"Would any society be tolerable, young man, where the ministers of justice are to be opposed by men armed with rifles? Is it for this that I have tamed the wilderness?" (344)—is unanswerably met with the reply, "Had you tamed the beasts that so lately threatened the life of Miss Temple, sir, your arguments would apply better" (344). Oliver and Temple share a deep sense of the importance of law and authority, and their disagreement here, irresolvable as it is, fully accommodates the issue. Cooper ensures the readers' sympathy with Oliver by giving them Oliver's "prying miscreant" to recognize.

The present in which Natty's case will be tried is, then, placed under great stress: Natty's saving action questions the law's prematurity from a position in a figurative "past," the wild that Temple had thought to have tamed but which is yet present and threatening; the sensible compromise of Natty and Kirby, significantly reenacted at the trial, is ignored; Doolittle and his confederates call in question the future, for, if the law is to find its precedents in cases like this, what price democracy? And Temple is deeply involved: the high Jeffersonian principle he invokes in employing Oliver is hardly consistent with his preferment as sheriff of Jones, who is behind the whole calamity.

As their altercation intensifies, Oliver's bitter outburst offers a larger dimension of criminality than the judge had in mind, and recalls Elizabeth's words in chapter 25 (280) and Mohegan's in chapter 16 (185): "Ask your own conscience, Judge Temple. Walk to that door, sir, and look out upon the valley, that placid lake, and those dusky mountains, and say to your own heart, if heart you have, whence came these riches, this vale, and those hills, and why am I their owner? I should think, sir, that the appearance of Mohegan and the Leather-stocking, stalking through the country, impoverished and forlorn, would wither your sight" (345). Temple's response claims his impeccable legal right and his right by agrarian deistic principle: "I appeal to Heaven, for a testimony of the uses I have put them to" (345). Temple here completes the pattern of the problem that animates the entire work. The narrative concealment that is so irritating to the novel's "interest"—its suspense is made to depend solely on the word Oliver does not speak—is in fact crucial to the work's meaning. Without that reticence, the ambiguities that enrich Oliver's responses here would be impossible. That Temple will later reveal the probity of his dealing does not eliminate the force of the dilemma presented. Here, Temple will prevail by the "might" of the law.

The problematic pattern is at once enacted again: Natty's hut is invaded under the colors of Jones's and Temple's "law" and suspicion of "other misdemeanours and offences against private rights" (355), and Oliver's outburst is matched by Natty's oration at the hut, now burnt by his own hand. His eloquence and bitter, exhausted resignation establish with unqualified poetic authority the price exacted by the advance of European imperium—Temple's vision of a future that will emulate Europe's industrial revolution, the fulfillment of the promise of the opening paragraph. The speech is unanswered; no convincing answer is conceivable.

> "What would ye have with an old and helpless man?" he said. "You've driven God's creaters from the wilderness, where his providence had put them for his own pleasure, and you've brought in the troubles and diviltries of the law, where no man was ever known to disturb another. You have driven me, that have lived forty long years of my appointed time in this very spot, from my home and the shelter of my head, lest you should put your wicked feet and wasty ways in my cabin. You've driven me to burn these logs, under which I've eaten and drunk, the first of Heaven's gifts, and the other of the pure springs, for the half of a hundred years, and to mourn the ashes under my feet, as a man would weep and mourn for the children of his body. You've rankled the heart of an old man, that has never harmed you or yourn, with bitter feelings towards his kind, at a time when his thoughts should be on a better world; and you've driven him to wish that the beasts of the forest, who never feast on the blood of their own families, was his kindred and race; and now when he has come to see the last brand of his hut, before it is melted into ashes, you follow him up, at midnight, like hungry hounds on the track of a worn-out and dying deer! What more would ye have? for I am here—one too many. I come to mourn, not to fight; and, if it is God's pleasure, work your will on me." [356–57]

His charge against human violence is reiterated by Mohegan on Mount Vision. His surrender is not merely a narrative event but the culmination of all his complaints and the recognition of his defeat. The placing of these events before the trial imposes an intolerable burden on the legal process: how can justice be done, or even seem to be done? The sentence on Natty is seen as a dreadful cruelty; the epigraph to chapter 33 refers to the sentence by alluding to the stocking of Kent in *King Lear* and a point in that play where evil seems indomitable. Against the cruelty of Natty's suffering, Cooper's evocation of the gathering on a warm July morning of the citizens of an idealized new order to witness justice, to form a jury of peers, stands in almost shocking contrast. Cooper's inclusion of a jury tamperer is not, in context, idle mischief. It is perhaps fitting that Natty's opening plea focuses not on the deer—he will even admit assault—but on his rights of privacy assured by the Revolution that brought this new community into being.

That Temple's charge to the jury is brief and clear, and his sentence harsh and just, cannot make the privileged reader any more comfortable with the witness on whose testimony the conviction is made. "Living, as we do, gentlemen," Temple maintains, "on the skirts of society, it becomes doubly necessary to protect the ministers of the law" (369)—but the reader must answer with a *quis custodet custodem*?

Also, as Natty clearly understands, the sentence means life in jail for him. The sentence may be just, and Temple may pay the fine; nevertheless, the sentence for *this* man is extreme. Temple's sensibility, of course, does him credit, but his "nation of laws" founders if justice can be found only by compensating interventions of men. Natty confronts Temple, ad hominem, with an appeal to the bond forged through Elizabeth and at Temple's first arrival in the valley; he submits to the sentence but craves mercy and humanity. Pump's recognition in this scene of a precisely similar bond tries Temple's feelings profoundly. The sentence is handed down and placed in execution, but the issue is not thereby resolved—it has received only its most resounding expression. Whatever consolation may attend Pump's beating of Doolittle, it is the latter's ascendancy that makes the beating necessary. Cooper's desire to keep the perversion of his legal process before the reader is evident in his pointed comment: "The air with which Mr. Doolittle delivered this prophetical opinion was peculiar to his species. It was a jesuitical, cold, unfeeling, and selfish manner, that seemed to say, 'I have kept within the law,' to the man he had so cruelly injured" (377). The dismay is compounded when Natty in his shame reminds us that the bond is not merely with Temple, Elizabeth, and Pump but with the nation itself; his service in the wars of 1756 and 1776, colonial and revolutionary, goes for nothing. His complicity with the forces who effect his own downfall merely adds a further dimension of melancholy, a further source of social guilt. When Natty submits to his sentence, "bowing his head with submission to a power he could not oppose," Cooper recognizes not merely Natty's shame but the "power" that brings him to it.

Cooper, at one juncture, points to Temple's capacity for "examining both sides of a subject" (321); it is a virtue that he forces on the reader. Virtually every time the law is invoked, a serious exception to it is raised; this is not simply a matter of balance but invariably a rendering of the proposition problematic, a denial of the conclusion Temple embodies. Each time the importance of the law in principle is affirmed, questions of the law as it is seen in operation emerge. If Temple has a certain amplitude and generosity of understanding, he is no match for his daughter's grasp of the price exacted from Natty and Mohegan. For him, Natty is at best an affecting anachronistic obstacle; when he resists the law, his actions are seen as whimsical or "obstinate" (Oliver's outburst is deserved, one must feel). And, finally, Cooper makes us aware at many points that law serves property above all. Although Mohegan recognizes intuitively the fundamental honesty of Temple, Temple does not recognize the validity of the Delawares' gift to Effingham but simply Effingham's right to property. The law is not simply a lofty principle that transcends more mundane social, political, and worldly matters but the instrument of the settlers' power. It would of course be false to infer from this that Cooper is anything but conservative, that he is some sort of closet Marxist, perhaps; rather, he is concerned to present things as they are, and he does it with a peculiar thoroughness.

Cooper's determination to adhere to the historical imperatives that have brought him to this point in the novel is immediately apparent in chapter 35, and his conceptual grasp is beyond dispute in the brief debate he fashions between Temple and Elizabeth.[35] Temple argues "the sanctity of the laws" (382); Elizabeth retorts that their inflexibility for "a man like the Leather-stocking" argues their imperfection. Her insistence that law not exist apart from its human victims and ministers is met by a short rejection of her female excess of feeling and lack of reason. While Cooper may appear to endorse Temple's substitution of an *in feminam* irrelevancy for argument, he may equally mean, given the drift of the exchange and the narrative to follow, that her "logic that contained more feeling than reason" points to the law's inadequacy. Elizabeth identifies the judge with the law, accuses her father of oppressing Natty, and employs a tone of command we have heard her use before—less winningly—to Remarkable Pettibone. It is the tone the naturally superior are allowed in Cooper's mores to take with their inferiors. Temple's plea that "the laws alone remove us from the condition of the savages" (383) receives a shocking blow from Mohegan's relentless criticism, again to Elizabeth, on Mount Vision and from the action of Jones's "posse of demons" (435). The discussion cannot reach a terminal point, and it is the most dramatic expression of the problematic issue so far in that it divides father from daughter. Temple's position is also undermined in two other respects. First, he arranges the payment of Natty's fine—a tacit denial of the law's adequacy without men of feeling like Temple; while Temple is clearly tempering public justice with private compassion, his personal kindness cannot remove the historical burden that renders it necessary. Second, in his final injunction to Elizabeth that she remember in *her* judgment that Natty's judge is her father (383), he makes precisely the plea on his own behalf that he rejects when Elizabeth makes it on Natty's. In this reversal, Cooper makes Temple's confusion clear. Perhaps confusion is inevitable, but Cooper at least is not confused about it.

In two further exchanges, Elizabeth acts her father's role as proponent of the decent, rational, Christian agrarian world of the opening paragraph. In offering to rebuild the hut and maintain Natty in "ease and plenty" (387), she already knows (280) that like Mohegan he must refuse, as he will once more in the final chapter. Natty is not insensitive to her kindness and is sad at the apparent frustration of the romance between Elizabeth and Oliver, but he is consistently realistic: his "Can ye raise the dead, child!" (386) is withering. The civilization out of which she speaks has already rejected him and, as she has much earlier recognized, cannot restore the conditions in which his life has meaning. In the following chapter (36) she repeats the pattern and is again rejected, now by Mohegan at his death; the feelings that she previously expressed to Oliver and that Oliver has so recently echoed again in anger to Temple are now expressed directly to Mohegan. Her concession of his "natural right" is met by an evocation of the life he has lost; her affirmation of her civilization's values that she supposes his conversion to imply acceptance of, "to fear God and to live at peace," receives its most detailed and contemptuous questioning so far: Mohegan may have fallen victim to rum, but his mind is undimmed as he ruthlessly deconstructs her presumption and reveals, in a passage already quoted in full (401), how violent, fearless of divine retribution, and unpeaceful the white man is to red and white alike.

Elizabeth is "embarrassed," as well she and what she speaks for might be. Her response, "If you knew our laws and customs better, you would judge differently of our acts" (402), is as forlorn and vulnerable as Temple's arguments to her. Her self-evident, unquestioned truth has been turned back on her, as Cooper had turned her father's back on him. Intention aside, the insistence of this reiterated structure, which is both conceptual and narrative, cannot be dismissed.

Mohegan's death scene effectively emphasizes not the regretful sigh at the inevitability of things but the impossibility of reconciliation. The imperium may conquer, destroy, and supplant, but Cooper does not permit erasure. Grant finds consolation, reiterating Elizabeth's words, in the pagan's supposed conversion, only to be met by John's reversion to Indian religion and Natty's unrelenting response, "Flesh isn't iron, that a man can live for ever, and see his kith and kin driven to a far country, and he left to mourn, with none to keep him company" (419). History is as unforgiving to its beneficiaries as it is to its victims; if the latter must suffer, their oppressors and dispossessors are denied the consolation of a Christianized Chingachgook and a pensioned-off Leather-Stocking. They, at least, are not candidates for hegemonic co-option, the spontaneous consent of the governed.[36]

In the narrative, it is striking testimony to Elizabeth's consistency that, rejected by Natty, she feels obliged to aid his escape. It is no mere romantic escapade. The level of her commitment in breaking the law ("his daughter shall be accountable, sir") implicitly insists upon imperatives beyond the law. There is nothing eccentric in this: it is a principle vital to republicanism and has its most famous reaffirmation in the Nuremberg trials. In this light, that the "posse of demons" use "Yankee Doodle" as their anthem is of more than passing interest; it is used here against those resisting oppression. More important, this episode unites Elizabeth, Oliver, Pump, Louisa, Kirby, and Natty and isolates Temple with Jones and Doolittle (even though Temple had—in Effingham's interest—evaded, or at least thwarted, the law). That Elizabeth leads in this is profoundly significant of the transitional and problematic state that the novel describes.

The fire on Mount Vision, in which Riddel will die as well as Mohegan, is the result of the improvidence of Natty's pursuers; it is fed by the litter of the settlers' wood gathering. An earlier fire, we recall, had permitted Temple's first entranced view from the Vision. More significantly for the plot, the fire brings Oliver and Elizabeth together to sing the old songs of romance: nobility and piety in extremis, and the truth of their love revealed under conditions that promise no worldly consummation. Elizabeth is more and more etherealized as her death impends; her vision of racial union—in an afterlife or at death—is almost enthusiastic. Oliver tames his proud spirit and aligns himself completely with her pieties. Their love is declared in the most elevated fashion.

The fire also of course allows Natty to save Elizabeth once more, and inscribe the bond of obligation with Temple yet again. By resisting arrest and shooting at Doolittle, Natty totally duplicates the earlier situation. Cooper will not let the issue go away.

Notwithstanding Natty's pardon, Cooper does not dismantle the problematic complex his text has established. Rather, the action insists upon it. Not merely has Natty's action in the fire and its aftermath duplicated and intensified his previous crime, but also the dénouement reveals that his motives for all his actions are identical with Temple's—the protection of Effingham's rights. As we have noted before, however, their immunities are different. Might does make right, and the "sanctity of the laws" stands revealed as nothing if not secular—they sanctify property. It is also true that Elizabeth's crime as an accessory to jailbreaking requires neither trial nor pardon.

In *The Pioneers* Natty has not reached the full endowment of the poetic possibilities Cooper will find for him in *The Prairie*, although there are signs that, by the end, Cooper has recognized his opportunity. Natty is called a hero only once, by Oliver, who half laughs at "the old hero's" first defense of the hut, and yet, by a strange irony, Natty, the Revolution's victim, in his defenses of his right to privacy and against unlawful search and seizure, is a less equivocal hero of the Constitution than Temple is; in defying the law, Natty is the law's ultimate defender. That is what Natty's speech at his burnt hut addresses; his exile then is not merely his personal misfortune but the misfortune of the nation on whose behalf the prophecy on the novel's opening page is delivered.

Cooper offers two last chances for that nation, that ideology, to gather Natty and Mohegan to its bosom as willing servants of hegemony. The first of these chances is expressed by Elizabeth. As we have shown, her offer of "ease and plenty," "fear[ing] God" and "liv[ing] in peace," is made only to be rejected. That is to say, the most cherished gesture society can muster is of no avail against history, Christian dispossession cannot be compensated for by Christian charity, and forgetting is impossible. The second possibility for including Natty and Mohegan proves empty as well. The fudging of the law that Natty's pardon represents no more ensures the gathering in of Natty than his trial and sentence ensure the protection of society; in giving license to Doolittle, Natty's conviction rather imperils society. To assimilate Natty, to own him, would be to evade history; his going forces civilization's beneficiaries to swallow their pill. Temple's pursuit of Natty is futile, an evasion that deserves to fail. Temple's society wants Natty only as a totem of its unimpaired virtue. That is why it can stomach him *only* as a myth. That is also why we should stop making his mythical status the first thing we say about him. The novel in which he is more nearly mythic, *The Prairie*, must be qualified and demystified by our memory of what the tale *The Pioneers*—first written, first read—actually tells.

THREE * *The Last of*

the Mohicans (1826)

THE DEATH OF A NATION,

THE DENIAL OF A GENRE

*The rights of the savage have seldom been properly appreciated
or respected by the white man. In peace he has too often been the dupe
of artful traffic; in war he has been regarded as a ferocious animal
whose life or death was a question of mere precaution and convenience.
Man is cruelly wasteful of life when his own safety is endangered, and
he is sheltered by impunity; and little mercy is to be expected from him
when he feels the sting of the reptile and is conscious of the power to
destroy. . . .*

*"We are driven back," said an old warrior, "until we can retreat no
farther—our hatchets are broken, our bows are snapped, our fires are
nearly extinguished: a little longer and the white man will cease to
persecute us—for we shall cease to exist!"*
– Washington Irving, "Traits of Indian Character," in The Sketch Book

While we can be reasonably sure that Cooper never had a fully formed
prior intention to write the five novels comprising the Leather-Stocking
tales, late in his life, as he collected his works, he was prepared to offer
them as a whole in the chronological order of Natty's life, complete with
an introduction to the entire series. And we can be certain that by 1827, in
The Prairie, he was fully aware of the immense significance that the
character of Natty could carry; Natty's hieratic death scene and the
concluding chapters of that novel seem emblematically to contain and
signify so much for American history that they form a fulfilling conclusion
for the series as he intended at that point to end it. However, *The Prairie*
could not have been written in the way it was immediately following *The
Pioneers*, most obviously because *The Pioneers*, while projecting Natty as

a virtuous man and a pathetic victim, offers too little to sustain the elevated hero fit for legend that *The Prairie*, at its conclusion, requires. Some may argue that *The Last of the Mohicans* does too little for Natty's reputation to satisfy that particular requirement. But perhaps these questions arise only because the matter is made to depend too personally upon one character; the common custom of looking at Natty as a figure of significant myth is largely to blame for our following that particular wraith. Although Cooper himself did after all in the end place Natty in the general title of the series, as the novels appeared, only in the last two did he inscribe the character in their titles. However, Natty's virtues, his self-sacrificing behavior, his generosity of spirit, and his actions in their display of appropriate skill and valor seem insufficient—especially in their consequences—to justify fully the image projected in *The Prairie* of Natty as a kind of symbolic father of the nation; yet it can hardly be denied that Natty, at his death, is a moving figure of great significance. We are affected, we are sorry for him, and we share in the prevailing admiration of him and his legend; but the elevated dimension is conferred not by rhetoric, not by a series of personal actions and their consequences remembered, but by the momentous history with which he alone of those assembled is fully intimate. Awe gathers about him when we remember his association with the series of events that brought America as nation and society to birth—and destroyed Natty. It is what he has been witness to that allows the sense of wonder to surround him; he can embody for a moment the history of the nation—whatever its consequences for him personally may have been. It is, then, through both a particular and a generalized memory that this great scene makes its impact, and such would be the case whether *The Prairie* is taken as the third or the fifth in the series, whether the series is addressed in the order of composition or in that of the chronology of Natty's life. Similarly, the order does not affect the vast historical scope the series encompasses, which forms such an important element in its impact.

The chronological sequence from *The Deerslayer* to *The Prairie* makes for a quite different—and less critical—emphasis. Of course, it focuses our attention more consistently on Natty's life and fortunes (and in either order the story is a doleful one) and to that degree tends toward simplification of the historical text; the priority given to consecutive historical time conveys a sense of inevitability. History, in the French war of the 1750s, finds employment for Natty's skills in *Mohicans*, but, to simplify, cannot in *The Pioneers*. If Natty remains useful for the purposes of the particular fiction in *The Prairie*, he is presented much more to be honored in epic terms for his past, for his legend, at his death rites, and in Middleton's recital of Natty's virtues. When in *The Pioneers* Natty is driven to reflect on the service he has done, we share his memory and justify his complaint; his pathetic fate is not obscured but rather intensified by the chronological treatment of his life. Our memory is his. I do not suggest, however, that the rearrangement of the order of publication shears the series of all its more complex effects: one might, in this order, reflect on how the almost Spenserian projection of virtues in *The Deerslayer* is reduced to mere function in *Mohicans*.[1] Natty's sense of discontent and ingratitude in *The Pioneers* would be more firmly anchored and deepened in the reader's sense of a history; the element of understandable revenge would be more evident, as the massacre at Fort William Henry is set against the previous massacre in the forest at the end of *The Deerslayer*.

If, however, *The Deerslayer* is addressed as the final novel, Natty's memory cannot align with the reader's; we remember what Natty cannot—a slaughter that has not in this novel's time yet taken place; we revise and reassess Fort William Henry and confirm the judgment of the opening passage of *Mohicans* upon the European colonizer. In either order, the two massacres make painfully clear that both white and red men are capable of relentless cruelty; nothing is done to justify the slaughter meted out by Warley; and, in the chronological order, the dyspeptic opening paragraphs of *Mohicans* follow naturally on Warley's atrocities in the forest. However, that connection was not possible for the first readers of *Mohicans*, since *The Deerslayer* was not to be written for another fifteen years. In the order of publication the critical connection must be made by the reader, the chronology of whose reading never synchronizes with the chronology of Natty's life. That constant chronological disjunction demands the critical action of the reader and confers a freedom with the text and its meaning which are released from the author's exclusive control. Similarly, to read Natty's betrothal to nature in *The Pathfinder* and his laborious demonstration and acquisition of virtues in *The Deerslayer* against the background of his treatment in *The Pioneers*, in which the destruction of his bride is already in progress and his virtues are traduced, makes for a quite different effect: we are forced by our awareness of the futility of his sacrifice, in practical and in moral terms, to criticize the society which he serves and whose highest aspirations in certain senses he is said to embody. Even the Christian values, Cooper insists within the individual novels, cannot stand immune from criticism, and the extent to which they animate the society as they should is consistently questioned.[2]

Such questioning arises far more urgently between the novels, *against* chronological sequence, than it does from the perspective of Natty's fictional chronology. One further example will suffice here: when Natty, early in *Mohicans*, uses the name of Major Effingham as a card of identity with Heyward, it has no significance from the perspective of Natty's fictional chronology, while for the reader who reads in the order of composition, the word Effingham summons the entire history of *The Pioneers* and Natty's subsequent fate—it is thus prior fact for the reader but unavailable to Natty in this novel. The reader will tend to see his alignment with the forces that will destroy him, while Natty cannot. Cooper's intention in this must remain problematic, although we must not deny him the insight and recognition he enables us to exercise. Certainly, his contemporary readers had no choice in the matter, and his early reviewers—even the antagonistic ones like John Neal—assumed a knowledge of his work previously written and even of the novel under review. As the eloquent anonymous reviewer of March 1826 in *The New York Review and Atheneum* has it: "Whoever has not read [*The Last of the Mohicans*] by this time, is either a Galleo about such matters, or an exceedingly wise man, who does not come to dilute his graver meditations with the notions of your ballad-mongers and romances."[3]

No review is here necessary of the contemporary criticism, for Dekker and McWilliams have collected much of it with an excellent expository introduction, but it is worth saying that Cooper's early reputation had more to do with his willingness to address American life and history than with any critical spirit his works may have manifested. In fact, for the most part, this critical attitude was overlooked; where it was noticed or suspected, it was dismissed or mentioned in passing, as it is by the excellent W. H. Gardiner (Dekker and McWilliams, *Fenimore Cooper*, 118). With the exception of the contemptuous—and contemptible for his envy—John Neal (80–88), Cooper's reputation stood high by 1826; whatever reservations his critics made, most of them admired his virtues and above all were proud of him as an American author. But they did make reservations, and a reading of Dekker and McWilliams's compilation will dismiss any suspicion that his contemporary American reviewers were naive, unlettered, and unsophisticated. The stipulations they make against him, or for him, are most often eloquently expressed and sharply focused on such matters as probability, narrative coherence, variety of invention, character, and the criteria of romance;[4] rarely do they touch on the social, historical, mythological, structural, or thematic issues twentieth-century critics have addressed, and when they do it is either tangentially or in a manner that we might be tempted to disdain as simpleminded—wrongly, I think. Cooper's contemporaries' uneasiness (not universal) about Cora's mixed blood, the possibility of Cora's and Uncas's marriage, or Gardiner's testimony to the sense of reality *The Pioneers* conveyed to him must be respected as confirmation of feelings expressed within *Mohicans* and evidence of Cooper's success in the purely "descriptive" aspects of *The Pioneers*. At the same time, it must be noted that criteria that value consistency or expound the extent to which Cooper did or did not fulfill the prescriptions of romance formulas do not serve well the kind of arguments that I wish to advance for Cooper: that, for example, the contradictions within his texts serve ends that are profoundly critical of American history and its most deeply held ideals or— the substance of the present chapter—that romance criteria, along with their informing Christian European principles, are shown to be debilitated, betrayed, and profoundly misleading.

When in the 1830s Cooper's critical political spirit became quite explicit, his inclination was deplored, both on literary grounds—politics having no place in polite literature—and on patriotic and political grounds,[5] and yet the political and historical criticism enfolded in the Leather-Stocking texts was not dealt with. Hiram Doolittle was regarded by O. W. B. Peabody as simply an unrealistic aberration (Dekker and McWilliams, *Fenimore Cooper*, 9). Cooper's political republicanism never came in question in these works. What the critics of his later fiction and his political statements did not grasp was that Cooper's criticism was invariably in the interests of the political health of American republican virtues as manifested or betrayed in action. Nor did they detect its ubiquitous presence in dramatic and fictional form in the Leather-Stocking tales. Cooper is in fact so frank, perceptive, and revealing, that, in whichever order we take the novels, they embody a radical critique of the very principles his questions and criticism desire to protect.[6]

Read in the order of their composition, Cooper's novels echo in one another's space, back and forth; the reader is constantly remembering, but often what the reader remembers has not yet taken place in this novel's time. The present novel may confirm and justify, or call in question, what we already know is asserted only at a later date; *Mohicans* supports what Natty remembers of his service to the crown in *The Pioneers*, as well as his resentment that it should be forgotten or left out of account. The account of his assistance to Temple before the settlement of Templeton, and the vulnerability of the settler without him, is underscored repeatedly in his rescues, protection, and guidance in *Mohicans*.[7] When Heyward reflects upon the liberality and justice of the English settlements, the reader will recall similar sentiments on Temple's tongue and wonder at how little principle has changed and—on the evidence of *The Pioneers*—at how little effect these sentiments have had, in a way that Heyward at that point cannot. The reader is critically distanced at such moments by anachronism as surely as he might be by deliberate twentieth-century techniques of disjunction and alienation. Before turning to a more thorough exploration of the links between *The Pioneers* and *Mohicans*, it might be useful in setting the tone to look at a particular link in a particular way.

Chronology aside, what in *The Pioneers* gives rise to *Mohicans*? The latter's title might lead us reasonably enough to refer to Mohegan's lamentations over the decline of his race and his loss of a pristine idealized unspoiled nature; that matter, as will later appear, is rendered in a sustained and highly complex manner. But *Mohicans* begins in a manner extraordinarily different from that of the calm, ideologized landscape of *The Pioneers*. Its epigraph from *The Merchant of Venice* sets at once the racial element before us; the epigraph to the first chapter, from *Richard II*, with its reference to a "kingdom lost" (whose kingdom? Chingachgook's? Cooper's? The French and English kings'?) introduces a passage of remarkable power. And epigraphs should not be overlooked, for however much we may doubt intention within the text, or on theoretical grounds, epigraphs import intention into the text; here the intention of the epigraph is evidently meaningfully obscure and complex. The opening pages deglamorize and dechivalrize history in comprehensive fashion: the rhetoric of anticlimax registers military action and high chivalric intention as futile, the military virtues as declining into shame, courage as replaced by fear or base policy, and the imperial adventure as hollow, greedy, and about to fail. Now, much of this—with its allusion to the peerless young Washington—might be seen as postrevolutionary republican reevaluation (though even such a view is subject to the censure of the reader's memories

of *The Pioneers*); however, that will not account for the passage's animated insistence on violence and bloodiness, its stress on the "cruelty and
fierceness" of man as he stains the beauty of forest and lake red. But as
Cooper's voice sets the tone for this violent and bloody book, the reader
recalls Elizabeth's exchange with Mohegan on "peace" just before his
death. Always responsive to justice and to the victims claimed as the price
of her inheritance, she listens in embarrassment to Mohegan's instruction:
"Since John was young, he has seen the white man from Frontinac come
down on his white brothers at Albany, and fight. Did they fear God! He
has seen his English and his American Fathers burying their tomahawks in
each other's brains, for this very land. Did they fear God, and live in
peace!" (*Pioneers*, 401). As he strikes the opening chord, then, Cooper
endorses the old Indian's view of the matter—not, perhaps, merely out of
sympathy with the plight of the Indian but rather in a spirit of a profound
criticism he shares with Mohegan as well as with Elizabeth of the history
he inherits. The link forged here between the two books is never abandoned and determines both Cooper's views of the making of America and
the romance genre he seemed to his contemporaries to be using. What
seems undeniable is that the connection here at least is not primarily one
of chronological narrative.

The connections between *The Pioneers* and *Mohicans* are many;
Cooper in his introduction of 1831, from a vantage point beyond *The
Prairie*, draws attention to Natty as the principal link and "witness" to the
passage of history:

> To portray an individual as a scout in the wars in which England and
> France contended for the possession of the American continent, a
> hunter in that season of activity which so immediately succeeded the
> peace of 1783, and a lone trapper in the Prairies after the policy of the
> republic threw open those interminable wastes to the enterprise of the
> half wild beings who hang between society and the wilderness, is
> poetically to furnish a witness to the truth of those wonderful alter-
> ations which distinguish the progress of the American nation, to a
> degree that has been hitherto unknown, and to which hundreds of
> living men might equally speak. In this particular the fiction has no
> merit as an invention. [*Mohicans*, 7][8]

Natty claims several times in *The Pioneers* that without his aid Temple
could not have made the settlement, and his value as protector of the

uninstructed in the wilderness is frequently evident there. In incident after incident in *Mohicans*, the aid of Natty and the two Indians alone preserves the lives of Heyward, Cora, and Alice, while Heyward's romantic virtues are futile, and the lesson of *Pioneers* is further substantiated.[9] It is not necessary to insist that European power would have prevailed anyway; within the fiction Cooper's point is clear enough—the Europeans depend for their lives on those whom they will displace, whose way of life they will destroy, and, of course, whose very acts cooperate with the process that will destroy them. The reader viewing *Mohicans* with the privilege of hindsight afforded by *The Pioneers* can hardly miss the point. It is worth noting here that although Natty does not complain yet on his own behalf, he does on behalf of the Indians, and so does Chingachgook almost as soon as he appears. The "settlements" to which Heyward takes Alice, in which her tears shall be dried and whose spread Natty fears (210), are made to depend very firmly on the aid of Natty. The indebtedness is acknowledged and stressed again in *The Prairie*.

While Natty in *Mohicans* is expert in the ways of the wilderness, he is not the displaced child of an unspoiled nature that is suggested more strongly in *The Pioneers*, although—as in the extraordinary description of Glenn's Falls (55)—we do occasionally see that side of him. However, the threat to nature, powerful though the presence of the forest is, is clear enough; from the novel's first page the threat of European arms to nature itself is made clear: "There was no recess of the woods so dark, nor any secret place so lovely, that it might claim exemption from the inroads of those who had pledged their blood to satiate their vengeance, or to uphold the cold and selfish policy of the distant monarchs of Europe" (11).[10] The epic struggle, it is clear, has at its end the defilement of nature. The destruction effected by peaceful settlement in *The Pioneers* is made to depend upon the violent military efforts the white Christian European hordes will expend. "Nature," as Natty muses, "is sadly abused by man, when he once gets the mastery." The connection with *The Pioneers* is evident, but it cannot go much beyond an occasional hint, since Natty is so thoroughly implicated in the destruction taking place.

The principal narrative element—the preservation of Alice and Duncan for the settlements against the background of the French wars—coexists with the novel's dominant theme of the decline of the Indian peoples. However, the theme is played in the reader's mind along with the aware-ness that it has already happened in Chingachgook's death in *The Pi-*

oneers. The reader of the series is most commonly as primed with prior knowledge of main events as was the audience of Greek tragedy and epic. The links are again specific and striking, and more complex than at first sight they may appear. The complaints against and uneasiness attending the dispossession of the Indian peoples are frequent in *The Pioneers* and need no repetition here: they involve Natty, Mohegan, Oliver, and Elizabeth. The 1826 preface to *Mohicans* makes the point instantly: Dutch, English, and French are offered not as explorers, settlers, and colonists but as "conquerors," dispossessors, and robbers (2–3); in the 1831 introduction the "inroads of civilization" are seen as "a nipping frost" (7) to the Indian, in an image that unites the destruction of nature with the elimination of the Indian. Cooper's position is scarcely in doubt.

Cooper here echoes Irving's "Traits of Indian Character" both in meaning and image: "Society has advanced upon them like one of those withering airs that will sometimes breed desolation over a whole region of fertility" (*Sketchbook*, 273). Oliver's bitter outbursts against white cupidity and Elizabeth's guilty reflections on her right of possession are frequently reinforced by Natty's insistence, in *Mohicans*, on the predations by Europeans upon Indian lands and the confusion wrought among the Indians by the "white cunning" (196) of the invader; "for it is not to be denied," Natty observes, "that the evil has been mainly done by men with white skins. But it has ended in turning the tomahawk of brother against brother, and brought the Mingo and the Delaware to travel in the same path" (227). This evil is, in fact, the topic of Natty and Chingachgook's opening conversation in the novel; Chingachgook prevails, as Natty earlier has in *The Pioneers* with Temple, in inscribing early in the novel white acquisitiveness and ingratitude, and the European technology of fire water and firearms, that have proven fatal to the Edenic vision he evokes. Chingachgook's terms are precisely those he had used in the "Christian beast" outburst in the tavern in *The Pioneers*.

While Cooper's romance requirements cast Uncas and Chingachgook as good Indians against Magua's bad Indian (and how intensely the satanic evil of Magua is insisted upon, as is the idealized heroic virtue and appearance of Uncas!), that simple opposition is not allowed full dominance in this novel. Heyward, as the novel begins, has fatally and inattentively dismissed Magua's tale as "idle"; his inattention means, of course, that the Indian does not matter. In chapter 11 when Magua tells his tale, it is anything but idle. His story is one of lost glory, dispossession, relentless

pursuit and harassment, liquor, decadence, and, eventually, the humiliation of the flogging for which he will exact vengeance. We do not need to
sympathize with Magua in a general way to understand him and receive
his point; it is not merely what Cora sees as Munro's "imprudent severity"
but the injustice it implies: "Is it justice to make evil, and then punish for
it?" (103).[11] Montcalm will later recognize the problem Munro's flogging
raises for *his* honorable discharge of his undertaking. While it cannot
exculpate Magua, from one standpoint we are allowed to see Munro as
partial creator of the massacre. Magua's accusation—as did Mohegan's—
runs together English and French as "whites"; all white Europeans, servants of the Christian kings Cooper has condemned on the first page, are
accused. Even more important is the term-for-term alignment that emerges
here between Magua and Chingachgook and scars across the romance
grain: as victims, as Indians, their fate at European hands is the same.
Under the severely equal law of Tamenund, again the artificial romance
oppositions evaporate, and Magua and Uncas are rendered equal justice
under law. Cora's embarrassed silence and incapacity to explain so as "to
suit the comprehension of an Indian" (103) precisely match Elizabeth's
before Mohegan's unrelenting characterization of the warlike nature of
the whites. While we are clearly not meant to sympathize entirely with
Magua or to endorse the vengeance he purposes, Cooper clearly intends
the perplexity the reader encounters at this point. In effect, Cooper's
procedure reverses the perverted racist assumption that treats all red men
as alike, as enemies, upon its white adherents.

Just prior to this in chapter 10, Heyward[12]—for all his futile, chivalric,
romance gestures—is in the face of necessity reduced to precisely those
"political practices" of Montcalm that, in an apparent digression by
Cooper, "do not always respect the nicer obligations of morality, and
which so generally disgraced the European diplomacy of that period"
(94); Heyward in fact offers prime evidence of what Magua (as well as
Chingachgook) complains of. He offers money,[13] trinkets, firearms, and
powder and even promises rum that will make the Indian's heart "lighter
than the feathers of the humming-bird, and his breath sweeter than the
wild honeysuckle" (96). That this is not merely policy for the dire moment
is made clear in his instructions to Cora: she "must be prodigal of [her]
offers of powder and blankets. Ardent spirits are, however, the most
prized by such as he" (101). Magua's narrative (102–3) instantly follows,
and his accusation is attended by the evidence for his view. Heyward is

here not a mere romance hero but the fully qualified and typical colonizer and dispossessor.

In romance terms, Cora is faced with death or dishonor; the dishonor refused, Magua is left only death to deal to satisfy his vengeance. But before we too hastily reject vengeance as beyond the moral pale, we should perhaps call to mind Natty's frequent invocation of it—and he, as we know, is "a man without a cross"[14]—and, if we are in any doubt, the sanguinary encounter that rescues Cora, Alice, and Heyward, with its scalping and Natty's abuse of the slain, should cure us of it. Cooper's exaltation of Uncas, whose eyes were "beaming with a sympathy, that elevated him far above the intelligence, and advanced him probably centuries before the practices of his nation" (115), complicates the texture unendurably; the reader must take the liberty of doubting the racial superiority implied, and in so bloody a context—Chingachgook flaying the scalps, Natty stabbing the corpses, the slaughter, the flogging of Magua—in the exposure of military chivalry shortly to follow at Fort William Henry and in the reading of Natty's advice to Gamut, must raise a skeptical eyebrow. Natty may not actively seek out vengeance, but his violence is carefully noted in his response to Gamut's Calvinism:

> "Do you take me for a whimpering boy, at the apron string of one of your old gals; and this good rifle on my knee for the feather of a goose's wing, my ox's horn for a bottle of ink, and my leathern pouch for a cross-barred handkercher to carry my dinner! Book! what have such as I, who am a warrior of the wilderness, though a man without a cross, to do with books! I never read but in one, and the words that are written there are too simple and too plain to need much schooling; though I may boast that of forty long and hard working years." [117]

Placed between one passage of biblically based theology and another of faith according to "the lights of nature" (117), Natty's choice of violent metaphor is significant. Such complications are not infrequent in Cooper, nor, I suggest, can they be unintended.[15]

Much later in the text, in the epic[16] set piece of Tamenund's first appearance, the strand begun by Mohegan in *The Pioneers* is extended with marked consistency. Once more, Magua is given the ascendancy; he is allowed to give a racial history of America:

"The Spirit that made men, coloured them differently," commenced the subtle Huron. "Some are blacker than the sluggish bear. These he said should be slaves; and he ordered them to work for ever, like the beaver. You may hear them groan, when the south wind blows, louder than the lowing buffaloes, along the shores of the great salt lake, where the big canoes come and go with them in droves. Some he made with faces paler than the ermine of the forests: and these he ordered to be traders; dogs to their women, and wolves to their slaves. He gave this people the nature of the pigeon; wings that never tire; young, more plentiful than the leaves on the trees, and appetites to devour the earth. He gave them tongues like the false call of the wild-cat; hearts like rabbits; the cunning of the hog, (but none of the fox), and arms longer than the legs of the moose. With his tongue, he stops the ears of the Indians; his heart teaches him to pay warriors to fight his battles; his cunning tells him how to get together the goods of the earth; and his arms enclose the land from the shores of the salt water, to the islands of the great lake. His gluttony makes him sick. God gave him enough, and yet he wants all. Such are the pale-faces."
[300–301]

It is a massive expansion of Mohegan's complaints and evocations in *The Pioneers*; it encompasses Munro's condemnation of a "luxurious people" (158), Elizabeth's—and Cora's—sense of injustice, Oliver's condemnations, the conversation of Natty and Chingachgook in chapter 3, and much else. The speech goes unchallenged.[17] Once more the easy moral polarization of romance formulation is forbidden in favor of an insistence on the common Indian fate. The power and truth of Magua's words quite overcome for the time being our sense of his cruel intentions as the villain of the romance, especially as his narrative finds further and less compromised expression in Tamenund's ruminations. They override Cora's pleas and evoke in clouded poetic memory the history of Indian victimization at the hands of the white man and include his resentment of white attitudes toward miscegenation. Again it is given to Cora to concede the point— and it could not be more touching that *she*, of mixed blood, is the recipient of these particular words. And their relevance to Natty's and Heyward's attitudes should not go unnoticed.[18]

This strong thread then is unbroken from *The Pioneers* through to the end of *Mohicans*, and it is one that offers no consolation to the whites as they confront their history. The juxtaposition of Uncas and Tamenund in chapter 30 holds out for a moment a wondrous, poetic, and delusory hope that time may be turned back. Tamenund is entranced by a vision of youth restored, a time before the history given in the previous chapter; Uncas's death will only ring a more definitive knell for Indian fortunes for that, and Chingachgook's death—which, for the reader, has already happened—assures us that no poetry, "dream" or delusion will reinstate past glory.

Cooper, then, in *Mohicans* does not shirk the implications of his preface; the book consistently projects—and endorses—the Indian view of white European imperium: the conqueror, English or French, is as greedy a destroyer as any conquistador. Even the best of them, Miquon—Penn, that is—falls under this censure. The Europeans—without a cross, to a man (if not a woman!)—do not, of course, share this view. We have already seen Heyward as he exhibits the very attitudes that have brought the Indian low. When, in chapter 19, Uncas kills and scalps a marauding Oneida, Heyward's trust in white legal alliances is shown as naive, as was his trust earlier in Magua and his reluctance to act without assurance of the Indian's guilt (40). It is not that Cooper wishes to endorse lawless action but that he wishes us to see the irrelevance—or worse—of mere principle in the circumstances.[19] The issue for Heyward is simple: for Natty to kill the Oneida "would have been an abuse of our treaties, and unworthy of [his] character" (196). Natty coolly blames "white cunning" for throwing the tribes into "great confusion"—a view that Cooper at once endorses (197). Natty prefers the pristine, unconfused clarity in which people know their own enemies and answer threats to their lives appropriately. Notwithstanding Natty's white, Christian love of justice, only the night saved the Oneida from Killdeer. Heyward's rather stuffy response is pathetically naive—even funny: "I had believed, those natives who dwelt within our boundaries had found us too just and liberal, not to identify themselves, fully, with our quarrels" (197). His assumption is that since whites are just and liberal, their ideals—manifest in word, thought, and action—must recommend themselves to the Indians. There is little in *Mohicans* to support his assumption and much to lay it open to doubt. Gamut, speaking for the party, introduces them as "Believers in religion, and friends to the law and to the king" (36). Heyward would concur; but Natty affirms his identical beliefs precisely: "Now, for myself, I do love justice; and therefore—I will not say I hate a Mingo, for that may be unsuitable to my colour and my religion—though I will just repeat, it may have been owing to the night that 'Kill-deer' had no hand in the death of this skulking Oneida" (197)—and denies them in the same sentence. *If Natty may be thought confused here, there is no reason to find Cooper so.* Natty's implicit denial is only typical, if more frankly stated, and of sounder motive than that of his fellow whites. God, justice, and the king—along with other European pieties—have a rough ride in this novel.

Heyward is naive not merely in the Oneida episode; the reader will recall how ineffective white justice and liberality are in Templeton and in the fate of Mohegan and Natty in *The Pioneers* as in this novel he attends to Magua's complaint and Heyward's conduct. He will shortly, too, have to measure white ideals of law and politics against the magisterial even-handedness of Tamenund in his community; Marmaduke Temple and his community suffer by the comparison. Once more, Cooper simplifies the reader's task by juxtaposing at once the rational and orderly consider-ations of Uncas, Chingachgook, and Natty with Heyward's simplicities.

> Notwithstanding the increasing warmth of the amicable contest, the most decorous christian assembly, not even excepting those in which its reverend ministers are collected, might have learned a wholesome lesson of moderation from the forbearance and courtesy of the dispu-tants. The words of Uncas were received with the same deep attention as those which fell from the maturer wisdom of his father; and so far from manifesting any impatience, neither spoke, in reply, until a few moments of silent meditation were, seemingly, bestowed in deliberat-ing on what had already been said. [198]

Cooper enforces the point with a scornfully sarcastic sentence at the expense of the European values Heyward so blissfully accepts: "In short, Uncas and his father became converts to his way of thinking, abandoning their own previously expressed opinions, with a liberality and candour, that had they been the representatives of some great and civilized people, would have infallibly worked their political ruin, by destroying, for ever, their reputation for consistency" (199).[20] The point is further endorsed by a comparison with Munro and Heyward shortly after this:

> The impatient Duncan now made several hasty and desperate propo-sitions to attempt the release of the sisters. Munro seemed to shake

off his apathy, and listened to the wild schemes of the young man, with a deference that his gray hairs and reverend years should have denied. But the scout, after suffering the ardour of the lover to expend itself a little, found means to convince him of the folly of precipitation, in a matter that would require their coolest judgments and utmost fortitude. [227]

Given Cooper's manifest republican hopes and conservative attitudes, we might easily conclude from a reading of him that, while he is capable of regret, since he cannot change the historical record, he will make his peace with it and live with equanimity within the emergent republic. In fact, at every point, he offers a radical critique of that history—its values and its results.

It might be argued for example that *Mohicans* represents merely an honest recognition of the nature of historical events and their driving principles now blessedly buried in the past. It seems to me, however, that the connections between *The Pioneers* and *Mohicans* are too carefully forged for that. One such link is the Effingham name, only on the face of it a minor one. Effingham makes no appearance in *Mohicans*, but his name is invoked several times; the first mention establishes Natty's credibility with Heyward, while the others have no great significance in themselves, but the name itself establishes a firm link between the two books. It reminds us of the servant status Natty enjoys on Effingham's memorial stone, of the dependence of the plot of *The Pioneers* on Effingham, passive though he is, and of his grandson Oliver's alliance with Elizabeth Temple and his inheritance of the land in Otsego County. The name joins the colonial period with the early republic; that Loyalist is so easily reunited with revolutionary, and that Cooper should have been at such pains to make the union under the conventions of romance, is of great significance. If, as we have observed, French and English are so often viewed only as "white," it is equally true that "white" Anglo-European identity overcomes in short order the political differences of the Revolution. Perhaps, too, they should. And certainly Natty does not inquire about the political allegiances of the whites he serves.

On the legal issue in *The Pioneers*, we have already seen that Temple finds himself isolated with Jones and Doolittle; in the political dimension the alignments are quite different, and that between Effingham and Temple represents all that is fatal to Natty. His service to Effingham, as scout in

Mohicans and as protector in *The Pioneers*, is equally service to Temple. It is not merely ironical that Temple and Natty share motives—the gesture is not literary but political and historical; for Natty, *no* action of his can affect the center of power. His most selfless actions are rendered acts of complicity with those who displace him. Natty's service is not enforced; he is a willing servant of Effingham and the English king; his acts are dedicated, valiant, considerate, and violent—but above all self-ruinous. I do not mean to suggest that Natty *could* hold his ground or turn back the march of European empire, or that the powerful should be more grateful, or that if they were Natty could or should accept their charity. Cooper merely makes it impossible for us to miss the point, unless we choose to be bemused into an uncritical assent by the opening of *The Pioneers*.

That opening could hardly offer a more striking contrast with the opening of *Mohicans*. The carnage that suffuses this passage and the entire novel is intimately connected with the process that establishes the European gentleman, Oliver Effingham, at the head of Templeton. The mere name Effingham calls the connection to mind in *Mohicans*; Cooper will use the gesture again in making the hero of *The Prairie* the descendant of Heyward and Alice. The appalling violence of *Mohicans* casts a long shadow on future achievements and, in the reader's memory, on Templeton. In chapter 20, very shortly after the massacre and the visit to the sickening killing field, Cooper adds a footnote (1831) that reminds us of what we already know: that settlements would eventually arise on the shores of the lakes, "well known to every American tourist"; "on most of these lakes, there are now beautiful villages, and on many of them steamboats." The reminder is meant perhaps as a long-view consolation after all the blood we have seen shed, but at the same time we are reminded unsettlingly of a connection between the two.

I am interested in what Cooper gives us in these novels in their order of publication. While my emphasis is not primarily on his intentions, I do credit Cooper with knowing what his text meant, even when I am sure we would not agree on how those meanings should be taken. When Cooper fell out with his audience, it was precisely over the unsparing critiques he offers of American society. It must be understood that Cooper never abandons fundamental principles, or derides them; his animus is always directed against the betrayal of values or, where there is no betrayal, the failure of principles, or the elimination of one set of values by others that are less worthy. Frequently, one senses his own discomfort at his critical view of the matters at hand, but this never leads him to back away. If the reader is drawn to question the principles themselves when they so often fail, there is provided ample evidence on which to do so. In *The Pioneers* it is republican values and actions that are scrutinized and found wanting; in *Mohicans* the colonizers' values, particularly in their essential military projection, are subject to critique, as is the genre which embodies them—romance.

Aside from the frequent charge of improbability, which has been made against *Mohicans* from the beginning,[21] it can hardly be denied that this novel proceeds with dispatch into its tale, is full of inventive incidents that, even when improbable in themselves, are developed with great lucidity, and is expressed with a full deployment of romance and epic gesture. While the romance elements may be seen as merely conventional, even as resulting from weakness and imperfectly realizing something Cooper found in his models, I shall maintain that they, and the deconstruction to which they are subjected, are integral to the massive historical criticism the novel expresses. The epic[22] permeates the style of this novel—which teems with literary echoes of all sorts, but most obviously of Homer, Milton, and Shakespeare—and is integral to the novel's tragic theme.

The opening pages of *Mohicans* are not merely bloody, although the carnage they announce and prefigure involves everyone in the work—even Gamut. Its noblest figures, Indian and white alike, Christian and pagan, participate zealously in adding to the volume of blood let, and it would be legitimate to maintain that blood itself is the principal theme in this novel about the making of America. Cooper, however, focuses more precisely than this view would allow.

The opening paragraph seems to offer an epic view of the courageous struggles of the "adverse hosts" in the colonial wars of North America with each other and with the difficulties of the terrain: they encounter "toils and dangers," "struggle" in the face of rapids and mountains, seek "opportunity to exhibit courage" in "martial conflict," and exhibit "patience and self-denial"; only at the end of the paragraph does Cooper release their anticlimactic motive: "to satiate their vengeance, or to uphold the cold and selfish policy of the distant monarchs of Europe" (11). There is not even "any secret place so lovely" that it "might claim exemption" from the carnage. Cooper draws no distinction among Englishman, Frenchman, and colonist, and his view coincides well enough with the views of Magua and Tamenund later. In short, the battles to protect and establish the frontiers of the nation are denied their epic stature—as are the pieties of Christianity—in one word, "vengeance." The religious and patriotic zeal of the renamers of Lake Horican is mocked. The settlers withdraw in fear. Gallantry and military virtue suffer death and abject defeat. The "bloody arena" affords no triumphs or defeats of honor, only futility. Romance virtues go uncelebrated and are seen as vacant of meaning. Neither England nor France can retain the land they fought and bled over. Military virtue and political will are in a condition of decadence and craven folly; the British subjects are fearful and lack manliness. The Indians are thrown into confusion and are on the warpath in the service of white paymasters. It is in such a war that our heroes and heroines are implicated. Such courage as there is can only be wasted or frustrated. Where is the possibility of *aristeia*?

There is, of course, in all this more than a little republican rejection of the imperial power in North America in decline, but Cooper's wholesale demolition of a war in which the settlers in the English colony had an interest, and which was of importance in preserving its integrity, and his disparagement of the virtues that are usually in evidence in all wars are important clues to all that follows. They set a tone not merely bloody but ashamed and dismissive of the white European imperium with which, I have maintained, the republican nation is rendered continuous.

Wars in history, romance, and epic—all of which Cooper is engaged with—conventionally justify themselves in their motives. Cooper is at great pains here comprehensively to disallow the justification. That absence renders personal virtues futile; youthful valor and self-sacrifice are extinguished in dust and ashes: "Glades and glens rang with the sounds of martial music, and the echoes of its mountains threw back the laugh, or repeated the wanton cry, of many a gallant and reckless youth, as he hurried by them, in the noontide of his spirits, to slumber in a long night of forgetfulness" (12).

Heyward's romance virtues, which qualify him as Alice's partner, are constantly in view: "Yes, sweet innocence," whispered the youth; "Duncan is here, and while life continue, or danger remain, he will never quit thee" (65–66). As Cora approaches Magua in chapter 11, Heyward alludes to his own "insatiable longings . . . after distinction" (102). Such petrified protestations receive formally appropriate response from the ladies—and Cooper intends no mockery of Heyward's appropriately dedicated sense of his protective mission. His personal valor and noble self-sacrifice, however, usually avail him—and Cora and Alice—not at all. Occasionally, it is true, as upon the party's arrival at Fort William Henry, Heyward's virtues are given the free play appropriate to them as he leads his battalion to repulse the attackers; Natty too has a moment appropriate without qualification to a romance hero as he speaks of his attachment to Uncas:

> "I have heard," he said, "that there is a feeling in youth, which binds man to woman, closer than the father is tied to the son. It may be so. I have seldom been where women of my colour dwell; but such may be the gifts of natur in the settlements! You have risked life, and all that is dear to you, to bring off this gentle one, and I suppose that some such disposition is at the bottom of it all. As for me, I taught the lad the real character of a rifle; and well has he paid me for it! I have fou't at his side in many a bloody skrimmage; and so long as I could hear the crack of his piece in one ear, and that of the Sagamore in the other, I knew no enemy was on my back. Winters and summers, nights and days, have we roved the wilderness in company, eating of the same dish, one sleeping while the other watched; and afore it shall be said that Uncas was taken to the torment, and I at hand—There is but a single Ruler of us all, whatever may be the colour of the skin; and him I call to witness—that before the Mohican boy shall perish for the want of a friend, good faith shall depart the 'arth, and 'kill-deer' become as harmless as the tooting we'pon of the singer!" [265–66]

Most often, however, such feelings are rare in Natty and useless to Heyward and his party—as Cooper makes plain. Heyward is "helpless" in the mysteries of the forest (45); an Indian lurks in their wake by the end of chapter 2.

Duncan at one point is tempted generously to save the life of an enemy and prevented from dangerous folly only by Natty's unrelenting realism: "Would ye bring certain death upon us, by telling the Mingoes where we lie?" demanded Hawk-eye, sternly; "'Tis a charge of powder saved, and ammunition is as precious now as breath to a worried deer! Freshen the priming of your pistols—the mist of the falls is apt to dampen the brimstone—and stand firm for a close struggle, while I fire on their rush" (69). At another, his instincts are gratified as Natty allows himself to use his last bullet to put a wounded Indian out of his misery. The act is virtuous, to be sure, but worse than useless. Heyward fights his adversaries with great courage in hand-to-hand combat, but only the intervention of Uncas saves his life—and his mission. Heyward valiantly remains with the sisters when Cora's brave common sense—itself cast in heroic terms—has persuaded Natty and the Indians to withdraw. She dismisses his self-sacrifice as "idle subtleties and false opinions" (80). His "useless exposure" of himself to enemy fire in the canoe (207) receives a similar reproof from Natty. Only the efforts of Natty and the Indians can save the wearied Heyward and the crushed Munro. Cooper's awareness of the limits of romance, and the ineffectuality and frailty of its associated virtues, is explicit when—as Duncan insists on sitting guard—he sleeps to dream of romance wakefulness:

> At instants of momentary wakefulness, he mistook a bush for his associate sentinel; his head next sunk upon his shoulder, which, in its turn, sought the support of the ground; and, finally, his whole person became relaxed and pliant, and the young man sunk into a deep sleep, dreaming that he was a knight of ancient chivalry, holding his midnight vigils before the tent of a re-captured princess, whose favour he did not despair of gaining, by such a proof of devotion and watchfulness. [129]

Even Gamut is more effective at staying alive than the European party unaided. When, against Natty's better judgment, Heyward undertakes in disguise to rescue Alice from the Mingo camp,[23] Natty praises his romance virtues but urges that he "remember, that to outwit the knaves it is lawful to practise things, that may not be naturally the gift of a white skin" (224). Chivalry, in the circumstances, is clearly to Natty a liability.

Natty's reflections on the "gift of a white skin" are often deliberately exposed as silly, as when he is about to put his knife into the supposedly dead Magua. More telling, perhaps, at the beginning of chapter 26, is Cooper's account of Natty's reason for leaving Magua alive: "Nothing but the colour of his skin had saved the lives of Magua and the conjuror, who would have been the first victims sacrificed to his own security, had not the scout believed such an act, however congenial it might be to the nature of an Indian, utterly unworthy of one who boasted a descent from men that knew no cross of blood" (267).[24] Chingachgook shows no such weak-willed mercy to the French patrol. Surely we are intended to see the discrepancy: Natty is incapable of taking his own advice to Heyward. Coming so late in the book, the incident deserves closer scrutiny. Cooper

has told us that it is the whites above all who have drenched the forest in
blood; Natty himself has hardly been laggard in dealing death, though
usually in open skirmish. Perhaps, the incident illustrates how pervasive
romance virtues, often recast in racial terms, are, here and everywhere in
the novel, and how they can—it is quite explicit—amount simply to lack
of foresight and caution. After all, the results of Natty's forbearance are
the deaths of Cora and Uncas; if the plot required that Magua survive the
episode, it did not require Natty's complicity and the attendant explanation. Natty's espousal of the culture's dominant virtue is as dangerous in
him as it is in Heyward. It is hard to avoid the conclusion that Natty's
alignment with the European-Christian romance values of Duncan con-
tributes to the death of the last of the Mohicans. This attitude is not even
consistent with his vengeful character, already cited from chapter 19.

Whatever Natty may say about the conduct appropriate to a white
Christian,[25] in fact, the Natty we see in this novel is dedicated to the
morality and necessity of the rifle. In chapter 26, Natty's promise to David
of revenge, and its rejection, offers a curiously still moment in which Natty
sees with unusual clarity what he is and what he cannot be:

> "Hold!" said David, perceiving that with this assurance they were
> about to leave him; "I am an unworthy and humble follower of one,
> who taught not the damnable principle of revenge. Should I fall,
> therefore, seek no victims to my manes, but rather forgive my de-
> stroyers; and if you remember them at all, let it be in prayers for the
> enlightening of their minds, and for their eternal welfare!"
>
> The scout hesitated, and appeared to muse.
>
> "There is a principle in that," he said, "different from the law of the
> woods! and yet it is fair and noble to reflect upon!" Then, heaving a
> heavy sigh, probably among the last he ever drew in pining for the
> condition he had so long abandoned, he added—"It is what I would
> wish to practyse myself, as one without a cross of blood, though it is
> not always easy to deal with an Indian, as you would with a fellow
> christian. God bless you, friend; I do believe your scent is not greatly
> wrong, when the matter is duly considered, and keeping eternity
> before the eyes, though much depends on the natural gifts, and the
> force of temptation." [274]

In an earlier exchange with Gamut, already referred to, Natty explicitly
rejects scripture in terms that, while they refer to survival in the wilder-

ness, are securely aligned with the instruments and technology of the European empire. While David intones "Northampton," Natty "coolly adjusted his flint and reloaded his rifle"; "the sounds . . . failed to waken his slumbering emotions" (118). Gunpowder and rifle represent this book's true values. They explode Natty's motivation for sparing Magua and offer an index of the extent to which Christian virtues have failed in the colonies—are abandoned, betrayed, or, like the pieties of romance and chivalry, are pointless or of no avail. Cora embodies and displays the heroic virtues of a strong and valiant romance protagonist in a world where the credit of those virtues has been canceled.

The survival of Munro, Heyward, and Alice—and Cora, as long as she lives—is made to depend on the gifts of Natty, Uncas, and Chingachgook, who consistently set at naught the romance virtues that coincide with the published values of the society they serve—Christianity, chivalry, the law of alliances, and personal valor and honor. Natty shows such virtues, usually, only as a last resort—most movingly when he offers to substitute himself as Magua's prisoner and when he departs to save Uncas, who is the most nearly successful conventional romance character on view, contrary to the stereotype of his racial character.

It is important to understand that it is not only a genre that undergoes implicit demolition but also what that genre encodes. Public virtue in the martial setting is identical with the virtue that informs romance and is therefore equally cast in doubt. However, the severe condemnation is not left merely implicit; it is rendered explicit in the massacre at Fort William Henry and the events surrounding it.

The decline of the noble virtues is closely associated with the book's all-embracing bloodiness; while the "bloody and vindictive warfare" (148) of the siege and the ensuing massacre at the fort is at the book's physical center and is the most impressively violent episode in the text, it is by no means exceptional to the "cruelty and fierceness" (11) that pervades the whole. Before it we have witnessed two deadly skirmishes, and in chapter 14 immediately preceding the central episode, Natty recounts two previous episodes of slaughter—actual historical events of 1755—which occurred in one day and in which he is made gleefully instrumental (135–36). In the second, the French were slaughtered as they ate and their bodies unceremoniously dumped into the Bloody Pond. It is here, too, that the agreeable French patrolman is killed by Chingachgook (137) and thrown into the water. Natty's reflection is: "'Twould have been a cruel and an unhuman act for a white-skin; but 'tis the gift and natur of an Indian, and I suppose it should not be denied! I could wish, though, it had befallen an accursed Mingo, rather than that gay, young boy, from the old countries!" (138). Given his own just-concluded narrative, this is ludicrous—and we are surely meant so to see it. However often Natty is admirable in *Mohicans*, it is difficult to elevate him very far. He may be unable to control the larger powers of empire at work, but he is surely not less than a willing servant of his master and the most articulately violent man in view. If Natty is a figure of significant myth, he is used to expose a large part of that myth as exploded. It should be noted that in the episode under discussion he is willingly under the orders of Sir William Johnson and Major Effingham, who is memorialized at republican Templeton in glamorous terms.

However, the focus rapidly moves from Natty to Munro and Montcalm, whose impending encounter is treated at once as a test of "honour" and "civility" (152) between Scotland and France. Montcalm's virtues are advanced: he is "distinguished as much for his attention to the forms of courtesy, as for that chivalrous courage, which . . . induced him to throw away his life on the plains of Abraham" (153). The ironical possibilities of "forms" and "throw away" are evident. Munro is dedicated in letter and spirit to chivalric values but is not above a petty and competitive contempt about the relative *titles* to European chivalry: "A pretty degree of knighthood, sir, is that which can be brought with sugar-hogsheads! and then your two-penny marquessates! The Thistle is the order for dignity and antiquity; the veritable 'nemo me impune lacessit' of chivalry! Ye had ancestors in that degree, Duncan, and they were an ornament to the nobles of Scotland" (157).[26] The note is struck again a little later when Munro, thinking that Montcalm has no English, insults Montcalm's nobility. Neither Munro nor Montcalm emerges from the passage with honor intact. Clearly, even in principle, "honour" is not given a clear run; Munro's spleen in the quotation may be short-lived but suggests a pointless vanity and is little superior in tone to the nationalistic inanities of Temple and Jones in *The Pioneers*.

The meeting between Munro and Montcalm is carried out with all the "forms of courtesy": "faith" is "plighted"; the word of "un gentil-homme Français" given and accepted; French "patents of nobility" and the seal of "true honour" are doubted, only to be affirmed. Montcalm offers terms of "unexpected generosity" for Munro's surrender, and lofty considerations are introduced: "There is a destiny in war, to which a brave man knows how to submit, with the same courage that he faces his foes" (164). All this is only slightly impaired by Montcalm's devious concealment of his knowledge of English—and Munro's assumption of his ignorance.

It is of course General Webb's betrayal that crushes Munro, who expresses his outrage in chivalric terms: " 'The man has betrayed me!' Munro at length bitterly exclaimed; 'he has brought dishonour to the door of one, where disgrace was never before known to dwell, and shame has he heaped heavily on my gray hairs!' " (164). Webb's cowardice confirms the crabbed commentary of the novel's opening paragraphs. Munro's world of honor is in ruins: "I have lived to see two things in my old age, that never did I expect to behold. An Englishman afraid to support a friend, and a Frenchman too honest to profit by his advantage!" (165). The ensuing massacre will annul even the final phrase.

The entire exchange is prefaced by Heyward's wide-eyed chivalry: "You forget, dear sir, that we confer with an officer, distinguished alike in Europe and America, for his deeds. From a soldier of his reputation we can have nothing to apprehend" (163). "Reputation" in Heyward's mouth is only a word, though for him heavily fraught with all romance assumptions; Cooper is not so bound and has Montcalm muse on his "tarnished" reputation: "Already has his fair fame been tarnished by one horrid scene, and in circumstances fearfully resembling those, under which he now found himself" (170). The allusion is repeated ten pages later. The incident referred to had taken place at Oswego in the year previous to the novel's present. The point is not merely that Heyward and Munro should have known about the historical event, but that "reputation" in this case is only a word. Munro concedes to Heyward in precisely Heyward's terms; Munro's distrust derives "from a sort of hereditary contempt of his enemy."

When Magua reveals the unsuspected presence of personal vengeance toward Munro, Montcalm resorts to a characteristic philosophical reflection: "As he mused, he became keenly sensible of the deep responsibility they assume, who disregard the means to attain their end, and of all the danger of setting in motion an engine, which it exceeds human power to control" (170–71). While it is true that Munro is reaping the results of his own actions, Montcalm's indifference to the dangerous implications of what he has heard is culpable. As with Heyward, verbal formulations are allowed to substitute for meaningful action that might avert the catastrophe. For Munro, nobility is the very principle of life, and its absence crushes him utterly; but the most crushing defeat is that suffered by the chivalric categories themselves. After the sickening slaughter, Cooper concludes:

> The cruel work was still unchecked. On every side the captured were flying before their relentless persecutors, while the armed columns of the Christian King stood fast, in an apathy which has never been explained, and which has left an immoveable blot on the, otherwise, fair escutcheon of their leader. Nor was the sword of death stayed, until cupidity got the mastery of revenge. Then, indeed, the shrieks of the wounded, and the yells of their murderers, grew less frequent, until finally the cries of horror were lost to their ear, or were drowned in the loud, long and piercing whoops of the triumphant savages. [179]

Perhaps the "apathy" "has never been explained" because it is inexplicable in such a way as to preserve the "forms of courtesy," "reputation," and "chivalrous courage"; the difficulty fades if we see—as Cooper compels us to—that the forms are only forms, both in Munro and Montcalm. Surely the words applied to Montcalm equally characterize the entire chivalric circumstance:

> Pages might be written to prove, from this illustrious example, the defects of human excellence; to show how easy it is for generous sentiments, high courtesy, and chivalrous courage, to lose their influence beneath the chilling blight of selfishness, and to exhibit to the world a man who was great in all the minor attributes of character, but who was found wanting, when it became necessary to prove how much principle is superior to policy. [180]

Cooper's intrusion into the preserves of the sister muse, Clio, is noted as he retires—and his purpose is clarified; Cooper's awareness of the issue is not in doubt.

As prelude to the return of the five men to the scene of the massacre, Cooper offers a highly wrought set scene. The soil is "fattened with human blood," and images of stiffness, pollution, deformity abound; nature's outrage is figured in a storm that angrily rejects the corpses. It is a "pictured allegory of life, in which objects were arrayed in their harshest but truest colours, and without the relief of any shadowing" (181). The hideous enlargement here puts the particular event into a cosmic setting: man seems to have uncreated his world into chaos. Natty's words apprise us of the blasphemy involved: "Nothing but vast wisdom and unlimited power should dare to sweep off men in multitudes" (184). The particular action of the Indians is permitted by Montcalm, the general of the Christian king. Whether Natty's own involvement in wholesale slaughter can be immune from his stipulation is hardly an open question.

The bodies of the dead—here as before and later—are left unburied, a revolting feast for the ravens. Such scenes engrave themselves on the memory, perhaps to be summoned again at the end of *The Deerslayer*. The last rites and respects are in evidence only at the novel's end and in the strange pastoral interlude after the rescue in chapter 12 at a ruined stronghold where Indians long ago were buried. The decencies are not always—or by everyone—neglected.

The other generic issue present in *Mohicans* has to do with epic, from which of course romance borrows many of its characteristic gestures. Through most of the text, epic offers Cooper a means of elevating descriptively the daring actions of Natty and the Indians; it provides a form of legitimization for some of the more improbable events and a stylistic resource for the description of noble Uncas. Epic also, however, offers Cora an idiom for her heroic role and lofty conduct and for the sentiment that immunizes her from the bias always implicit against romance.

Cooper himself was later to claim a Homeric precedent for his idealization of Chingachgook and Natty which seems to me not particularly relevant in the present novel. But the novel does have the epic theme of the death of a nation, and it is as that theme moves into predominance in the Delaware encampment that the epic note is most consistently struck, as it is in the obsequies of the final chapter. Cooper in these chapters admirably sustains that expansive sense of time that characterizes epic by elaborating and elevating his characters' speech, appearance, and deportment. All is filled with an atmosphere of awe and wonder as Tamenund hears his petitioners and delivers his judgments, lyrical prophecies, and evocations of times past. Even Magua—always an orator of epic proportions—participates in the general elevation. Contempt and critique are set aside for the victims of European imperium; they are rarely absent for the dispossessors and their values. The point, for Cooper, is not a purely literary ambition to construct a heroic elegy over the decline of the Indians. The tone is entirely appropriate for the elevated and, for Cooper, the exemplary love of law and heroism their behavior manifests. For the reader who remembers Templeton, Heyward's temptation of Magua, or Munro's scourging of Magua—and Montcalm's reflection on it—or who cares to set this world of complete respect for law and justified traditional usage against the charade between Munro and Montcalm, the value of Cooper's resort to epic will be only too apparent. It is absorbed into his general critique of American history.

Natty's way of coping with the racial issue may serve him, but it is not a satisfactory one to the reader. To reduce the matter to one of cultural— religious and racial—difference, white gifts and Indian gifts, with a sign that Indians, in effect, know no better, endorses the difference as well as roughly explaining it, as Natty intends. When Natty uses such arguments to excuse violent action or in the face of Uncas's "white" behavior, it seems merely condescending at best; indeed, Uncas's permission to enter white civilization centuries before it could be thought possible (115, cited above), considering how superior his conduct is to everyone else's, stands in an ironical relation to Natty's categories. Natty shares the sense of white superiority with all except Cora and Munro among the whites— even Heyward's noble disavowal of racial prejudice is accompanied by a consciousness he cannot deny: "'Heaven protect me from a prejudice so unworthy of my reason!' returned Duncan, at the same time conscious of such a feeling, and that as deeply rooted as if it had been engrafted in his nature" (159). That superiority cannot be sustained against white be- havior in the book; even Natty, as I have suggested, is not exempt from this charge—his views are self-contradictory, and his actions likewise do not accord with his racial position. Chingachgook's small debating vic- tory in chapter 3 is deserved. Just as Natty often blames the white man for sowing confusion among the Indians, the reader might well conclude that the enveloping action of white imperial struggle, and its motives, render such attempts at fine discriminations on racial issues, as well as romance virtues and "white gifts," unavailing.

Cooper, as narrator, sometimes seems as uncomfortable with the issue as were—with lone voices excepted—his contemporary reviewers.[27] But there is nothing tentative about Cooper's views on the dispossession of na- tive peoples and on white "luxurious people," in Munro's phrase, or about the conflation of Magua, Chingachgook, and Tamenund into a single voice on genocide. Cooper seems to endorse the more sharply expressed outrage of Irving in the two Indian sketches in *The Sketch Book*.

The issue is most directly addressed in the matter of Cora Munro's mixed blood. Cooper's reviewers were swift to recognize the issue[28] and to couch their discomfort in literary terms; they usually found it at least awkward, an unnecessary intrusion on the immunities of romance. And miscegenation is gratuitous in the sense that Cooper did not have to include it—the story does not require it; we may therefore assume it to be deliberate, and the final chapter renders that conclusion indisputable. That Munro who is so vehement on the issue in chapter 16 should also be the scourger of Magua complicates the issue; however, this complication proves not Cooper's awkwardness but his awareness of the issue's complexity, which resists simple characterizations based on romance criteria of unwavering virtue and vice (even Magua fails to kill Cora!).

In the final chapter Natty's insistence on racial difference even beyond the grave isolates him until the final frame; he is a minority of one, set against the song of the Indian maidens, against the recent bitter denunciation of Tamenund on the subject of white attitudes on marriage, and against himself, as the reader has known him at a greater age in *The Pioneers*. His role in the earlier novel is assumed by Munro here: "Say to these kind and gentle females, that a heart-broken and failing man, returns them his thanks. Tell them, that the Being we all worship, under different names, will be mindful of their charity; and that the time shall not be distant, when we may assemble around his throne, without distinction of sex, or rank, or colour!" (347). But Natty is unrelenting: "To tell them this," he said, "would be to tell them that the snows come not in the winter, or that the sun shines fiercest when the trees are stripped of their leaves!" (347). Natty's final avowal—and moving the moment is—not merely affirms his love for Chingachgook and Uncas but undoes much that he has said before and predicts the concurrence with Munro that we have already seen in *The Pioneers*.

The scene is an affecting one, enacted out of sight of Alice and Heyward, but the two men are so isolated. While moved, the reader is caught between a gratified sense of the racial union projected and a sense of the fragility of the promise against the massive demolition of idealism the novel embodies, and the knowledge of what the two men will face, have faced, together in *The Pioneers*. Uncas dies in this novel; he is mourned by his father, Chingachgook, whose death the reader has already witnessed, after Chingachgook's decline into the drunkenness that also allies him with Magua. The consolation the scene offers is profoundly qualified.

Late in life, in his "Preface to the Leather-Stocking Tales" (1850), Cooper was to claim the authority of Homer for rendering Natty as a "*beau idéal*." Enough has already been written here of the weakness of that position in *Mohicans*. Natty's complaint in *The Pioneers*—his first words and almost his last ones there, that might is right—is made concrete by the beginning of *Mohicans*. The palliative hope of a heavenly judgment in which might and racial difference are erased in the sight of the Almighty is given to Munro in this novel. But it must be remembered that Natty is in the willing service of that bloody-minded might that stains his native forest and lakes. The consequence of that allegiance we already know from *The Pioneers*; we do not therefore say simply that it was his own fault and withhold the sympathy he deserves, but we do recognize his wholehearted complicity with the forces that have already canceled Chingachgook. His alliance with the Indian at the end is not merely a gesture of human fraternity but an embrace of defeat. If Natty does not see his own fate in that of Uncas and Chingachgook, the reader must. This must also be part of our consciousness when, in *The Prairie*, Middleton rehearses Natty's legend.

Middleton, Heyward, Oliver, and their ladies are saved not by their romance values, which are class possessions, their white gifts, or their Christian European virtues but by Natty, Uncas, Chingachgook, and Hard-Heart, whose ways of life—and actual lives—are forfeit in the very act. Cooper's great achievement, it seems to me, lies in his refusal to privilege his own European-republican allegiance so as to idealize history, his "sister muse." In *Mohicans* and *The Pioneers* he severely mauls the principles that should animate the republic; though thus exposed, the white republic prevails. In the ideological ruin Cooper has fabricated in *Mohicans*, only Washington, unnamed in the text in 1826 and known only by his virtues and actions, remains unscathed—the Revolution is yet to be. The reader has seen its early fruits already in *The Pioneers*.

On the evidence *Mohicans* offers, it is difficult not to conclude that the Indian is superior by the white man's own highest standards—in law, polity, and human conduct. The superiority offers no insurance whatsoever against elimination. One might be pardoned for wishing to see a comprehensive sardonic joke. It is Cooper's great merit as a novelist that such a response is even conceivable.

FOUR * *The Prairie* (1827)

THE USES OF MEMORY

The Struggle of Man against Power is the Struggle of Memory against Forgetting.
– *Milan Kundera,* The Book of Laughter and Forgetting

    I am far from finding fault with your not having written a purely socialist novel, a Tendenzroman, *as we Germans call it, to glorify the social and political view of the author. That is not at all what I mean. . . .*
    Well, Balzac was politically a legitimist; his great work is a constant elegy on the irreparable decay of good society; his sympathies are with the class that is doomed to extinction. But for all that, his satire is never keener, his irony never more bitter, than when he sets in motion the very men and women with whom he sympathizes most deeply—the nobles. And the only men of whom he speaks with undisguised admiration are his bitterest political antagonists, the republican heroes of the Cloître Saint Méry, the men who at that time (1830–1836) were indeed representatives of the popular masses.
    That Balzac was thus compelled to go against his own class sympathies and political prejudices, that he saw the necessity of the downfall of his favorite nobles *and described them as people deserving no better fate; that he saw* the real men of the future where, for the time being, they alone were to be found—*that I consider one of the greatest triumphs of realism, and one of the greatest features in old Balzac.*
– *Engels to Margaret Harkness*

When I insist that the Leather-Stocking tales reveal the importance of property and class structure in the American society Cooper projects and that he, implicitly and explicitly, subjects that society to a damning critique, I do not mean at all to imply that Cooper *intended* as criticism all that a reader may put to critical use but only that Cooper's intention is not necessarily the issue. Cooper was certainly not opposed to private property and class distinction: virtuous conduct in *The Pioneers* for Temple, Oliver, Natty, and even Chingachgook relies to a large extent on the protection of private property. In *The Prairie*, class could hardly be insisted upon with less embarrassment; it is integral both to the romance, to the developing settlements, and to their class structure that Inez and Middleton be present, pallid and unsatisfactory as characters though they are.[1] The point I insist on throughout is that the works themselves contain far more than Cooper's own ideological positions or his intentions, narrowly construed; they also permit the most radical questioning of the very principles Cooper would embrace. That is their merit. *The Prairie* gives great prominence to the word "civilization," insisting on its virtues, but at the same time it shows repeatedly that the settled real property on which civilization is founded depends upon theft and cupidity, protected under the letter of the law. That law itself is likewise submitted to an interrogation, positively thrust upon the reader by the present text and the other texts it explicitly summons to memory.[2] Intention only confuses the issue by simplifying it. Cooper does endorse certain civilized virtues and institutions, but he also ruthlessly exposes them as betrayed, ill founded, inert, or ineffective. It does not matter except to the biographer that Cooper, in *Notions of the Americans* (1828),[3] is far more accepting of the fate of the Indians than he is in *Mohicans* and *The Prairie*; the novels tell a very different story from *Notions* and *The American Democrat*, just as the latter must qualify the former, much more explicitly reflecting, as most of Cooper's later work does, a good deal of the critical subtext of *The Pioneers*. The issue is not what Cooper in person thought at this point or that but what he wrote, what he saw, what he insists the reader see. What Engels asserts of Balzac in the epigraph to this chapter, I aim to demonstrate is largely true of Cooper. Only the self-constraints imposed by those critics who resolutely insist on the superseding merits of myth, who resolve the issue into one of a biographical dilemma among conflicting political beliefs, or who fail to get behind the transcendentalized pieties of law and "civilization" obstruct the emergence of Cooper, in these novels famed as romances, as a historical realist. As such, he would be unable to resolve the matters he addressed as Henry Nash Smith would have him do.

In an interesting critical note to his excellent new edition of *The Prairie*, James P. Elliott offers the kind of resolution Smith sought in vain. Elliott's detailed treatment of Cooper's search for social and moral meaning finds in Mahtoree, Hard-Heart, Ishmael, and Natty a range of options for civilization:[4] "Cooper's Indian and white societies range symbolically through human history to present spectrums of governments attempting to render justice" (xxxvi). There is obvious merit in the suggestion, and the allegorical implications sit well with Cooper's practices elsewhere. Elliott finds that various "stages" in "civilization" are represented. Bush is seen as yielding to "a law greater than himself"; he grows "in stature and maturity" (xxvi). Elliott cites Wasserstrom to the effect that Bush, after his judgment, "is no longer a kind of Hebrew nomad chieftan; instead he speaks as a Christian who has received God's word and knows what he must do in order to gain salvation" (xxxii–xxxiii). The highest stage is represented in the wedding of Middleton and Inez (we remember that of Oliver and Elizabeth), which combines the accumulated experience of the Old World and the New, primitive and civilized values, which in the legislature of the Union will inform Middleton's reflections, as, in "the lower branch," the example of Natty will Paul Hover's.

Elliott's construction of the matter captures the conceptual closure that eludes Smith, and it reflects a sound understanding of Cooper's own position; Natty's words to Paul at the end lend strength to the view as well. However, the novel gives much more than that resolved conclusion. "Man's search" for justice is all very well, but Elliott's view is far too oriented to the unquestioned superiority of Western Euro-Christian civilization. To accept closure in what Middleton represents is to eliminate the problematic rendering of civilization that Cooper's novels relentlessly provide. Elliott has Cooper's ideological tendency correctly situated, but I suggest that he quite misses the extent to which the reader is drawn to distrust the ideology. The weight of subversion is such that it cannot be argued away and remains unassimilated by the text's primary ideology, and in this it accurately reflects history.

One can quite see the allegorical pattern that determines the defeat of Mahtoree by Hard-Heart; he "must fall" because Hard-Heart is "stronger and more just." But Cooper also allows us to see how attractive (and just) to Hard-Heart Mahtoree's arguments are, and the whole series makes us wonder how confident we should be that Washington will smile on Hard-Heart's petition. The history of the Indians in the 1820s is not encouraging, as Cooper must have known and as Tocqueville was soon definitively to point out. The promise of civilization is no more sunny. To omit this dimension of the work is for me as great as the omissions of which Elliott complains in the traditional reception of the novel.

Henry Nash Smith's influential chapter on Leather-Stocking[5] offers a cautionary instance of the perils of arguing from intention and of not examining the texts of the novels closely enough.[6] Smith is sensitive to the close relationship between genre and social class and to the embarrassment caused when the hero, Leather-Stocking, is not of a class appropriate for the hero of a romance and thus not eligible for the essential romantic involvement with a heroine, and when those who are appropriate and eligible are incompetent to survive in frontier conditions (Oliver Effingham is an exception to the rule). Smith develops a persuasive scenario that has Cooper aware of his problem and modifying his practice in *The Pathfinder* and *The Deerslayer* to accommodate the discrepancy. Smith sees the issue in terms of determinate "problems" of fulfilled or unfulfilled "intention"; he is fully aware of Cooper's divided allegiance on the issues addressed and finds Cooper unable to "solve" them. Smith is anything but uninformed or unresponsive in all this, but his governing criterion is evident here: "[Cooper's] conflict of allegiances was truly ironic, and if he had been able—as he was not—to explore *to the end* the contradictions in his ideas and emotions, the Leatherstocking series might have become a major work of art" (*Virgin Land*, 66, italics mine). He demands a determination of the issue impossible in historical reality, not merely in Cooper's divided sensibility. Cooper's Leather-Stocking novels do not resolve "to the end" what cannot be so decisively resolved, and it is this irresolution, so fully captured, that makes them valuable to us in a way that a forced resolution could not. To attempt it would be to misrepresent.

Smith is led by his premise to propose that in *The Pathfinder* Cooper tries to find a credible mate for Natty in Mabel Dunham; it does not work, not because Cooper's resources failed him (he was not often deterred on principle by improbability, after all) but because Cooper had no intention of finding a human bride for Natty. Mabel's wedding with Jasper Western reinscribes that of Ellen and Paul in *The Prairie*. What possible motive could Cooper have had to confer a cabined domesticity on a character who had so resolutely resisted settlement in *The Prairie* and *The Pioneers*?

Cooper did not serve (or subserve) genre but reality, both that which he had made and that which he experienced.

Smith, a disciplined and careful scholar whose book gave a generation a reliable way of understanding the idea and the historical actuality of the American frontier, is much less exacting in the reading of Cooper's texts than he is in the reading of history. He is given to the quick "take" rather than comprehensive detailed reading (or is it that he cannot circumvent his liberal affiliations?). When he quotes Elizabeth's exclamation—"the enterprise of Judge Temple is taming the very forests! How rapidly is civilization treading on the footsteps of nature!"—he fails to note how seriously this view is questioned in the novel. Citing with approval Temple's remonstrance to Elizabeth, "Thy heart lies too near thy head," and his payment of Natty's fine, Smith quite fails to show how thorough is the novel's interrogation of civilization's laws that "alone remove us from the condition of the savages"; still less does he indicate how much more effective Ishmael Bush's eventual resort to "law" is than Temple's.

Finally, to lead us to *The Prairie*, Smith notes Temple's reception of Oliver into his house in chapter 18 of *The Pioneers*, "the influences of more sacred things" which the wilderness cannot offer, and Natty's spirited and predictable response: "As for honesty, or doing what's right between man and man, I'll not turn my back to the longest winded deacon on your patent" (202). "Cooper," says Smith, "is unable to solve" the issue "and resorts to a compromise statement that represents his inability to accept the full implications of the conflict he has stated" (69). The "compromise statement" is, of course, Temple's, not Cooper's (although it may be true that in life Cooper would have agreed with Temple). Cooper has fully registered both the conflict and the condescending and class-ridden compromise. Why should he fraudulently resolve what his society has not resolved? And how much of a compromise is it to reassert his assumed *moral* superiority: "This youth is made of materials too precious to be wasted in the forest"? (70). It is not at all that Smith does not respond to Temple's "Falstaffian instinct" about Oliver's class but that he does not adopt criteria appropriate to literary fictions. Just as important, I think, is the fact that Middleton in *The Prairie*—in his own name and in the words of his grandfather, Duncan Heyward—repeats Temple's compromise: "In short, he was a noble shoot from the stock of human nature, which never could attain its proper elevation and importance, for no other reason, than because it grew in the forest" (114). Clearly Cooper regards the sentiment as characteristic of the ruling class on the frontier over three generations, and Natty here accepts it as honorific. Given the origin of this self-flattering theory of the moral benefits of society in Temple, Heyward, and Middleton—all of whom owe their very lives to Natty and none of whom demonstrates either the *effective* virtue of the park settlements where human trees grow to their full elevation or his right to make the adverse judgment of Natty's life—it is at the very least patronizing, and, whatever Cooper's intentions and private convictions may have been, the reader must be free to perceive its emptiness and to deploy his memory critically among the books. Certainly *The Prairie* abounds in opportunities where it is difficult not to do so, to the extent that the reader's most valuable resource in receiving this text reliably is memory. We need not suppose in this that Cooper was deliberate in his designs on the reader; but we must suppose that he was conscious of what he included. He has not made a free text in which the reader constantly makes and remakes the text; indeed, after the first novel, Cooper and his reader are both constrained by a restrictive memory that enforces a certain range of meanings. Within that range, differences in reading are possible, but they cannot include taking seriously a human bride for Natty or a resolution of the historical conflicts Cooper faced as fact.

It is because so many critics—like Smith, Elliott, and, earlier, Parkman—assume with Cooper the absolute value of "civilization" and, as a result, choose to underrate the critique the novels contain[7] that in what follows I must insist, sometimes laboriously, on how pervasively this novel brings the countervailing view before the reader.

Little space need be spent in the discussion of the narrative elements of *The Prairie*; while it contains many well-developed, exciting, or affecting episodes, its defects as a continuous narrative are evident enough. We need not dwell upon the abundance of filler, the awkwardness that results from Cooper's lack of direct familiarity with his chosen locale, the improbable contrivance of his major plot, his difficulty in managing his multipronged story line, the absence of any conceivable tension in his major plot lines (except perhaps for the murder of Asa Bush), and the feebleness of some of his central characters, especially Middleton. Even Natty, whose presence dominates the book at its spectacularly posed opening and close, is hardly a *narrative* consideration at all, except episodically. Perhaps Ishmael Bush and his tribe offer the most interesting narrative possibilities; Natty excepted, Bush is certainly the most active, resourceful, and competent character on view, for all his faults and Cooper's frequent and determined disparagement of him. Moreover, as opposed to the evident importance of what they are, what *happens* in the stories of Ellen and Paul, Inez and Middleton is of little significance in itself—except insofar as Bush's disposal of their cases carries serious meaning; what happens in the Bush story, however, is highly significant, and is made—as I shall later show—integral to the novel's ideological thrust.

In part, the lack of narrative impetus in *The Prairie* can be attributed to the weight of the past that Cooper makes it carry by constant allusions to *The Pioneers* and *Mohicans*, made explicitly and implicitly, by incessant paralleling that the reader can hardly miss, and by repetition of thematic issues. If we grant the epic stature Cooper seems so willing to confer on an idealized Natty at the end of his life, which in hindsight Cooper was to confirm in his invocation of Homer in the "Preface to the Leather-Stocking Tales" and in the 1849 introduction to *The Prairie*, such a mustering of the past is entirely appropriate—epic heroes, who have by definition great historical and national significance, rarely come to the reader unattended by their past. The classical analogy is reinforced by the audience's possession of that past already. The placing of the events of this novel—and its predecessors—in a historical perspective that relates past, present, and a desired future involving the material and moral destiny of a nation is likewise appropriate to epic. Even a casual reading of *The Prairie* and *Mohicans* must reveal Cooper's frequent and skillful resort to the heroic style—in rhetoric, description, and the treatment of his episodes. Many of the longueurs attributed to Cooper result from his courting of a leisurely and elevated epic mode.

The links Cooper forges with the previous novels are immediately apparent: the provision of an analytical historical opening parallels similar passages in the two preceding novels; the counterposing of the "swarms of restless people" and "the tide of instant emigration" (9–10) with the legendary "distinguished and resolute forester . . . seeking for the renewal of enjoyments which were rendered worthless in his eyes, when trammelled by the forms of human institutions" reinscribes at once an already familiar theme; even the enveloping of Daniel Boone, unnamed amid his periphrases, recalls the similar summoning of Washington's republican reputation at the expense of the Royalist context of *Mohicans*.

No sooner has Natty been introduced, enlarged, and spectacularly backlit by a setting sun, than we see him reluctantly engaged in giving aid to migrants as he had done to Temple and his military superiors, at such eventual cost to his way of life. By this time in the series there are few events which fail to summon memories and, as a result, to assume a preexisting load of significance.

Among Bush's "prodigal and ill-judged ornaments,"[8] which themselves constitute a kind of symbolic historical anthology, shines his "keen and bright wood-axe." Like Hover's rifle, the axe is for Natty a portentous symbol; in the nation's history there are no more potent icons than the rifle and the axe, which for Bush are mere instruments of convenience—the axe's longer range symbolic freight of construction and destruction that Whitman projects in "Song of the Broad-Axe" would be lost on Ishmael and his tribe. For Natty, the axe summons thoughts of a past laid waste and a future to be dreaded. The symbol is simple and almost instantaneous in its impact on the reader. As the novel proceeds, it is clear that the axe is the starting point of a linked series of pictures, episodes, and rhetorical commentary that are dominated by Natty. The opening characterizations of the terrain are bleak indeed—the perspectives "long, narrow, barren," the vegetation "withered," "sour," "coarse" even where it is relatively "luxuriant"; the natural desolation is almost at once augmented by the improvident purposefulness of the sons of Ishmael: "They stripped a small but suitable spot of its burden of forest, as effectively, and almost as promptly as if a whirlwind had passed along the place" (19). Natty's complaint is silent but predictable: "As tree after tree came whistling down, he cast his eyes upward, at the vacancies they left in the heavens, with a melancholy gaze, and finally turned away, muttering to himself with a bitter smile, like one who disdained giving a more audible utterance to his discontent" (19). Natty cannot be silent long; Ishmael's view of the prairie as a natural "wide tract of clearing" elicits this response from Natty:

> "You may travel weeks, and you will see it the same. I often think the Lord has placed this barren belt of Prairie, behind the States, to warn men to what their folly may yet bring the land! Ay, weeks if not months, may you journey in these open fields, in which there is neither dwelling, nor habitation for man or beast. Even the savage animals travel miles on miles to seek their dens. And yet the wind

seldom blows from the east, but I conceit the sounds of axes, and the crash of falling trees are in my ears." [24]

Here, Ishmael's "clearing," itself a dread word for Natty, contains a divine prophetic warning,[9] as well as Natty's memory of what man's folly has already wrought; the prophecy is foretold and remembered both and, of course, is actually present in the Bushes' destruction for "temporary comfort." Such is the operation of frontier development that Natty, at a later date than that of *The Pioneers* and in flight from Templeton's settlement, is forced to endure an "earlier," more primitive experience—more brutal to nature, more extreme, and lacking Templeton's social motivation. The movement here strikingly recalls that already noted in Crèvecoeur. The apocalyptic note struck in "whirlwind" is intensified in Natty's later discussion with Ishmael:

> "They scourge the very 'arth with their axes. Such hills and hunting grounds as I have seen stripped of the gifts of the Lord; without remorse or shame! I tarried till the mouths of my hounds were deafened by the blows of the choppers, and then I came west, in search of quiet. It was a grievous journey, that I made; a grievous toil to pass through falling timber, and to breathe the thick air of smoky clearings week after week, as I did. 'Tis a far country too, that State of York, from this!" [75]

The chopping is a mockery of "the gifts of the Lord," says Natty in his pious absolutism, and he offers the denuded prairie as a projected retaliation by the divine hand: "Look around you, men; what will the Yankee choppers say, when they have cut their path from the eastern to the western waters, and find that a hand, which can lay the 'arth bare at a blow, has been here, and swept the country, in very mockery of their wickedness" (76).

In this conversation, Natty traverses his life in space and time across the continent and confers a divine and human significance on what he sees and has seen. He imagines for the restless pioneers a parodic Pilgrim's Progress. As the Bushes decamp and make for their rock fortress, he ruefully eyes the waste they leave behind and mutters:

> "I might have know'd it! I might have know'd it! Often have I seen the same before, and yet I brought them to the spot myself, and have now sent them to the only neighborhood of their kind, within many

long leagues of the spot where I stand. This is man's wish, and pride, and waste, and sinfulness. He tames the beasts of the field, to feed his idle wants, and having robbed the brutes of their natural food, he teaches them to strip the 'arth of its trees, to quiet their hunger." [83]

His realistic noting of his own complicity[10] raises memories of Templeton, and of Temple's failure to eliminate the wasteful destruction of the forest.

Natty's later observation to Middleton that he has come to the plains "to escape the sound of the axe" marks the futility of his flight, as does the casual reference to Lewis's surveying expedition. Enough has been said then to establish the powerful presence that the axe, with its various extensions, has in the novel and to extend its significance beyond this novel's specific time frame. It might be observed, however, that the biblical terms Natty uses are considerably expanded in the discussion between Natty and Bat about God's garden (197–98). The symbol of the axe also serves to align Natty with the Indian—not merely with Hard-Heart but also with Weucha and Mahtoree, for, whatever differences there may be among these four men, all share a common fear and resentment at the relentless expansion of white settlement power that the axe embodies. Natty's consistent view of the spoliation of nature as a notable evidence of impiety, the sure mark of man's fall, also associates readily with *Cooper's* insistence here, and in the other novels, on the failure of white Christian principle in the march of civilization and on the dominance of cupidity in white conquest. Although the refrain may seem over familiar, its contexts insist on the repetition.[11] Simpler instances of links among the novels may readily be found, of course; Natty's competent dominance in reason and knowledge over Middleton and Hover,[12] whose chivalrous feelings and impatient bravery are so often useless, reenacts Natty's similar relationships with Heyward and, to some extent, Oliver. Likewise, the opposition of Delaware and Mingo is transformed into that of Pawnee and Sioux—as Natty specifically reminds us; Uncas and Magua become the Hard-Heart and Mahtoree of this novel.

As in *Mohicans*, however, the matter is rendered less simply than a good Indian/bad Indian opposition would permit. Weucha's thirst for liquor reminds us of Magua's and Mohegan's, but sin and malignity aside, they all—including Hard-Heart and Mahtoree—share a justified resentment at their dispossession by "white adventurers" (107), "Christians" who "rob the heathens of their inheritance" (190). Once more we see Cooper working gratuitously across the grain of the romance opposition. His insistence on this theme is so great in the novel that it will receive separate treatment later. Suffice it to say here that this reiterated strain renders it highly problematic that Hard-Heart's plea (367–68) will be heard, notwithstanding the peerless hospitality which leads him to reject Mahtoree's invitation to common cause against "the robberies of the long-knives" (334–35). *Mohicans* affords enough evidence on which to doubt.[13]

The question of land rights is explored in all three novels—and not exclusively in relation to the dispossessed Indians. Cooper is never friendly to squatters; neither is Natty, but he has a freer tongue and his absolutism allows him to reflect, "It is greatly to be mourned that colour, and property, and tongue, and l'arning should make so wide a difference in those who, after all, are but the children of one Father" (58). While this touches on frontier vengeance and violence and on human weakness, its wider application to artificial human political, economic, and racial distinctions is obvious, as is its alignment with Bush's words: " 'Owners!' echoes the squatter, 'I am as rightful an owner of the land I stand on, as any governor in the States! Can you tell me, stranger, where the law or the reason, is to found, which says that one man shall have a section, or a town, or perhaps a county, to his use, and another have to beg for 'arth to make his grave in. This is not natur and I deny that it is law. That is, your legal law' " (61). Natty instantly concedes the point but also qualifies it shrewdly by applying it to the Indians.

We need approve of Bush no more than Cooper does to give serious attention to his claim to equal rights to land—here with the Indians, elsewhere with others:

> "The Teton and the Pawnee and the Konza, and men of a dozen other tribes claim to own these naked fields."
>
> "Natur gives them the lie, in their teeth. The air, the water and the ground are free gifts to man, and no one has the power to portion them out in parcels. Man must drink, and breathe and walk, and therefore each has a right to his share of 'arth. Why do not the Surveyors of the States, set their compasses and run their lines over our heads as well as beneath our feet? Why do they not, cover their shining sheep skins with big words, giving to this land-holder, or perhaps he should be called air-holder, so many rods of heaven, with the use of such a star for a boundary mark and such a cloud to turn a mill!" [78]

Such rights he maintains are above the law, whose sanctions he rejects. As a position, it is not less valid than legitimized views of property—by deed, by appropriation, by United States law, by royal patent, or, even, by Indian custom. In order to prevail over such a view, one must posit a view of society that one may prefer but whose superiority cannot be demonstrated in absolute terms. What Bush says here is not really very different in its nature from complaints about white Christian acquisitiveness by Natty and the Indians—in this book and in its predecessors.[14] Cooper also allows his squatters in the Littlepage manuscripts similar moments. Ishmael's wastefulness may not make him admirable, but, in that particular, he is no worse than the inhabitants of Templeton, we remember; and, in any case, his waste does not destroy his argument. And we must recall in such a discussion how crucial to the resolution of *The Pioneers* the matter of property is. Cooper may call Bush's words a "wild conceit" and find his sons' merriment "frightful"; he may well find it a threatening idea, since it attacks the very basis of capitalism—not perhaps in a very attractive cause, but one that is not in itself more sinister or more acquisitive than anyone else's—so Cooper, here as elsewhere, at least allows equal time to Bush. The passage casts a cold light on the legitimacy of the march of civilization that the novel seems to endorse. One may, in short, oppose Bush in principle, but little evidence in civilized practice exists in these books to set against him.

That civilization must find its values in its dominant classes; the claim, unspoken of course, of Middleton, Heyward, and Oliver to rule lies in their character as chivalrous, courteous, considerate gentlemen. While Cooper allows us to question the effectiveness, in frontier circumstances, of those values, he never questions those values themselves. Middleton gains access to his insipid bride on those terms:

> The haughty and reserved Don Augustin was by far, too observant of the forms of that station, on which he so much valued himself to forget the duties of a gentleman. Gratitude for the kindness of Middleton, induced him to open his doors to the Officers of the Garrison, and to admit of a guarded but polite intercourse. Reserve gradually gave way before the propriety and candor of their spirited young leader, and it was not long ere, the affluent Planter rejoiced as much as his daughter, whenever the well known signal, at the gate, announced one of these agreeable visits from the commander of the post. [157]

The alliance of property, class, and gentlemanly values is insisted upon. While Temple's welcome is more instinctual and open in manner, it too depends on his recognition of Oliver as a gentleman. Cooper registers two kinds of reality with his women. Alice and Inez are mere romantic, pious apparitions—these "first ladies" have no apparent function but to look the part and be capable of pious platitudes. In Ellen Wade and Elizabeth Temple, however, a different pattern emerges: Christians both, they are capable, vigorous, independent, outspokenly moral, and clearly fit for a more active role in the affairs of their societies. Ellen's deference to Inez's social class ill fits her vigorous personality and gifts.

The male potential leaders, Heyward and Middleton, have strikingly similar introductions: the former and his party are heralded by Gamut as "believers in religion, and friends to the law, and to the king" (36); the latter introduces himself as "a friend, a white man, and, I hope, a Christian" (106), and the "U.S." on his knapsack, like the commission he bears, declares his allegiance to established authority and law. The links to Oliver are also clear, though not so neatly encapsuled. The similarity is of more than passing significance, given the reiterated questionings in all three works of the virtues of law, state, and religion by which they identify themselves. Cooper, as narrator and through Natty, constantly draws into question not only the law but also Christianity; when speaking of his white European acquisitors, Cooper very frequently provides the epithet "Christian." In a heated discussion with Bat (234–39) which resolves itself into a series of fundamentalist reflections on human pride, Natty rejects Bat's claim for the history "in morals" of "Christiandom:" "I am no great admirer of your old morals, as you call them, for I have ever found, and I have liv'd long, as it were, in the very heart of natur', that your old morals are never of the best. Mankind twist and turn the rules of the Lord, to suit their own wickedness when their devilish cunning has had too much time to trifle with his commands" (238). Bat's clarification of "morals," "the practices of men, as connected with their daily intercourse, their institutions, and their laws," draws from Natty the contemptuous dismissal, "And such I call barefaced and downright wantonness and waste" (238). While Natty may be more absolute here than he is in his farewell to Paul Hover, he does have—as the reader of *The Pioneers* recognizes—some reason for his vehemence and failure to recognize the improvements wrought by law and state. Bat may often be stupid, but here he speaks with all the assurance of Judge Temple.[15] Cooper never merely eliminates or shirks the question raised. He even, in the chapter following, has Natty—recalling Tamenund for us—thus characterize the colonizer: "the first christian that plac'd his wicked foot in the regions of York!" (250). Those who despoil his wilderness garden are Christians. Here too, as in *Mohicans*, the conduct and the legal and political practices of the Indians, both Sioux and Pawnee, are seen as superior in their consistency to those of the whites.

The question of race, which so vexed Natty in *Mohicans*, is addressed yet again in *The Prairie*. Natty's assumption of the father's role with Hard-Heart (278), like the linking of hands and sharing of sorrow at the end of *Mohicans*, is among the most touching episodes in the entire series. It is not here left to another, as it is left to Munro in *Mohicans*, to announce the meeting of all men and women in equality before God: "You believe in the blessed Prairies, and I have faith in the sayings of my fathers. If both are true, our parting will be final; but if it should prove that the same meaning is hid under different words, we shall yet stand together, Pawnee, before the face of your Wahcondah who will then be no other than my God" (382). The reader remembers the even more forceful words of Natty at the end of *The Pioneers*: "I pray that the Lord will keep you in mind—the Lord that lives in clearings as well as in the wilderness—and bless you, and all that belong to you, from this time, till the great day when the whites shall meet the red-skins in judgment, and justice shall be the law, and not power" (455). We are surely expected to reflect upon the discrepancy between principle and practice, the heavenly state and the earthly.[16]

Incidents and characters are explicitly recalled from the previous two novels, and incidents in *The Prairie* recall, by their similarity, earlier ones. When this occurs, the action of memory is not restricted by what is specifically written—the allusive field may extend to all the reader recalls. When Natty excitedly shares with Middleton his memories of events we know from *Mohicans* (232–33), the reader is free to recall also Natty's complicity in his own destruction, the elimination of the Delawares, and Heyward's impatient and useless chivalry. To recall the Bloody Pond of *Mohicans* (170–71) is also to recall the entire bloody history of the nation registered in that book. Natty, remembering bitterly the courthouse scene of *The Pioneers*, is nevertheless inclined to forgive; the casual word "court-house" provokes this outburst:

"Ay Court-Houses are the 'happy hunting grounds' as a red-skin would say, for them that are born with gifts no better than such as lie in the tongue! I was carried into one of the lawless holes my self, once, and it was all about a thing of no more value than the skin of a deer. The Lord forgive them, the Lord forgive them; they knew no better, and they did according to their weak judgements, and therefore the more are they to be pitied. And yet it was a solemn sight to see an aged man, who had always lived in the air, laid neck and heels, by the law, and held up as a spectacle for the women and boys of a wasteful settlement to point their fingers at!" [323]

"Court-houses" or "lawless holes"? The criticism of law and settlement is here vividly and unsparingly recalled. The reader must supply the intensity of debate that surrounds the earlier incident. The presence of the *Pioneers* in *The Prairie* must disturb the complacencies of our view of the society to which Middleton, Hover, and the Bushes return.

If Natty's specific recall late in the novel is insufficient, the allusions proliferate as the novel draws to its close. Natty again must face a judge—this time one whose verdicts, conduct, and consistency, unexpectedly, outstrip Temple's. Natty bequeaths Killdeer to Oliver Effingham. Middleton and his companions attempt—like Oliver, Temple, and Elizabeth before him and with the same lack of success—to reclaim Natty for the civilization. He is predictably adamant: "Settlements, Boy! It is long sin' I took my leave of the waste and wickedness of the settlements and the village. If I live in a clearing, here it is one of the Lord's making, and I have no hard thoughts, on the matter; but never, again, shall I be running wilfully into the danger of immoralities" (370). He will bless Hover and Ellen, wish Godspeed to the nation, but maintain—necessarily, for himself and the book—his separation from it.

It is Natty in himself, of course, who constitutes the strongest connecting fabric among these novels. As he recalls, repeatedly, the events of his life, the fifty-year span of which we know and the longer one of his whole life, over which we run several times in *The Prairie*—his registration of his spatial movements from sea to sea, from forest, to settlement, to prairie, to river and lakes, always linking his experience with that of the Indian—his words and his life bear eloquent witness to the birth of a nation.[17] Only in the eulogium of Middleton is Natty seen unblemished, honored by and an honor to the country making itself.[18] In Natty's words, experience, and thoughts, republican though he is, the nation is born deformed. Cooper offers no convincing witness to the contrary. The question that lurks unanswered is whether Middleton's witness is enough, whether it conveys a force of meaning sufficient to counterbalance or qualify Natty's own doleful account within the novel of his life of displacement and flight. Can Middleton's idealization of Natty compensate for his elimination? If it does not, it is a sample of his society's hypocrisy, or, more kindly, self-deception and bad conscience, and it serves to affirm not society's piety but its failure.

Francis Parkman, in his 1852 essay on Cooper,[19] admires the character of Leather-Stocking, and observes, recalling Crèvecoeur and Irving,

> "Civilization has a destroying as well as a creating power. . . . Exterminating the buffalo, and the Indian . . . [it] must eventually sweep from before it a class of men, its own precursors and pioneers, so remarkable both in their virtues and their faults, that few will see their extinction without regret." [Dekker and McWilliams, *Fenimore Cooper*, 252–53]

The bias of Parkman's view is evident by his "must" and in his failure to qualify "civilization," even by an article—"this" would make a considerable difference to the tone of his remark. Civilization is magnanimous enough to feel "regret" but not to make the regret unnecessary. Parkman's detachment (and that is too weak a word) is miles from Cooper's divided feelings and the rigorous requirement his novels exact that we scrutinize that "must" and assess the cost of that civilization's sweeping of all before it. It is surely noteworthy that Cooper nowhere shows us that civilization flourishing according to its stated principles; it remains an object merely of desire, of a future unfulfilled.

In *The Prairie*, as at the opening of *The Pioneers*, there is no question that Cooper's emphasis is on the future, the anticipated civilization. As has often been observed,[20] Cooper had difficulty in resolving the conflicting claims of traditional "aristocratic" values and his democratic convictions, but he was in no doubt at all about the governing principles of the new republic; they are the political currency issued by the Declaration and the Constitution—the triumph of European rationalism in America—and they are present throughout the text. The civilization must be founded on laws and be governed by white European Christian principle, which also, of course, imbues the heroic romance values of truth and honor; equality is asserted for all, and the avenues to advancement are open to all through education; reason rather than prejudice and superstition prevail; property is protected; the industry, reason, and virtue of the republican citizen in circumstances of unparalleled opportunity ensure the prosperity of the civilization. Few—if any—of these principles emerge unscathed from *The Prairie*; even if they were affirmed without qualification, they would have to be submitted to the experience of *Mohicans* and *The Pioneers*, and, although *The Pioneers* is chronologically prior to *The Prairie*, it is also the most advanced future state of the civilization that Cooper offers in the series and must therefore qualify even hope and desire. As Natty remarks, man's "gifts are not equal to his wishes" (240).

A well-known passage from *The Prairie*, from the standpoint of 1827, when "the vigorous swarms are culling the fresher sweets of a virgin world" (65), expresses the desire as in the process of fulfillment:

> Although the citizen of the United States may claim so just an ances-try, he is far from being exempt from the penalties of his fallen race. Like causes are well known to produce like effects. That tribute, which it would seem nations must ever pay, by way of a weary probation, around the shrine of Ceres before they can be indulged in her fullest favors, is in some measure exacted in America, from the descendant instead of the ancestor. The march of civilization with us, has a strong analogy to that of all coming events, which are known "to cast their shadows before." The gradations of society, from that state which is called refined to that which approaches as near barbar-ity as connexion with an intelligent people will readily allow, are to be traced from the bosom of the states, where wealth, luxury and the arts are beginning to seat themselves, to those distant, and ever-receding borders which mark the skirts, and announce the approach, of the nation, as moving mists precede the signs of day.[21] [65–66]

The confidence of this is at once set against a somewhat confused passage on the mixture of virtue and vice in the "borderers," of whom Bush is a prime example: a lawless despoiler without religion (66). However, in this novel, Bush is civilized far more successfully than Twain dared civilize Huck. Civilization is less seriously threatened in the end by Bush than it is, in *The Pioneers*, by forces from within.

Cooper's introduction to the 1832 edition of *The Prairie* inscribes strongly his confidence in American political and material progress: "The power of the republic has done much to restore peace to these wild scenes, and it is now possible to travel in security, where civilized man did not dare to pass unprotected five-and-twenty years ago" (5). By 1849, railroads are contemplated "that men have ceased to regard . . . as chimerical" (6); the "barrier" that in the 1820s he thought "the comparative desert" of the prairie to pose has been comprehensively breached, and " 'the settler,' preceded by the 'trapper,' has already established himself on the shores of that vast sea." Against this, however, is set the "desperate resignation" of Natty—idealized though he is in the final sentence—driven west from "his beloved forests" by "the sound of the axe" with "the remnants of the Mohicans and Delawares, of the Creeks, the Choctaws, and Cherokees . . . destined to fulfill their time on these vast plains," which the following text depicts as a wasteland. Cooper's tone is strangely muted here about the Indians—he is less restrained in the text of the novel; he certainly lacks the bite of Tocqueville, who was writing so shortly after the appearance of *The Prairie* and whom Cooper certainly knew and had read by 1850: "The Secretary of War, in a letter written to the Cherokees, April 18th, 1829 . . . declares to them that they cannot expect to retain possession of the lands, at that time occupied by them, but gives them the most positive assurance of uninterrupted peace if they would remove beyond the Mississippi; as if the power which could not grant them protection, would be able to afford it them hereafter" (Tocqueville, *Democracy* 1:353). It is useful to bear Tocqueville in mind when reading Hard-Heart's final message to the Great White Father through Middleton.

The buoyant hope that sustains the 1849 introduction is immediately confirmed in the first chapter, as Cooper at once outlines the political and economic advantages to the United States of the Louisiana Purchase: it offers a vision of political and social control, the peace and security of the States, the solution of Indian problems, and the enormous economic advantages of the opening to the West and of the acquisition of the "great thoroughfare of the interior" (9); and, "if ever time or necessity shall require a peaceful division of this vast empire, it assures us of a neighbour that will possess our language, our religion, our institutions, and it is also to be hoped, our sense of political justice" (9). The ideological interest of Cooper could not be clearer, and it characterizes the entire work; at the same time there is a stylistic hesitancy before "our sense of political

justice" that locates it in future subjunctive. Those who remember the
preceding novels may have some difficulty finding an effective sense of
political justice. However, the hopeful note is sustained by the bursting
forth of the restless energies of the adventurous settlers. Once more,
though, the counterpoint of the introduction is sustained by the evocation
of Daniel Boone "seeking the renewal of enjoyments which were rendered
worthless in his eyes, when trammelled by the forms of human institution" (10).

The imprinting of republican values and aspirations given in the novel's
initial paragraphs and reinforced at the opening of chapter 6 (65–66,
cited above) makes its mark even more boldly with the entry of Middleton, "a white man and, I hope, a Christian," in chapter 10, with "U.S."
marked on his equipment and bearing a commission signed by Jefferson
and sealed by the state, and a name showing the impress of Uncas and
Heyward (the transition from monarchy to republic is as intact here as it is
in the union of Elizabeth and Oliver). In his memory he carries the verbal
honors bestowed on Uncas and Natty by his grandfather. In his marriage
to Inez, the account of which is given in chapter 15, he registers the
blending of cultures, religions, and traditions that is taking place in civilization's march and the raising of benighted Catholic "subjects, to the
more enviable distinction of citizens in a Government of Laws" (156). The
"political tie which had made a forced conjunction between people so
opposite in their habits, their educations, and their opinions" is cemented
by family unions and cultural and class considerations—the proper behavior of gentlemen, "the forms of that station, on which [Don Augustin]
so much valued himself" (157) and which override those differences. For
all the freight of significance he is made to bear, Middleton is inert and
ineffective in action as a character; were it not for the need to rescue Inez
he would be supernumerary. At best, he is a *commis*, a master of cere-
monies, perhaps. But it is perfectly obvious why he is there.

The role of Bat is less easy to see; he has usually been viewed as a boring
windbag who is not funny enough to offer comic relief, and that view is
understandable. What he does and says in the novel is a gross parody of
the spirit of experimental reason and education that is so much a part of
the revolutionary republican sentiment. But he is not invariably ludi-
crously parodic: his words do not too seriously misrepresent—if they
overstate—some eighteenth- and nineteenth-century notions of the capacities of human reason, *Verstand* or *Vernunft*: "Man may be degraded to

the very margin of the line which separates him from the brute, by ignorance; or he may be elevated to a communion with the Great Master Spirit of All by knowledge—nay, I know not, if time and opportunity were given him, but he might become the Master of all learning, and consequently equal to the great moving principle" (180). The passage oddly conflates Franklin and Jefferson with Emerson and Whitman. Bat's project is nothing less than to reform human depravity—"It is much too certain that certain facts will warrant a theory which teaches the natural depravity of the *genus*; but if science could be fairly brought to bear on a whole species, at once, for instance, education might eradicate the evil principle" (240). Natty rejects Bat contemptuously: "That, for your education!" We should hesitate to dismiss these exchanges, so passionate on Natty's part, as marginal debates in which thick-headed rationalism meets encrusted fundamentalism and is defeated. Bat does embody reason and a belief in the power of education, and it is not merely a convenience of plot that entrusts him to speak in the name of "the Confederacy of the United, Sovereign States of North America" and "the laws" (148): " 'I demand of thee, the surrender of this rock, without delay or resistance, in the joint names of Power, of Justice and of the—Law,' he would have added; but recollecting that this ominous word would again provoke the hostility of the squatter's children, he succeeded in swallowing it, in good season and concluded with the less dangerous and more convertible term of Reason" (149). And Natty's opposition to him is not made simply on the grounds of his own submissive piety; he associates Bat's reason—his blasphemy, as he sees it—with the engrossing greed and destructive power of the settlements, of the civilization, and interprets it as an insult to divine reason. It is not difficult to understand—on the evidence—why Natty should think so; it is more difficult to see on what, other than words, a civilization can mount the case for its superiority. Natty's attack on Bat, then, is also an attack on Middleton and all he embodies; a more direct attack would produce a fictional chaos, but the charge is made and is anything but marginal.

That the future Cooper contemplates is white hardly needs exhaustive demonstration. The assumption of a specifically racial power and superiority is made by all the whites at one time or another; it is a consideration that connects the gentleman, Middleton, even with the coarse squatter, Bush. It is implied throughout and is in *The Prairie*, as in the two previous novels, explicitly recognized by the Indians. Mahtoree must trim his desire for revenge by calculating the force that lies behind Middleton, in his proud whiteness, as Natty makes clear: "Could the red nations work their will, trees would shortly be growing, again, on the plough'd fields of America, and woods would be whitened with christian bones. No one can doubt that, who knows the quality of the love which a red-skin bears a Pale face; but they have counted our numbers until their memories fail them, and they are not without their policy. Therefore, is our fate unsettled; but I fear me there is small hope left for the Pawnee!"22 (276). What Natty knows Mahtoree must consider is endorsed by Hard-Heart:

> "Tell me, Pawnee, have you ever, in your traditions heard of a Mighty People, who once lived on the shores of the Salt Lake, hard by the rising sun,—"
> "The earth is white, by people of the colour of my father."
> "Nay, nay, I speak not, now, of any strollers who have crept into the land to rob the lawful owners of their birth-right." [277]

What the white man brings—other than dispossession, theft, and eventual elimination—is the kind of deracination noted in Mahtoree; he loses his own racial and religious identity and receives in return only the debased forms of an acquisitive and godless conqueror:23

> We have every where endeavored to show, that, while Mahtoree was in all essentials a warrior of the Prairies, he was much in advance of his people, in those acquirements which announce the dawnings of civilization. He had held frequent communion with the traders and troops of the Canadas, and the intercourse had unsettled many of those wild opinions which were his birth-right, without perhaps substituting any others, of a nature sufficiently definite to be profitable. His reasoning was rather subtle than true and his philosophy far more audacious than profound. [288]

It is hardly surprising that, at the end, Hard-Heart is given some tactfully reserved doubts about the white civilization's will to allow his existence.

Religion and morality are central to Cooper's vision of the future republic, and we have already noted how frequently Cooper admits into his novel criticism of their practice. Natty's rejection of the settlements' immoralities and twisting of Christian principle is ubiquitous. In *The Pioneers* Christian charity is a virtuous but futile afterthought—and can be nothing else. It is tempting to see Inez, a "bright vision," and her piety on the rock as an emblem of that futility, but she does inspire Middleton to scale the rock; she will live to perform the queenly pious functions of her station in life. Her consort, though the novel renders him as usually ineffective without the aid of Natty, does exhibit values and virtues which we admire and must see as animating principles for the society he is made so comprehensively to represent. His magnanimity and respect for law and honor are nothing if not dignified: "I should forget not only my gratitude, but my duty to the laws, were I to leave this prisoner in your hands even by his own consent, without knowing the nature of his crime, in which we may have all been his innocent accessaries" (351). His gratitude to Natty, like Elizabeth Temple's, is sincere, of course—"take all, or anything!"—and the moment is a moving one. He can give Natty his dog but cannot give back to Natty what he has lost, any more than Elizabeth could. It is, perhaps, Ellen Wade who offers the best moral hope for the settlement life; she is capable of the fullest moral response. She meets her dilemmas robustly; she is conscious of her obligations to Ishmael and cannot, with ease, simply make the best of the opportunity that offers. Even in making her choice of Hover, she is sensitive to the Bushes' feelings and capable of a dignified rendering of her consciousness of gratitude to them.

> "You took me a fatherless, impoverished, and friendless orphan," she said struggling to command her voice, "when others, who live in what may be called affluence compared to your state, chose to forget me, and may heaven in its goodness bless you for it. The little I have done, will never pay you for that one act of kindness. I like not your manner of life; it is different from the ways of my childhood and it is different from my wishes, still, had you not led this sweet and unoffending lady from her friends, I should never have quitted you, until you yourself had said, 'go, and the blessing of God go with you!'"
> [349–50]

She has a moral consciousness that is a model of liberal democratic principle.

Cooper's future state clearly will not be free of class considerations in some way related to religion. He rarely fails to mark class distinctions: between Ellen and Esther in their appearance and language, between yeoman Hover and gentleman Middleton, between Inez and Ellen. Ishmael fully recognizes—and early—that Ellen is better suited to settlement life than to that of the raw frontier, and, though he does not intend it to be so, it is a class recognition. Bush's specific rejection of law and church religion is related to class. Ellen's religious and moral scruples, so clearly the result of education and upbringing, are likewise class markers.

The distinction made between Inez and Ellen has clearly a romance basis: Inez is the aristocratic beauty of ethereal aspect, a fitting bride for a romance hero, while Ellen, ever willing to serve Inez, exists on a more humanly estimable plane—hers is an active rather than a described virtue. But for all her virtues, she is of a lower class and accepts that she is. Natty is often clearly shown as of the servant class and is so taken by Inez; Natty is quite conscious, too, of class limits, of what is—and is not—appropriate to propose to a gentleman, although of course this is not permitted to impair his leadership role in appropriate circumstances in the narrative.[24]

The most striking instance of Cooper's class distinctions appears when we are told of the future destinies of Paul and Ellen, Middleton and Inez; the distinctions are carefully maintained. Middleton rises in the governmental structure and shows Paul favor and opportunity, and he in turn rises—but never to Middleton's level—through his own merits and industry, by a process of Jeffersonian improvement. The message of both class and republican national progress is conveyed with great directness.

Middleton was soon employed in various situations of responsibility and confidence, which both served to elevate his character in the public estimation and to afford the means of patronage. The bee-hunter was among the first of those to whom he saw fit to extend his favor. It was far from difficult to find situations suited to the abilities of Paul in the state of society that existed three and twenty years ago in those regions. The efforts of Middleton and Inez in behalf of her husband were warmly and sagaciously seconded by Ellen, and they succeeded, in process of time, in working a great and beneficial change in his character. He soon became a landholder, then a prosperous cultivator of the soil, and shortly after a town-officer. By that progressive change in fortune, which in the republicks is often seen to be so singularly accompanied by a corresponding improvement in knowledge and self-respect, he went on, from step to step, until his wife enjoyed the maternal delight of seeing her children placed far beyond the danger of returning to that state from which both their parents had issued. Paul is, actually, at this moment, a member of the lower branch of the Legislature of the state where he has long resided, and he is even notorious for making speeches, that have a tendency to put that deliberative body in good humour, and which as they are based on great practical knowledge suited to the condition of the country, possess a merit that is much wanted in many more subtle and fine spun theories that are daily heard in similar assemblies, to issue from the lips of certain instinctive politicians. [376]

This summary conclusion, based, we are told, on Middleton's information, is an exemplary wish fulfillment of Cooper's hopes for the future. It also conveniently evades the questions raised by *The Pioneers*. What happened? Hover rose by his own merits and the patronage of a benevolent member of a superior class, as it is written that such as Hover should. But while we accept the fiction, it cannot eliminate the memory of Templeton, and Temple's patronage there.[25]

The beneficiaries of the future Cooper desires and projects do not bear its costs, nor can they alter its consequences. Set against Cooper's hopes for a civilization is Natty's exclamation: "What this world of America is coming to, and where the machinations and inventions of its people are to have an end, the Lord, he only knows" (250). Collapsing his own experience with that of Tamenund, he implicitly insists that what will happen can be no different from what has happened over the past century and more:

"I have seen in my day, the chief, who in his time, had beheld the first christian that plac'd his wicked foot in the regions of York! How much has the beauty of the wilderness been deformed in two short lives! My own eyes were first opened on the shores of the Eastern sea, and well do I remember that I tried the virtues of the first rifle I ever bore, after such a march, from the door of my father to the forest, as a stripling could make between sun and sun, and that without offence to the rights, or prejudices, of any man who set himself up to be the owner of the beasts of the fields. Natur' then lay in its glory along the whole coast, giving a narrow stripe between the woods and the ocean to the greediness of the settlers. And where am I now! Had I the wings of an eagle, they would tire before a tenth of the distance, which separates me from that sea, could be passed; and towns, and villages, farms and highways, churches, and schools, in short all the inventions and deviltries of man are spread across the region! I have known

the time when a few red-skins shouting along the borders, could set
the Provinces in a fever, and men were to be armed, and troops were
to be called to aid from a distant land, and prayers were said, and the
women frightened, and few slept in quiet, because the Iroquois was
on the war path, the accursed Mingo had the tomahawk in hand.
How is it now. The country sends out her ships to foreign lands to
wage their battles, cannon are plentier than the rifle used to be, and
trained soldiers are never wanting in tens of thousands, when need
calls for their services. Such is the difference atween a Province and a
State, my men; and I, miserable and worn out as I seem, have liv'd to
see it all!" [250–51]

The advance of United States empire, signaled by the presence of Middleton and by the Lewis survey (twice referred to—117, 187), foretells the
iteration of Natty's and the Indians' past experience: "It will not be long
afore an accursed band of choppers and loggers will be following on their
heels to humble the wilderness which lies so broad and rich on the western
banks of the Mississippi, and then the land will be a peopled desert from
the shores of the Maine sea to the foot of the Rocky Mountains, fill'd with
all the abominations and craft of man and stript of the comfort and
loveliness it received from the hand of the Lord!" (187). The injustice
implicit in the Louisiana Purchase is specifically registered by Hard-Heart:
"And where were the chiefs of the Pawnee-Loups, when this bargain was
made. . . . Is a nation to be sold like the skin of the beaver!"[26] (188). The
future forlornly envisaged by Natty and the present resentment of the
Pawnee are referred to the past for the authentication of a pattern that
Natty sees as unlikely to change: "Right enough, right enough; and where
were truth and honesty also. But might is right according to the fashions of
the 'arth and what the strong choose to do, the weak must call justice. If
the Law of the Wahcondah was as much hearkened to, Pawnee, as the laws
of the Long knives, your right to the Prairies would be as good as that of
the greatest chief in the settlements, to the house which covers his head"
(188). The echo of *The Pioneers* rings loud in *The Prairie*: "Might is
right." While nature, Natty, and the Indians are destroyed by white civilization, with them goes a kind of absolutism about moral and legal issues
that the civilization requires and sentimentally respects; in *The Pioneers*
and *The Prairie* repeated attempts are made to absorb Natty, and they fail
not because they are insincere but because they are merely sentimental.[27]

The rule of law is fundamental to Cooper's civilization; it is the largest part of "our sense of political justice"—it beds uneasily with Natty's "might is right." It is coherent with religion and morality. In *The Prairie* early on, Natty confides to Ellen his sense that the law is necessary: "The law—'Tis bad to have it, but, I sometimes think, it is worse to be entirely without it. Age and weakness have brought me to feel such weakness, at times. Yes—yes, the law is needed, when such as have not the gifts of strength and wisdom are to be taken care of" (27). His reluctance recalls for the reader his experience with a wretchedly inadequate law in *The Pioneers*, which Natty will relate more explicitly and bitterly later in the novel. The extension of central power announced by the arrival of Middleton and Lewis in the West announces also the arrival of the law; it is not accidental that Bat comes to the rock to help release Inez in the name of the central government and the law. To Phoebe Bush, defending the stronghold, the word "laws" is sufficient to identify an "enemy"; she sees clearly Ellen's affiliation: "I know you, Nelly Wade; you are with the lawyers in your heart, and if you come a foot nigher, you shall have frontier punishment" (153). While Cooper will never endorse lawlessness, he concedes that Esther Bush's gleeful resistance to the law is "not without its secret charms" (119), and, in any case, he has a longer and more significant tale to tell of the Bushes and the law. It is immediately following the rescue of Inez that Cooper so firmly endorses "the enviable distinction of citizen in a government of laws" (156). When Middleton chooses to remain in the Bush encampment for Natty's trial, he does so out of a sense of an obligation both moral and legal; Hard-Heart too, we suppose, shares that sense.

Those laws are under severe stress on the far frontier: they are threatened by the violence and evil of Ishmael and Abiram, what Natty in another place characterizes more generally as "human weakness"; although Ishmael may not have murdered, lethal violence is commonplace on the frontier, as Hover makes clear (58). Ellen's shudder of revulsion marks her for the settlement. While Natty's response to the issue of vengeance is more philosophical, what he says points, in its terms, to a radical fault in "political justice": " 'Each one knows the ties which bind him to his fellow creatur's best,' he answered. 'Though it is greatly to be mourned, that colour, and property, and tongue, and l'arning, should make so wide a difference in those who, after all, are but the children of one Father!' " (58). Ishmael's claim to an equal right to the land, as has already been noted, also places some stress on the legitimization of property; Natty's conversation with Hard-Heart—"Is a nation to be sold like a beaver"?—operates even more strongly to question the coherence of justice with law. For Natty, whatever his particular quarrels with the law have been, the ultimate criticism of those laws is the offense they offer to divine law in their legitimization of the willful destruction of God's creation and of the impoverishment of his children of color.

The history of the Bushes is perhaps the most revealing tale told in *The Prairie*; it is a tale of progress to civilization into which, at the end, they are absorbed.[28] This result is not in the least predictable at their introduction to the reader: they do not in any way fulfill the expectations of the opening paragraphs. They seem a brutal tribal force opposing the energetic ambitions delineated at the outset; they are quite without an animating motive, neither that of the swarming settlers nor that of Daniel Boone. Ishmael Bush and his family are animalistic, thriftless, and brutal—ruled only by the time of day and the needs of the moment, their animal needs for food and shelter. Bush has no vision of the future; he will continue west, he says, "Until I see reason to stop, or to turn again" (24). Although he seems so marginal to civilized life, his sons' "whirlwind" spoliation of a small woodland growth reminds Natty and the reader of how typical he is. His opposition to and contempt for institutionalized law is everywhere apparent; he regards it as an intrusion on his freedom. Esther concurs and raises his children to express a hearty contempt for the law. As patriarch-tyrant, as a matter of explicit policy, Ishmael rules his tribe, ruthlessly, by force. In one particular, however, he finds common cause with "civilization": he aligns himself with white Christian power. When Natty judges himself harshly for participating in battle, without knowing "the right of the quarrel, as well as a man of three score and ten, should know the reason of his acts afore he takes mortal life, which is a gift he can never return!" (64), Ishmael comforts him: "It is of small account what may be the ground-work of a disturbance, when it's a Christian against a savage" (64). Is Ishmael more primitive than Warley?

In the ideological opening paragraphs of chapter 6 in which "the march of civilization" is so confidently affirmed, Cooper most clearly characterizes Bush as its enemy:

Ishmael Bush had passed the whole of a life of more than fifty years on the skirts of society. He boasted that he had never dwelt where he might not safely fell every tree he could view from his own threshold; that the law had rarely been known to enter his clearing, and that his ears had never willingly admitted the sound of a church bell. His exertions seldom exceeded his wants, which were peculiar to his class, and rarely failed of being supplied. He had no respect for any learning except that of the leech; because he was ignorant of the application of any other intelligence, than such as met the senses. [66]

In each particular Bush is so defined: he builds nothing; he is a thriftless destroyer and purely a creature of the senses, resistant to the restraints of law and religion. And yet, though an enemy, he is, as white Christian, an ally. His absorption by civilization is possible, while Natty's is not.[29]

The murder of Asa Bush stirs new feelings among the family; along with the desire for vengeance, there is an affecting display of human grief.[30] However awkward the Bushes are with their pieties and emotions in chapter 13, they seem only the more genuinely human for being so. As their tale proceeds, we note that Inez carefully distances Ishmael from Abiram as less culpable in her abduction, as Ishmael himself earlier had done; under the pressure of the loss of her son, Esther's Christian principles become more evident and influential. As the moment approaches when Ishmael must assume the role—if not the robes and institutional office—of judge, the tone perceptibly changes. Cooper signals his intention: "Circumstances were about to transpire that might leave a lasting impression on the wild fortunes of their semi-barbarous condition" (341). Esther's coarse maternal chiding is "tempered by something like the milder dignity of parental authority" (342). The role forced on Ishmael by crime within the tribe confers on him an unsought dignity:

> There is something elevating in the possession of authority, however it may be abused. The mind is apt to make some efforts to prove the fitness between its qualities and the condition of its owner, though it may often fail, and render that ridiculous which was only hated before. But the effect on Ishmael Bush was not so disheartening. Grave in exterior, saturnine by temperament, formidable by his physical means and dangerous from his lawless obstinacy, his self-constituted tribunal excited a degree of awe, to which even the intelligent Middleton could not bring himself to be entirely insensible. [343]

Crude as his knowledge of the law is—an eye for an eye, a tooth for a tooth—he dispenses his judgments "without fear or favour" and finds

Middleton's offer of favor offensive (344); "reason"—and Esther—have shown him the error of his ways, and he releases Inez. His rationalizations do not always hold water and are even comic, but his judgments are remarkable in their consistency. He respects the right of Hard-Heart to his prisoners and piously lays to rest Esther's lingering doubts of his fidelity. He is magnanimous in his treatment of Ellen and rational in not wanting to set himself up as "a ruler of inclinations"; he concedes her right to choose Hover and the settlement over the nomadic life Bush himself has to offer her. He treats Abiram, his brother-in-law, in exactly the way he had intended to treat Natty and is proof against Esther's plea for mercy without being insensitive to the dilemma she is in.

Clearly, in all of this, Cooper is preparing the Bushes for the settlement—civilizing them. It is curious that, uninstructed and awkward as he is in the law which is so crucial to civilization, Bush performs more convincingly than Temple did in *The Pioneers*. We are bound to remember the earlier trial since it too involved Natty, and when we do we must register the conviction that, for consistency and for lack of favor, Temple is no match for Bush. Although Bush can offer no mercy on rational or biblical grounds, he is deeply enough stirred in his spirit to return to the place of execution to afford Abiram decent burial. Doubtless, the piety that emerges in chapter 32 is clumsy—it is new to the Bushes; but it is hard—and at variance with their performance—to maintain that they did worse with the law and the Bible than far better qualified, civilized practitioners. As Cooper remarks of Esther's fitful Bible reading, "In this manner Esther had made a sort of convenient ally of the word of God, rarely troubling it for counsel, however, except when her own incompetency to avert an evil was too apparent to be disputed. We shall leave casuists to determine how far she resembled any other believers in this particular" (357). What they take with them as they disappear into the civilized settlements is not worse than what they will find. I do not wish to glamorize them as they depart, but simply to note that on the whole, in the outcome, they are able to exhibit a far better understanding of some basic tenets of civilization than the civilization itself has so far shown. We need not, in drawing attention to the effect, assign that specific intention to Cooper; nor should we be foolish enough to imagine that the Bushes will be any less greedy, destructive, and racist than the civilization they have joined.

For if, detail by detail as in the story of the Bushes, Cooper casts a somber light on the prospects for civilization, his relentless inscribing of its cupidity invites wholesale condemnation. Early in the first chapter the note is struck—but only in passing:

> In the pursuit of adventures, such as these, men are ordinarily governed by their habits or deluded by their wishes. A few, led by the phantoms of hope, and ambitious of sudden affluence, sought the mines of the virgin territory; but by far the greater portion of the emigrants were satisfied to establish themselves along the margins of the larger water-courses, content with the rich returns that the generous alluvial bottoms of the rivers never fail to bestow on the most desultory industry. [10]

Cooper sets against the industrious husbandmen, exemplars of rational agrarian principle, the "few" drawn ever by gross acquisitiveness, who must remind the reader that Doolittle preceded Natty in the movement west. At this juncture it is "a few"; in the text at large the developing civilization itself is charged with "cupidity," a word first heard, ambiguously, from the mouth of Oliver.

The issue of greed is addressed most insistently in relation to the Indians. Natty and Cooper concur in calling the Indians "the rightful owners" (27), "the ancient, and perhaps more lawful occupants, of the country" (107).[31] Natty thus expresses his disaffected acceptance in his old age of human greed: "Natur is much the same, let it be covered by what skin it may. Do you ever find your longings after riches less when you have made a good crop than before you were master of a kernel of corn. If you do, you differ from what the experience of a long life, tells me is the common cravings of man" (77); his assessment is massively supported by the insistence of all the Indians on the predations of white European Christian settlers. The romance distinction of good Indian and bad Indian withers before the issue, in *The Prairie* as it did in *The Last of the Mohicans*. Weucha, the craven and deceitful Sioux, first raises the issue: "Have the pale faces eaten their own buffaloes, and taken the skins from all their own beavers . . . that they come to count how many are left among the Pawnees?" (44). Mahtoree, his chief, with his first words reiterates the point:"The earth is very large; . . . why can the children of my great white father never find room on it?" (45). At one of Mahtoree's most menacing moments, in the night visit to the Bush encampment, resentment at white greed constitutes his motive; he is "jealous and resentful of the inroads of the stranger."

Just as Magua is aligned on this issue with Chingachgook and with Tamenund (whose presence in *The Prairie* is so strongly recalled in Natty's oration, "I have seen in my day, the chief who, in his time, had beheld the first Christian that placed his wicked foot in the regions of York!" [250]), so Mahtoree and Weucha align with Hard-Heart, Le Balafré, and Natty. Hard-Heart and Le Balafré, like Chingachgook before them, have peaceable instincts, Hard-Heart specifically prides himself on Pawnee hospitality, and Natty's entire history identifies him in this with Hard-Heart; even so, all are conscious of those who "rob the lawful owners of their birthright" (277), "the Christians [who] rob the heathens of their inheritance" (190), to produce, in Cooper's words, "this wronged and humbled people" (185). Hard-Heart's indignation at being "sold" by the whites has been cited. Although his direct knowledge of the whites is sparse, his ears are open; he "even alluded to the steady march, which the nation of his 'Great Father' as he courteously termed the government of the States, was making towards, the hunting-grounds of his tribe. It was apparent, however, by this singular mixture of interest, contempt and indignation that were occasionally gleaming through the reserved manner of this warrior, that he knew the strange people, who were thus trespassing on his native rights, much more by report than by any actual intercourse" (189). He knows perfectly well what this movement portends, and the knowledge draws from him a condemnation of the arrogant greed of the invader: "The Red-skins find the Big-knives as easily as the stranger sees the buffaloe, or the travelling birds, or the falling snow. Your warriors think the Master of Life has made the whole earth white; they are mistaken. They are pale, and it is their own faces that they see. Go, a Pawnee is not blind, that he need look long for your people!" (195). It is not without point that Cooper inserts into this exchange between Hard-Heart and Natty a dignified memorial of "that once mighty but now fallen people, the Delawares of the Hills" (191). The destroying power, as we have noted, is a Christian power; as Natty remarks of "kings," "Them did [God] create men; but they have eaten like famished wolves" (107). If religious principle should lie at the heart of the civilization Cooper desires, one must conclude that it is rotten at the heart. Although Le Balafré, like Chingachgook in his age, speaks for peace, he too shares that sense of white cupidity: "Why cannot his people see every thing, since they crave all" (314).

The Indians, here the Sioux, do not understand the process that is engulfing them: "[Mahtoree] had heard of a Great Council, at which the Menahashah, or Long knives and the Washsheomantiqua, or Spaniards, had smoked together, when the latter had sold to the former their incomprehensible rights over those vast regions, through which his nation had roam'd, in freedom, for so many ages. His simple mind had not been able to embrace the reasons why one people should thus assume a superiority over the possessions of another" (223–24).[32] But Mahtoree, in his final exchange with Hard-Heart, understands the political consequences only too well; he assumes the worst, as Hard-Heart in his generosity of spirit cannot: "Where a Pale-face comes, a red-man cannot stay. The land is too small. They are always hungry. See, they are here already" (335). Although Hard-Heart refuses the alliance against the white even as he bids farewell to Middleton, he does not in the least lose his consciousness of the threat: "With a delicacy, that none knew better how to practise than an Indian warrior, he made no direct mention of the rapacious temper, that so many of them had betrayed, in their dealings with the red-men" (367). Two pages earlier, Cooper openly endorses Hard-Heart's misgivings: "In short, the victors seemed to have lost every trace of ferocity with their success, and appeared disposed to consult the most trifling of the wants of that engrossing people, who were daily encroaching on their rights, and reducing the red-men of the West, from their state of proud independence to the condition of fugitives and wanderers" (365). Cooper's determination that the reader not lose sight of the *continuing* process constructively damages our view of the civilization he desires.

Natty's refusal to join the party bound eastward for civilization is not simply a preference for the prairie. Like Crèvecoeur, with different motives but similar reasons, he withdraws in his "desperate resignation" to an Indian village. His passing of his last days with his Indian "son" is not merely a gesture of sentimental affinity for the wild but rather one of solidarity with those whom the civilization must destroy. He constantly aligns the destruction of his natural habitat with the destruction of the Indians. He sees clearly that the same hand wrought both results and that what has been is what will be.

Cooper's irresistible sense of the terrible destiny the Indian faces is put succinctly by his contemporary, Tocqueville:[33]

From whichever side we consider the destinies of the aborigines of North America, their calamities appear irremediable: if they continue barbarous, they are forced to retire; if they attempt to civilize themselves, the contact of a more civilized community subjects them to oppression and destitution. They perish if they continue to wander from waste to waste, and if they attempt to settle they still must perish. The assistance of Europeans is necessary to instruct them, but the approach of Europeans corrupts and repels them into savage life. They refuse to change their habits as long as their solitudes are their own, and it is too late to change them when at last they are forced to submit. [*Democracy* 1:354]

The evidence of *The Prairie* does not suggest that Cooper could reach a more optimistic conclusion or would assign the blame any less forcefully and scornfully than Tocqueville did. Just as Tocqueville is certain that the eloquent Cherokee appeal will fall on deaf ears, we may be sure that Hard-Heart's will go unheard.

So much has already been said here of Natty and it is so clearly his book that his ubiquity speaks for itself. His successive encounters with Bush, Hover, Bat, Middleton, and Hard-Heart each brings out a familiar facet of his character and specific points of reference to his past. Each has been touched upon incidentally, and no summary is required. But Natty, now in advanced old age, conscious of his closeness to death, affectingly nostalgic for white company despite the consequences it has had for him, is treated quite differently in *The Prairie* from what we observe in the other books.

He is, at last, capable of carrying the mythic significance so often assigned to him. His introduction into the novel and his death scene are almost enough alone to confer epic stature upon him, melancholy but grand. More important, his years of life allow him to survey with authority the past as he repeatedly evokes it into the novel's present; his particular memories, pleasurable and disaffected, summon the previous novels into *The Prairie*. His more generalized sense of his own life—and the life of the nation—enables us, more than any other factor does, to assess the history to which he has been witness and of which he is the victim. For all Cooper's hopes for the civilization, he frequently and specifically acts to endorse Natty's view of that history.

Natty's piety is so often shown, he orates so often on the subject, that we are apt to become bored and take it for granted simply as a characteristic of Natty at death's door. That would be a mistake. His radical belief is always associated with his account of history and mankind, and stands in a hostile and critical relationship to a civilization that, in its making, abandons its pieties, its very laws. He insists to the end on society's "immoralities." Even when he bids Hover back to the settlements, he says, "Forget anything you may have heard from me, which is nevertheless true, and strive to turn your mind on the ways of the inner country" (373). Natty's suggestion that to thrive we must forget challenges James P. Elliott's suggestion that Hover's value as a legislator stems in part from his experience of Natty (xxvii). While Elliott may be right, his reading is only pious, while Natty's is more realistic. He knows that his voice will be heard only as a piety and will have as little effect as it has already had. Natty's distrust of human reason is not the result of prejudice; he judges human society and human nature not abstractly but by its fruits, and, in spite of what he knows, he continues to aid his fellow creature. Natty's submission to God is the result of his concluding that God at least can be trusted and, on the evidence of his life, almost nothing or no one else can. Nor is his a coarse literal fundamentalism; his responses to Bat evince not a superstitious belief in the Word but an active and imaginative sense of a garden despoiled in verified experience. He accepts the lesson of the Bible, remembered from the "good Moravians'" lessons: "I remember to have heard it, then and there said that the blessed Land was once fertile as the bottoms of the Mississippi, and groaning with its stores of grain and fruits; but that the judgment has since fallen upon it, and that it is now more remarkable for its barrenness than any qualities to boast of" (239). His own prophecy of America's desert is founded on observation. He has, as Hard-Heart remarks, "seen all that there is to be seen in this country."

Notwithstanding, Cooper offers Natty in *The Prairie* as father to the States, to which Natty professes explicit allegiance. His function in blazing the trail and aiding the settlers is clear enough, but here he is made an adopting father to Ellen, Paul, Hard-Heart, and Middleton—as he was before to Uncas and Oliver—and by implication to the nation itself. When "the old man, with his own hands, shoved the boat into the current, wishing God to speed them" (374), the implicit blessing is on the nation itself.

For all this, is he the "figure of significant myth" so routinely claimed? If so, what does the myth signify? His status as victim or witness, even prophet, can quickly be assented to. His example of absolute piety and submission to God will not be emulated—that much is clear in the book.

A community that respects Natty will be the better for it, but there is in the books no evidence that his example *is* actively respected and plenty that it is ignored.

Is Natty yet, in *The Prairie*, the "*beau idéal*" that Cooper was later to claim him as? While he is pious, brave, considerate, far above the blood-thirsty servant-scout he so often was in *Mohicans*, he offers an ideal that society's practice finds profitless. He is not then an ideal for his society but only an idealization. Even the life of integration with nature he has lost is never seen as *lived*. Only as lyrical *recall* in *Mohicans*, *The Pioneers*, and *The Prairie* is it present; it is marked by its absence.

Does Natty then embody the nation's values, its highest virtues? Middleton specifically denies it; Natty could never attain his "proper elevation and importance, for no other reason, than because [he] grew in the forest" (114). But the clearings have no better to show; Natty does not—cannot—animate a civilization that disparages him. The strength of the novels is that they frankly offer this; it is not *their* embarrassment that Cooper does not, so to speak, make *his* point, if indeed he did intend to offer Natty as the embodiment of national values.

D. E. S. Maxwell is drawn, along with other critics and biographers, to discuss Cooper in terms of his reflection of the postrevolutionary debate among Jefferson, Adams, and Hamilton between agrarian and commercial positions. Maxwell is correct, I think, in asserting that Hamilton and Cooper are fundamentally more in agreement than Cooper would have cared to allow. Usually critics who take such approaches mark his embrace in theory of Jeffersonian and Jacksonian democratic principles and his countervailing leanings to aristocratic notions, and to institutions and laws as being of supreme importance to society; they note also the failure of laws to control, by their wholesome principles, the democratic body politic and the emergence of a materialistic acquisitive spirit, cupidity, and demos run wild. Cooper's inability to resolve for himself such issues and his lapse into defeatist conservative positions, both social and religious, are clear enough in his career as a novelist.

Cooper's dilemma—embodied in the novels by the conflict between Natty's radical conservative piety and absolutism, and Temple's civilized Christian rule of law—is real enough but is not really the issue. It is rather his unflinching *registration* in the novels of such dilemmas. History had already disallowed a resolution of the dilemma, and resolution would amount therefore to misrepresentation. Maxwell certainly is respectful of the value of Cooper's refusal "to force a comprehensive reconciliation on the successive and distinctive parts of the historical process from anarchy to order" (*American Fiction*, 120). He compares Cooper in this to Keats's negative capability, and to T. S. Eliot's impersonality. The comparison is revealing in its aesthetic and conservative preferences, as it is in its failure to scrutinize the "order" and laws Maxwell assumes to be unquestionably monolithic. By the same token, Cooper's politics, liberal or conservative, or his psychology, his willing assumption of guilt, are not the issue either; his critical spirit, his honest seeing and representing, allows the reader to see the basic cupidity, partisan interests, and racism—including his own—that ideals, which are usually unexamined however liberal and charitable they may be, serve usually to conceal.

Seeing Natty only as an ideal doomed to futility fails to capture how integral Natty is to an understanding of the civilization Cooper wishes to endorse. While a resolution eludes Cooper, Maxwell is willing to hazard one—and he is not untypical in doing so; the idea that he offers as a resolution is implicit in the attitudes of Oliver, Heyward, and Middleton: "Imperfect though they may be, only institutions can preserve a social harmony; and only such ideals as Natty represents can preserve institutions from autocratic abuse" (*American Fiction*, 138–39). So, in effect, Natty is marginalized. I decline to scrutinize more closely the assumptions behind that "social harmony," hoping that my view of that is already apparent. But one must say that there is no *social* harmony in *The Deerslayer*, and the reader, who recalls from *The Pioneers* the society erected near the site of the Redcoats' bloody slaughter (to which Maxwell is here referring), can only with severe qualification accept the phrase.

In the light of this, we must finally ask what is to be made of an idealized Natty, whom we may well realistically see—without cynicism—as a superannuated, marginal simpleton whose fate is pathetic rather than heroic. And, if he is *that*, what possible value can he have? His example is not followed, and, in any conceivable society adumbrated in the works it could not be. History erases Natty; society refuses him. That America will and must destroy what sustains Natty is freely conceded, if, as in Parkman, with regret. The regret, it goes without saying, comforts and ennobles those who express it. It has the weary tone of Eliot's "constitution of silence." Cooper's novels are not part of that "constitution" that Maxwell endorses.

The solution offered by Maxwell then is this: Man is imperfect by Natty's exacting standard, and man's society is inevitably flawed; but if it remembers Natty—if it does not forget the presocial virtues Natty embodies—the society will be the better for it. This sentimental reconciliation is only too clear in Middleton's remonstrance and eulogy of Natty, in the headstone he erects and in the one Oliver erects to his grandfather, in the desire of the society to take Natty in at the end of both *The Prairie* and *The Pioneers*—futile gestures—and in the legendary remembrance of him in *Home as Found*.

Why is it that America, Cooper's desired "civilization" that is to say, so adept at absorption, at co-option, cannot stomach Natty? While Natty's *life* cannot be replicated and, therefore, poses no problem—except as a museum piece, an appropriate object for melancholy reflection in idle moments, or a "stump of time"—the radical *meaning* of Natty's life, its economy and its morality toward nature and man, is *at enmity* with a society based on acquisition of wealth (in land or money), cupidity, and profit, and on class, exploitation, and genocide.[34] How can a society endorse and emulate an example that denies its very nature? Temple's idealism about the law and the future, however well-meant, masks a society whose driving concern is the ownership of property; the alliance of Temple and Jones already noted is not simply an ironic mischance or the result of Temple's weakness—Jones is only more coarse and frank about it all. It is not then anything so polite as a dilemma but a historically unresolved and theoretically unresolvable opposition. Each must render the other a lie.

Whether Cooper intends this opposition or not is not now important; that his novels allow us to see it is. To say this is not at all to "solve" the problem of Cooper's dilemma but to render its value. This view forbids a dismissal on grounds of generic, aesthetic, or political confusion; it enforces Cooper's value as an expresser of political conflict, not as a defective solver of political problems in fictional forms. It also forbids the consignment of Natty into the margins of myth, however significant. It invites America to confront its greed and racism. The invitation is usually not answered.

While any reading of *Mohicans* is profoundly affected by the memory of *The Pioneers*, and by the complication afforded by the achronological order of the appearance of the two books, the operation of memory is both extended and intensified in our reading of *The Prairie*. In 1827, Cooper was as much at the mercy of what he had already written as are his readers at the mercy of what they have already read. Cooper had chosen in *The Pioneers* to proceed dialectically; in *The Prairie*, while Cooper has clearly not abandoned that choice, in a certain sense he had no choice. As he approached what seemed then the final book, the fifty years spanned between *Mohicans* and *The Prairie* exerted their own power. We are compelled to remember.

The republican values Cooper expresses everywhere are, if anything, more pronounced in *The Prairie* than they were in *The Pioneers*, but they do not erase the past. Memory is constantly pitted against the forgetting that a single-minded republican ideology would represent. Indeed it is not too much to say that Cooper makes of the necessity he has constructed for himself a virtue, and even a technique, in the acts of both writing and reading. We are not merely free to remember but are constantly and deliberately reminded. As we recall, we are protected against the seductive power of civilization's pieties and enter inevitably into critique. It is not, I believe, possible in an attentive reading to sustain the view that all that Cooper offers is sad testimony to the pathos of history; rather, he gives profound and fearless insight into the dialectic that must precede historical understanding. He is as relevant in the reading of today's speech by George Bush (or yesterday's by John Kennedy) as he is to the understanding of the tract of history that he directly addressed.

Fixed in his own guiding ideas, Cooper knew that history was not fixed and could not guarantee, and had not guaranteed, the fulfillment of ideology. Memory afforded him—and his readers—that. When Natty instructs Paul Hover to "forget" what is nonetheless "true," he is prescribing what is—patently, I suggest—an impossibility to which Cooper's novels, for the reader at least, attest.

FIVE ✳ *The Pathfinder* (1840)

A MATTER OF CHOICE

Try to forget all that is disagreeable, and to remember only the pleasant part of the matter.
– James Fenimore Cooper, The Pathfinder

The conclusion to my chapter on *The Prairie* may seem strident; what I have done there is to gather and place on an equal footing with the mythicized Leather-Stocking all those elements in which the civilization that rejects Natty stands condemned. In the context of a critical tradition that has usually stressed Natty as *beau idéal*, it must seem harsh, at the moment of Natty's greatest elevation, to insist upon what Natty means and why the civilization which he blesses, and which celebrates him, is clearly incapable of absorbing him. I am as responsive as the next critic to Cooper's desire to idealize Natty and to the attraction of the imposing figure Natty constitutes in isolation—but Natty *is* isolated; his very isolation registers the distance between the idealization of Natty and the historical reality. The evidence for that, as I hope I have shown, abounds in the text, and to allow the idealization to dominate the text is to misrepresent and impoverish it.

Orm Overland, among recent critics, offers the fullest reading so far of *The Prairie*; it is detailed and subtle, and he is fully aware of the novel's contradictions. He draws attention to Cooper's strongly inscribed hopes for American civilization, citing the return, at the novel's final episode, of Middleton and Hover to the Pawnee encampment:

> At length the cavalcade, at whose head rode Middleton and Paul, descended from the elevated plain, on which they had long been journeying, to a luxuriant bottom, that brought them to the level of

the village of the Loups. The sun was beginning to fall, and a sheet of golden light was spread over the placid plain, lending to its even surface, those glorious tints and hues that, the human imagination is apt to conceive, form the embellishment of still more imposing scenes. The verdure of the year yet remained and herds of horses and mules were grazing peacefully in the vast natural pasture, under the keeping of vigilant Pawnee boys. Paul pointed out, among them, the well known form of Asinus, sleek, fat and luxuriating in the fulness of content, as he stood with reclining ears and closed eye-lids, seemingly musing on the exquisite nature of his present indolent enjoyment. [*Prairie*, 377]

Overland observes: "The Great American Desert has become the Garden of the West—and Cooper has presented us with a reversal of the mythic Fall" (171). He gives full weight to the necessity of Natty's exile and his opposition to "the orderly progress of the Middletons of America" (172). He shrewdly points to the justification of Mahtoree in his final exchange with Hard-Heart and the curiously disparaging implication it has for our assessment of the latter's wisdom and foresight. And he is memorably skeptical about Middleton's ineffectual piety in Natty's epitaph, "*May no wanton hand ever disturb his remains*": "The advancing plow, to which one side of Cooper's mind hardly objected, was sure to turn up the remains of the trapper as it in fact did those of the historical Hard-Heart, the admired and noble, but nevertheless doomed Petalesharo" (172). This is well said and registers the distance the critic must take (and Cooper enables) from the novel's dearest pieties. As he says, agreeing with D. E. S. Maxwell and Henry Nash Smith in a line of critical judgment extending back to Francis Parkman, "While [Cooper] could lament the destruction of the natural forests and the decimation of the Indians, he was not prepared to face the fact that these evils were in effect an important part of the foundation of his and the Middletons' way of life" (165). While that may be true of Cooper the man,[1] Overland—like many other critics—converts Cooper's personal dilemma into a critical, interpretive tool, and thus obscures the sheer energy of Cooper's insistent expression of the violence of that "way of life," its palpable lack of the "orderly" in its "progress." Such a position ends by merely echoing the "lament"—which like Natty's epitaph sounds sincerely, but feebly—against what history has told and will have to tell. The rejection of Natty, the destruction of the forest, and the genocide are not just "an important part" of civilization; they are essential to that civilization's empire. The destruction is not just a regrettable byproduct of civilization's construction but essential to it. This common critical position diminishes Cooper's complex unresolved text to a biographical detail of Cooper's psyche, and it disallows the clear sight Cooper affords us in favor of what Roland Barthes characterizes as "*Neither-Norism*":

> It is on the whole a bourgeois figure, for it relates to a modern form of liberalism. We find again here the figure of the scales: reality is first reduced to its analogues; then it is weighed; finally, equality having been ascertained, it is got rid of. Here also there is magical behaviour: both parties are dismissed because it is embarrassing to choose between them; one flees from such an intolerable reality, reducing it to two opposites which balance each other only insomuch as they are purely formal, relieved of all their specific weight. [*Mythologies*, 153][2]

I do not argue here that Overland—or those who agree with him, as I, in almost all his insights, would—is a bad critic or is wrong about Cooper. Nor is my disagreement merely one of emphasis. I argue rather that whatever Cooper's problem might have been and whether he "faced" it or not, his *work* does not encourage its reader to flee the "intolerable reality" but renders reality with striking fullness; it forbids "a magical act ashamed of itself, which verbally makes the gesture of rationality, but immediately abandons [it]" (Barthes, *Mythologies*, 153); it enables Overland's choicest critical points, which are the product not of Cooper's flight from but of his confrontation of the "intolerable reality."

An unsigned review of Cooper's *The Monikins* (1835) observed, "It is the unhappiest idea possible, to suppose that politics can be associated in any effective way, with romance or fiction. One is the *reality*, the other the *ideality* of life. Cohere they cannot; . . . [Cooper] must keep [his works of *fancy*] divorced from all association with the abortive works of *fact*."[3] While we need not here dispute the evaluation of *The Monikins*, the review could hardly make clearer the soothing functions assigned to fiction, then as now. Apart from the poverty of the critical reading of "romance and fiction" it implies and entails,[4] it is not an unusual view of the matter, and it has at least the merit of frankness, so often absent in both the writers and critics of fiction. It freely concedes the release from ugly fact expected of fiction and the elevation of the aesthetic, the ideal, and the fanciful over reality—that is, the social and the political. Given the prevalent criteria available to him,[5] this critic's view is understandable, as is the inclination of Cooper's contemporaries to respond to the Leather-Stocking novels in their romantic elements, but it should make us skeptical about contemporary readings of him. The outrage that greeted his more overtly political novels of the 1830s indicates how little his audience had grasped the political content of his earlier work.

H. Daniel Peck's *A World by Itself* shares the same limitation: "Studies of Cooper's pictorialism, then, are as unsatisfactory as examinations of his social thought and historical consciousness. All of these tend to hold his fiction at a distance, to place it rather than engage its imaginative qualities directly" (xi). Peck goes on to say, "We need a more flexible and responsive criticism, one which takes fuller account of the writer's literary power. . . . For too long, attention has been focused on these secondary roles, and in this study I have attempted to address the artist" (xii). It is true that much attention has been paid to Cooper as social critic[6] and—as in American literary history and criticism generally—to establishing various refractions of "the dominant myths of our culture" (x);[7] it is also true that Peck's book usefully draws attention back to certain virtues of Cooper praised most notably by Balzac but also by Conrad and Lawrence—his construction of spatial worlds. Peck's is a reasonable ambition to have, and many of its critical consequences are estimable. However, his virtual banishment of the political and historical from his text reveals our academy's preference for the "imaginative" as the sole qualifying criterion for "fiction," for "literary" power, for the "artist"; everything else is "secondary" and may be overlooked. What remains unexamined and unargued is only everything: the necessarily secondary nature of the political; the, of course, unpolitical privileging of the literary, narrowly construed; that fiction to be fiction must be "imaginative" (that is, not political, not historical); that the "artist" is not really an artist at all when he engages in "argumentation" or allegory. It should not need to be pointed out that Peck's suppression of the political, the argumentative, and the historical, if applied beyond Cooper, entails the elimination of much that is already in our canons and ensures the continued omission of much that we do not include.[8] The most important consequence, however, of suppressing these concerns is that it leads to a too hasty reading of those elements that do not lend themselves to Bachelard's injunction to "study poetic images in their exalting reality." "The image, in its simplicity . . . has no need of scholarship. It is the property of a naive consciousness" (17).[9] Exclusive attention to Bachelard's "youthful language" leads Peck, as I shall later argue, to a reading of *The Pathfinder* and Natty's significance in it that is seriously misleading.

And yet the appeal of Peck's approach as we open *The Pathfinder* is evident; here, as in *The Deerslayer*, Cooper rejoices the eye with images of lake, forest, and river, which entrance Mabel Dunham. A dozen years have clearly wrought a difference in Cooper.[10] It is immediately evident in the absence from the opening depiction of the terrain of any of the historical, ideological, or political implications we have noted in *The Pioneers*, *The Prairie*, and *The Last of the Mohicans*. Even so, Mabel's response to the landscape in such terms of the sublime, the picturesque, and the beautiful qualifies as an accomplishment of an educated young woman; it, therefore, has for Cooper a class significance and is hence political. The descriptive terms are highly conventional and, as such, can hardly be naive.

The simplicity in tone and texture of *The Pathfinder* is disconcerting after a reading of the three novels that precede it and disallows the somewhat stringent approach I have so far assumed. Notwithstanding its passages of intense emotion and violent action, the plot line is developed in a calm and orderly way; its various elements are well proportioned, clearly related to one another, and, though not without some narrative awkwardness and artificiality in the handling of Muir's deceit and Arrowhead's tale, clear in their outlines. The dénouement neatly resolves the three major elements: the military action, the romance, and the intrigue. The settings—forest and river, lake, fort, and island—are in no sense marginal to the plot, but nor do they bear the same measure of symbolic or prophetic weight they often have in *Mohicans* and *The Prairie*. The novel's central significance, as far as Natty is concerned, is securely anchored in its central romance plot, which is rendered in a pervasive idyllic tone; its morality, centered upon a highly idealized Natty, is coherent and elevated. Not the least of the work's attractions, in fact, lies precisely here: Natty's morality is essential to the tale, and his impeccable response to it is profoundly moving; he is, for once, not merely a choric witness, not a complaining and outraged victim, but the active forger of his own fate, a man making a willing and conscious sacrifice whose full impact is convincingly felt in his own emotions.

The insistent addressing of the issues of ownership of land, by Indian or settler, the bloodshed attending the early struggles of the nation, the spoliation of the land, the price exacted by the march of European civilization from Indian or woodsman, the betrayal of principle—Christian and chivalrous, legal and political—all these issues, so naggingly present in the earlier novels, are omitted, muted, or reduced to mere hints.

The reader who takes the Leather-Stocking tales as a single work—as we are doing—must take the hints offered; Cooper does, after all, concede in both prefaces to the novel the existence of the series and the discrepancies "in the facts" among the separate works, and he obviously makes no attempt to immunize the series from disjunctions in tone or to isolate the novels from each other. At the same time, *The Pathfinder*'s difference is marked. The Natty who deplores so bitterly, for himself and for the Indian, his own humiliation and the destruction and degradation of the Indian is totally absent here. Clearly enough, a romance story line, in which Natty's idealization is essential, is allowed dominance. We may say, then, that there is a disjunction from *Mohicans* and *The Pioneers*, and a centralizing in *The Pathfinder* of the idealization of Natty which is one of the most striking features of *The Prairie*. It is tempting to suspect here a defensive reticence, or psycho-political suppression on Cooper's part, to see the intense mythicization of Natty as his further marginalization.

The muting of the Indian presence in *The Pathfinder* would lend strength to this point of difference: Chingachgook is reduced to a mere actor in the adventure story, not often present except when needed— Cooper accounts for the omission surprisingly in the 1839 preface by noting what he perceives as the lack of variety in Indian character.[11] The Delawares are lamented and extolled but carry little of the stress of complaint evident elsewhere in the series; the Mingoes are predictably excoriated by Natty but act simply as the enemy within the military plot line and the threat in the forest scenes, and—Dew-of-June excepted— they receive little of the complexity of treatment that attends Magua and the Sioux Mahtoree. Likewise, as I have noted, the terrain presented at the opening contains little ideological or historical weight. However, that element is displaced into the prefaces, where what was merely future in *The Pioneers* is inscribed (in 1839) and reaffirmed (in 1851) as achieved and beyond question: "Since that day, light may be said to have broken into the wilderness, and the rays of the sun have penetrated to tens of thousands of beautiful valleys and plains, that then lay in 'grateful shade'.

Towns have been built along the whole of the extended line of coasts, and the traveller now stops at many a place of ten or fifteen, and at one of even fifty, thousand inhabitants, where a few huts then marked the natural sites of future marts" (4–5). Cooper's confidence is qualified: "That great results are intended to be produced by means of these wonderful changes, we firmly believe; but that they will prove to be the precise results now so generally anticipated, in consulting the experience of the past, and taking the nature of man into the account, the reflecting and intelligent may be permitted to doubt." The tone is philosophical and reticent, however, as compared to the implicit and explicit condemnations of the earlier work. In this it is entirely characteristic of the marginal reflections in *The Pathfinder*.

In one sense, the mythicization of Natty is a sort of compensation offered for his elimination, as is coherent with Cooper's firm alliance with civilization expressed in the prefaces; at the same time, it must be recognized that only his elimination can validate the total idealization, the removal from him of all political and historical significance—to affirm this, after all, is only to assume what takes place in the novels. If one wished to speculate psychologically, his idealization of Natty could be seen as balm for a burdensome conscience, Cooper's as well as that of the society he so resoundingly endorses in the novels, the prefaces, and *Notions of the Americans*.

The marginalization into myth of Natty renders more frankly than Cooper intended, perhaps, the ambiguity I addressed at the end of the previous chapter: if a society acts in the way the text says it does, it cannot at the same time meaningfully endorse Natty, and yet the text requires us to receive both propositions. Indeed, the romantic tale told contains and expresses particularly well the mutually exclusive options of civilization and settlements as against nature unspoiled—the perfect life, divinely given; it becomes a matter, precisely, of Jasper *or* Natty, equal in their love for Mabel; it cannot be both,[12] and Mabel must choose. The nearest proximation Natty makes to settlement life in this work is a forest hut; there is certainly no convincing future projection for him of marriage, family, and integration into society. Mabel attempts an accommodation of her dilemma by contemplating Jasper as husband and Natty as surrogate father, which clearly parallels the attempts of Middleton and Elizabeth Temple to retain Natty as a pensioner of civilization. But this is of necessity rejected by Natty, and this rejection is rendered in *The Pathfinder* in emotionally convincing terms. The strain of bearing the memory of his role as committed lover along with the tutelary role of father is too great,[13] as he affectingly recognizes in the final chapter. The polarization necessary both to romance and to Cooper's thematic preoccupations is peacefully accomplished within the love story.

However composed and peaceful the progress of this tale and its enfolding and exposition of theme may be, the reader sees the difference, reads the suppression, and discerns that the love contest of two separate virtues elides the "disgrace" of the historical tale told elsewhere. We know and we remember what has happened, what will happen.[14] At issue is not simply changes of tone, manner, or fictional genre (or, as Henry Nash Smith has argued, a revision of genre); rather, we have a concentration, a more intense focusing of an already familiar set of radical alternatives into a fully realized romance that succeeds in reducing its historical content almost to zero. The reader of the whole series cannot collude in any censorship of memory or any compromise that Cooper's intentions may seem to require but deploys the testimony offered by *The Pathfinder* against that of the other works in the series. That memory has been constituted by Cooper himself.

Cooper, ever sententious, occasionally reflects abstractly on the events taking place. When he does, he sometimes arouses the reader, sensitized to the suggestion by the previous novels, to recall central episodes; for example, in the shooting contest, which itself recalls the turkey shoot of *The Pioneers*, Cooper gratuitously observes: "Nothing [is] so attractive to the unsophisticated as the appearance of rigorous justice; and nothing so rare as its actual administration" (156). Upon Lundie's suspicions of Jasper, Cooper generalizes: "Of all the feelings of the human mind, it is that which is the most treacherous in its workings, the most insidious in its approaches, and the least at the command of a generous temperament. While doubt exists, every thing may be suspected, the thoughts having no definite facts to set bounds to their wanderings, and distrust once admitted it is impossible to say to what extent conjecture may lead, or whither credulity may follow" (197). While Cooper doubtless is here sounding a high Augustan, Cowperian note (see the epigraph to chapter 17), these aids to reflection must surely awaken recollection of the defective justice of Templeton and the operation of suspicion and circumstance there which so torment Natty.

Some of these reflections occasionally show streaks of bitterness:

This truth is just as apparent to-day, in connection with the prodigies of the republic, as it then was in connection with those distant rulers, whose merits it was always safe to applaud, and whose demerits it was treason to reveal. It is a consequence of this mental dependence, that public opinion is so much placed at the mercy of the designing, and the world, in the midst of its idle boasts of knowledge and improvement, is left to receive its truth, on all such points as touch the interests of the powerful and managing, through such a medium, and such a medium only, as may serve the particular views of those who pull the wires.[15] [212]

Others show hints of gratuitous satire: "Of the veracity of the former he entertained the highest respect, while of the latter he thought, as the more observant and intelligent classes of this country are getting pretty generally to think of certain scribblers among ourselves, who are known to have been so long in the habits of mendacity, that it is thought they can no longer tell the truth, even when they seriously make the effort" (405). The biographical foundation[16] of these is not hard to find, and we do not feel constrained to transform them into commentary that deeply disturbs the texture of the romance in hand. While some of Cooper's most profound misgivings about the development of republican democracy are occasionally expressed, in situ they are clearly marginal, as is typical of such moments in the work. A conversation between Muir and Lundie is brought to its close thus: "In truth, while all men act under one common law that is termed human nature, the varieties in their dispositions, modes of judging, feelings and selfishness are infinite" (151). Like the remark on progress and the "nature of man" (5) already given from the 1851 preface, this reflection is so generalized as to be capable of finding its place in a hundred other novels. Unlike the more narrowly directed commentary of the other Leather-Stocking novels, such moments do not usually in *The Pathfinder* elicit any profound perturbations about history.

This critical reticence is also usually evident when memory is explicitly summoned by the text or at other points whose potential for critical extension is left undeveloped. When Natty introduces himself to Mabel it is as the possessor of a deserved reputation, just as later Captain Sanglier recognizes him by his deeds:

"I'm a man well known in all these parts, and perhaps one of my names may have reached your ears. By the Frenchers, and the red-skins on the other side of the Big Lakes, I am called la Longue Carabine; by the Mohicans, a just-minded and upright tribe, what is left of them, Hawk Eye; while the troops and rangers along this side of the water call me Pathfinder, inasmuch as I have never been known to miss one end of the trail, when there was a Mingo, or a friend, who stood in need of me, at the other.". . .

"So they call me, young woman, and many a great lord has got a title that he did not half as well merit." [18]

Natty, as he does throughout the series, engages himself in service to European settlers, here Mabel and the military. Whereas, in the preceding works, the reader is drawn insistently to consider the darker consequences of such service, here we are not. There are many moments in *The Pathfinder* where the reader is led to recall *Mohicans* by Natty's specific or oblique memory of events and themes from the earlier book: Effingham (96), Washington (192), and Cora Munro (54) are specifically brought to mind; Sanglier's request for "honorable retreat" (409) and his world-weary indifference, Natty's caution as he remembers "massacres" (412), and his contemptuous rejection of military notions of "honor" (410), which recalls Jennie's outcry in the block house to her dead husband (341)—all call up a comprehensive memory of *Mohicans*. But, in *The Pathfinder*, Cooper does not insist as he does earlier; the introduction of Natty with his republican sentiments does not involve the massive criticism of the ruling class and race that we found in *Mohicans*. Incidents are usually recalled biographically; reflections on human behavior and such matters as "honor" are incidental and belong to the speaker, and do not penetrate the romance to become preoccupying. The burden for critics of Cooper, however, is not merely to respect the tone of a particular novel in the series; when memory is stimulated as it is here—even if at a low pitch of implication—the question must arise as to how far the reader's memory can be controlled. If *The Pathfinder*'s allusions to *Mohicans* lead to total recall, then the reader either will be perplexed at the difference or will read *The Pathfinder* much more darkly than the written text alone specifically endorses.

This issue is perhaps still more clearly seen in the events surrounding the unjust suspicion of Jasper; it obviously recalls for the reader events that in Natty's life have not yet occurred—the suspicion of Natty as murderer in *The Prairie* and the circumstantial accusation of Natty in *The Pioneers*.

The suspicion of Jasper is eventually as quickly disposed of as that of Natty in *The Prairie*. The dark villainy of Muir matches exactly that of Abiram White. In both *The Pioneers* and *The Pathfinder* Natty is willing to exert physical force as a last resort. But since Jasper and Natty are both innocent victims, the center of interest is the suspicion itself and those who harbor it. Both rulers, Lundie and Temple, are vulnerable to unworthy suggestion; both know that unsigned letters and unfounded rumor should not be trusted but succumb just the same. Both are only too inclined, like Heyward, to offer to buy the satisfaction of their will and desire; both indulge in nepotism and prefer unworthy candidates, knowing their weaknesses.

The differences are only too clear: in *The Pioneers* the issues are addressed much more seriously—the law is invoked by Temple with such conviction that the events must be measured against the most stringent moral criteria and the future that he sees as dependent on them. In *The Pathfinder* the events are isolated from any consequences they might have for the ensuing civilization; the novel's dénouement simply eliminates them. Lundie's letting loose of Muir on Mabel may be remembered to his discredit, but that is all. The reader of both novels is under greater constraint; as he already knows, if, like Cooper's contemporaries, he reads *The Pioneers* first, such frailty has dire consequences and is not merely a matter of character or narrative; if he reads *The Pathfinder* first, then, in *The Pioneers*, he should recognize the germinal earlier pattern now repeated in a context that confers greater significance upon it. The critic's task here can only be to point to the parallel and to suggest its range of significance; to characterize and limit its impact on readers of the text is clearly impossible. However, it is reasonable to suggest that a reading of the tales that omits this consideration is inadequate. One is free to doubt whether or not the effects are those of deliberate art, but that they are properties of the extended texts is hardly debatable.

Natty's preference for unspoiled nature over the life of the settlements is affirmed in all five novels, and, of course, in this novel it is central to the choice both Natty and Mabel must make. It is a constant in our awareness of Natty as in Natty's awareness of himself, and no insistent argument is needed to establish it as a link, and an irritant to the reader's memory. "That towns and settlements lead to sin, I will allow, but our lakes are bordered by the forests, and one is every day called upon to worship God, in such a temple" (24)—this statement represents an opinion that is so

pervasive in the series that, unidentified, it would be easy to ascribe to
Natty, but to place it in its specific context, or even the novel it appears in,
would be more taxing. In *The Pathfinder* there are several such passages,
but, although the polarity it addresses underlies the tale's dénouement, the
expression of it is made not by direct reference to the polarity but in terms
of the feelings the principals have for one another. The replacement of
nature unspoiled by settlements is simply not the crucial historical issue it
is elsewhere, and to take its full measure one needs the memory of *The
Pioneers*, *The Prairie*, and *Mohicans*; with that memory, *The Pathfinder* is
immeasurably deepened. Near the end, with Natty's vehement "wasty
ways of the settlement" (444), it is difficult not to muster *The Pioneers*
into full consciousness, and when one does the romantic and noble tale of
Natty in the toils of the "master passion" (3) is subjected to an enriching
decline into the "reality" of Templeton forty years on.

The reduction in *The Pathfinder* of reference across the books to matters of narrative and character is matched by the diminished energy with
which issues of history and political thought are addressed. That "the
Indian character has so little variety" (1) is inadequate to explain the
reduction of Arrowhead to mere villain; contact between Indian and
European is noted neutrally (11) and no longer seen as the source of
inevitable degradation and deprivation that it was to Magua, Tamenund,
Mohegan, and Mahtoree. Chingachgook's loss of his son and his tribe is
reduced to his "trouble," and although Natty unfailingly extols the virtues
of the Delawares, "what is left of them," and remembers the tears he shed
with Chingachgook, the vast impact of *Mohicans* finds its strongest overt
expression in Natty's words: "Ah's! me! no shoot of the old Mohican stem
remains! He has no children to delight with his trophies; no tribe to honor
by his deeds; he is a lone man in this world, and yet he stands true to his
training and his gifts!" (79). References to Christian European greed in the
other novels are reduced here both in number and force: Arrowhead is,
without comment or qualification, one of "the native owners of the soil"
(8), and only once is reference made in such a way as to detain the reader's
attention.[17] Dew-of-June says to Mabel: "'Yengeese too greedy—take
away all hunting grounds—chase Six Nation from morning to night;
wicked king—wicked people. Pale Face very bad.'" And Mabel acknowledges the validity of this complaint: "Mabel knew that, even in that
distant day, there was much truth in this opinion, though she was too well
instructed not to understand that the monarch, in this as in a thousand

other cases, was blamed for acts of which he was most probably ignorant. She felt the justice of the rebuke, therefore, too much to attempt an answer, and her thoughts naturally reverted to her own situation" (346). The moment passes quickly, however, to be replaced by the dominant narrative. The European arrogance that undergoes such strictures in *Mohicans* is here referred to only infrequently and marginally, except where it is made to have narrative consequences—as in the case of the death of Corporal McNab.

There are other elements, however, that are more urgently charged. In a conversation between Natty and Jasper, the question of settlements and the spoliation that invariably attends them arises: Natty observes, "The things they call improvements and betterments are undermining and defacing the land! The glorious works of God are daily cut down and destroyed, and the hand of man seems to be upraised in contempt of his mighty will. They tell me there are fearful signs of what we may all come to, to be met with, west and south of the great lakes, though I have never yet visited that region" (98). The Prairies, Natty continues, are "marked by the vengeance of Heaven": "I have heard as honest Delawares as I ever knew, declare that the finger of God has been laid so heavily on them, that they are altogether without trees. This is an awful visitation to befal innocent 'arth, and can only mean to show to what frightful consequences a heedless desire to destroy may lead" (98). Jasper's agrarian response is met by Natty's absolutism and Cap's uncomprehending coarse materialism. The discussion serves to lay a foundation for the difference between Jasper and Natty, important in the tale's resolution. But it also seems unlikely that any reader will fail to make the obvious connections with *The Pioneers* and *The Prairie*. We might not, when Mabel is so certain that "no Christian, seeing a woman approach alone, would fire upon her," recall the exploits of Hutter and March in *The Deerslayer*, or, if we follow the order of composition, Montcalm's indifference in *Mohicans*—though I am impelled to do so—but when, in the final chapter, Mabel views Natty from a distance and hears his legend "after the Revolution" (468), it seems impossible not to recall *The Pioneers*. Likewise, while the extended idealization of Natty at the end of chapter 9 serves his role in this romance admirably, it cannot in its stress upon "his beautiful and unerring sense of justice" fail to raise memories of *The Prairie* and *The Pioneers*—the various problems that surround his idealization in the former and the way in which another view of justice besets him in the latter.

It might be held that I exaggerate the problem. While the main purpose has been to assert that there is abundant opportunity offered by this text to make connections with the others in the series yet at the same time to mark the differences between it and them, I am quite aware that it is possible to ascribe the differences to a difference in the dominant genre—a simplified romance of Natty in love, bearing, as the contemporary *Burton's* reviewer suggested, the same relation to the rest that *The Merry Wives of Windsor* has to *Henry IV*.[18] The issue must, perhaps, remain moot—or determinable only by each reader of the text. My view is already clear: although the familiar issues are muted, they are raised, and when they are they are difficult to ignore. I shall later argue that the development of the romance plot so intimately enfolds the other issues that, while entertaining them is disturbing, to do so deepens its implications to the benefit of this particular work and the series as a whole.

Since the striking change of tone in *The Pathfinder* from that of its predecessors has led to a tentative critical stance[19] in this chapter, it might be appropriate to address more fully the problem of the order of the tales at this point. While it is impossible to be exhaustive or definitive about the issue—to answer for all the differences each reader might register in thinking of the books either in the chronological order of Natty's life, as late in his career Cooper offered them, or, as Cooper and his contemporaries had no choice in doing until after 1841, in the order of their composition and publication—it should be possible to indicate the major considerations that must arise.

In either case, of course, the *fabula*, the sum total of events, does not change, but the order and the reader's reception of the events does. In the order of Natty's life, the reader must—along with much else—experience a linear disappointment, a growing dismay that the virtuous Natty is treated as he is in *The Pioneers*, that the pristine wilderness is despoiled and the Indians eliminated; the civilization that is held to justify all the destruction that is factual at the time of composition is never seen in its fully developed state in the series. The conclusion achieved by *The Prairie* affirms Natty as a tutelary, paternal, mythical figure. In *Home as Found* (1838) he is remembered posthumously in purely idealized terms against a society in which materialism is rampant and the worst implications of *The Pioneers* are fulfilled. On the other hand, the order of publication, while it to a degree confuses historical time for the reader, projects a supralinear reality, in which succession in time is subsidiary to the overriding forces shaping history and forming its myths; and the reader—forced to consider what is transpiring in the context both of what has transpired and will transpire—is placed in the privileged position of making the fiction, and making sense of it, to a far greater degree than usual. While Cooper was undoubtedly aware of this and seems in *The Pathfinder* to act to "correct" it, he—as much as his readers—is compelled by his achronological logic; it is, sometimes, *used* by Cooper, but not, I think, as a freely embraced pervasive technical consideration for the shaping of his fiction. His final wish to adopt the chronological sequence makes that clear.

In the order of fictional chronology, *The Deerslayer* at once establishes the idealization of Natty and ensures that the almost allegorical parade of his virtues will be what we shall always first remember. The work itself operates in a context neither of memory nor of a conceivable future.[20] The rendering here is ahistorical, absolute and almost exclusively moral; although Natty's enmity to the "settlements" is affirmed, it has no locus. The appalling slaughter at the end, while it does have historical significance, has none of the resonance it must take on for the reader who can recall the massacre at Fort William Henry in *Mohicans*. Natty's refusal of Judith is apt to seem merely priggish, lacking the preparation offered by *The Pathfinder*.

The move from *Deerslayer* to *Mohicans*, while it is coherent with the Redcoats' carnage in the forest, is extreme—from idealization to relentless realism. The violence of imperial combat and conquest invades the stillness of lake and forest and is allowed to occupy them unopposed; the outcome of the French wars is left unsettled in favor of the working out of the romantic tale and the extermination of an indigenous people. If *Mohicans* thus follows *Deerslayer*, certain questions arise: what sort of fulfillment does the Natty of *Mohicans* represent of the rites of passage of *Deerslayer*? Why is the reluctant slayer of *Deerslayer* so soon a mere willing instrument of the bloodthirsty Redcoats?[21] Natty's assistance in the establishment of the power that is to destroy him and the terrain as he knows it is conveyed with far less force if the reader cannot draw on the implications of the invocation of Effingham's name and on what *The Pioneers* has depicted of Natty's and Chingachgook's fate. Even so, the criticism of the advance of European civilization offered by *Mohicans* is massive.

It is principally for this reason that, even in the order of the tales' fictional chronology, *The Pathfinder* makes for a difficult adjustment. The past of *Mohicans* is often enough invoked to establish sequence, but its total force is hardly mustered into *The Pathfinder*. Chingachgook is there and useful but is hardly the most active character; Cooper shrewdly uses Natty's love for Chingachgook and Uncas to set against that of Mabel and Jasper for each other, but that is useful for plot resolution and character development and would be equally valid whether considered in the order of publication or that of fictional chronology.

The Pathfinder* erases almost completely the critical note of *Mohicans*; the Natty who shared the grievance and grief of the Indians is replaced by the idealized Natty of *The Deerslayer*; his extended debates with Bat are abbreviated into the less searching differences with Cap. When he muses on his newfound "craving after property" (432),[22] it is less a reflection upon human acquisitiveness and more an item in the development of the plot, as Natty mentally withdraws from the domesticity of a future with Mabel. Likewise the trial of Jasper is worked out as a matter of plot; although Cooper is sententious about "suspicion," "circumstance," and foolish rumor, there is no radical discussion of law and power—as there is in *The Pioneers*, *The Prairie*, and *Mohicans*—but only the repeated declarations of Natty's and Mabel's trust in Jasper. While there is considerable novelistic interest in Cooper's treatment of Mabel's relationship to her father, it is the romance element that is fully played out; the central issue is resolved simply in terms of Natty's superior virtue. The effect of that resolution—like the effect of almost every character's rhetoric in the book—is further to idealize Natty and to set him firmly apart from civilization and its institutions. If the security of hegemony rests upon its success in persuading its subjects into complicity with its power, Natty remains in this novel immune—but it is an idealized immunity and less, as so often elsewhere, a critical rejection.

In *The Pioneers* the effects of the passage of time, so insisted upon in the novel's opening paragraphs, are evident not merely in the most advanced state of settlement the series offers (in this its sequence with *The Pathfinder* is useful) but most strikingly in the decline of Natty and Chingachgook; the reader remembers the valiant and morally peerless Natty and the brave and romantic young Chingachgook against their present decrepitude and lack of power. Natty's and Chingachgook's luminous evocations of an unspoiled wilderness now have the authority conferred upon them by *The Deerslayer* and *The Pathfinder*. At this point too Natty's complaints that his services to the nation have been forgotten and Chingachgook's condemnation of the vision of the white man's bloodiness can be endorsed by the reader's memory, even though the characters' memory largely lacks specification. The reader might well establish the parallel between Temple's nepotistic preferment of Jones and Lundie's favors to Muir, but reading in the order of composition disallows that specific recall. Reading *Mohicans* after *The Pioneers* gives a complex—and clearly intended—force to the early mention of Effingham's name; in the context of fictional chronology, however, it is more simply an item of biographical continuity and is hardly needed.

From work to work, whatever the order, Natty's morality remains constant and clear, but the focus in the order of fictional chronology is not on an isolated incident in which Natty figures as a justifiably aggrieved victim but on a developing community that does not fully value the idealized and serviceable Natty, with whose history and merits the reader is now completely familiar. The reader is made to recall, but the citizens—even the most virtuous—do not recall in any way that leads to *effective* restraint. In whichever order we read the novels, then, the weight of the critical questioning of civilization remains the same, but in the context of fictional chronology that questioning has to work against a prior, intensified idealization, now to be taken literally—Natty actually was and did all these things. At this point, then, the failure of the civilized community is perhaps more striking. What the series loses in this order is its original founding in a radical criticism which suffuses all that follows; to read *The Pathfinder* and *The Deerslayer* in the light of *The Pioneers* makes an enormous difference—we do not admire Natty less but know, throughout and at every point, that his virtues are futile.

In both orders, *The Pioneers* and *Mohicans* are prior to *The Prairie*, but, in the order of fictional chronology, *The Prairie* has to cope with an idealization inscribed in the two works written after it; the idealization, first fully enunciated in *The Prairie*, now is made to rest upon what is most fully advanced in *The Deerslayer* and *The Pathfinder*, and more fully balances the critical spirit in the whole series. The failure of the civilization is not eliminated, but it is muted by forceful insistence—in the first, the third, and the fifth novels in the series as Cooper finally presented them—on the cherished ideal.

In the order of publication, as my previous chapters indicate, the first three works, however virtuous Natty is in them, encompass a massive criticism of an American civilization that, whatever its merits and aspirations, is destructive and seriously flawed in its principles and practice: it erases in deed the ideals it ennobles in words. The relationship enforced upon the reader against the fictional chronology—remembering what will come, engaging what has not yet happened, as well as what has—gives the reader a peculiar privilege and authority; the text is enriched by a freer play, against chronology and cause and effect, with the forces at work in the society's development.

In the order of publication, which I have embraced, *The Pathfinder* constitutes a critical moment. Cooper returns to the historical time of *Mohicans* and, specifically, in the first novel named for him, to Natty. Cooper picks up the idealization of Natty from *The Prairie* and intensifies it; it is constantly affirmed by all—it is *the* issue in the book, which has a still, almost abstract tone. The tale Cooper tells draws Natty out of his elected marginality onto a wrong path, innocently misled by an equally idealized Mabel Dunham. He is fully humanized and moving in his love, romantic generosity, and heartbreak, but even in the alien world into which he has taken a false track, his virtue proves adequate to the test; it is perhaps the greatest of all his merits that he alone is capable both of recognizing its falseness and of restoring a just order—his virtue is not passive or merely idealized but is fully active. Society in this novel is not notably criticized (and only mildly when it is), nor does civilization reject Natty, or so express itself as to make life within it for Natty intolerable. The break with civilization is made by Natty himself—it is *his* recognition, *his* will. While we may agree that the idealization of Natty is fully achieved in *The Pathfinder* and, indeed, amplified beyond all other presentations of Natty to this point, it is far less clear that the reader can eliminate Natty's past embodiment in *Mohicans* or his future victimization in *The Pioneers*, whatever Cooper's intentions might have been. It is difficult not to recall Templeton, and Natty's bitter memories of his experiences there even in *The Prairie*, when we are told of Jasper's future as a merchant in New York.

Whatever the reader's memory may supply, the pervasiveness of the idealization of Natty in *The Pathfinder* makes it impossible to ignore. There is no chapter that does not sound his praise. Cap's first sight of him as "half-rigged; neither brig nor schooner" (16) quickly gives way to Natty's own listing of his own skills reflected in his "names"—La Longue

Carabine, Hawkeye, Pathfinder—in the last of which Mabel recognizes him. He is known then by a reputation deservedly earned by deeds, as he is quick to point out, in distinction from merits assumed by rank or inheritance. His first note then is stoutly republican, some decades too early.[23] This moment in the text, perhaps, reflects Cooper's expression to his daughter of his dissatisfaction with characters like Middleton, as Henry Nash Smith has pointed out; certainly, the exclusion of the likes of Middleton enables a distribution of the chivalrous virtues to Jasper and Natty, and, significantly, to Mabel Dunham.

After his introduction, each new episode is made to reveal another aspect of Natty's virtue. Mabel finds "his smile attractive, by its simple ingenuousness, and the uprightness that beamed in every lineament of his honest countenance" (37). His habitual expression of "simplicity, integrity and sincerity, blended in an air of self reliance, that usually gave great confidence to those who found themselves under his care" (48–49). At the moment of Mabel's first rejection of Natty she praises him in these terms: "Your truth, honesty, simplicity, justice and courage are scarcely equalled by any of earth" (270). Such generalized commendations of his virtues abound, but they do not lie inert. When Natty renders moral judgment—say, of Mabel (128) or of June (19)—it is discriminating and generous, if, as we always have to, we except the Mingoes! His modesty about his achievements and his unwavering submission to providence are everywhere apparent; nor will he take exclusive credit where it should be shared with Jasper or Chingachgook. He follows the dictates of his practical reason, a gift of God, and when his prejudices or limitations are exposed he is quick to concede (117). Although his sense of piety requires humility before adversity, his is a rational, self-regulating morality—even if at times excessively scrupulous. For example, Natty seems too ready to condemn himself for idling, "listening to the sweet tones of Mabel's voice, as she sang ballads to her father" (207), while he might have been on watch; this is quite consistent with his character, but the neglect of duty he condemns is also one aspect of Natty's "false trail" in his infatuation with Mabel.

If it falls to Natty's duty to kill, he will do so only lawfully and out of necessity (73); this is most notable in his rational mercy in permitting the "honorable retreat" (409) requested by Sanglier. His virtue here is seconded by Mabel in the name of "our holy religion, and the God whom we profess to worship in common" (410). Natty and Mabel stand against Cap's "prize-money, head-money, and honor" (410), and, of course, against the memory, here recent, of the massacre at Fort William Henry. For Natty, honor lies in "doing what's right"; it is very different from the honor of Munro, Montcalm, and Heyward. The differences between the virtues of Natty and Jasper and those of military chivalry and honor are frequently implied; while Natty and Jasper vie for the attentions of Mabel, their competition is always quite lacking in meanness of spirit. Their conduct to one another is always generous; they are both capable of forbearance and forgiveness. Their virtue is personally held and referrable to conscience and deed, and not just to a word. When they fall short—as both do in the shooting match and its aftermath—the failings are human enough and in each case motivated by love.

Natty's physical strength, his skills, courage, and stamina are unfailing; he is proud only of his ability to serve. His gallantry, self-sacrifice, delicacy of feeling, and nobility are beyond question, and his actions are always without ulterior motive. Much as he desires Mabel, he refuses to regard her hand as earnable by his actions. Given his possession of virtually every conceivable human virtue, it is not surprising that he seems to some superhuman, to bear a "charmed life," and that Sarjeant Dunham finds it inconceivable that Natty should die by human hand.

But Natty's virtue is not superhuman. Even though he is on the wrong path in craving Mabel and domesticity, from the first he is not without a sense of his error; his desire to find a mate is shown as natural enough, but it is Dunham who arouses that feeling. Even as Natty responds, he is equally aware that it is unsuitable for him and that he and Mabel make an unlikely match. Upon Mabel's refusal, he characteristically recognizes its rightness: "I have indeed, been on a false trail, since we met!" (272). However, that merely articulates decisively what one part of his mind has known all along as "misgivin's"; his awareness is evident early and continues throughout. His concession is rational, generous, gentle, and considerate; above all, it is just.[24] Although he does woo Mabel despite his reservations, he does not endorse her father's folly in thinking that Natty's military accomplishments—or even his unequaled virtue—ought to guarantee Mabel's amorous affections (130). In this his view is reasonable and just; in his final recognition, he is fully capable of acting upon it.

It is immediately after this early exchange with Dunham, at the end of chapter 9, that Cooper delivers himself of an extraordinary encomium to Natty's virtues; he is "a sort of type of what Adam might have been supposed to be before the fall, though certainly not without sin" (134):

The most surprising peculiarity about the man himself, was the entire indifference with which he regarded all distinctions that did not depend on personal merit. He was respectful to his superiors from habit, but had often been known to correct their mistakes and to reprove their vices, with a fearlessness that proved how essentially he regarded the more material points, and with a natural discrimination that appeared to set education at defiance. In short, a disbeliever in the ability of man to distinguish between good and evil, without the aid of instruction, would have been staggered by the character of this extraordinary inhabitant of the frontier. His feelings appeared to possess the freshness and nature of the forests in which he passed so much of his time, and no casuist could have made clearer decisions in matters relating to right and wrong; and yet, he was not without his prejudices, which, though few and coloured by the character and usages of the individual, were deep-rooted, and had almost got to form a part of his nature. But the most striking feature about the moral organization of Pathfinder was his beautiful and unerring sense of justice. [134]

It must be recognized here that, while Natty's virtue is not the result of instruction, most of the qualities that Cooper ascribes to him and that I have placed in the foreground are not primitive virtues but make up a virtual anthology of desirable human attributes *in any society*. *The Deerslayer* insists on this even more forcefully. And it is this fact, rather than merely his profound attachment to nature unspoiled, that casts so questionable a light on American civilization's inability or unwillingness to accommodate him.

Comparing Natty to Captain Sanglier, Cooper observes: "One served for money and preferment, the other because his life had been cast in the wilderness, and the land of his birth needed his arm and experience" (419). The duality is clearly noted: Natty as man of the wilderness and as the "arm" of his nation. The epic implications of the latter are too obvious to require comment; Natty's conduct in the book—military, social, and personal—constitutes an extended *aristeia* for the society which he serves, and which fails to recognize him—except in word, in reputation, and in "legend."[25] Society's self-amputation is clear enough if we bear in mind *The Pioneers* and *Mohicans*.

However, the wilderness side of the duality is not, for Natty, unintegrated with his national duty but is its very foundation. While Natty occasionally registers the polarity between nature and the settlements and their "wasty ways" (444) in a fashion already familiar from the other novels, *The Pathfinder* locates itself clearly in a rapt celebration of un-spoiled nature—forest, lake, river, islands, trees and rocks—rather than the settlements. The epigraph by Moore to chapter 1 sets the tone:

> The turf shall be my fragrant shrine;
> My temple, Lord! that arch of thine;
> My censer's breath the mountain airs,
> And silent thoughts my only prayers.
>
> [7]

Cooper's opening pages, redolent of a cultivated response to the sublime, picturesque landscape, clearly define Mabel, who, "wondering but pleased" (9), responds sensitively but in an educated way to nature. Later, as she views in turn the lake and the forest, "Nature had appeared to delight in producing grand effects, by setting two of her principal agents in bold relief to each other, neglecting details; the eye turning from the broad carpet of leaves, to the still broader field of fluid, from the endless but gentle heavings of the lake, to the holy calm, and poetical solitude of the forest, with wonder and delight" (109). Cooper at once gives her response the social context that is to disqualify Natty:

> Mabel Dunham, though unsophisticated, like most of her country-women of that period, and ingenuous and frank as any warm-hearted and sincere-minded girl well could be, was not altogether without a feeling for the poetry of this beautiful earth of ours. Though she could scarcely be said to be educated at all, for few of her sex at that day, and in this country, received much more than the rudiments of plain English instruction, still she had been taught much more than was usual for young women in her own station in life, and, in one sense certainly, she did credit to her teaching. The widow of a Field Officer, who formerly belonged to the same regiment as her father, had taken the child in charge, at the death of its mother, and under the care of this lady, Mabel had acquired some tastes, and many ideas, which other-wise might always have remained strangers to her. [109]

It is this education that qualifies her to rise in the class structure and fits her for the status Jasper Western's industry and acumen will win for her as a city merchant's wife.

Natty's relationship with nature could hardly be more different. As he assumes control in chapters 1 and 2, the forest is seen in more intimate detail, and, at the same time, as his place of worship: "That towns and settlements lead to sin, I will allow, but our lakes are bordered by the forests, and one is every day called upon to worship God, in such a temple" (24). All is of "the ordering of God's Providence, and these salt and fresh water lakes are some of them. . . . I think it the duty of all to believe in them" (25). His submissive piety is everywhere insisted upon. Natty does not find his piety in "worship garrison-fashion," which fails to raise within him "the solemn feelings and true affection, that [he] feel[s] when alone with God, in the forest." "There I seem to stand face to face, with my master; all around me is fresh and beautiful, as it came from his hand, and there is no nicety, or doctrine, to chill the feelin's. No—no—the woods are the true temple a'ter all, for there the thoughts are free to mount higher even than the clouds" (92). His piety and his other virtues are equally founded in nature, which never fails him, is never absent from him; the voice he responds to in nature is a quiet one: "I want no thunder and lightening to remind me of my God, nor am I as apt to bethink me most of all his goodness, in trouble and tribulations, as on a calm, solemn, quiet day, in the forest, when his voice is heard in the creaking of a dead branch, or in the song of a bird, as much in my ears at least, as it is ever heard in uproar and gales" (93). This voice is identical with the one that expresses the "commission from God to act right, and to deal fairly with his fellow creatur's" (426), which is superior to civilization's highest command, invoked by Jasper, "His Majesty's commission" (426). The "commission from God" is unvarying—to use Natty's word, "stationary" (97). "And yet God is unchanged—his works are unchanged—his holy word is unchanged—and all that ought to bless and honor his name should be unchanged too!" (98). All the virtues advanced in Cooper's encomium are reducible for Natty to this, and if Mabel's response to nature suggests Natty's disqualification, his disqualifies her. The difference is not in the quality of her virtue, sensitivity, and feeling but in their source; Cooper has chosen the book's epigraph shrewdly:

> —Here the heart
> May give a useful lesson to the head,
> And learning wiser grow without his books.
> [Cowper, *The Task*, 6.ll.86–88]

Cooper is very close both to Cowper's response to nature and to his moral dignity.[26]

Nature in *The Pathfinder* is still in its unspoiled, precivilized state, still abounding in "venison, salmon and trout" (36)—of which the military vanguard of civilization so quickly tire; "every thing was in its natural state" (47), "teeming with all the living productions of nature" (123) but not unthreatened by the materialistic views of Cap, who "were it not for ship-building and now and then a house,—can see no great use in a tree" (99). It is interesting that, at this point, Jasper and Natty differ, Jasper taking a more agrarian view of the issue: "You relish your bread, Pathfinder, and yet wheat will not ripen in the shade" (98). The difference is one of the determinants that make Jasper a suitable match for Mabel.

However, the initiative is with Natty, and Cooper is careful to depict Natty as easily distracted from Mabel by nature, his true bride: "Of all on board, the Pathfinder viewed the scene with the most unmingled delight. His eyes feasted on the endless line of forest, and, more than once that day, notwithstanding he found it so grateful to be near Mabel, listening to her pleasant voice, and echoing, in feelings at least, her joyous laugh, did his soul pine to be wandering beneath the high arches of the maples, oaks and lindens, where his habits had induced him to fancy lasting and true joys were only to be found" (287). The liturgical echo is hardly accidental. This comes just after Mabel's rejection of his proposal. When he finally has resigned Mabel to Jasper, he observes, "Yes, natur' seems to have made [women] on purpose, to sing in our ears, when the music of the woods is silent!" (453–54). But it must never be forgotten that nature is for him, always and invariably, "the great school of Providence" in which all his virtue has been learned (27). Nature is never for Natty a means of escape to a region free of care and responsibility.

In the 1840s, his daughter tells us, Cooper had come to think Inez and Middleton "a great blemish" on *The Prairie*.[27] While it would be pointless to debate that issue, one might observe that Middleton is hardly a persuasive representative of what, at its higher social ranks, American civilization might mean and that its idealized merits are far more satisfactorily indicated in *The Pathfinder* by Natty and Mabel, who because she returns to participate with Jasper in the formation of the nation might well be seen as a civilized American ideal. She is certainly much more than an inert romance heroine, the helpless consort of the male hero and the justification of his heroic actions.[28]

Mabel is in some ways like an Ellen Wade freed of the deadening presence of Inez, to whom she must show a demeaning servility. It is not at all that Cooper shows no interest in class considerations; indeed they are constantly placed before the reader. Natty, Mabel, Dunham, Lundie, and Muir are all in their different ways very conscious of the demands of class and rank, and the wooing of Mabel is always seen as in part a class issue. Mabel's education places her above Natty and her father—and Mabel is appropriately embarrassed when she makes the difference clear (303); Mabel and her father are both conscious of the dangers of her marrying above her station, which would alter if Dunham were to step into Muir's commissioned shoes. But, however important class is for Cooper, it is never, without merit, sufficient to command respect, and it must be evident that rank deserves little respect in *The Pathfinder*: Lundie's moral languor and Muir's duplicity represent nothing of value. Although Dunham and Natty respect rank and are appropriately obedient in their stations, they transcend, by their merits and knowledge, the artificial distinctions of rank; Lundie trusts Natty and Dunham above any commissioned officer. Natty, of course, as we are often told, will never make his sense of right bend before the obligation of obedience. Natty, after his rejection, commends Jasper to Mabel and observes, "I know Davy Muir well, and though he may make you a lady, he can never make you a happy woman, or himself a gentleman" (274). The distinction is neatly made and is not lost on Mabel, whose intelligence and moral judgment hardly need this instruction: "I would rather remain as I am, to my dying day, than become a lady at the cost of being his wife" (274). And Cooper's intention in the repetition is transparent.

A similar point is apparent in the shooting competition which is given as a frontier version of a chivalric contest. When Jasper presents her with the calash he has won, she accepts it with all due chivalric grace: "I do accept it, Jasper, and it shall be a sign of the danger I have passed in your company, and of the gratitude I feel for your care of me—your care and that of the Pathfinder" (167). Against her unaffected generosity, the patronizing envy of the ladies of rank stands condemned. Although Mabel knows her place, her sense of merit and independence prescribe the limits she must observe. She is anything but servile. In this she resembles Elizabeth Temple, who recognizes the imperative of filial obedience and at the same time places limits upon it.

If Mabel's education clearly marks her capacity to rise within her society, it is not something she immodestly insists upon, and it is hardly her sole qualification. Her Christianity—like that of Ellen and Elizabeth, and even Inez—animates all her actions and utterances, most notably at her father's deathbed and at Sanglier's surrender but more generally in her sensitivity to the suffering of others, her active charity and love toward Dew-of-June, and her consciousness of the debt of gratitude she owes to the love of others. Her grief at the wound she must inflict on Natty is not the conventional response of a heroine's display of sensibility but an expression of her ample Christian spirit. The sustained and deliberate delineation in fiction of moral qualities is often received today with irritation; such feelings are quite foreign to Cooper, and a failure to take his moral intentions at full value must misrepresent him.

Mabel has all the feminine graces: education, piety, gentle sensibility, "modest gentility" (136), and obedience. However, like Ellen, Cora, Judith, and Elizabeth, she also possesses American female frontier virtues of bravery, stamina, and resourcefulness, in the face of danger from the Indians in chapters 6 and 7 and later at the blockhouse. While her reading might have prepared her sensibility for a response to landscape, her response to the wilderness and the divine presence in it is her own; her breadth of sympathy embraces "this remote frontier" and "our own Manhattan" (173); if she brings a responsiveness to the sublime from the city's bookshelves, she will return with an experience of nature and universal piety at first hand. If she is sensitive, broad, and flexible in her sympathies, stout and unflagging in her morality, Mabel also has wit, intelligence, and discrimination, as her interventions in the discussions of Cap, Dunham, and Natty reveal. It is to Mabel that the single reference made in this book to Indian dispossession is given—her response, quoted earlier, to Dew-of-June's accusation of English greed; while the issue is marginal here, Mabel's response to it is not and, coherent with Elizabeth Temple's response, qualifies her in her role as a fit American heroine. If this treatment of Mabel seems overextended, it respects the care Cooper gave to her moral delineation and gives no more than its due to her, gender apart, as the most fully equipped citizen-hero Cooper offers us for the republic she would live to see. It is Cooper's insistence on the issue that has determined the thoroughness of my exposition in regard to both Natty and Mabel. The high moral drama enacted at the novel's climax depends totally upon Cooper's insistent moral empowerment of the two. It is simply not enough to affirm in general terms their high moral character and Cooper's typical didacticism.

Mabel's virtue is put to its severest test in the conflict between love and duty with which she is faced. Her duty to her father is sealed by a double promise to him; her love for Jasper is more fully evident to the reader than it is to Mabel herself; her affection and admiration for Natty, although it is not love, would sustain the marriage she has promised. She can be firm in her resolve, but romance demands that love triumph; it is an impasse that only Natty can resolve, since Jasper's romantic unwillingness to declare his love to her (he does so only reluctantly to Natty) would not allow the issue to emerge. The manner in which this is managed deserves the closest attention, because it involves much more than the satisfaction of the generic requirements of a romance tale.

Throughout the novel, Natty and Jasper, as the candidates for Mabel's hand, are kept constantly in view, and their claims as to the love they hold for her and their personal merits are given equal weight. Although Jasper and Mabel never until the end declare their love, Cooper develops their reciprocal love from the beginning and even brings it very close to the point of open declaration during the storm (251); even if he did not, the play of Mabel's and Jasper's eyes would be indication enough.

What is most interesting is the depiction of male attitudes toward Mabel; for men—Natty excepted—she is an object of desire to be won or awarded. Her father is most important in this because he can exact a duty of obedience from the virtuous Mabel; he is willing to confer her as a gift upon Natty, whose merits, in Dunham's eyes, are converted into reasons for her compliance. Natty has misgivings, well-founded ones. It is to her credit that, left free, she is able to make the taxing decision to reject Natty's suit, and Natty recognizes the justice of it and that "the sarjeant was wrong"; his judgment is repeated three more times. Natty attempts without success to bring Dunham to allow Mabel's free choice; although Dunham raises Natty's hopes once more and Natty agrees to continue his suit, his words are carefully chosen. He exacts a promise that Dunham will not "meddle" and guarantees that "all will come right in the end" (280). Natty's use of words like "right" and "wrong" is never to be taken lightly. But Dunham does meddle; in fact, he exacts every ounce of Mabel's daughterly affection and duty. His moral and emotional coercion of her amounts to paternal tyranny.[29] It is an ugly scene that reveals dramatic and novelistic powers Cooper rarely displays (although his registration of Natty's conflicting emotions [277–78] at his rejection shows a complexity of characterization that Cooper is not usually credited with). The promise is reiterated in more melodramatic fashion on Dunham's deathbed; the significance of his unawareness that he is grasping Jasper's hand and not Natty's is not missed by the reader and prepares for the encounter between Natty and Jasper that immediately follows. This and the subsequent events surely have a multiple appeal, involving as they do declarations of love and duty and acts of self-sacrifice whose attraction lies largely not in the happy ending but in the moral purity they express.

Jasper's restraint in the face of Natty's elated infatuation is tender and admirable, as is his renunciation of his ambitions to marry Mabel. His eventual insuppressible declaration of his love brings on the ultimate test of Natty's virtue and "sense of justice"—"this noble trait," Cooper has instructed us earlier, without which "no man can be truly great, with it no man other than respectable" (134). Natty, of course, is equal to the test. Mabel's will cannot resolve the issue; Jasper's will is to silence, for the noblest of reasons. Natty cannot behave as if he does not know. Not merely does he fashion the confrontation but even puts Jasper's own case along with his own. Natty perceives the inadequacy of Mabel's motives for marrying him, for they are the very basis of his own earlier misgivings; his response to Mabel includes neither that wordless exchange of love of which Jasper tells nor the word "love" itself. But Natty does understand "talking without the use of tongue" (448); he has known it in nature, and with Uncas and Chingachgook, but not with Mabel.

Mabel's sense of duty to her father and her promise to Natty are not so easily overcome. Natty forces her to choose freely between two who love her equally, but his coercion is different from Dunham's emotional blackmail. The issue is for him simple, even if it entails pain; the statement that governs the entire episode is Natty's response to Mabel's complaint of Natty's impropriety in forcing the "cruel trial": "Every thing is proper that is right, Mabel, and every thing is right that leads to justice, and fair dealing; though it is painful enough, as you say, as I find on trial, I do" (453). Natty can insist upon her choice because "the sarjeant left me your protector, not your tyrant. I told him that I would be a father to you, as well as a husband, and it seems to me no feeling father would deny his child this small privilege" (455). Mabel's resort to her obedience, her promise "to do all you desire" prompts only Natty's reconstruction of the choice as his "desire." I find it impossible to imagine a more admirable, a more *mature* moral action than Natty's in the final episodes of *The Pathfinder*.

Daniel Peck's relentless psychologizing of Natty reduces him to " 'childish simplicity,' " his mind " 'almost infantine in its simplicity,' " and Mabel to "woman," who "in this respect, means the intrusion of the adult" (*A World by Itself*, 80). But Peck is unreasonably selective: the phrase "almost infantine in its simplicity" is removed from a context in which Natty responds with "emotions so painful and so deep, that they seemed to harrow the very soul." He can have those feelings only because he really at that moment wants Mabel as his wife. I agree that Natty frequently offers "a way back to the world of Glimmerglass" (Peck, *A World by Itself*, 80), but to see that as a kind of infantile regression, an escape from the real, adult world, misrepresents what the world of Glimmerglass means to Cooper and to Natty. The relationship with nature and with God in it is the source and foundation of all Natty's virtues, and those virtues are not merely personal but belong to "adult" civilization. I cannot deny the relevance of Bachelard's notions of "youthful language" and "naive consciousness" to Natty, but to ignore, as a result, Cooper's insistent didacticism is to interpret what Cooper did not write—an anthology of choice selections. To ignore Natty's exercise of an adult morality with regard to Mabel and to construe it as an infantile withdrawal from "sexuality and responsibility" strikes me as wide of the mark. It certainly makes it easier than Cooper found it to account for civilization's effective rejection of its own *mature* ideals as exemplified in both Natty and Mabel.

Natty, in the novels so far addressed, is often a father figure: he protects his weaker daughters and sons as they face the hazards of founding a nation; he fathers no children but adopts Hard-Heart and shares the fathering of Uncas with Chingachgook. All call him father in *The Prairie* in deference to his age but also sensing in him the father of the nation; in *The Prairie* and *The Pioneers* the children wish to adopt the parent—it is revealing that Hard-Heart can succeed with Le Balafré, while Elizabeth and Middleton fail with Natty. In *The Pathfinder*, Natty most truly fulfills that function with Mabel, and it is the moral high point of his life; in it he offers the highest example of justice in action that the series affords. When Natty returns to visit Mabel and Jasper he finds that the relationship of father, in human terms, is too much for him emotionally to bear. Here, his example and meaning are not rejected by the society he fathers. But if, at the point of composition, Cooper envisaged the place *The Pathfinder* would find in chronological sequence, Mabel's final view of Natty on the outskirts of the settlement prepares us for the rejection to be witnessed in *The Pioneers*; the reader, in the sequence we have adopted, already knows. For the reader who will address *The Deerslayer* last, to view Natty in his earliest and purest incarnation, the elimination of matrimony and the distractions of the flesh and the heart that *The Pathfinder* inscribes may seem an appropriate prelude.

In making the transition from my discussion of *The Prairie* and its predecessors to that of *The Pathfinder*, I noted the change in tone that characterizes *The Pathfinder* and *The Deerslayer*. This change is hard to miss. The substitution of the measured, composed tone for the more disputatious and troubled one of the first three books written is perplexing. Between *The Pathfinder*'s covers there is much less to disturb or question the dominant idealization of Natty than there is in earlier books. The question must arise whether or not Cooper had suffered a change in outlook. Certainly the unwillingness to stress the betrayal of America's ideals is evident enough; but then, in what he had already written and took no steps to censor, *that* is yet to come when taken in the order of the tales' fictional chronology, and to preserve the elevated tone can serve only eventually to stress the betrayal even more strongly.

The entire series, with the polarities that structure it, seems to insist upon the idea of choice. Choice is often implied in a general sense, quite apart from the tale being told; the main story lines of *The Pioneers*, *Mohicans*, and *The Prairie* do not involve choice to a significant degree for their evolution, but the reader—and the characters—are constantly exposed to opportunity for choice: between virgin land or social community, between respect for native rights or insistence on the "march of civilization," and so on. Whether the reader is aware of this as an objective presence in the text or chooses to enter the text as partisan, judge, or arbitrator, it is a disturbing factor. It is no less disturbing that there is equally registered in the books a context of historical necessity which establishes that no real choice exists. This lack of choice is inscribed early in the series in Elizabeth Temple's sense of her impotence to correct the injustice whose advantage she inherits. The questions, the implied choices, do not recede because their resolution cannot affect the outcome; they become the substance of a critique of history that reveals how certain effects, "civilization," were produced.

As my chapter on *The Prairie* maintains, Cooper's dilemma and literary history's treatment of it depends in part on a failure fully to recognize how complete the mutual exclusion between nature and civilization is. *The Pathfinder* implicitly renders that only the more powerful by the intensity of Natty's idealization, for what is idealized and marginalized is clearly identifiable as the set of values that traditionally animates a Christian civilization. The preference critics have often expressed for a mythical Natty, embodying an ideal but in the end impossible set of values, only to be enjoyed in a daydream of return to a bosky pastoral—"a landscape of the mind" (Peck, *A World by Itself*, 189), which because imagined is permanent—implicitly regards the novels as therapy or balm for society's melancholy, regret, and bad conscience. The regret—and the willingness to make the sentimental journey back to the pastoral moment—confers a tender virtue on those who share it. Peck puts it thus: "Today, more than ever, we feel the need to be inspired by a timeless vision of simplicity and childhood wonder. As our own environment becomes increasingly threatened by spoliation and our own 'difficulty' becomes more acute, we can turn to Cooper to recover, perhaps to cultivate for the first time, a sense of the pastoral" (190). What is interesting about such a view is the way it elides any agent, any exercise of choice or responsibility, in the making of the "difficulty" and the spoliation. This is quite at odds with Cooper's pervasive moral tone; Peck's book exacts a heavy penalty for his decision to eliminate the social, political, and historical from his treatment of Cooper. Peck's view also masks the inconvenient fact that civilization has destroyed the very landscape that generates Natty's significance and renders it the object *only* of reverie or literary tourism. Significance is reduced to a sigh or a gasp. Peck projects for us a postpastoral world (infantile?) in which things fall without being pushed, break without being dropped.[30]

Apart from the construction I place on *The Prairie's* dramatization of Natty's indigestible meaning for society, the choice is extrapolated there in Ellen Wade's preference for Paul Hover over the Bush sons, for life within society over that of the lawless frontier. Ishmael, to his great credit, permits Ellen's choice, himself chooses society, acts judge, and turns east. Even Hard-Heart in his final exchange with Mahtoree makes a parallel choice. Natty's final words to Paul Hover insist upon it: "Therefore, forget anything you may have heard from me, which is nevertheless true, and turn your mind on the ways of the inner country" (*The Prairie*, 373). In short, the march of civilization, the historical necessity that limits choice, is itself determined by choices: a choice to be a "citizen" or a "subject," to be enveloped by a law-abiding community or to be isolated as an outlaw—whether in Bush's or Natty's particular manner. Although Cooper and his text largely recognize and endorse the power of civilization, that power is registered also as both the object and product of choice.

In this light, *The Pathfinder* may be viewed as less discontinuous with *The Prairie* than it seems at first sight. In fact the process of choice lies at the thematic, generic, narrative, and structural heart of *The Pathfinder*, whereas in the earlier works it is peripheral to the main narrative interest. For the narrative resolution, Mabel must choose, romance-fashion, between two equally worthy competitors for her hand, but Jasper and Natty are also each involved in a choice as well. For Natty, the choice lies at one level between "protection" and "tyrant," justice and force; more personally, it lies between, on the one hand, nature—his bride, his way of life, his pastoral setting, a parade of cherished flora and fauna, the source of his virtue, God's voice—and, on the other hand, Mabel Dunham—the charms, pleasures, and responsibilities of domesticity, the yearning of his heart, the settlements, property, education, in a word, civilization. His choice of justice is, in fact, for *him*, a choice of nature. When he enforces choice upon Mabel, he knows what her answer must be—as he had sensed what it *should* be throughout the novel.

Although Jasper is from time to time aligned with the agrarian settlement view, he makes a romantic choice between two courses of action: to declare his love for Mabel or to respect his profound love for Natty. His choice between Mabel and the sea reduces to that. His choice does not affect the outcome, but it does establish his worth. It is to be seen, then, as a choice determined by genre—romance.

Mabel's choice constitutes the resolution of the narrative, and it derives much of its attractive quality from the romance genre. But it is also determined by Natty's choice to allow it, by his sense of justice. Although she follows her heart, her choice is made between Natty, the wilderness scout, and Jasper, the Manhattan merchant-to-be. Her choice is no more reprehensible than Ellen's; it is the right choice, but it is more than a choice between two men. It embodies society's choice, and that is to reject Natty. *The Pathfinder* may have little of the darker shading of the earlier novels, little of their explicit historical critique, but the choice that lies at its center and its resolution is germinally the whole substance of that critique.

For a choice to be made, the opportunity must be offered, and in this novel it is Natty who provides it—his ascendant virtue dominates this novel's action as it does no other's. In this he is curiously aligned with Ishmael Bush, although Natty can proceed on a more secure moral base than he. Bush forgoes rule by force for rule by law, however primitive; Natty has replaced Dunham's tyranny—force—by justice. This determination of the issue is very different from the marrying of Elizabeth Temple who—like Florizel—discovers that her destined mate, Oliver, is princely and suitable.

While it may be held that Natty's weakness or attraction is his "infantine" innocence, his affinity to unspoiled nature, his insistence on Mabel's freedom, and his informed rejection of the role of tyrant in favor of "right" are unmistakably mature, adult. It is the kind of choice that civilization refuses to make and does not make. He is in this novel empowered; his determined, benign exercise of that power stands in itself as a criticism of a society that exercises power abusively or, like Lundie, languidly. America, as the future will tell—has already told—fulfills the promise of neither Natty's nor Mabel's example.

That prophecy is what the figure of Natty "after the Revolution," seen from a distance, portends—if not for Mabel, then surely for the reader. Cooper's apparent change of direction, then, that I noted at the outset— toward a more transcendentalized tone, toward a romance of great purity enacted on an insistently elevated moral plane—is not a deflection but rather a more concentrated crystallization of the unchanging issue that pervades the entire series.

SIX ＊ *The Deerslayer* (1841)

THE WORD AND THE ACT, THE

BEGINNING AND THE END

What we call the beginning is often the end
And to make an end is to make a beginning.
The end is where we start from. . . .
Every phrase and every sentence is an end
                          and a beginning.
– T. S. Eliot, "Little Gidding"

The 1850 preface to *The Deerslayer* and the 1850 "Preface to the Leather-
Stocking Tales" assume that readers in the future will follow the series in
the order of their fictional chronology, "the regular course of their incidents" (5); although he expresses in the 1841 preface some doubts as to
the reader's patience in confronting Natty for the fifth time, he insists on
the need that *The Deerslayer* is designed to satisfy, to present the "study"
from which all the succeeding tales are drawn. He cannot, obviously,
conceal the problem raised by the "first" novel's being the last to appear.
Although, especially toward the end of *The Deerslayer*, Cooper draws the
reader forward to the novels that will follow, he cannot—at the first use of
the name Uncas—avoid distinguishing in a footnote Chingachgook's father from his son and referring forward (backward?) to *Mohicans*. When-
ever Tamenund is mentioned it is impossible for the reader not to remember *Mohicans*; if Cooper's readers obediently follow the order of fictional
chronology, the associations that surround the name are unavailable to
them—Cooper's contemporaries did not suffer that limitation. In the
antepenultimate paragraph of the novel, Cooper clearly leads the reader
forward by allusions to *Mohicans* and *The Pioneers*, but just as, at that
moment, Cooper draws Natty and Chingachgook back in time, from the
mid-1750s to the early 1740s in which the previous chapters had been set,

it is impossible for Cooper to control his reader's memory—or for that matter his own—of all the novels he had already written. Whatever the differences are in the reader's experiences of the series in the two possible orders, it is quite clear that neither the reader nor Cooper can release himself from the imperative of the series as a whole—and that is a historical imperative, determined not only by the events Natty witnesses in his life but also by Cooper's view of the century that separates the composition of *The Deerslayer* in 1840–41 from the events of the 1740s he depicts in the novel; the span is broadened still further if we include the prefatory material of 1851 and Tamenund's evocation of his own past— and, what Cooper could not take account of, his readers' consciousness of history, of *this* history and its aftermath over a further century and a half. What might be seen as a merely technical difficulty—and Cooper is aware of that—in making the five-novel narrative work is, in truth, much more than that. While, like all the novels in the series, *The Deerslayer* itself is highly problematic in the relationship between the "timeless" idealization of Natty and the society he eventually elects to enter, the reader who comes to it first is prevented from fully addressing the complexities of the novel that can be enjoyed only by the reader who comes to it last.

Judith Hutter's wooing of Natty is *known* to be futile by anyone who has read the previous novels—or only one of them. In a significant sense, the testing of Natty under the stress of romantic love in *The Pathfinder* is a preparation for the perfect, pure Natty we find in *The Deerslayer*. When Natty predicts for himself a forest grave (533), his actual grave in *The Prairie* is evoked. Cooper observes at Hetty's obsequies, "Thus died Hetty Hutter, one of those mysterious links between the material and immaterial world, which, while they appear to be deprived of so much that is esteemed and necessary for this state of being, draw so near to, and offer so beautiful an illustration of the truth, purity, and simplicity of another" (535); on reading this it is difficult for us not to remember that Natty is already dead and that these words might just as well apply to him. Her burial might well seem to inter Natty while he still lives. The affinity between Hetty and Natty that is sustained throughout the book makes this of more than incidental significance.

When Natty, Chingachgook, and Hist invoke the presence and authority of Tamenund, the reader invokes the memory of *Mohicans* and *The Prairie*. It is of course true that the chronological reader will shortly meet Tamenund and hear his history, prophecy, and law in the "next" novel, but this reader cannot experience the appalled consciousness that the hope for the Delaware nation embodied in the wedding of Chingachgook and Hist is already blighted, that the fear of white power expressed by Rivenoak and Hist alike is already realized, that the Uncas we meet in the final pages is, like his father, already extinguished.[1] Even more important, the entire manifestation of an idealized Natty is subverted by what the reader remembers of *The Pioneers*: Natty's service to the colony which begins in *The Deerslayer* has been, for both Cooper and the reader of 1841, already ignored in *The Pioneers* in 1823; for all the massive establishment of Natty as an ideal of behavior, he can *only* be ideal. The sense derived is anything but consoling: we cannot help admiring Natty, but at the same time we wonder what he is for, other than to inscribe with an irresistible force what civilization wills *not* to be. If James F. Beard found it "appropriate . . . that the Deerslayer has often been considered the personification of the American spirit," one can only ask why; it is true that Natty "encompasses much of the highest wisdom in the history of Western culture. The Deerslayer and the action of this romance interpret aspects of the concept of 'Higher Law' from which American political institutions derived their early sanction" (Beard, introduction to *The Deerslayer*, xvi). But Cooper stresses over and over again that Natty's virtues are active ones; in him word, action, and spirit are united. How can one suggest that virtues consistently betrayed by the nation in its history—rather than the betrayal—constitute "the American spirit"? The entire series implicitly forbids this and inscribes what America chose not to be. Thus America—Temple, Elizabeth, Middleton—fails figuratively in all its attempts to appropriate Natty: one cannot exile and adopt at the same time. I think that Cooper did wish to preserve in the republic, in civilization, what Natty means; what he wrote, however, inscribes its impossibility.

Cooper never abandons the civilization he endorses in the opening pages of *The Pioneers*, but he does fail[2] to concede fully that the actions of that civilization reveal its *nature*. He wishes to see Natty and Chingachgook as regretted victims of aberrations of that society; the destroyers, Jones and Doolittle, Thomas Hutter and Harry March, constitute a force within society to be controlled by Temple, Effingham, Heyward, and Middleton. He does not explicitly accept that the threat of these destroyers to Temple and Effingham at the end of *The Pioneers* is as great as that to Natty. He does not see that idealism like his own or Natty's is doomed by the same impulse toward exploitation, progress, "improve-

ments," accumulation, and destruction; that Jones and Doolittle are typical, not exceptional; and that at root this civilization, by its nature,
justifies doing the very things he deplores. To make Natty an ideal within
civilization's psyche, as it were, is a massive self-deception; it reveals
civilization's schizophrenia. Cooper's refusal to resolve fictionally what
history has not resolved and to reconcile intellectually or emotionally the
mutually exclusive claims of Natty and the civilization that destroys him
enables the reader to grasp the unendurable conflict. Cooper's account of
the matter is so full and so true to the contradictions that we can perhaps
see what he could not. It is a wonder that his critics have so often been
willing to center the interest in the fiction on Cooper's dilemma—perhaps
it is because it reflects their own: sorrowfully to recognize the shortcomings of civilization, to endorse the ideal embodied by Natty, and to see it,
with a sigh, as impossible or infantile, the proper object of polite yearning.

That Cooper knows the nature of the impulse wantonly to kill Indians is
clear: "[Harry's] conscience accused him of sundry lawless acts against the
Indians, and he had found it an exceedingly easy mode of quieting it, by
putting the whole family of red men, incontinently, without the category
of human rights. Nothing angered him sooner, than to deny his proposition, more especially if the denial were accompanied by a show of plausi-
ble argument, and he did not listen to his companion's remarks, with
much composure, of either manner, or feeling" (59–60); later Cooper
goes on to say, "But, neither Hutter, nor Hurry was a man likely to stick at
trifles, in matters connected with the right of the aborigines, since it is one
of the consequences of aggression that it hardens the conscience, as the
only means of quieting it" (88). Cooper's instruction to the reader as to
how to judge Harry and Hutter could not be clearer. That their forays
after scalps are countenanced and encouraged by both the English and
French colonies is equally evident. While, of course, civilization does not
inscribe genocide in its founding principles, it is difficult to conclude, given
the evidence here and elsewhere, that the ethics of genocide are not
endemic to this civilization. I do not suggest that Cooper endorses genocide—or that Temple, Heyward, Effingham, or Middleton would—of
course, he does not; but he shows us, unmistakably, that the civilization he
and they endorse has practiced it and found it endurable. We know that
the practice continued, in fact and in spirit, long after the period of which
Cooper speaks and during Cooper's own lifetime. It is common to say that
North America has a bad conscience about its aboriginal peoples; here

again, Natty is a firm point of reference—when he betrays his own principles, he sees it, regrets it, makes recompense, and does penance. In this, as in most other things, he stands in contrast to society and is one of our principal means of mounting the critique of it. What I maintain here is not offered as a sermon based on Cooper's text, nor, I would suggest, is it merely thematic. I shall maintain not only that what Cooper has given leads us—if not Cooper—to an inevitable conclusion but also that *The Deerslayer* is structured and formed not merely by the systematic idealization of Natty, but also by the adverse critical relationship it establishes with the society in which it is placed. It does not matter that Cooper—so determined in his didactic, allegorical presentation of moral issues and of Natty, their embodiment—does not determine so fully the historical and political issue; the novel he wrote will take care of that.

In treating each of the novels, I have reflected on the relationships among them—the manner in which each raises the memory of the others as well as the question of the order in which they are best to be addressed. In only two cases is the order not an issue: in the first to be read, since at that point there cannot be an order (although I have already indicated that in *The Deerslayer*, written to be read first, Cooper is unable altogether to avoid the impact of the novels already written) and in *The Prairie*, in that all that has been written prior to it is also chronologically prior, and the reader's awareness of past history matches the protagonist's. What is suggested here is that, while the achronological approach through the order of composition is no serious impediment to our sense of chronology, the chronological approach must sacrifice certain specific effects that result from the former approach. Two brief examples will remind the reader of the kind of effect I have in mind: first, while a reader endowed with a long and retentive memory may, reading *The Prairie* last, recall at Natty's death his anticipation of a forest grave in *The Deerslayer* and register the disappointment, a quite different effect results from reading Natty's anticipation in the knowledge that it has not been fulfilled; second, Natty's intimate alliance with unspoiled nature in *The Deerslayer* and *The Pathfinder* is received quite differently by those who have already read *The Pioneers* and *The Prairie* and by those who have not—those who have done so experience fulfillment and disappointment in the same moment of time.

In *The Deerslayer*, as in the other novels, there are many moments at which the reader may—or must—recall the other novels. Harry March's noisy clatter, prejudice, and moral obtuseness may bring to mind Richard Jones; Natty's rapturous joy in nature, which "the hand of man had never yet defaced, or deformed" (36), with its undiminished abundance of game—still a source of the purely positive morality Natty always draws from it—must call up for the reader the saddening memory of the less consoling landscapes of *The Pioneers* and *The Prairie*. When Natty calls on the memory of Tamenund, or, provoked by le Loup Cervier, concedes white complicity in massacre, we remember *Mohicans*. Cooper participates, perhaps unwillingly, when Killdeer is examined by Natty by telling us that the rifle "subsequently became so celebrated, in the hands of the individual who was now making a survey of its merits" (389) or by anticipating Natty's legend before it has been established: "In after life, when the career of this untutored being brought him in contact with officers of rank, and others entrusted with the care of the interests of the state, this same influence was exerted on a wider field, even generals listening to his commendations with a glow of pleasure that it was not always in the power of their official superiors to awaken" (216–17). While these are clearly intended as forward references, they operate for us also as backward ones. The past and the future coexist.

While the attentive reader will register such instances of cross-reference among the novels and consider the question of order, the process of doing so reveals that in this novel those issues are less preoccupying. The greatest benefit of reading the novels in the order we have chosen is the privilege and obligation that the procedure places on the reader to constitute the sense of the series without the narrative tyranny of the chronological passage of Natty's life or the restraint of considering history simply as a series of events that happened in a certain order. We are freed from an objective diachronic sequence and are released cumulatively into an awareness of the pervasive historical forces and issues that operate across time. While Cooper is customarily quick sententiously to draw attention to the significance of the actions, characters, and events he describes, the continual reemergence and reiteration of patterns, sentiments—both Cooper's and his characters'—and issues work far more effectively than any series of single authorial instructions can.

Cooper's opening of *The Deerslayer* marks a difference. While he early sets the action "between the years 1740 and 1745," he is at pains to give Natty a setting in an "eternal" nature that is a fitting stage for his allegorical presentation in the novel:

> Whatever may be the changes produced by man, the eternal round of the seasons is unbroken. Summer and winter, seedtime and harvest, return in their stated order, with a sublime precision, affording to man one of the noblest of all the occasions he enjoys of proving the high powers of his far reaching mind, in compassing the laws that control their exact uniformity, and in calculating their never ending revolutions. Centuries of summer suns had warmed the tops of the same noble oaks and pines, sending their heats even to the tenacious roots, when voices were heard calling to each other, in the depths of a forest, of which the leafy surface lay bathed in the brilliant light of a cloudless day in June, while the trunks of the trees rose in gloomy grandeur in the shades beneath. [16–17]

Later, as Natty goes to his appointed meeting with Chingachgook, Cooper offers,

> Many of the trees stretched so far forward, as almost to blend the rock with the shore, when seen from a little distance, and one tall pine in particular overhung it in a way to form a noble and appropriate canopy to a seat that had held many a forest chieftain, during the long succession of unknown ages, in which America, and all it contained, had existed apart, in mysterious solitude, a world by itself; equally without a familiar history, and without an origin that the annals of man can reach. [149]

Thus it is suggested that Natty can be seen exhibiting his ideal timeless virtues in a setting that transcends time, even though by the novel's end the impending threat to that landscape will have been fully inscribed.[3]

However, in the novel's first paragraph, a less ethereal view of time is advanced. Instead of the clear historical coordinates given at the beginning of *Mohicans* and *The Prairie* or the orderly prediction of the opening of *The Pioneers*, Cooper, from the standpoint shared with the first readers of *The Deerslayer* in 1841, reflects on changes wrought by the passage of a century since 1740, the novel's historical moment, and even back before it:

On the human imagination, events produce the effects of time. Thus, he who has travelled far and seen much, is apt to fancy that he has lived long; and the history that most abounds in important incidents, soonest assumes the aspect of antiquity. In no other way can we account for the venerable air that is already gathering around American annals. When the mind reverts to the earliest days of colonial history, the period seems remote and obscure, the thousand changes that thicken along the links of recollections, throwing back the origin of the nation to a day so distant as seemingly to reach the mists of time; and yet four lives of ordinary duration would suffice to transmit, from mouth to mouth, in the form of tradition, all that civilized man has achieved within the limits of the republic. [15]

The process he alludes to—the achievement of a sense of antiquity without the fact of it—the compression of events in time, and their availability to memory and recent record suggest that American history can be viewed whole. The evidence of what took place a hundred years before is still to be met with.[4] That progress, development, and growth place New York State alone on a par with European nations suggests that America is "modern," if still developing, in the sense that Europe is "modern," without regard for the actual passage of years from the time of its settlement.[5] That America can recall its "savage state" more easily than Europe can does not make it closer to that state in any real sense. Such a view does not impose upon the reader the need to regard what follows as merely particular to the primitive history of one nation's development but as expressive, in perhaps more dramatic and compressed form, of the forces that determine the modern Western world and all the worlds it has touched. It is as well to bear in mind here too the continuity with Europe that Cooper has so often insisted upon and inscribed so fully. The issues need no longer be seen simply as interconnections or promptings to memory among the books but as common to them all and as characterizing the entire history he addresses.

In the discussion in chapter 3 between Harry and Natty about scalping and the bounty offered for scalps, we confront an ascertainable, historical fact; it might recall for us the whole cluster of condemnations of white depredations upon the Indians composed in the course of the series; it might prefigure the state of mind that could rob, exploit, and exterminate the race, especially in *Mohicans*—Cooper certainly insists on *that* in *The Deerslayer*. Harry appeals to "reason": "Just hearken to reason, if you please, Deerslayer, and tell me if the colony can make an onlawful law? Is'n't an onlawful law more ag'in natur', than scalpin' a savage? A law can no more be onlawful, than truth can be a lie" (51).[6] Natty's response condemns not merely Harry but society itself, for its betrayal of white gifts—that is, Christian principle—for its legitimization of cupidity in a particularly brutal form, and for its failure to adhere to law. It is Natty's version of the Nuremberg judgment:

> "That *sounds* reasonable, but it has a most onreasonable bearing, Hurry. Laws don't all come from the same quarter. God has given us his'n, and some come from the colony, and other some from the King and parliament. When the colony's laws, or even the king's laws, run ag'in the laws of God, they get to be onlawful, and ought not to be obeyed. I hold to a white man's respecting white laws, so long as they do not cross the track of a law comin' from a higher authority, and for a red man to obey his own red-skin usages, under the same privilege. But, 'tis useless talking, as each man will think for himself, and have his say agreeable to his thoughts." [51]

If, as Temple insisted, it is civilization's laws that separate us from barbarism, then it is clear that this society falls short in the essential matter. The issue is not confined to this incident or to this novel but is repeated in various forms throughout the series—and without regard for chronology. While the society and the series of events that bring Natty down in *The Pioneers* do not exhibit so crass a brutality as we see here, they manifest some of the same features and the shaky hold civilization has upon its legal principles. It might be noted that there are bounties only for Indian scalps, not white ones—French or English. Similarly, the immunities offered by the law to Temple and to Natty in the protection of Effingham's property are—as we have noted—very different.[7] Harry may dread "the approaches of civilization as a curtailment of [his] own lawless empire," but in this novel civilization legitimizes, rewards, and encourages his lawlessness.

Natty distances himself, even at this early stage of his life, from that civilization. He is pleased that Lake Otsego has "no pale face name, for their christenings always foretel waste and destruction" (45). Examining Hutter's sextant, he takes it as a surveyor's instrument and expresses *his* fear of "the approaches of civilization," which has a surer foundation than Harry's: "I've seen all their tools often, and wicked and heartless enough are they, for they never come into the forest but to lead the way to waste and destruction; but none of them have as designing a look as this!" (222). Hutter is not a surveyor, but Natty is not far off the mark as to what the likes of him—or surveyors—mean. Natty's fullest statement of his position is made in response to Judith's yearning for the society of "civilized beings . . . farms and churches, and houses built . . . by Christian hands," for "the sweet and tranquil" rest of a settlement. After denouncing the moral dangers of the forts and extolling the ageless beauty of nature, he observes:

> "It seems to me that the people who live in such places, must be always thinkin' of their own inds, and of univarsal decay; and that, too, not of the decay that is brought about by time and natur', but the decay that follows waste and violence. Then as to churches, they are good, I suppose, else wouldn't good men uphold 'em. But they are not altogether necessary. They call 'em the temples of the Lord, but, Judith, the whole 'arth is a temple of the Lord's, to such as have the right minds. Neither forts nor churches make people happier of themselves. Moreover, all is contradiction in the settlements, while all is concord in the woods. Forts and churches almost always go together, and yet they're downright contradictions; churches being for peace, and forts for war. No—no—give me the strong places of the wilderness, which is the trees, and the churches, too, which are arbors raised by the hand of natur'." [266]

The "contradictions" of civilization are evident to him. He is fully aware of the constant compromise of Christian principle in white action; he even confesses as much to Rivenoak: refusing Rivenoak's invitation to deceit as unfitting to his Christian birth, Natty continues,

> "Sarcumventions in war may be, and *are*, lawful; but sarcumventions, and deceit, and treachery among fri'nds are fit only for the pale-face devils. I know that there are white men enough, to give you this wrong idee of our natur', but such are ontrue to their blood and gifts, and ought to be, if they are not, outcasts and vagabonds. No upright pale-face could do what you wish, and to be as plain with you as I wish to be, in my judgment no upright Delaware either. With a Mingo it may be different." [296]

"Or ought to be, if they are not" makes the point precisely; it is what brings Natty down in *The Pioneers*—as it taints Temple's rule there, it taints civilization generally.[8]

The internal contradictions of the settlements express themselves not merely in the destruction of nature but in the corruption of "the high innate courtesy" of the Indian warrior (124), in the robbery of native people (38, 46), and in the encouragement of Indians "to commit their excesses" (147). Natty—and Cooper, explicitly, too—recognizes as clearly as Rivenoak what "the increase of our colour" (135) means to the Indians. When Rivenoak rejects Hetty's pious appeal, it is not simply because it does not correspond to Indian morality but also because white actions do not manifest white principle:

> "This is the pale face law," resumed the chief. "It tells him to do good to them, that hurt him, and when his brother asks him for his rifle to give him the powder horn, too. Such is the pale-face law?"
>
> "Not so—not so—" answered Hetty earnestly, when these words had been interpreted—"There is not a word about rifles in the whole book, and powder and bullets give offence to the Great Spirit."
>
> "Why then does the pale face use them? If he is ordered to *give* double to him that asks only for one thing, why does he *take* double from the poor Indian who ask for *no* thing? He comes from beyond the rising sun, with his book in his hand, and he teaches the red man to read it, but why does he forget himself all it says? When the Indian gives, he is never satisfied; and now he offers gold for the scalps of our women and children, though he calls us beasts if we take the scalp of a warrior killed in open war. My name is Rivenoak." [194]

Cooper observes blandly that "abler heads" than Hetty's "have frequently been puzzled by questions of a similar drift" (195)—like those of Elizabeth and Cooper himself. Nor is Rivenoak's cold criticism an isolated example in this book: it is endorsed by Hist, Chingachgook, and Natty—recalling the alignment on this issue, earlier noted, of Magua, Chingachgook, Natty, and Tamenund in *Mohicans*. The point is made by virtually every Indian in the series—and by most of Cooper's Indians, good and bad, outside it. It is not merely the source of thematic linkage among the novels but a pervasive issue that helps to structure the novels' movement toward meaning. Cooper ensures that Rivenoak's criticism be substantiated by Hutter, who at once confirms it in his sullen and morally indifferent claim that his act is justified by "the government of the province" that "had bid high for scalps" (196). If Rivenoak rejects Hetty's undiluted biblical imperatives, so do Hutter and March and the government that legitimizes their actions. Even Hutter, in a gentler moment, sees Hetty thus: "You sometimes ask queer questions, Hetty! Your heart is good, child, and fitter for the settlements than for the woods, while your reason is fitter for the woods than for the settlements" (93). If Hetty's "reason" will find no place in the settlements, and what reason she has is founded upon a faithful pursuit of divine injunction, then the settlement is placed in opposition to the very legitimizing principles it claims.

It is a serious and pervasive error to suggest that Natty's primary appeal lies in his childlike desire to preserve an ideal, perfect life in an unspoiled nature—that he figuratively fulfills, in short, the reader's wish for a less complicated, purer life. Such views succeed in obscuring the fact that Natty embodies all the virtues that civilization endorses but pays only lip service to—Cooper insists on this. When a sincere recognition of and desire to correct manifest injustice are in evidence, as they are with Elizabeth Temple, they are presented as impotent against the forces of history. For Elizabeth to want peace and comfort for Chingachgook and Natty is to go against the grain of white history, as Chingachgook makes clear to her embarrassed understanding.

Natty's inability to compromise is a result not so much of a moral absolutism, a primitive conservatism, or an infantile regression[9] as it is of a radical opposition. For those of us who stand within society as the inheritors and beneficiaries of European conquest—and that includes most of those who have read Cooper and written about him—the question too frequently devolves into one of how much of the virtue idealized in Natty civilization can retain, of how it can so humanize itself, of how it can remember what Natty means as civilization marches forward. In the series, Elizabeth Temple best conveys that sense—and it is admirable, in its way, as a sentiment; she poignantly expresses civilization's desire to see itself as virtuous. But her defeated collapse into "Christian charity" in her discussion of the matter with Oliver parallels the defeat that her father's "law" sustains in *The Pioneers*; instead of resolving competing claims, her effort serves only to reinscribe civilization's authority (what Natty repeatedly calls "might") and to reveal that civilization lacks the means or the will to reconcile the issue. Natty can only oppose; his opposition to Hutter and March is of a piece with his opposition to civilization; no compromise is possible with, can be effective against, its destructive, wasteful, and deadly exploitation. The opposition is inscribed by Cooper; its terms are Natty's, and not the result of my interpretation. Nor is the opposition weakened by Natty's eventual willing complicity and alliance with the power that will destroy him. It requires the naiveté of the liberal academy merely to reaffirm Cooper's dilemma as virtuous in the face of the durability of the problem he confronted when, as I have shown, Cooper's active critical practice is so pervasive. Which is not to say that we are wrong to prefer the defeated hope so frequently ascribed to Cooper to the predatory cruelty of Hutter, or the idealism of Temple to the cupidity of Doolittle.

In *The Deerslayer*, Natty cannot complain with the same conviction that he shows in *The Pioneers* about the effect of settlement upon the wilderness, even though the reader remembers his complaints there, as in 1740 Natty condemns the settlements and forts—again the series works as a whole rather than as a series of historical chronological events; the justification is adduced without regard for chronology. Nowhere is this more telling or apparent than in Natty's sentence after the shooting of the eagle: "What a thing is power! . . . and what a thing it is, to have it, and not to know how to use it" (447). It is a conscientious judgment upon his own "unthoughtful" act. It should also recall Natty's opening complaint in *The Pioneers*, so often returned to, that "might is right"; though Natty exercises his own might, he is capable—as the "great" (447) are too often not—of recognizing the wrong as wrong and of acting upon the recognition. The scene in question is a complex one in its effect. The deadly shot providentially brings about Natty's release and, in so doing, releases an exercise of unrestrained power far greater than his own, which occasions no self-reproach at all. Natty's observation "Then, how one evil act brings others a'ter it" is realized in ways far beyond his intention in making it.

While Cooper's treatment of the Indians cannot be as comprehensive here as it is in *Mohicans* or even *The Prairie*, it is nonetheless altogether consistent with them. They, in a sense other than chronological, authorize these "earlier" reflections. Natty early strikes the elegiac note in speaking of the Delawares as "a fallen race . . . a fallen people" (33–34); how fully his hopes of the marriage of Chingachgook and Hist, "that a great and ancient race like your'n shouldn't come to an end" (238), are fulfilled has already been recounted in *Mohicans*, as every reader in 1841 would have known. Indian resentment at white indifference and assumptions of superiority is present, almost intrusively, at Natty's expression of "innocent vanity on the subject of colour" (123) before the dying le Loup Cervier, as it is in Chingachgook's manifestation of "a feeling of colour" that overcomes "the ancient animosity of tribes" (321) at March's "unthinking cruelty" in killing a Huron girl, which provokes Hist's outraged reproof of Harry on racial grounds (322). Her words explicitly articulate what Harry always denies—the humanity of the Indians; his act conveys not merely his own callousness but that of the province. It is worth observing too that when white conduct is placed beside Indian—as we have noted before—the Indian is superior; Rivenoak's dignity in defeat silently rebukes Captain Warley's cynicism in victory (526).

Above all, Rivenoak's defeat at the hands of a merciless conqueror fulfills the fear he has expressed of his white nemesis: "When we gaze at the east we feel afraid, canoe after canoe bringing more and more of your people in the track of the sun, as if their land was so full as to run over. The red men are few already; they have need of help" (471). In this, tribal difference disappears; the Huron Rivenoak echoes the Delaware Tamenund. "The Yengeese are as plenty as the leaves on the trees! This every Huron knows, and feels," he says to Judith, as she appears in her regal finery in the Huron camp (511). Her action is no doubt a brave one, but her appearance, her rhetoric, and the manner she assumes identifies her with the fatal European power that oppresses the Indian. She speaks resoundingly for the colony's force, which Rivenoak and his Hurons are shortly to feel. Her imposture is true. The involvement of the Indians in wars between European powers is destructive to them, as it is to Natty; their nemesis is also his, as the whole series fully reveals.

Notwithstanding the irresistible force exerted by the whole series at the point of *The Deerslayer's* composition, Cooper in 1851 seems quite secure about the main emphasis of the book. Because it is to serve as "the study" from which the rest are drawn, he clearly emphasizes his intentional idealization of Natty; Natty cannot be exempted from the fall, and Cooper does not intend him as "a monster of goodness" but, like Chingachgook, as a *beau idéal*. He invokes the authority of "the elevation of romances" and of Homer for this, observing that to represent the Indian only in "squalid misery" and a "degraded moral state" would equally misrepresent. It seems to me that, for all the idealizing, by offering Doolittle, Hutter, Bush, and March along with Natty, and Magua along with

Uncas and Chingachgook in both his youth and his old age, Cooper earns some immunity from the charge he defends himself against. Even so, there can be no question as to the massive idealization of Natty to the point of a fully realized allegory that is manifest in *The Deerslayer*. At the same time, however, there is a realistic dimension of the book in which the history of colonial America makes itself insistently felt as counterforce to what the allegory develops.

Although the twentieth century has not in the criticism of fiction been especially friendly to allegory and the kind of explicit didacticism Cooper exhibits, Cooper had no such reservations. If we are to read Cooper at all, we must lay these prejudices aside and recognize that it is as fruitless to demand that Natty behave like a Merton Densher as it is to demand of the Lady in *Comus* that she exhibit the dramatic qualities of a Shakespearean hero; we must grant that it is unreasonable to require that Cooper be as reticent as Hawthorne or James.[10] Cooper's characters rarely run on a free rein; he always controls the moral characterization of his books, and his own voice is frankly heard steering his reader's moral attention. He, of course, did write explicitly allegorical works—*The Monikins*, *The Crater*, and *The Sea Lions*—and many other novels that are not fully realized allegories but frequently employ distinctly allegorical devices.

While *The Deerslayer* is not exclusively allegorical, many of its episodes are constructed with unmistakable allegorical purpose, and so is the entire presentation of Natty and Hetty; those with whom they are aligned or to whom they stand in marked contrast are also drawn into the allegory's field of force. Also, given the prevailing atmosphere of romance that surrounds the works—and especially the last two to be written—the presence of allegory should occasion no surprise. Since it might be argued that *The Deerslayer* is not properly to be called an allegory and since I do not want to engage in lengthy justification or debate along generic lines, I suggest only that the narrative, its characters, and its episodes, are, as in allegory, didactically driven to such a degree that allegory is a suitable term for the work. While its landscape is "real"—that is, is an identifiable place—and its characters historically believable, as is not always the case in traditional allegory, this work is as fully motivated by its afictional meaning as is *The Faerie Queene* or *Pilgrim's Progress*. Indeed, Natty is as thoroughly put through his moral paces as Christian is, even though his efforts find no terminus in an Eternal City. By allegory, then, I intend to note first that a high degree of didactic determination pervades virtually every event and character in the book, next that in the end we are explicitly invited to see the whole work in the light of that determination, and finally that certain episodes are treated as they are for solely allegorical ends, with no qualification of the term.

The allegorical direction of *The Deerslayer* is evident to the greatest extent in the treatment of Natty and Hetty and to a lesser extent in that of Hist and Chingachgook. Toward the end of the novel Cooper gives a pointed indication as to how they—and the entire work—are to be taken; as Hetty dies, he instructs us, "Thus died Hetty Hutter, one of those mysterious links between the material and immaterial world, which, while they appear to be deprived of so much that is esteemed and necessary for this state of being, draw so near to, and offer so beautiful an illustration of the truth, purity, and simplicity of another" (535). This speaks for itself. More comprehensively, taking account of the world as well as the spirit, the novel's final sentence somewhat defeatedly insists, "We live in a world of transgressions and selfishness, and no pictures that represent us otherwise can be true, though, happily, for human nature, gleamings of that pure spirit in whose likeness man has been fashioned, are to be seen relieving its deformities, and mitigating if not excusing its crimes" (548). While both these passages insist on the ideal dimension of Hetty and Natty, they may also be taken as suggesting, as Hutter has said earlier about Hetty, that their very otherworldly virtues disable them for this world, for society. Similarly, although Natty's gifts and character are extolled throughout the series, the defensive suggestion that these virtues can exist only in unspoiled nature, a presocial state, often attends the encomium—as it does for Temple and, most strikingly, in Middleton's rehearsing of Heyward's eulogy in *The Prairie*. At the same time, such reservations cut both ways, reflecting society's limitations as much as they do Natty's.[11] Cooper's awareness of the problem is evident in the uneasy, and unexplored, conjunction of "mitigating" and "not excusing."

Such reservations are not meant to question Natty's spotless virtue in spirit and in action, which is celebrated throughout the series. The circumstances differ, but Natty's virtue is never compromised; even when sorely beset he never sacrifices his moral sense. When virtue momentarily fails, conscience instantly operates in him to reveal and correct the failure. Even in *The Pioneers* and *The Pathfinder*, in which Natty is most novelistically rendered, confronting forces and issues he is ill equipped to manage, even at his highest moments of anger and outrage, he does not overstep the limits imposed by his moral sense.

Surely, none of Cooper's readers, then or since, can have missed the central part played by the idealization of Natty in the whole series, and especially in *The Deerslayer*. Beard puts the matter well:

> The main action of *The Deerslayer* is a sequence of ordeals or tests which initiate the young Leather-Stocking into the duties and responsibilities of manhood—a type of action as old in fiction as the Old Testament and as new as Hemingway's Nick Adams or Faulkner's Isaac McCaslin. While the ordeals of Cooper's knight of the wilderness must be developed from real-life situations appropriate to American circumstances in the 1740's, they have much the function and ritualistic quality of the artificially contrived ordeals of medieval romance. His theoretical training for life completed, the young hero, for whom Cooper confessed the affection of a living person, must kill his first enemy, demonstrate his valor and competence in the arts of warfare, display the delicacy and chivalry of his manners, show his willingness to sacrifice his own life in the service of others, vindicate his integrity at the risk of imminent death, and prove his chastity by resisting the blandishments of a sexually attractive woman. [Introduction to *The Deerslayer*, xiii]

His highlighting of the book's connection to the tradition of romance-allegory is to the point; it is beyond question in *The Deerslayer*, but it is open to question whether a "sequence" is represented and an achievement recorded. Tests may subject virtues to stress in order to prove (or disprove) their strength; although Natty, manifesting modesty rather than doubt, may properly question his own powers in action under test, the reader does not.[12] All his moral actions are surefooted; even under Judith's "blandishments" or the threat of Huron torture, he knows exactly what he is to do, knows exactly how to think and feel. His moral and religious equipment is as complete as the Lady's in *Comus*, and the outcome of his ordeals as little in doubt; they are undergone simply to demonstrate the virtues he is so fully in possession of from the instant he first appears. Beard's view also raises the question of the purpose of such an initiation, and I shall return to that later.

Natty's virtues are transmitted to us constantly, through the praise of others, through his actions, and through Cooper's explicit commentaries upon them: the parade of his merits seems endless, and they are as complete as is possible for a man after the Fall. His virtue may even fatigue the reader, who receives it piecemeal and repetitively, but its completeness is coherent with the notion that the prime source of his morality is nature, and God in nature—it is received from the source whole: Hetty's or the Moravians' Bible and his mother's instruction (43) can only confirm what he has already received and is constantly offered.

Harry's intemperate early shot at a buck echoes among the mountains: "When a few moments of silence had succeeded the sudden crack, during which the noise was floating in air across the water, it reached the rocks of the opposite mountain, where the vibrations accumulated, and were rolled from cavity to cavity, for miles along the hills, seeming to awaken the sleeping thunders of the woods" (56–57). Natty answers Harry's regret thus: "Never lament it, as the creatur's death could have done neither of us any good, and might have done us harm. Them echoes are more awful in my ears, than your mistake, Hurry, for they sound like the voice of natur' calling out ag'in a wasteful and onthinking action" (57). Natty displays every virtue that Christian civilization or secular morality has endorsed; he is an embodiment of the books of chivalry, the decalogue, and the Sermon on the Mount, and he rarely shows doubt or lack of resolution, except in his racial vanity and in his confusion about Indian "nature" and "gifts"—but that *is* registered as a confusion.[13] Incident after incident is so constructed as to reveal a particular quality in him: his honesty that earns the love of all others but exposes him to the contempt and manipulations of Hutter and March; his purity, truth, justice, and loyalty—even to March; the piety that informs his every moral judgment; his high notion of friendship; his discriminating conscience; his pity; his lack of envy, malice, and vengefulness; his manliness, reason, frankness, and ingenuousness; his modesty and humility; his prudence in action; his strictness and gentleness; his patience, courtesy, discretion, and generosity; and his unfailing perseverance in all of them. While Natty's conduct usually conveys its own message, Cooper is not embarrassed to underline the virtue (or vice, in Hutter or March) on display: "He did not feel impatient, for the lessons he had heard, taught him the virtue of patience, and most of all inculcated the necessity of wariness in conducting any covert assault on the Indians" (107). While such passages as these are the acts of an author concerned that his meaning shall not be lost, they are also instructions to the reader on how to address the text.

As we have seen in other novels—in Middleton's praise of Natty in *The Prairie*, in Mabel's and Cooper's in *The Pathfinder*—Natty is the subject of comprehensive eulogy:

> Deerslayer, on the other hand, manifested a very different temper, proving by the moderation of his language, the fairness of his views, and the simplicity of his distinctions, that he possessed every disposition to hear reason, a strong, innate desire to do justice, and an ingenuousness that was singularly indisposed to have recourse to sophisms to maintain an argument, or to defend a prejudice. Still he was not altogether free from the influence of the latter feeling. This tyrant of the human mind, which rushes on its prey through a thousand avenues, almost as soon as men begin to think and feel, and which seldom relinquishes its iron sway until they cease to do either, had made some impression on even the just propensities of this individual, who probably offered in these particulars, a fair specimen of what absence from bad example, the want of temptation to go wrong, and native good feeling can render youth. [49][14]

Judith, whatever her faults, whatever her ulterior motive, is profoundly moved and even, in a shrewd shift, frightened by the comprehensive virtue of Natty: "'It is a hard thing to fear truth, Hetty,' she said, 'and yet do I more dread Deerslayer's truth, than any enemy! One cannot tamper with such truth—so much honesty—such obstinate uprightness! But we are not altogether unequal, sister—Deerslayer and I? He is not altogether my superior?'" (313–14).

Natty's virtues are not isolated; his principles and practice are emulated or confirmed by others—especially Hetty, Hist, and Chingachgook—or are set against contrasting actions. His ubiquitous modesty and humility about his appearance and his achievements stand in stark contrast to Judith's manipulating vanity and lack of discrimination:

> As this was said, a singularly handsome and youthful female face was thrust through an opening in the leaves, within reach of Deerslayer's paddle. Its owner smiled graciously on the young man, and the frown that she then cast on Hurry, though simulated and pettish, had the

effect to render her beauty more striking, by exhibiting the play of an expressive but capricious countenance; one that seemed to change from the soft to the severe, the mirthful to the reproving, with facility and indifference. [63][15]

At her first appearance, in a small matter, a moral point is made that confirms all we have heard so far of her and that is fatal to her growing affection for Natty. More seriously, Hutter's moral confusion—he can attempt to scalp an innocent female victim and enjoin Natty to protect Hetty and Judith (112)—stands against Natty's unfailing steady grasp upon his morality:

> "My gifts are not scalpers' gifts, but such as belong to my religion and colour. I'll stand by you, old man, in the Ark, or in the castle, the canoe, or the woods, but I'll not unhumanize my natur' by falling into ways that God intended for another race. If you and Hurry have got any thoughts that lean toward the colony's gold, go by yourselves in s'arch of it, and leave the females to my care. Much as I must differ from you both on all gifts that do not properly belong to a white man, we shall agree that it is the duty of the strong to take care of the weak, especially when the last belong to them that natur' intended man to protect and console by his gentleness and strength." [85–86]

Hutter and March are utterly innocent of any feelings of mercy; Hutter understands his brutal indifference to the pain of others only after a *physical* lesson, his own scalping alive. Natty's refusal to strangle the old Indian woman who guards Hist leads to his own capture. His generosity and loyalty to Harry similarly stand in contrast to Harry's self-serving contempt for and disgraceful abandonment of Natty. At Harry's intemperate killing of the Indian girl, Judith catches a glimpse of Natty by the light of the torches, "standing, with commiseration, and as she thought with shame depicted on his countenance, near the dying female" (318). This serves no narrative purpose; its end is only allegorical. Set at once against this is Harry's sickening response:

> Hurry himself was startled at these unlooked for consequences, and for a moment he was sorely disturbed by conflicting sensations. At first he laughed, in reckless and rude-minded exultation; and then conscience, that monitor planted in our breast by God, and which receives its more general growth from the training bestowed in the

tillage of childhood, shot a pang to his heart. For a minute, the mind of this creature equally of civilization and of barbarism, was a sort of chaos as to feeling, not knowing what to think of its own act; and then the obstinacy and pride of one of his habits, interposed to assert their usual ascendency. He struck the butt of his rifle on the bottom of the scow, with a species of defiance, and began to whistle a low air with an affectation of indifference. [321]

The contrast is obvious enough, but while Harry's moral "chaos" is personal to him, Cooper also inscribes it as belonging to one "equally of civilization and barbarism," implying a distinction that in this novel is difficult to sustain. This episode should be remembered, along with Natty's refusal to kill the Indian woman, during the Redcoats' slaughter of the Hurons.

Natty's response at this point is static and correct—he is pictured almost in freeze-frame. However, the distinctive feature of Natty's morality is precisely that it is not abstract but always *active*: he infallibly sees the moral point or the correct behavior and acts upon it. He observes to Hetty, "[The Hurons] hold up avarice afore me, on one side, and fear on t'other, and think honesty will give way, atween 'em both. But let your father and Hurry know, 'tis all useless; as for the Sarpent, *he* knows it already" (306). As to Natty's relationship to March and avarice, Judith says, "No one— man or woman, could think of naming your honest heart, manly nature, and simple truth, with the boisterous selfishness, greedy avarice, and overbearing ferocity of Henry March" (267). The rejection of avarice, a vice that allegorically suffuses the whole of chapter 15, is accompanied by Natty's resolve to act upon his honest feeling. Natty's virtuous friendship with Chingachgook commands his active self-sacrificing assistance in freeing Hist, although Natty is taken prisoner in the episode. Similarly, the word he gives to the Huron to secure his furlough will be scrupulously kept; few of the Ark's company can even begin to understand this. They understand his giving of his word but not his keeping of it in deed.

The issue here is much more than a further addition to Natty's repertoire of virtues. Without the capacity to act upon his sense of right, Natty must betray the word he constantly gives to others and receives from nature. He would also lose what precisely distinguishes him from civilization; even Temple, one of society's more admirable representatives, believes in not wasting nature's resources, but, having the power, he lacks the will and capacity to forbid and prevent. Civilization does not in this series manifest Natty's active virtue—indeed, it frequently acts deliberately against the virtues it endorses, breaking its promises; and, as shall shortly emerge, in no other novel in the series is this deceit more striking than in *The Deerslayer*. It is interesting that immediately after Natty makes the observation to Hetty just given, Cooper ends the chapter by having Rivenoak, in all his disingenuousness, "sit in" for "civilization" against Natty's honesty: "The Huron resumed his seat by the side of his prisoner, the one continuing to ask questions with all the wily ingenuity of a practised Indian counsellor, and the other baffling him by the very means that are known to be the most efficacious in defeating the finesse of the more pretending diplomacy of civilization, or by confining his answers to the truth, and the truth only" (307). For all Natty's active moral power, he is occasionally rendered powerless, as, for example, when he sits in the canoe, helpless to resist the scalping expedition of Harry and Hutter; his ingenuousness renders him vulnerable to their manipulation of him and unable to act upon spoken principle. His response to their call upon his help to gather the hidden canoes places him unwittingly as their accomplice in the crime. Their "civilized" sophistication destroys the simplicity of his categories.

The comprehensive opposition that Cooper elaborates between Natty and Hurry Harry—in character, conduct, and opinion, covering virtually every major issue in the work—is a device typical of allegory. It is part of a pervasive patterning in the book, in small matters as in the largest ones, that relies on pairing. The oppositional pairing of Natty with Hutter and Harry is matched by the thoroughly explored counterposing of Hetty and Judith, which covers not merely their natures, mental capacities, characters, morality, and dress but even their living quarters; the extent to which this pairing operates allegorically may be readily seen even in the search for the key to Hutter's chest. Chingachgook and Hist—frank, chivalrous, resourceful, courageous Delawares—are set against both Harry March and the devious Huron Rivenoak; but all three Indians are set against whites. The pairings are not always of adversaries. Hist, at her first appearance, draws attention to the pairing of herself with Hetty as parallel to that of Natty and Chingachgook. Perhaps the most important pairing, for Cooper's allegorical purposes, is that of Hetty with Natty, which stretches from the opening conversations with Harry March to the book's end.

Even before he has met Judith, Natty has rejected her as subject to the settlements' influence and impervious to the nature in which she lives— nature which "will not deceive you, being ordered and ruled by a hand that never wavers" (27). Hetty is one of those, as is said of Natty in *The Pathfinder*, "that the Lord has in his special care" (27). The sight of Hetty's simple attire brings his mother to Natty's mind, and "a tenderness of feeling to which he had long been a stranger" (43). If her eyes are "sometimes vacant," "they were signs that attracted sympathy by their total want of guile" (178). The style with which she is first introduced strikingly recalls similar summary celebrations of Natty's virtues:

> It had often been remarked of this girl, by the few who had seen her, and who possessed sufficient knowledge to discriminate, that her perception of the right seemed almost intuitive, while her aversion to the wrong formed so distinctive a feature of her mind, as to surround her with an atmosphere of pure morality; peculiarities that are not unfrequent with persons who are termed feeble-minded; as if God had forbidden the evil spirits to invade a precinct so defenceless, with the benign purpose of extending a direct protection to those, who had been left without the usual aids of humanity. [66]

The affinity between the two is shown in the unaffected tenderness he shows to her, and in her efforts to persuade the Hurons to release him. The common allegorical purpose they share, which may be felt in the closing sentences of each of the last two chapters, is endorsed by Hetty's dying words to Natty: " 'I feel, Deerslayer,' she resumed,—'though I couldn't tell why—but I feel that you and I are not going to part for ever. 'Tis a strange feeling!—I never had it before—I wonder what it comes from!' " (533).

The piety and simple morality of Hetty are the result of a childlike submission that is more a matter of instinct than reason, but, like Natty's morality, hers is willed and active, if not understood. Both trust, but Natty acts as he does with a fully operating reason, choosing and willing his course of action. When Hetty's unaffected truth explodes Judith's superficial imposture, we recognize an authentic moral act, even if it is instinctive.[16]

As the novel proceeds, Hetty assumes a moral authority parallel to that of Natty; it is she who construes Hutter's scalping as in Cooper's words "retributive Providence." Judith feels it, but it is left to Hetty to utter it in words appropriate to her: "The Bible might have foretold this dreadful punishment!" (356). As for Natty, for Hetty nothing is "too dreadful to speak of." She even gains the ascendancy over her imperious sister:

> Judith spoke with decision, and she spoke with authority, a habit she had long practised toward her feeble-minded sister. But, while thus accustomed to have her way, by the aid of manner and a readier command of words, Hetty occasionally checked her impetuous feelings and hasty acts by the aid of those simple moral truths, that were so deeply engrafted in all her own thoughts and feelings; shining through both, with a mild and beautiful lustre, that threw a sort of holy halo around so much of what she both said and did. On the present occasion, this healthful ascendancy of the girl of weak intellect, over her of a capacity that, in other situations, might have become brilliant and admired, was exhibited in the usual simple and earnest manner. [379]

At Natty's shooting of the eagle, it is Hetty who delivers a reliable moral verdict: "God will be more apt to remember your sorrow for what you've done, than the wickedness itself. I thought how wicked it was to kill harmless birds, while you were shooting, and meant to tell you so; but, I don't know how it happened,—I was so curious to see if you *could* hit an eagle at so great a height, that I forgot altogether to speak, 'till the mischief was done" (447). Her verdict is not weakened by her own momentary excitement. Her judgment is even transcendentalized by Cooper: "Though timid, and shy as the young of the deer, on so many occasions, this right-feeling girl was always intrepid in the cause of humanity; the lessons of her mother, and the impulses of her own heart,—perhaps we might say the promptings of that unseen and pure spirit that seemed ever to watch over and direct her actions—uniting to keep down the apprehensions of woman, and to impel her to be bold and resolute" (501). Although she is at a loss in dealing with her affection for Harry and must be protected from the world by Natty and Judith, she is entirely capable of delivering an affecting and definitive rendering of the dominant leitmotiv of the whole series: "I don't like the settlements—they are full of wickedness and heart burnings, while God dwells unoffended in these hills! I love the trees, and the mountains, and the lake, and the springs; all that his bounty has given us, and it would grieve me sorely, Judith, to be forced to quit them" (376). One important consequence of the allegorical alignment of Hetty with

Natty, and her counterposing to Judith, is that Judith is exiled from any conceivable resolution within the moral structure Natty and Hetty inhabit. The allegorical pairing, then, while simple in itself, enables the management of more complicated issues like that of Natty's treatment of Judith, which is allowed to remain unresolved even at the end—a mute testimony to the fracturing effect of settlement.

Often, in allegory, incident may bear only the slightest connection with narrative development. Hutter's scalping, graphic and dramatic as it is, is hardly necessary to the tale told and exists primarily as evidence for the divine retribution Cooper, Judith, and Hetty find in it. At the close of the final chapter, the return to Glimmerglass, where Cooper's primary narrative motive seems to be to lead the reader from *The Deerslayer* forward into *Mohicans* and *The Pioneers*, Natty finds a piece of Judith's ribbon and attaches it to Killdeer. It is a mysterious gesture that the final sentence goes some way toward clarifying; it brings together Natty and Judith at a level of allegorical abstraction, however the reader may interpret it.

While Natty's first warpath is integral to the plot and has extended narrative consequence, its treatment is highly allegorized. In the early pages of the novel we are repeatedly reminded of Natty's innocence of human blood and his reluctance to shed it, as well as of the circumstances that might justify bloodshed. The episode is preceded by a discussion of the morality of retaliation and revenge; as he attempts to justify his scalping, Harry's moral confusion leads him to pervert the folk-wisdom of "one good turn deserves another" into "one *bad* turn deserves another" (91), as Judith is quick to point out. Natty converts the terms into "Moravian doctrine" with the biblical injunction "to turn the other side of the face"; Harry's response, "Do as you're done by . . . that's ever the Christian parson's doctrine," is a perversion, as Natty insists, of "Do as you *would* be done by." Natty's awareness of what must guide a Christian's conduct with an adversary is clearly uttered, and his encounter with le Loup Cervier will put those principles into action. It is worth noting that this is a more than local issue; it informs Hetty's naive design to evangelize the Huron to the doctrine of "return good for evil" (169) and underlies the revision Natty resorts to in justifying his killing of le Loup Cervier and the Panther: "This is nat'ral law, 'to do lest you should be done by'" (494).

As Natty, "a novice," approaches his testing ground, Cooper stresses that he is "alone," "thrown on his own resources, and . . . cheered by no friendly eye, emboldened by no encouraging voice" (116). He carefully enumerates Natty's practical and moral qualities, and the reputation that will accrue to his name from this and similar exploits that will follow it: "Equally free from recklessness and hesitation, his advance was marked by a sort of philosophical prudence, that appeared to render him superior to all motions but those which were best calculated to effect his purpose" (116). His conduct stands in marked contrast to that of Hutter and Harry in the scalping episode that immediately precedes this. We note his moral hesitation to kill an "unprepared foe"; he demonstrates an exquisite blend of epic chivalry, Christian scruple, and pious resignation; Cooper's moral delineation is nothing if not exact. The "lofty courtesy" of the antagonists' exchanges is not allowed to descend into a squalid "quarrel about the own-ership of a miserable canoe" (119). When virtue must yield to necessity, the coup de grace is delivered with dispatch. Natty regrets his deed, rejects scalping (a sign of cupidity, not honor), and shows sympathy and gentle-ness toward the Indian's travail. He submits to his ritual naming (recalling his first conversation with Hetty about his names, which express his virtues) and refuses, shortly, a further opportunity to kill. His soliloquy after the killing expresses his unfailing adherence to his white Christian gifts, his rejection of Hutter and Harry's explicit denial of them, and his disapproval of the colony's "[forgetting] from what they come, and where they hope to go" (125). His conscience is divided between heroic and Christian values,[17] whether to flaunt his triumph or to regret it. By leaving his name to providential care, the meed of praise for his virtue from Judith and Chingachgook is all the sweeter for his humility. Cooper's allegorical improvement of a simple scene could hardly be more comprehensive.

Hetty's first visit to the Huron camp is in itself something of a narrative deflection; if its occurrence is coherent with her character, it is also unexpected, to both the reader and the other participants in the scene. Her actual journey to the encampment is full of purely allegorical significance. Once more, the conversation that precedes it anticipates much of its content. Judith's fears at midnight of "woods [that] are filled with savages and wild beasts" (168) are answered by Hetty's affecting faith in divine tutelage: "Neither will harm a poor half-witted girl, Judith. God is as much with me, here, as he would be in the Ark or in the hut. I am going to help my father, and poor Hurry Harry, who will be tortured and slain, unless some one cares for them" (168). Her submission recalls that of Milton's Lady. As she prepares for sleep, Cooper observes, blending real-ism with moral improvement,

She knew that wild beasts roamed through all the adjacent forest, but animals that preyed on the human species were rare, and of dangerous serpents there were literally none. These facts had been taught her by her father, and whatever her feeble mind received at all, it received so confidingly as to leave her no uneasiness from any doubts, or skepticism. To her the sublimity of the solitude in which she was placed, was soothing, rather than appalling, and she gathered a bed of leaves, with as much indifference to the circumstances that would have driven the thoughts of sleep entirely from the minds of most of her sex, as if she had been preparing her place of nightly rest, beneath the paternal roof. [171]

Her security within the natural world is at once combined with the divine protection she seeks in her two prayers. She sleeps tranquilly. On her awakening into "the freshness of a summer's morning" (172), she finds herself attended by a bear cub and its family at a honey tree. The mother bear menaces, and Hetty mildly prays once more. Pacified, the mother suckles her young. As she resumes her path to the Indian camp, the bears file after her. It is impossible to miss the allegorical conjunction of the pious girl and compliantly peaceful nature. The passage serves that end and no other. If the Christian idealism she expresses in the encampment is rejected by the Indians, it is also rejected by Harry and Hutter, who are quite free with the word "Christian" when it suits them (for them it means only "white"—and that permits all). So—as Hetty makes quite plain—it is by the express permission of "the wicked governor and the province" (190) that the catastrophic scalping expedition takes place. Only she and Natty adhere to the word and its spirit.

Shortly after this when Natty, Chingachgook, and Judith search Hutter's chest for a suitable ransom, Cooper again takes the allegorical bit between his teeth.[18] Before the decision is taken to open the chest, there is a serious moral discussion of propriety which frames the entire incident; at its close, with the arrival of the Indian youth and the danger he might have offered, Natty finds an occasion to reproach their "prying into another man's chist" (227). The procedure within the episode is more miscellaneous than is the case with Hetty's journey. The search for the key and its discovery in itself constitutes a small perfect allegory, as the hiding place reveals, quite incidentally to the main purpose, a judgment upon the relative merits of Judith and Hetty—as Judith's blush registers her resentment and shame. The splendid coat betokens vanity, firmly rejected by Natty, as well as the uniforms of the colony and empire; the brocade dress later reveals Judith's vanity and envy, and, notwithstanding his recognition of Judith's beauty in it, Natty turns aside from the the sight as indecorous for her and a temptation to him; the pistols reveal "white neglect"; the sextant, though he mistakes its function, is an appropriate emblem for the "waste and destruction" (222) that follow the "heartless" surveyors; the elaborately carved ivory chessmen with their suggestions of chivalry, warfare, and empire draw from Natty a denunciation of idolatry and false gods. Natty's mistake is comical, but, as Judith sees, he is not too far off the mark: "My poor father carries his God with him, wherever he goes, and that is in his own cravings" (224).

By far the most protracted allegorical episode is that of Natty's furlough, and, in that, narrative and allegorical import are held closely together. The episode occupies almost a sixth of the entire novel and reinscribes Natty's virtues comprehensively. It enters the narrative at the point of Hutter's death; although Natty is about to face Indian torment himself he at once manifests his generous presence. Addressing the girls' bereavement he evinces a stoic, pious submission to the almighty will and shows pity for their plight. He offers consolation, and, simple as his expression is, it is no cold spiritual lesson: "I can't bring the dead to life, but as to feeding the living, there's few on all this frontier can outdo me, though I say it in the way of pity and consolation, like, and in no particular, in the way of boasting!" (383). His honesty is at once insisted upon— it is the overriding virtue he displays in the entire passage; it is a virtue affirmed by Judith, who nevertheless is "puzzled" at this "unaccountable being" (383). Cooper always registers her alertness to and admiration of Natty's virtues but separates her from full identification with them. They remain external to her. Although her active concern for him and her will to save him are entirely admirable, they are purely practical and unintegrated with her clear sense of his consistency; "her feelings" are "revolted at the cruel fate that she fancied Deerslayer was drawing down upon himself, while the sense of right, which God has implanted in every human breast, told her to admire an integrity as indomitable and unpretending as that which the other so unconsciously displayed. Argument, she felt would be useless, nor was she, at that moment, disposed to lessen the dignity and high principle that were so striking in the intentions of the hunter, by any attempt to turn him from his purpose" (385). What she admires but finds "unaccountable" is to Natty a simple moral imperative—the keeping of one's word—which, as Natty patiently explains it, finds more whole-hearted acceptance with Hetty (459) than it can with Judith (384–85).

In his scrupulousness, Natty places himself firmly against Harry, who, unlike Chingachgook, cannot understand the issue involved (405). It is Harry whose "cruel murder" (386) is responsible for Natty's seemingly fatal predicament; Harry's unregenerate lack of conscience about the scalping (404), his blunted feelings, and his lack of chivalry and protective concern for Hetty and Judith stand condemned by Natty's example. "I heartily wish old Hutter and I had scalped every creatur' in their camp, the night we first landed with that capital object!" Harry says. "Had you not held back, Deerslayer, it might have been done, and then you wouldn't have found yourself, at the last moment, in the desperate condition you mention" (404). His coarse self-justification receives its direct rejection from Natty: "'Twould have been better had you said, you wished you had never attempted to do what it little becomes any white man's gifts to undertake; in which case, not only might we have kept from coming to blows, but Thomas Hutter would now have been living, and the hearts of the savages would be less given to vengeance. The death of that young woman, too, was oncalled for, Henry March, and leaves a heavy load on our names if not on our consciences!" (404). While Natty will not accept a burden on his personal feelings for Harry's act, he clearly registers the racial complicity he will have to accept. Cooper's contempt enjoins the reader's compliance: "Resentment at what [Harry] considered Judith's obstinacy, was blended with mortification at the career he had run, since reaching the lake, and, as is usual with the vulgar and narrow-minded, he was more disposed to reproach others with his failures, than to censure himself" (400–401).

Natty fully discharges his errand from the Hurons and receives the responses he will bear back at the appointed termination of his furlough. Harry is unable to understand Natty's firm determination to act upon his promise: "What's an Injin, or a word passed, or a furlough taken from creatur's like them, that have neither souls nor reason!" (405). There is something almost psalmlike in Natty's extraordinary response:

> "If they've got neither souls nor reason, you and I have both, Henry March, and one is accountable for the other. This furlough is not, as you seem to think, a matter altogether atween me and the Mingos,

seeing it is a solemn bargain made atween me and God. He who thinks that he can say what he pleases, in his distress, and that twill all pass for nothing, because 'tis uttered in the forest, and into red men's ears, knows little of his situation, and hopes, and wants. The woods are but the ears of the Almighty, the air is his breath, and the light of the sun is little more than a glance of his eye. Farewell, Harry; we may not meet ag'in, but I would wish you never to treat a furlough, or any other solemn thing that your christian God has been called on to witness, as a duty so light that it may be forgotten according to the wants of the body, or even accordin' to the cravings of the spirit." [405]

The moral reproof to Harry blends with a prophetic biblical note that Cooper strikes with a sure hand. It is important to understand too that the admonition and accusation laid here at Harry's door are, on the evidence of the entire series, equally applicable to civilization,[19] which so often infracts the absolute principles that sustain Natty: "Sustained by his principles, inflexible in the purpose of acting up to them, and superior to any unmanly apprehension, he regarded all before him, as a matter of course, and no more thought of making any unworthy attempt to avoid it, than a Mussulman thinks of counteracting the decrees of Providence" (405–6). His calm and firmness, even at their parting, stands in contrast to Harry's "want of caution"; when the latter returns it will be with the still heavier, still more careless tread of the Redcoats.

Natty's perfection and constancy of will in thought and action, so fully given here, pervade the entire episode and are frequently reiterated. He remains protected by his lack of sophistication and effortlessly impervious to the temptation Judith offers; it is not merely that he does not love her but that his allegorical role requires his immunity to her charms. His resignation to what seems a certain death is registered simply as his pious submission to the divine will that has so ordained all things in nature; the doctrine he applies at Hutter's death applies equally at his own. The reader who recalls *The Prairie* will respond to this more fully than the reader beginning with *The Deerslayer* can.

This resignation appears in a less somber note in a remark to Judith that seems to me to set the moral tone for what is shortly to follow: "My edication has been altogether in the woods; the only book I read, or care about reading, is the one which God has opened afore all his creatur's in the noble forests, broad lakes, rolling rivers, blue skies, and the winds, and tempests, and sunshine, and other glorious marvels of the land! This book I can read, and I find it full of wisdom and knowledge" (418). Again nature is his "school of Providence." Shortly, his respect for nature is closely aligned with the moral imperative to respect his furlough; that he has "never, yet, pulled a trigger on a buck or doe . . . unless when food or clothes was wanting" (437) gives him a clear conscience which makes his word easier to keep and his ordeal easier to face: "Nothing truly makes a bolder heart, than a light conscience" (437). It is precisely the lack of such moral constancy which makes Harry a brute bully and a coward.

Passages like these make the name bestowed upon Natty by Judith, King of the Woods, entirely appropriate; the man perfect for his setting is bequeathed the perfect weapon, Killdeer. His childish betrayal of the name and the weapon forms the basis of the most highly charged allegorical passage in the novel. He thoughtlessly shoots a nesting eagle; it is a great shot and a disgraceful act. It is made to contain vast significance. It might recall (what has not yet happened) his impulsive killing of the deer out of season in *The Pioneers*—and at the same time, the insensitive shooting of the pigeons in that novel and of the two seagulls in *The Pathfinder*. Certainly it emblematically marks too the potential antipathy of the settlers' technology toward nature.

The act exists on the allegorical level not merely to register Natty's human imperfection but to reveal fallen man's indispensable virtue of conscience, which Natty's self-judgment so fully sets forth. He sees quite clearly not only his personal fault, the affront it constitutes to his respect for nature, but also what it means—the immoral exercise of power— which is so central in the entire series. What distinguishes Natty, of course, is his capacity to see it and act upon it. The colony cannot or, if it can, does not.

Natty's error here and the conscience that answers it do not impair Natty's moral authority; in the parade of wisdom as he bids each of his friends goodbye, his command is only the greater for his knowledge and conscience. Indeed, the central allegorical point of the entire episode is precisely to reveal conscience, not as an abstract virtue recommended but as an active virtue practiced. By him we may measure acts that do not satisfy the central criterion that should govern civilized Christian behavior.

The narrative consequences of the shot, governed by "the inscrutable providence" (448) Natty everywhere submits to, are highly ambiguous: they lead not only to his release but also to the dire slaughter "in which neither age nor sex forms an exemption to the lot of a savage warfare" (522). The soldiers, we note, do not share the concern for "nestlings" that Natty shows after his shameful act.

Natty is always in this novel infallibly placed in relation to a nature "which the hand of man had never yet defaced or deformed any part of" (36)—beautiful, abundant, calm, and ruled by providence; the softened light of dawn is at one with the moral sense: "It is the moment, when every thing is distinct, even the atmosphere seeming to possess a liquid lucidity, the hues appearing gray and softened, with the outlines of objects defined, and the perspective just as moral truths, that are presented in their simplicity, without the meretricious aids of ornament, or glitter" (332). Nature is not merely Natty's bride or "sweetheart" (139) but the source of all his morality, his very life blood; this "man of strong, native, poetical feeling"

> loved the woods for their freshness, their sublime solitudes, their vastness, and the impress that they everywhere bore of the divine hand of their creator. He rarely moved through them, without pausing to dwell on some peculiar beauty that gave him pleasure, though seldom attempting to investigate the causes, and never did a day pass without his communing in spirit, and this too without the aid of forms, or language, with the infinite source of all he saw, felt, and beheld. Thus constituted in a moral sense, and of a steadiness that no danger could appal, or any crisis disturb, it is not surprising that the hunter felt a pleasure at looking on the scene he now beheld, that momentarily caused him to forget the object of his visit. [278][20]

However, to note that nature in 1740 was not yet "defaced or deformed" is to allow that it is now, a hundred years later. "The holy calm of nature" is constantly threatened and disturbed; the first voice we hear is Harry March's; the Castle stands as mute testimony to the invasion. The alternation between the concord of nature and the contradictions of the settlement is constantly referred to; indeed, one of the most striking structural features of the work is the alternation of peace and violence: the innocent sounds of nature, like the cry of the loon, and the curdling shrieks of Man's violent incursions, like the cry of Hist threatened by the scalping knife of Hutter. Man with his forts, settlements, and civilization always threatens nature; the soldiers, manslayers by profession, as Hetty points out, stand in contrast to Natty, the deerslayer; Judith, by contact with the forts and the soldiers, is irreparably spoiled. In short, within the allegorical structure man stands against nature and therefore against God. If the settlements fail on the allegorical level, they fail comprehensively; if they deny what Natty means, his organic integration with god and Nature, they amputate that potential within themselves. It simply will not do to suggest that what Natty has been made so painstakingly to represent—the highest values civilization lays claim to—is a primitive childlike state that must give way to an adult reality which can only yearn for those virtues. To do so is to render *The Deerslayer* nonsensical. In fact, it is on this point, between an idealized Natty and the antagonist "settlement," that the entire novel turns. The cumulated force of Natty's allegory is irresistible as the novel's prime concern, but from the outset it is challenged and threatened by the colony. While the colony prevails, in the narrative and in the history, what it prevails over is indelibly described; it constitutes an allegorical negative force. In whatever order we read, the ruthless cupidity and cruelty which Cooper depicts as characterizing the first steps of the march of civilization must qualify the decent aspirations and ambiguous actions, "contradictions," of Templeton. At the very least, it must be concluded that, from the outset and by intention, civilization exacted as its price the destruction of the possibility of an organic relation between man and the created world. It would hardly be news that one of the primary agonies of nineteenth-century fiction was precisely to heal the rupture. Part of Cooper's significance in literary history lies in the power with which he felt and embodied the breach.

If, at the allegorical level, settlement and colony stand as negative forces against the positive force represented by Natty, Hetty, and pristine nature, the colony also constitutes in material terms a historical force that is irresistible and stands condemned not merely in abstract moral terms but in its acts, verifiable in the fictive and actual history. The colony's presence is felt throughout the novel and dominates its final phase. The irreconcilable conflict of the two elements does not disrupt the novel but is an indispensable feature of its form.

Scalping is crucial both to the thematic issue and to the narrative— everything stems from it, and it serves as a focal point for virtually every central concern of the entire series.[21] Harry March, at his departure from the Castle, shows no remorse for his scalping exploits that prove so nearly fatal; he regrets only that he was not more successful, as we have already seen. If Natty's spirited response raises a moral feeling in Harry, it is one he quickly sheds; he is as impervious to such considerations at the end as he is at the beginning. Hist's shriek, which breaks the stillness of the forest and which is registered so graphically by Cooper (108), does not deter him any more than Natty's moral remonstrance does when, before the action has fairly begun, the issue is first raised. Scalping is the focus for repeated discussion of Indian and white Christian gifts, for Natty's condemnation of man's betrayal of God's law and—by extension—for his indictment of the colony itself to which he and Chingachgook are loyal; it is the meeting point of moral discussion—especially about revenge—and of the themes of settlement and Indian dispossession, and it provides the most blatant example of the presence of white greed and cruelty in the entire series. That Hutter suffers divine retribution (or more simply, human revenge) does not settle the moral bill. The placing of a bounty on human scalps reduces the human to the animal level; Hetty, childlike as she is, takes the point as Hutter cannot: "Sell your skins, and get more if you can; but don't sell human blood!" (92). But, of course, Hutter and Harry do not consider Indians to be human—neither do the colonies, English or French. Cooper insists on this—as he does on the ineffectuality of Natty's words and actions; neither the colonies nor his companions are ever touched by Natty at all. Cooper's thoroughness in addressing the matter requires a more careful examination.

Natty, of course, rejects scalping and needless bloodshed repeatedly; he is never without scruple or reason. In response to Harry's racism and lack of logic—"You'll not say that a red man and a white man are both Injins"—Natty logically observes, "No; but I *do* say they are both men. Men of different races and colours, and having different gifts and traditions, but, in the main, with the same natur's. Both have souls and both will be held accountable for their deeds in this life" (59). His principles are witnessed in action in his encounter with the Huron le Loup Cervier and in his refusal to kill a second Indian needlessly.

The indifference of Hutter and Harry to Natty's or the missionaries' arguments is ubiquitous; human life has no special value to them—even the threat to their own scalps is greeted with stoical indifference. Their personal greed in seeking scalps is the direct cause of all that follows; it provokes a not particularly aggressive Huron hunting party, and the cruelty of it all is not engaged in unaware. Hutter consciously calculates that "this encampment contained the women and children of the party": " 'That's not a warrior's encampment,' he growled to Hurry, 'and there's bounty enough sleeping round that fire to make a heavy division of head-money. Send the lad to the canoes, for there'll come no good of him in such an onset, and let us take the matter in hand, at once, like men' " (105). Harry and Hutter are not simply boisterous, careless frontiersmen but are deliberately and unprovokedly heartless and cruel; they find their man-hood in such actions. Natty puts the matter plainly to Chingachgook:

> "It surely can do no harm to a red skin's honor to show a little marcy. As for the old man, the father of two young women, who might ripen better feelin's in his heart, and Harry March here, who, pine as he is, might better bear the fruit of a more Christianized tree, as for *them* two, I leave them in the hands of the white man's god. Wasn't it for the bloody sticks no man should go ag'in the Mingos this night, seein' that it would dishonor our faith and characters; but them that crave blood, can't complain if blood is shed at their call. Still, Sarpent, you can be *marciful*. Don't begin your career with the wails of women, and the cries of children. Bear yourself so that Hist will smile, and not weep, when she meets you. Go, then; and the Manitou presarve you."
> [262]

Cooper shortly endorses Natty's view of Harry and Hutter:

> But, neither of these two rude beings, so ruthless in all things that touched the right and interests of the red man, though possessing veins of human feeling on other matters, was much actuated by any other desire than a heartless longing for profit. Hurry had felt an-gered at his sufferings, when first liberated, it is true, but that emotion soon disappeared in the habitual love of gold, which he sought with the reckless avidity of a needy spendthrift, rather than with the ceaseless longings of a miser. In short, the motive that urged them both so soon to go against the Hurons was an habitual contempt of their enemy, acting on the unceasing cupidity of prodigality. [263][22]

However, if they were merely exceptional villains, the civilization could not stand condemned in their actions. Unfortunately, this is not the case. The colony, the source of civilization on this continent, authorizes their actions; indeed, their actions are completely coherent with the will of the colony which rewards them. Their indifference to age and sex anticipates that of the Redcoats.

Harry finds "the consciences in the settlements pretty much the same as they are out here in the woods" (111); even with his limited understanding of conscience it is only too easy to agree. Hutter's cruelty and greed are provoked by the colony, as Cooper notes with contempt:

"The bounty—" returned [Hutter], looking up at his attentive companion, in a cool, sullen, manner, in which, however, heartless cupidity, and indifference to the means, were far more conspicuous than any feelings of animosity, or revenge. "If there's women, there's children, and big and little have scalps; the Colony pays for all alike."

"More shame to it, that it should do so," interrupted Deerslayer; "more shame to it that it don't understand its gifts, and pay greater attention to the will of God." [87]

Cooper is at some trouble to see that we do not miss the point: "The morality that presided over their conference . . . was in truth that, which, in some form or other, rules most of the acts of men, and in which the controlling principle is that one wrong will justify another. Their enemies paid for scalps, and this was sufficient to justify the colony for retaliating. It is true, the French used the same argument" (88). Cooper insists that "neither Hutter, nor Hurry was a man likely to stick at trifles, in matters connected with the right of the aborigines, since it is one of the consequences of aggression that it hardens the conscience, as the only means of quieting it" (88). In doing so, he makes Hutter and Harry typical; they are as loyal, in principle and in action, as they think they are. As Hist shrewdly recognizes in a different context, "Governor tell no difference" (176); and if the governor cannot or will not, why should Harry and Hutter be expected to do so? Harry often invokes the colony's law to justify his actions: "Here was old Tom, your father, and myself, bent on a legal operation, as is to be seen in the words of the law and the proclamation, thinking no harm; when we were set upon by critturs that were more like a pack of hungry wolves, than mortal savages even" (186–87).[23] Natty, much earlier, has given the definitive answer to that, and it bears repeating, for at this juncture it is not merely an affirmation of his own sense of abstract virtue but amounts to a total condemnation of the colony and with it Harry March, its apologist, for his moral confusion is not less than the colony's: "Laws don't all come from the same quarter. God has given us his'n, and some come from the colony, and others come from the King and parliament. When the colony's laws, or even the king's laws, run ag'in the laws of God, they get to be onlawful, and ought not to be obeyed. I hold to a white man's respecting white laws, so long as they do not cross the track of a law comin' from a higher authority, and for a red man to obey his own red-skin usages, under the same privilege" (51). If this is not meant to guide the reader's response, it is pointless. The identification of Harry and Hutter with the colony makes it impossible to assign violence merely to the conditions of a rough unformed frontier. It is part of policy. Judith sees the scalping of Hutter very clearly, as she angrily tells March, "[The Hurons] have done that for *him* which you and he, Harry March, would have so gladly done for *them*. His skin and hair have been torn from his head to gain money from the governor of Canada, as you would have torn theirs from the heads of the Hurons, to gain money from the governor of York" (362). Harry's loud presence with the Redcoats when they arrive is entirely fitting.

Judith is herself a touching victim of the colony's influence. From the outset she is so presented to the reader: her vanity and her flightiness are clearly ascribed to the influence of the forts and their officers, and she is condemned by Natty even before their first encounter. However, she is a character of great strength; her merits remind us of Ellen Wade, Cora Munro, and Mabel Dunham, those courageous and ready frontier women. She is highly susceptible not only to the officers' libertine flattery but even more to the saving power of Natty's elevated morality—indeed, she is quite overcome by him. The reader appreciates her lively tongue, the forthrightness with which she sees and condemns the actions of Harry and Hutter, and her determination not to be beguiled by Harry's purely physical attractions. Also, her reform under Natty's influence presents a generic problem for the reader; should Natty not have accepted her proposal? In not doing so, he seems priggish, and it does not quite meet the case to say that just as she did not love Harry, Natty did not love her. The romance genre invites the match of a reformed Judith with the reforming Natty.

The match must fail on the level of allegory because she is not good enough for Natty, and, however reformed, she remains irremediably flawed; the nature of her fault is perhaps well illustrated in the passage in which she comments on the scalping exploit: " 'A cruel errand it was! But what will you have? Men will be men, and some even that flaunt in their gold and silver, and carry the king's commission in their pockets, are not guiltless of equal cruelty—' Judith's eye again flashed, but by a desperate struggle she resumed her composure. 'I get warm, when I think of all the wrong that men do,' she added, affecting to smile, an effort in which she only succeeded indifferently well" (137). She is exasperated and embarrassed here by the uneasy coexistence of her moral condemnation with her compliant sense of civilization's reality. She never quite resolves it, and it disables her as Natty's mate as surely as does our knowledge, at the narrative level, that Natty did not marry and that he is betrothed to nature.[24]

Her unfitness to be Natty's mate is made even clearer in her most impressive act, her imposture at the Huron camp. The act, self-sacrificial and courageous, is carried out with great presence of mind and would have succeeded but for Rivenoak and Hetty. The scene operates on the allegorical level: her deviousness is met by Rivenoak's suspicion and by Hetty's truth. Even more important, the *substance* of her attempted deception aligns her once more with the colony. The allegory of power that she so effectively embodies in her regal appearance and imperial rhetoric falls before Hetty's allegory of truth. But if she fails at the allegorical level and disqualifies herself for Natty's hand, she does figure forth a historical truth which Rivenoak recognizes at once, even as he sees through her pretense.[25] She *means* European power. Her "young men" (512) are no fiction; she threatens with them—and her threat is made good; the young men with their bayonets are led there by Harry, and she heralds their arrival. Her intentions notwithstanding, the scene brilliantly reveals her affiliation and tells us why Natty and she are an unsuitable match. What shortly follows indelibly inscribes what that power means—in numbers, violent force, and superior technology. Coming after it, the opening of *Mohicans* requires no gloss; if we have read *Mohicans* earlier, the final page of chapter 30 gives gruesome and particular substance to what is only generalized there.

Natty's wanton shot at the eagle is rendered ambiguous indeed by the actions of the colonial troops: they are heard before they are seen, and their sound is awesome—the moccasin is replaced by the boots, whose sound is "measured," "menacing," "regular," "heavy," "as if the earth were struck with beetles [mauls or sledgehammers]" (521); only Harry and the released Natty use firearms—the soldiers, their royal livery scarlet among the forest's green, do their imperial duty with the bayonet. "That terrible and deadly weapon was glutted in vengeance" (522). The scene is startling in its swiftness, but it is offered not as exceptional but as typical, even in its failure—precisely like that of Harry and Hutter—to discriminate about who is killed: "Presently, however, the shrieks, groans, and denunciations that usually accompany the use of the bayonet followed. That terrible and deadly weapon was glutted in vengeance. The scene that succeeded was one of those, of which so many have occurred in our own times, in which neither age nor sex forms an exemption to the lot of a savage warfare" (522). The word "savage" here is applied not to the Hurons but to the forces of the king's colony. The episode is merely continuous with the actions of Hutter and Harry. The legitimization by the colony of scalping is easy to accept if cynics like Captain Warley are in power. That Cooper is single-minded enough to bestow Judith on *this* man is almost shocking, even though, on the allegorical plane, it is not incongruous. This squalid conqueror, we note, is later knighted by a grateful sovereign.

Cooper nowhere else expresses so graphically the ruthless and violent exercise of white power as he does in *The Deerslayer*; whether it is read at the beginning or the end, it is unforgettable and must loom over the entire series. Whether we experience this account as we remember the Huron carnage at Fort William Henry in *Mohicans* or remember it as we read the latter, Cooper's imputation as to who initiated the savagery cannot be mistaken. Nor can the massacre's dreadful fitness as a completion of the historical counterforce, the colony, to the allegory of Natty be denied.[26] The book's closing word is "crimes."

If the indictment of civilization is more severe and unremitting in this novel, the inscription of Natty's complicity with historical process is equally emphatic. Natty, as *Mohicans*, *The Pioneers*, and *The Prairie* make plain, exists in Cooper's fictionalized history and is not merely a product of a civilization's idealizing allegory. While he sustains the constant, unfailing moral power the allegory equips him with, he cannot resist the force of history or of race. His complicity, however, is willed. We have noted time and again the assistance Natty gives to the forces that destroy him; in this he bears a striking resemblance to Faulkner's Ike McCaslin and Sam Fathers, and Faulker's treatment of Indians generally in *Go Down Moses* and *Requiem for a Nun* is reminiscent of Cooper's.[27] But, in *The Deerslayer*, Cooper goes much further than he has before in the series.

Natty wills his affiliation with the colony as firmly as he does his rejection of Judith.

Natty's alliance with the colony is early established; his first warpath is entered upon as a result of an encounter with "an officer of the crown." He tells Hutter that, after meeting Chingachgook, they will "go [their] way together, molesting none but the king's inimies, who are lawfully [their] own" (73); we note that even this early he sees himself as the colony's lawful subject. His alliance is not a passive one; he is soon to feel the excitement of his first encounter on the Ark with his "lawful" enemies. This is not at all to say that Natty becomes uncritical of what the colony does or abandons his principles; he remains the colony's most effective critic, as we have already seen: "When the colony's laws, or even the king's laws, run ag'in the laws of God, . . . [they] ought not to be obeyed" (51). He severely rejects "the colony's gold": "I'll not unhumanize my natur' by falling into ways that God intended for another race" (85–86).

While Natty never personally seeks the opportunity to shed blood, the occasions when he must—though they are rendered as personal encounters—are all to be seen as resulting either from the hostilities between the colonies or, more specifically, from colonial laws that countenance scalping for bounties. At the personal level, he is able to meet Hetty's remonstrance at his failure to return "good for evil" in the killing of The Panther with the argument of self-defense: "'Twould have been a'gin natur' not to raise a hand in such a trial, and 'twould have done discredit to my training and gifts. No—no—I'm as willing to give every man his own, as another, and so I hope you'll testify to them that will be likely to question you as to what you've seen this day" (486). His reply to Sumach is similar: "This is nat'ral law, 'to do, lest you should be done by'" (494). Sumach accepts the justice of the excuse. It is also, precisely, Hutter's justification for scalping: "We kill our enemies in war, girl, lest they should kill us. One side or the other must begin, and them that begin first are most apt to get the victory" (92). Hutter, of course, in his version of the preemptive strike takes the issue a stage further than Natty would or needs to do; it is, nonetheless, surprising, making all the obvious allowances, to note the identity of their starting points. Once Natty enters history, even his clear moral categories are compromised. The late twentieth-century reader has some reason to be chilled by what *The Deerslayer* inscribes: the amputation of moral decision by the logic of empire.

In his final conversation with Judith, Natty declares his full affiliation with the colony and justifies it by saying: "If the young men of this region stood by, and suffered the vagabonds to overrun the land, why, we might as well all turn Frenchers at once, and give up country and kin. I'm no fire-eater, Judith, or one that likes fightin' for fightin's sake, but I can see no great difference atween *givin' up territory afore a war, out of a dread of war, and givin' it up a'ter a war, because we can't help it, onless it be that the last is the most manful and honorable*" (540). The italics do not indicate the emphasis of Natty's tone of voice but the emphasis of Cooper. Thus to emphasize, within direct speech, is an unusual intervention for an author to make. It represents Natty's and Cooper's recognition of necessity. But the way in which the necessity has expressed itself in indiscriminate slaughter must raise larger questions than the resolution attempted in Natty's speech, which appears to validate Warley's preemptive strike. The morality and the expediency at work here draw Natty and the colony, with Harry and Hutter, into a closer affinity than is comfortable. We know that Natty will never *approve*—has never approved—the colony's or the nation's excesses, but he recognizes that he has no choice but to ally himself. The recognition is early inscribed, in *Mohicans*, in the sigh with which he greets Gamut's rejection of his promise of revenge for a possible death. The choice is so painful and perplexing because of the context of the colony's indiscriminate slaughter; we silently object—"but to ally with *this*"?—and recognize the typically imperial gesture in Natty's words in which the invaded is transformed into the invader. If Natty's own dilemma is unsparingly registered here, Cooper does not spare himself— or the reader—his implication in the settlements' "contradictions." No exemptions are allowed. Whatever Natty's shot at the eagle may imply about the ways of providence, it also unerringly implicates Natty with the civilization that will prove his and Chingachgook's nemesis. Cooper's honesty and sincerity in this embrace not merely his loyalty to the republic but also his reading of history; the combination imposes a dilemma he cannot escape, cannot resolve, but must inscribe.

The Deerslayer's final sentence fashions a rhetorical balance that the book itself does not fully bear out; it borders on intellectual platitude, a facile resignation to the imperfections of human nature. While it might seem to come as close to evasion as Cooper ever comes, it is placed as I hope to have shown, at the end of a book, and in a series, that is anything but evasive. Nonetheless, many readers are so overwhelmed by the ideal-ization of Natty, "gleamings of that pure spirit in whose likeness man has been fashioned," that they, in various degrees, omit the "deformities" of the divine image. Cooper's daughter Susan, in the preface to the 1899 London edition, accepts—and rather affectingly improves upon—Coop-er's almost mythical Natty and, ignoring the explicit criticism of *The Pioneers*, projects for the reader an idealized picture of Otsego in her grandfather's and father's day—an unspoiled landscape, set side by side with a harmonious agricultural community, much as Cooper had done in *Notions of the Americans*. Certainly, Cooper's loving presentation of his country and landscape and the imagining of an ideal Leather-Stocking possess great appeal, but not everyone susceptible to them needs to be as naive as Susan Fenimore Cooper understandably was.

James F. Beard, Cooper's most knowledgeable and sympathetic reader, offers in his introduction to *The Deerslayer* an excellently framed view of the matter. Fully conceding the force of the allegorical rites of passage Natty undergoes, he is not the less aware of the "pervasive irony" that results when what Natty represents, the possibility of "an ideal or divine harmony," must confront the real world. As Beard puts it, "Man . . . is precluded by his human and social nature from achieving an Adamic innocence." In human conflict, "the characters convert their earthly para-dise into a battleground." The "Edenic image" is transformed,

> with its implication of universal rational order, which justifies man's hope of creating a new, rational order, appropriate to his condition, in which the goal of innocence is superseded by the goals of personal responsibility and justice. By cultivation of his aesthetic faculties and by careful study of the laws of physical and human nature, the Leather-Stocking is, in this sense, able to achieve a remarkable har-mony with nature, though he must remain a killer to discharge his responsibility. Insofar as the other characters are oblivious of or indifferent to their opportunity to develop their moral consciousness, they cut themselves off from the possibility of their own salvation. [xiv]

While I am not sure that "innocence" can be a "goal," Beard's view makes good sense in its own idealistic terms. One can accept the substitution of "goals of personal responsibility and justice" for "innocence," but are the goals merely personal? Does not "innocence" mask what Natty means—

an embodiment of all the virtues a Christian civilization must claim? Is it man's "social nature" or his social choices that obstruct Natty's meaning? Does Beard state as strongly as Cooper the abject failure of "a new rational order"? He construes the purpose of Natty as a kind of trans- formed exemplar, a sort of social beacon. I agree that he is, but he only illuminates how fully his example is betrayed. It is not just themselves that the other, indifferent characters cut off from the possibility of salvation but the entire civilization. This may seem to overstate pessimistically Cooper's case against society, but is it any more overstated than the unrealistic view that America took much notice of Natty or the optimistic one that it would? The extreme idealization of Natty must be taken, if it is to have its full effect, in the context of how in the entire series Natty, nature, and the Indians are treated by civilization. Moral idealism mis- represents the books.

There is inevitably a rather sour taste in the reading of *The Deerslayer*; what is all the idealization for if Natty joins the cause of such a wretched colony and if that colony and its successors exile him so completely— physically and spiritually? After all, it is quite clear what Parsifal's rites of passage are for. What correlative does *The Deerslayer* offer for Amfortas's stricken kingdom? Can Natty redeem? Of course, he cannot. He is dressed for his own funeral; civilization buries him alive.

If it be argued that Natty figures only as the object of an atavistic and regressive desire to return to the childlike state, it must also be added that Natty marks the extent to which the century into which he barely makes his entry will disallow—has already disallowed—the organic life he rep- resents. Seen in this way, Cooper's Leather-Stocking novels imprint the central concern of nineteenth-century artists. Natty may be marginalized, but Cooper's concern with him is central.

Cooper's achievement was not at all that he could resolve the conflict inherent in the awful compromise he shared with Natty but that, in each and all of the novels, he was able to embody it so forcefully.

NOTES

1. There is a remarkable critical consensus about Cooper's impulse toward reconciliation that unites critics as different otherwise as Rogin, Sundquist, and Philbrick—even though the view of the reconciliation is different; some construe it as psychological masking of conflict, while others see it as an artistic accomplishment or a projection of a political hope.

2. Russell Reising ("Reconstructing") invites us to reassess Parrington. Reading Parrington on Cooper is to be aware of a man, graceful in his expression, fully appreciative of the poise and style of Cooper when he wrote about politics. Striking too is Parrington's admiration for Cooper's honesty and patriotism, since he obviously could not share Cooper's conservatism. Would that Trilling had shown Parrington as much courtesy. Parrington's style on Cooper may be illustrated by his treatment of *The Chainbearer*; after citing Thousandacres's defense of squatting, he says:

> No romance blends with the tale of their lives; no sympathy softens the picture of the stern old Yankee. He has set himself against law and order and must yield or be destroyed. It is the old story of the struggle for land . . . that went on for generations between speculator and squatter, between rich and poor, with much wrong and much right on both sides; yet Cooper's sympathies are cold to the squatter's plea and he enlists God, morality and the law, in defense of a title to forty thousand acres wheedled from the Indians for ninety-six pounds. [*Main Currents*, 226]

I largely share Parrington's view; guilt about the invasion, the theft, of America dies hard—for Cooper too. I would, however, rather stress that Cooper, by giving Thousandacres's argument full weight and letting us know how the land was acquired, enables the reader to respond as Parrington does.

3. Both Edgar Dryden (*The Form*) and Michael Davitt Bell (*The Development*) have recent books on romance that fail to mention Cooper.

4. See Waples, Outland, and the brief summary of the episode in appendix 1 to McWilliams's book on Cooper.

5. McWilliams characterizes the Cooper of the late 1840s in this way: "The Free Soil and Abolitionist movements, women's rights, Fourierism and the Fundamentalist revival, added to the spectacular illegalities of Anti-Rent, all seemed in Cooper's eyes, to prove the inability of Americans to govern their lives rationally or with regard for proven traditions" (*Political Justice*, 375–76). It is an appalled and appalling vision. I would argue, against Axelrad's view of *The Pioneers* as some version of pastoral, that Cooper registers from the beginning a powerful sense of what he sees as destructive of American idealism.

6. Railton, Sundquist, Rogin, Franklin, Clark (*History*), and, most recently, Motley in his excellent *The American Abraham* work out variations of this theme.

7. The strength of McWilliams's *Political Justice* resides in the clarity with which it shows how basic notions of justice come into conflict, and how those notions and conflicts pervade Cooper's texts. Since McWilliams is an honest and subtle reader on whom nothing is lost, I have little quarrel with him, except to question whether the novels are best served by being looked at in a way that privileges Cooper's political desire so completely. The distinguished peroration to McWilliams's analysis of *The Pioneers* commands assent, even as we note a rhetoric that favors Cooper's desire for civilization: "The greatness of *The Pioneers*, however, is that Cooper does not obtrude his own preferences upon the reader. . . . He allows the facts of Templeton to dictate that, inevitably, Templeton must deprive itself of Natty. . . . *The Pioneers* is one of those rare works in which an author has fully understood and successfully dramatized all the ramifications of a conflict that is crucial to his civilization's development" (129). McWilliams emphasizes the "inevitability"; Cooper does more—he forces us to scrutinize that notion. I find it odd that, on this novel, McWilliams has so little to say of the Indian, who places such duress upon the Christian assumptions that always for Cooper accompany "civilization."

For a more recent exploration of some of the territory McWilliams has occupied unchallenged for so long, see Brook Thomas's *Cross-Examinations*, an admirable book that considers Hawthorne, Stowe, and Melville as well as Cooper.

8. Warren Motley, in *The American Abraham*, like Slotkin and McWilliams though in different ways, stresses the providential nature of the American enterprise; it is noted by Tocqueville and is central to both the Puritans and the founding fathers. In this, whatever their differences, Winthrop, Bradford, Cotton Mather, Jefferson, Franklin, Cooper, and Crèvecoeur share an enormous amount. One half of Cooper's mind fully entertains the vision of a *destined* American civilization, while the other contests it. This is not simply a dark-light contrast. He clearly sees the future of America as dependent upon human will and responsibility; there is the course of history, but there is also human agency, will, and responsibility. He never seems quite to buy into narratives of inevitability, optimistic or pessimistic. It is this that impairs the neatness of the determinate narratives of both McWilliams and Axelrad.

9. For example, selectively, Philbrick's reading of *The Pioneers*, Axelrad's of *The Bravo* (in *History*), McWilliams's of *The Wept of Wish-ton-Wish* (in *Political Justice*), and Bewley's chapters on Cooper in *The Eccentric Design*.

10. In his urge to complete his myth-narrative, Slotkin in *The Fatal Environment* imposes a kind of philosophical closure on the novels that they do not sustain: "Here is a white man raised by the Indians, who on all occasions speaks for the immutability and sanctity of racial and class divisions. It is as if Nature herself speaks in validation of the peculiar compromises that characterize American society; and Natty's skill in bringing about the catastrophe of the Indian race reads this notion into the myth-historical record—Nature rejects her own children in favour of the Nature-transcending whites" (105). Interesting and provocative as this is, it depends upon overstatement and exaggeration. Does Natty *always* speak for the immutability of racial and class divisions? Is Natty to be credited with the "catastrophe"? Without extending the argument, I would simply maintain that Natty is much more varied than that. Similarly, Slotkin is quite right about who inherits the power "once the special conditions of race war and wilderness have been eliminated" (106), but in saying so he eliminates the dialectic of *The Pioneers*: clearly the Temple-Effingham line inherits the power, but that resolution is not permitted in my view to erase the conflicts and expropriations that precede it.

Even so, Slotkin is unfailingly illuminating on Cooper's ability to incorporate in his fiction "the major concerns of post-revolutionary republican ideology"; I disagree only that Cooper "fixed" the "explanation" offered by the myth of the frontier. By insisting on "myth codes," definitions, and explanations, he predictably ends with the notion of Cooper's "inadequacy"; for me Cooper's adequacy lies with his instinctive, ubiquitous refusal of the finality of definition.

11. The best arguments for following the order of Natty's life are given by David Noble, and, especially, by Axelrad (*History*, "Order").

12. Seeing Cooper as beset, like the Littlepages, with threats to his position, McWilliams in *Political Justice* tends to underemphasize the far from contemptible arguments having to do with use and property that Cooper gives to Thousandacres. This does not imply a lessening of Cooper's confidence in his own principles at a time when they were under severe attack, but rather his awareness of the possibility of a problematic element that he includes in his fiction without lessening the main didactic thrust. McWilliams is unfailingly evenhanded but always makes Cooper's beliefs his point of departure; McWilliams judiciously exposes the flaws in Cooper's positions but does not always allow that Cooper himself commonly exposes these contradictions. By construing always in terms of intention, McWilliams makes a failure to resolve a political position into an artistic failure, or a failure to resolve in artistic terms a polemical failure. Henry Nash Smith's well-known treatment of Cooper shows a similar error. By such criteria a novel may fail as a work of art, but the failure, honorably won, may be more deeply revealing, more truly representative of the world it addresses than any resolved novel could be. Demands for aesthetic closure of historical and political situations

are just as coercive and limiting as demands for political correctness, *Tendenzro-man*. If novels are not political pamphlets, still less are they sonnets.

13. I find myself here in close agreement with Brook Thomas—especially in the remarkable reading he gives of Melville's *Benito Cereno*. With admirable detach-ment he surveys the interpretative options and ends by supporting the deeply conflicted view of law, civilization, commerce, property, and "interest" that Mel-ville carries, unresolved, into his text. He insists on rejecting demands that Mel-ville's book take sides—not out of indifference or in service of a theory of un-decidability, but because it is not in the book. The value of Thomas's position—and the book's reversible ethnic situation, its central trope—is that it enables us to see the participants not understanding, and thus to understand. The result is deeply critical of the law and the attitudes that protect its dignity and is anything but quietist in its implications. It is undecidable only if the reader refuses to decide, *not* on black or white, *but* on slavery. It is unendurable only if we take the issue to be intractable to political solution.

On Babo, Thomas is brilliant; Babo's silence is construed not primarily as a literary gesture but as a truth of legal history. Melville cannot give a testifying voice to a slave and not defy verisimilitude. To do so would be to misrepresent. The silent Babo *signifies*, as no explanation could, the power of law, the suppression of the voice of the Other.

14. In the opening pages of *Cross-Examinations*, Brook Thomas demonstrates more lucidly than any other critic has the complications of a critical agenda that insists on the public and political obligation of art. He shows clearly how deeply contradictory many of the founding notions of the nation, accepted as simple pieties, were in political and legal fact. Whether we see Cooper as a realistic, romantic, or historical writer, he was inevitably involved in a highly problematic public debate; and resolving cannot serve and is not really involved. To be com-mitted to any public issue is to be entangled in an endless unresolved set of contradictions; an underlying realistic imperative must disqualify oversimplifica-tion, or reduction—political, mythic, or moral. Cooper cannot isolate himself, and does not isolate Natty, as the mythical interpretation guarantees; Natty is always surrounded by and participates in a credible situation or real events. However abstract he may sometimes be as a fictional construct, especially in *The Deerslayer*, however much he may stand for an idealized individualistic state (as near perfection of the moral life as may be permitted fallen man and, hence, exemplary), Natty fails in that exemplary function; the historical circumstances that surround him make his failure perfectly plain and turn Natty into mere myth; and this is equally the case whether the circumstance is represented by the well-meaning Temple, or the odious Warley, Doolittle, or Jones.

15. I am aware that I pass rather lightly here, as throughout, some very large theoretical issues having to do with narrative, representation, historicism, and the like. I find such matters of the greatest interest and importance, but, having resisted various sorts of barriers to a direct approach to my texts, I thought it inappropriate to erect others. However, a recent article by Hazard Adams touches

perceptively on my concerns here. Speaking throughout of a "visionary," "anti-thetical" position, standing against the polarization of aesthetics and power, he refers to our sense, expressed constantly, of an imposing presence that perhaps has more to do with the altered vision produced by works of art. There is nothing new in that (or in most theoretical writing), but what he says applies exactly to how I see Cooper (and Spike Lee): above unifying myth or political conviction, "the text continually challenges one to think further in a new light . . . even to the point of unresolvable contradictions."

16. I do not think the same argument could be made for a study of, say, the Home novels, or the Littlepage manuscripts: with *Homeward Bound* and *Home as Found* it would be necessary to offer at the minimum some biographical information, some account of the social and political changes that had overtaken America during Cooper's absence in Europe; the Littlepage trilogy requires con-textualization in the actual circumstances of the anti-Rent disturbances in the 1840s in New York state, the history of land ownership, and the party maneuver-ing that attended these issues.

McWilliams, Thomas, and Axelrad convincingly demonstrate the utility of giving priority to ideas and currents from outside the text. Indeed, it is difficult at this stage of literary history to imagine a study of literature isolated from social and political history, sociology, and the history of ideas.

17. McWilliams (*Political Justice*) deserves much credit for introducing an argument for incident as synecdoche: struggles for "bits of earth" become inquisi-tions of the nature of American civilization itself. Parrington is a possible forerun-ner. Motley recently takes it up with greater literary emphasis.

18. Including this discussion of the critical background in the text enabled me too to dispense with many notes, and to confine my notes to more recent critics.

CHAPTER I

1. Michael Gilmore interestingly reflects upon the effect of such growth on the American romantic artist; he hints at the impact of this on Cooper's literary practice (*American Romanticism*, 11). Wallace takes the matter much further.

2. Recent work by, among others, Robert Clark, Philip Fisher, Russell Reising, David Reynolds, Annette Kolodny, James Wallace, Warren Motley, and, most notably, Jane Tompkins suggests that this is changing. Earlier work by Nicolaus Mills and the too infrequently consulted David Howard also worked against the grain of established academic criteria.

3. Marius Bewley's *The Eccentric Design* offers the most intelligent and for-midably sensitive readings along this line; Bewley is also very alert politically.

4. It should be noted that while he has not altered his basic position, Peck's chapter on Cooper in the new *Columbia Literary History* shows a sharper con-sciousness of the claims of politics and history.

5. See Orians ("Romance"), and Rans ("Inaudible Man").

6. A reading of Theodore Parker's "Sermon of Merchants" and the controversy it aroused might raise similar reflections about the connection between transcendentalism and naturalism. See Miller's *The Transcendentalists*.

7. See Bewley, and Maxwell.

8. References to Crèvecoeur are not unusual among Cooper's critics, but usually they are only grace notes. Baym ("Women"), McWilliams (*Political Justice*), and Clark (*History*)—to name only three—refer to Crèvecoeur, but only incidentally. Kolodny is more penetrating and rather more detailed (*Lay*, 56–59). For a full analysis of the issue, see Rans ("Prolegomenon").

9. Mark Patterson's new book (*Authority*) should not be missed on this issue. His fourth chapter, on Cooper, is particularly relevant.

10. In the criticism of Crèvecoeur since Lawrence, the beast fables have often excited commentary, whereas the political text is only scantily addressed.

Jane Tompkins's restoration of the respectability of the didactic in her *Sensational Designs* seems to me an important moment in the historiography of American literature. Both Cooper and Crèvecoeur would respond negatively to Hayden White's rhetorical question, "Could we ever narrativize *without* moralizing?" ("Value," 23).

11. Obviously, questions of the law are often central in Cooper, especially in *The Pioneers*. Brook Thomas's opening pages are invaluable in opening up the problems that attend the law (and inevitably lead to the intensity of professionalization we see today). If, as Cooper explicitly did, one maintains the superior virtue of property and the law protects property, it is hard to maintain equality before the law, to restrict the *desire* for property, or to respect and balance "rights" that depend less on ownership than on use and occupation. McWilliams, and the more recent work of Robert Ferguson and Mark Patterson, should also be consulted.

12. Crèvecoeur's insistence on the willful, deliberate breach of the bonds of family, human affection, and sex unites him with the authors of authentic slave narratives, and with those of fictional ones like Stowe and Twain.

13. The question of the origin of, or the authenticity of, this letter is unimportant in my treatment of the *Letters*. If, however, it is "invented" or appropriated, it—like the "fictional" ending—only strengthens the argument for treating the *Letters* as a deliberate work of art. In this I find common ground with Winston, Chevignard, Philbrick (*Crèvecoeur*), Béranger, and Mohr.

14. My casual, conventional invocation of the "liberal" agrarian position should send the reader to Axelrad's *History and Utopia*, which instates conservative notions as other than aberrant in eighteenth-century thought. Axelrad draws careful distinctions—vital ones for Cooper—between a worldly, materialistic politics and a conservatism that distrusts meliorism. If one chooses to contest Axelrad's vision as too deterministic, even naturalistic, support will be found in Perry Anderson's *In the Tracks of Historical Materialism* (81).

15. At Crèvecoeur's "And after all who will be the really guilty," the reader might recall David Simpson's laconic remark cited in my preface about the intellectual prerogatives of victory.

16. An example is Mark Seltzer's recent work on James that brings Foucault and historical writing so brilliantly to bear—or the work of Baym, Tompkins, Kolodny, Bercovitch, and many of those collected in Elaine Showalter's recent anthology, as well as Ruth Bernard Yeazell's collection of English Institute essays. The exclusionary power of academic criticism may be indicated by the virtual ignorance of Carlos Fuentes's remarkable essay on Melville.

17. It is strange that he cites Orians's "Censure of Fiction" but not his "Romance Ferment."

18. By taking Cooper's ideas seriously, McWilliams (*Political Justice*), Motley, Philbrick ("*Pioneers*"), and Axelrad (*History*) produce serious readings of this novel as a work of art, whether it fails or not. Peck's determining assumption that Cooper's purpose is to construct an island paradise ensures his failure fully to read that novel. A charge similar to the one Peck levels at Cooper could obviously be leveled at him in this passage.

19. Bellah et al., *Habits of the Heart*, 144. In the two pages following the citation, the authors find—correctly, I think—a link between the Natty-Huck fugitive-outsider figure and figures in contemporary popular fiction, like Shane, the Lone Ranger, and the private eye. Their discussion of the movie *Chinatown* places the detective against so powerful a corruption that the only response is "unrelieved cynicism." They do not note that the particular form of evil is expressed through a perverted hypertrophic manipulation of the agrarian myth (orchards need water) and finds its expression on the level of personal behavior in the narrative line as murder and incest.

Patterson is only the most recent in a long line of critics to insist persuasively upon the "irreconcilable opposites" of myth and history.

20. While I share Mills's opposition to Bewley as an inheritor of Trilling who accepts that American social circumstances were inimical to fiction, I find that Mills overstates his case. Bewley remains one of Cooper's most sensitive readers, and he taught those who followed that Cooper's text rewards the closest reading.

21. Motley takes this idea as the central theme of his *American Abraham*; his book succeeds so well because he allows the psychological trope to be fully penetrated by Cooper's political and social ideas, consciously advocated. His textual demonstrations are of high quality indeed.

Patterson takes the matter still further and offers a skillful reading of *Home as Found*.

22. Axelrad ("Wish Fulfillment") provides the most thorough demolition of Lawrence on Cooper. He is lethally well mannered. He makes the routine respect paid to Lawrence difficult to sustain.

23. Tocqueville finds it easy to agree with Tamenund on miscegenation, as Cooper, a child of his Anglo-Saxon time (see Horsman), could not (*Democracy* 2:345). The issue, of course, is a vital one in much American fiction, both by whites and African Americans: Faulkner, Chesnutt, and Chopin are only three that spring to mind.

Tamenund, a historian artist within the text, finds not a merely literary opportunity, but an unending tale of European aggression, expropriation, and victimization.

24. My remarks here apply mainly to Slotkin's *Regeneration through Violence*. His more recent book *The Fatal Environment*, in its opening chapters, shows a sharp critical awareness of the dangers of the mythical approach. Similarly, a reading of Slotkin's introduction to his and James Folsom's compilation, *So Dreadfull a Judgment*, should qualify my remarks on Slotkin's attitude to Indians in *Regeneration through Violence*, where his omission of Tocqueville is significant.

25. Ross J. Pudaloff makes a similar point, finding that Cooper's romance could not accommodate both social aristocracy and political democracy. The most extensive exploration of this idea is to be found in McWilliams, of course.

Martin Green too speculates on Cooper's use of romance, and he finds that the reader is "represented by a regular Army officer . . . Captain Middleton" (*The Great American Adventure*, 221). Green does not see how insistently Cooper asks us to question what that officer really is, and how strong morally he is. By polarizing Empire and force (producing "adventure") on the one hand and industrialization, economics, and political considerations on the other, Green fails to bring out the implicit interrelation of the two sets of factors in the history Cooper inscribes.

26. Naturalism is currently receiving a great deal of serious attention. See especially the recent work of Walter Benn Michaels and of others—those, for example, represented in Eric Sundquist's compilation of essays on American realism.

The emphasis placed upon popular literature by both Fisher and Tompkins conclusively dismisses Moore's assumption that such work cannot be "the vehicle for scrutinizing the myth of progress" (*The Frontier Mind*, 183).

27. Carlos Fuentes illustrates this process admirably in his "Prometheus Unbound" (on *Moby Dick*), as does Brook Thomas in *Cross-Examinations*, which provides documentary underpinning for this observation of Fisher's.

28. It should perhaps be explained that the introduction was written after the five substantive chapters of the book; the reader might to some degree share my uneasiness at having presented as prolegomenon what is in fact the result of what follows. There is, I suppose, a certain twisted justice in that, given what I have concluded about the order of Cooper's five novels. Further, it should be mentioned that I read Tompkins, Clark, and Fisher—as well as others, like Axelrad, Thomas, Motley, and Wallace, who figure prominently in my notes—only after the completion of chapters 2 through 6.

29. There is no space here to develop this issue very far, nor would I be competent to do it. Fortunately there is no need to, since the appearance of Elaine Showalter's brilliant anthology *The New Feminist Criticism* should put the importance of the feminist enterprise for literary studies beyond question.

30. Cooper's very late novel, *Oak Openings* (1848), offers an Indian solution, in Scalping Peter's conversion to a secure piety, that the best efforts of the Reverend Grant failed to accomplish with John Mohegan.

31. Henry James's sense of this issue is unmistakably expressed in his notes for *Portrait of a Lady*; see his *Notebooks*, 18–19.

32. An interesting case in point is that, for generations of students, Crèvecoeur has meant only Letter III, "What is an American?," totally divorced from the context that informs it. Even Robert Clark (*History*), who is so responsive to contradictions in literary texts, alludes to Crèvecoeur in this way.

33. "Aristocrat" was a troublesome word in both Cooper's life and his writings. For a thorough discussion of it, see Waples, McWilliams (*Political Justice*), and Axelrad (*History*).

CHAPTER 2

1. This dimension of Cooper is of course most thoroughly advanced in Mc-Williams's influential book *Political Justice*; McWilliams makes Cooper's patriotic convictions the driving force for the fiction. More recently, there has emerged an inclination to see McWilliams's book as an oversimplification of the law, involving an underestimation of the partiality of the law, as well as of Cooper's capacity to see and register that partiality. See, especially, the work of Robert Clark (*History*), Charles Swann, Brook Thomas, and Richard Godden. The matter is crucial in *The Pioneers*, where too often Temple's merits have been taken at face value, his weaknesses understressed, and an identification with either Cooper or his father too readily assumed.

2. In a sense, this is the basic issue I offer the reader of my book; it is a matter not so much of what Cooper believed as of what he, as author, put in his text for the reader to hear and make sense of.

3. It cannot be sufficiently stressed that no easy assumptions about the meanings of these two words for Cooper should be made. McWilliams (*Political Justice*), Axelrad (*History*), and Waples offer clarification.

4. Since my prejudices against psychoanalytical readings tend to show rather blatantly (what might I be concealing?), a few words on the topic might put the issue behind me. Some of the best of Cooper's readers employ psychohistorical or psychobiographical formulae; Slotkin, Kolodny, Sundquist, Railton, Peck, Clark, Franklin, Godden, among others, in various ways and to varying degrees show this tendency. In some of them it is a continuation of a venerable tradition that seeks to find uniting conceptual formulae that enable the viewing of American writers in a context of defining American themes; and no one needs to deny the value of, say, Slotkin's efforts in that line. Often, however, it is a procedure that involves the insertion of a simplification to resolve a complex issue; once one introduces an Oedipal construction, it must eliminate or absorb other issues or be pointless. The more particular applications of psychoanalytic theories of, say, suppression have the drawback of being neither verifiable nor falsifiable. They tend to be merely asserted. Without disparaging Motley's excellent book, it does seem to me that while his major thesis holds up and is valuable to all readers of Cooper, his

254 ✳ Notes to Pages 49–50

speculation that Cooper in the creation of Temple had to struggle "to come to terms with his father's originality" (*The American Abraham*, 75), while interestingly pursued, is only distracting, at least to me, because, unlike most other things Motley affirms, it is not convincingly demonstrable. When, as it happens in Godden, we descend into psychoanalytical speculations about *Temple's* suppressions and secret, concealed recognitions, an important contribution to Cooper studies is maimed.

5. Among recent critics willing to allow for such an approach without unduly stressing prior literary demands about genre and plot are Tompkins, Fisher, Thomas, and Godden. The approach is not without danger of course; Godden, who is often illuminating, allows free flight for his own psychological speculation about Temple's motives on the slightest textual suggestion. Axelrad ("Wish Fulfillment") demolishes Lawrence's license with the text. All—and it is much—that is suggested here is that if we attentively follow Cooper's text, it yields not a personal confusion but an open-eyed skepticism about even the most basic republican assumptions. While Cooper as author is rightly credited with great foresight in raising the issue of conservation and the environment so early, and while Temple is anxious to establish himself as conservationist before his audience at the Bold Dragoon, we should not be surprised to find his conservationism tainted by self-interest. Kolodny (*Lay*, 91) offered a temperate view of this issue in 1975; ten years later Swann and Godden deconstructed Temple's pretensions as an unembarrassed fraud. Both approaches have their own appeal, but the extremes have the limitation of excluding the interest that inheres in the coexistence of two opposed motives in the same mind. It is this awareness that makes Kolodny's conclusion so persuasive, even if one balks momentarily at her calling Temple "kindly and well-intentioned" (he *is* that too): "The possibility of a human settlement harmonious with nature is rejected as early as the opening chapter; the possibility that a man could serve both as spokesman for civilization and as a protector of the natural world proved unworkable" (96). Clearly, she is right; it is, however, an open question whether or not Cooper set out to establish the "possibilities," as she suggests, or, as I prefer, to describe the impossibilities.

6. See Orians ("Romance Ferment") and Rans ("Inaudible Man") for more extensive treatment of this issue. Wallace's recent argument that Cooper did not aim only at the intelligentsia who contributed to the quarterlies but also at a more popular audience repays close attention.

7. Baym (*Novelists*) elucidates these categories comprehensively. Her remarkable book is required reading for those who would understand the critical terminology and assumptions within which Cooper and his contemporaries worked. That Cooper, especially in *The Pioneers*, appears often to defy them only makes the challenge of reading it more interesting.

Warren Motley is excellent on stylistic and generic matters in *The Pioneers*; one need not agree with a perhaps hypertrophic desire to prove his thesis about the dominance of the issue of authority in Cooper to appreciate the sophistication and force of his demonstration of the shift in *The Pioneers* from "Descriptive Tale" to the "dynamic frontier synecdoche he makes of Templeton later in the novel" (*The American Abraham*, 85).

8. Axelrad (*History*) gives the most convincing argument I have seen for reading the novels in the chronological order of Natty's life; he does this on the basis of a master narrative of a cyclical historical decline. He makes important counterarguments to McWilliams and others. The shortcoming of his argument is that it discourages the reading back of his thesis into *The Pioneers*, where, I believe, all the signs of decline and corruption are already in action. Axelrad's scheme requires Templeton to be a "proximate Utopia." Thomas sees Templeton as an agrarian idealization of land for sale, speculation, and exploitation (*Cross-Examinations*, 34). Kehler lists others who find Templeton "a disagreeable place" ("Architectural Dialecticism").

9. I do not think we should be too eager to construe Temple's act as *only* that of a generous man; Cooper's denial of its fulfillment is full of a more than emotional significance. The reconciliation that many have seen in the marriage of Elizabeth and Oliver is surely placed in question by Natty's refusal to be appropriated by "civilization." Kelly's formulation—Natty "exiles himself" (*Plotting America's Past*, 74)—is surely only partly true, and misleading; Natty does choose to go, but could he have chosen otherwise? What sort of novel would result?

10. Jane Tompkins's argument along these lines is the fullest and most convincing of several that make similar assumptions. See especially the contributors to Clark's collection.

11. While I cannot share Clark's Freudian leanings, his editorial introduction to his collection of essays on Cooper expresses my view exactly. Clark finds the genesis of Cooper's writing in "his radical uncertainties." Expressing the burden of the modern critic as many others today would, he writes "literature is a complex mediation of historical experience. . . . the problematic, the inconsistent . . . haunts [Cooper's] writing" (*James Fenimore Cooper*, 8). While his—and some of his contributors'—attitudes might seem aggressively theoretical, the theoretical considerations are fully founded in close attention to Cooper's text.

12. While most critics note the conceptual importance of this passage, until recently few shared my sense of how radically Cooper puts its assumptions to the question.

13. Motley and Ickstadt are only the most recent to affirm this, a commonplace of historical criticism. However, more recent critics are less inclined to swallow the legend whole or to take it at face value. See also Swann and Godden. Axelrad's providential view is quite different and, in effect, reinstates Calvinism into the largely deistic consensus (*History*).

14. McWilliams (*Political Justice*), who usually reads reliably for Cooper's intended sense, draws Temple close to his author—and there is good reason for doing so in chapter 1, and in Cooper's nonfictional writing. This practice has the effect, however, of limiting our sense of Cooper as capable of writing a *character* like Temple. Other critics have been far more ready to stress Temple's self-interest, which Cooper has also inscribed, rather than his disinterested principles—to lay

far greater emphasis on Temple as property owner and prophet of the entrepreneurial spirit, and in doing so to compromise Temple's always uneasy reception of Natty. Temple finds it difficult to know why Natty turned cold to him when he first discovered Temple's mission in the valley; the reader does not and is free to find Natty more intelligent and prescient than Temple, or to suspect Temple of being disingenuous.

15. Charles Swann ("Guns") forces a radical revision of our view of the game laws as conservationist. He shows that in New York as elsewhere they were an instrument for protecting privilege. Temple may well be well intentioned, weak willed, and ineffective; he may also be seen as self-interested and, in matters of business and property, anything but ineffective. Suffice it to say that his conceptions and words are out of keeping often with his deeds. A close reading of page 160 in Beard's edition will reveal unmistakably Temple's interest, complicated too by the fact that the "vigilant magistrate" is also the property owner; this should not be forgotten when we read Natty's retort and, later, Elizabeth's disagreement with her father about the law.

16. Peck's view of Jones as "comic" ("James Fenimore Cooper," 244) seems to me mistaken; Jones, arguably, can be seen as a comic character, but his commercialism, corruption, and cruelty cannot. Doolittle departs, it is true, but to do his damage on new frontiers. I cannot see that "*The Pioneers* contains these forces within its larger pastoral vision" (244).

17. I use the term "history" rather loosely. It is not part of my intention to involve myself in particular history, the "real" history of actual events, as it were, or even in any systematic history of ideas. I deal only with the history the novels contain, as the novels give it. I am aware that alterations and convenient repressions of real events may have taken place, but, for my purposes, the novels contain all the complications it is necessary to deal with. Cooper's sense of and response to actual events was always sharp, informed, and specific; but in the novels his approach is more general—it is, rather, the Revolution, the expropriation and removal of native peoples, the violence of colonial wars, the changing landscape and technology that he offers in a general setting in which human characters enact complex and recognizable responses having historical consequences if not in specific historically verifiable events.

Others offer a more comprehensive detailed historical background: Smith, Slotkin (*Regeneration through Violence*), Meyers, Cooper's biographers, Beard in the textual and introductory apparatus of his edition of the *Letters*, and the authors of the introductions to the individual volumes of the SUNY Press edition of Cooper's works.

18. This is a crucial moment in the text, and my response may seem harsh or cynical. McWilliams (*Political Justice*) sees it clearly as the proper exercise of the authority of the law, a bastion against barbarity. And obviously it responds to the need of the novel's plot. I would draw attention to the lengths to which Cooper allows lawlessness in the name of the law to go. His latitude in the matter serves of course a conservative law and order view of the matter: this is how far things can

go when the law sleeps. At the same time it reveals how slender the hope is that rational laws, *if* they are rational, will control this society. In any event, Oliver's immediate assent shows how clearly in the end he is aligned with Temple, and how appropriate an inheritor he is. His invocation of "Heaven" suggests confirmation of the basis of McWilliams's legal schematics.

19. Many critics of very different persuasions—Philbrick (*"Pioneers"*), Peck (*World*), McWilliams (*Political Justice*), and Kelly, for example—are attracted by the idea that the marriage accomplishes a satisfactory fictional and conceptual resolution; the romance ending unites the contending elements in the novel. There is strong reason to think so. Kelly sees it as an attempt to "defuse" or "resolve" the destructive conflicts (*Plotting America's Past*, 29–31). I do not see it that way. A bomb has been described, and it will explode; the evidence for thinking so is that it already has. Although a wished-for resolution is figured forth in the marriage, the fulfillment is, throughout Cooper's work, withheld—as McWilliams makes clear—except, temporarily, in the allegorical fantasia of *The Crater*. Given who the happy couple are, it is hard not to think that the new is old; the Revolution did not change too much, and certainly property did not change hands.

Eric Cheyfitz makes precisely this point in a very recent article (*"Tarzan"*). Although its title does not suggest its relevance here—it has to do with Tarzan and United States foreign policy—it is profoundly to the point about race, class, and property in Cooper as well as Burroughs. It is because I admire his work and regard it as indispensable in Cooper studies that I hazard an avuncular tone: I do not understand why, in his 1985 article (*"Literally White"*) and in places in the 1989 article (*"Tarzan"*), he employs a theoretical rhetoric that ensures that his important insights will remain the "property" of a small part of a privileged academic class instead of reaching the wider audience that might make a difference. The theory *is* important; it cannot, as Gerald Graff has insisted, be kept out of any discussion; but on/in whose terms? This is Cheyfitz's central concern, and it is vitally important that it be seen; I am not sure that Cheyfitz's language is not frequently masterful in a way that in other contexts he deplores.

20. The tendency of much recent criticism takes a line similar to mine. McWilliams (*Political Justice*) establishes with great clarity the importance of property to Cooper's political and legal thought. A more critical strain appears when Cheyfitz (*"Literally White"*) raises the question of appropriated and imposed languages and of what "legal" might mean to a colonized people; Brook Thomas's discussion of the close relationship of law and property should also make us cautious in affirming the protective function of law or equality before the law. Swann and Godden also dismiss the simpler pieties about the law—she is not for them the blindfolded figure with balanced scales. As Godden somewhat tendentiously puts it, "Law has always been Temple's battleground, and with it he teaches the rules of the market" (*"Pioneer Properties,"* 131).

21. This is for me a crucial point and an easy one to miss, for it can be seen simply as an emotional appeal. Elizabeth, unable to get Natty to do something for himself, tries to persuade him to do it for her. There is nothing discreditable in that,

but it is very revealing, since it stands for Natty's entire situation: he can only give; civilization can only take or, what is the same thing, offer something worthless in exchange. Natty's giving is so complete that he is a true model of Christian charity, and yet he is rendered as absolutely exceptional in a nominally Christian society. Cooper is utterly honest, a fearless witness, and absolutely ruthless; as Christian, he sees it as his duty to expose a Christianity of mere words, betrayed by Christians' deeds. As an advocate of civilization and of republican patriotic values he is equally unforgiving. The conflict is extremely disarming; it is important to recognize, however, that he is not confused or conflicted when he dramatizes it.

Cheyfitz ("*Tarzan*") shows clearly—if it still needs to be said—the relationship between commerce, property, law, and Christianity from the beginning. Cooper is exceptional only in the frankness of his recognition of it.

22. It seems to me that one way of approaching this novel is to see it as multivocal or multilingual rather than as the expression of a single or compound plot. In doing so one would attend to each voice on equal terms. Godden's suggestion of many plots and his equanimity about lack of sequence are also helpful. When one takes this approach, it quickly also becomes apparent who is *listening* to whom, and one becomes extremely sensitive to inconsistency. One is quick to see the absurdity—if one listens—of a court procedure in which the accused is acquitted of a crime he did commit and condemned for one he did not (Godden, "Pioneer Properties," 133). Philbrick in his comments on the sheer violence of argument in *The Pioneers* was perhaps the first modern critic attuned to this, in spite of the formalism of his justly famous article.

23. Swann's discussion ("Guns") of the legal historical background and foreground surrounding hunting laws and the right to hunt casts an entirely fresh light. It is a vital essay for the understanding of this passage. It certainly suggests limits to the property rights Temple would like his hearers to think he has, as well as pointing clearly to the advantages that accrue to the influential and landowning classes as a result of game laws. Godden ("Pioneer Properties"), relying on Swann, whom he exculpates from his own excesses, usefully invokes E. P. Thompson on the issue.

No serious criticism of this novel has ignored the legal issues, and in particular the confrontation at law of Temple and Natty: Grossman, Dekker, Smith, Ringe, and McWilliams (*Political Justice*) have all seen that as central. The conflict, whether construed as Cooper's own or simply as a fictional projection of a conflict between two equally virtuous views as to what constitutes a worthy life on earth, has one obvious, but not often discussed, peculiarity: the judge is also the plaintiff in this construction. Moreover, it has often been too readily agreed that Temple's view of the sanctity of the law is unassailable, even self-evidently true. I have never been convinced of that and welcome Wayne Franklin's rejection of it; a body of critical writing is developing that submits those assumptions to close scrutiny and in the process reveals a much more interesting novelist than had previously been thought. The crisis of belief, wherever we place it in Cooper's career, that produced openly polemical novels has all its elements present and deeply embedded as early as *The Pioneers*, and, I would suggest with others, even in *The Spy*. I hope in these pages to have contributed something to this revision.

A full pursuit of the legal issue would require as a first step a reading of McWilliams (*Political Justice*), Swann, Thomas, and the important sources Thomas cites in his *Cross-Examinations*—in both the main text and the footnotes. Thomas is, as Swann remarks in a footnote, too kind to Temple, but it is remarkable how well Cooper's text responds to Thomas's legal analyses.

24. McWilliams establishes this comprehensively in *Political Justice*; Cooper's own *The American Democrat* makes the matter quite clear. Indeed, the ownership and exploitation of land property is the basic telos of the agrarian narrative, as Crèvecoeur's "Andrew" shows. Cooper's resistance to the notion that political power should be attached to property is also well-documented (McWilliams, Waples, Axelrad [*History*]); that was the aristocracy he feared. I take it that the Charles-Town episode in Crèvecoeur's *Letters* indicates an agreement on that issue. Cooper, in McWilliams's rendering of his career, conceded only late in his life the intimate relationships among wealth, property, law, and political power and was even willing to accept them, if only as a necessary evil.

However, to speak of Cooper's beliefs should not blind us to Cooper's evident awareness, in my view early in his career, of what those relationships were, and to his revelation of them in *The Pioneers*. If Cooper's sympathies are intended to be with Temple, that only makes the matter more interesting and strengthens the argument for Cooper's artistic disinterestedness. The "shift in emphasis from creation [settlement] to acquisition . . . from retreat to territory" noted in *The Crater* by Motley (*The American Abraham*, 163), is equally evident in *The Pioneers*. Brook Thomas points to the failure of the laws to differentiate between Doolittle and Natty (*Cross-Examinations*, 40); I am not sure that I agree, but the point is less that they are *unable* to do so than that they are not called upon to do so. Cooper is only realistic when he points out this omission, which he is careful to let the reader see—but not the judge.

25. Swann indicates the legitimacy of the judicial search for the slain deer. In the novel, of course, the deer, which they *know* is there, is not the real object of search.

26. The reader is referred to Jane Tompkins for a very impressive argument for this position. She is not alone in the field; I believe that works like her *Sensational Designs*, Russell Reising's *Unusable Past*, Brook Thomas's *Cross-Examinations*, Philip Fisher's *Hard Facts*, Cathy Davidson's *Revolution and The Word*, and Carolyn Porter's *Seeing and Being* will change the way we see American literature more radically than Matthiessen did.

27. Cheyfitz ("Literally White"), notwithstanding his arcane rhetoric, is illuminating on this issue. The current active discussion of colonialism is very pertinent to Cooper. Rob Nixon is interesting on the point in an article on what Caribbean and African writers have seen in *The Tempest*. Leo Marx (*The Machine*, 72) and Cheyfitz ("Tarzan") pursue the issues raised by *The Tempest*.

28. It has always been difficult for white critics to write about matters aboriginal; it is the rare one—even among those aware of the problem—who can rinse

clean our inherited vocabulary of racial superiority and stand free of accusation. The problem began with the word "discovery" and continues into the present. It would not surprise me to find myself accused too. If I do not name critics who prefer civilized norms, the "better kind of life" that replaces the aboriginal, it is partly because this attitude is so pervasive and involuntary. Such citations certainly would confirm the continuing problem today, which Cooper first addressed in 1823, even in a time that has become critically conscious of the freight of bias that language carries. At a time when racism was pandemic, respectable, and supported by science (see Horsman), it is really quite astonishing that, when he had available stereotypes like the noble savage which he would use in later novels, Cooper, whose own writing contains evidence of his belief in the superiority of the white race, should choose the least admirable stereotype—the Indian degraded by liquor—and use it to convey so searing a critique of the entire ethos upon which the novel is founded.

Cheyfitz and McWilliams both have essays in Robert Clark's collection that address the issue of the problem that the Indian presented to Cooper.

The treatment of Scalping Peter in *Oak Openings* has struck several critics from McWilliams (*Political Justice*) to Ickstadt as a shocking abandonment of the problem so fully addressed in the passage under discussion.

29. Philbrick is authoritative on the presence in the text of the cycle of the seasons; he presents the matter very persuasively. Philbrick is aware of the conflicting forces in a period of intense social change, but his predilection for cycles, reconciliation, and civilization's view of the events in the novel deflects attention from the critique to which civilization is submitted.

30. At this point, I take this to mean simply: Temple is making the wilderness safe for everyone. A comforting thought in short. Godden ("Pioneer Properties") sees the "taming" and "civilization" as gestures of domination and exploitation. I agree, as I do also that McWilliams is too easy on Temple's presumed altruism (Godden, 126, 128). If McWilliams oversimplifies in reading, in Godden's words, "civil law" as "innocent of economic interest," however, so does Godden in rendering the issue univocally in the other direction. That Elizabeth's intended meaning coexists with the subtext Godden insists on enriches the fiction.

31. The moment of Oliver's "election" by Temple is a vital and complex one. It involves a sense of guilt and obligation that does Temple credit; it recognizes Oliver as a fellow gentleman—Oliver's later behavior confirms Temple's instinct; it provides as well a criterion that overrides class and property—contested by Jones; and it affirms the superiority of a "housed" civilization to that of the woods—contested by Natty—an affirmation that is repeated in Middleton's "epitaph" in *The Prairie*, where Natty is too moved to see it (although his equivocal valediction to Paul Hover may indicate a change in attitude). There are then several voices and views present. At that point, it becomes a matter of what the reader does with them.

If Oliver is elect, who are the excluded? Those assembled at the tavern? There is little that is Jeffersonian here—the improvident, vulgar, drunken patrons and their incorrigible demagogues, and yet they issue an important moment of critique. Is John Mohegan, degenerate and seemingly barely coherent, excluded? And yet he is given two resounding opportunities of critique too. And Miss Grant's final class marriage places her as fixedly as Elizabeth is placed—and merit has nothing to do with it. In short, again and again, a fixed position is beset by an invented circumstance that questions it.

It has always seemed to me odd that an author so set in his views and articulate about them should create a text that leaves the reader so much space to occupy. After all, Cooper did not always do so and did so less and less as his career developed. I find Axelrad's insistence on Cooper's conservatism helpful here. Cooper could never accept the Left's view of political and human possibility, but his rooted distrust of fallen man enables his clear sight of what there was to be seen. He is freed of a belief in man, and this freedom creates the unsparing critic he is. It enables his readers in their turn to take a view of what Cooper sees that is quite different from his own. Cooper may have had desires and dilemmas, but they did not impair his clear-sightedness. He could always see, and frame his perception of, corruption, but what he saw can be quite differently framed. What is order for Cooper is for others class privilege; what qualifies Heyward as superior, the reader is left to ask. Temple's order, law, must be met by Elizabeth, who in her turn must be met by Mohegan.

32. In this conversation, the secret of Oliver's identity enables Oliver to engage in some very provocative racial irony at Elizabeth's expense. The reader familiar with the racial views of Cooper and his contemporaries will recognize that these ironies do not spare their author. See also, Horsman's *Race and Manifest Destiny* and Cheyfitz's "Literally White."

33. While Elizabeth here clearly refers to Indians and Natty, the word "possess" must have a different or additional meaning for Oliver that the first-time reader cannot share: Oliver should "possess" the land. That he is thought to be Indian but is not nicely focuses the issue.

34. Temple's deviousness is apparent here; so is his evident desire to recreate in the New World the conditions which Franklin invited immigrants to escape from. The imputations of Thomas, Swann, Godden, and others about the relationship between law, property, power, and an industrial future, not transcendently inevitable but as the product of deliberate and interested will, find support here.

35. One of the most durable views of this episode involves Perry Miller's frequently alluded to "head"/"heart" distinction. This seems to me an unacceptable simplification. While it is true that this view is affirmed by an authorial voice, that need not mean that it has peculiar limiting authority. Elizabeth's subsequent action shows that this model of feminine propriety and sensibility is unconvinced by the masculine head. I also disagree with Nina Baym ("Women"), who with Annette Kolodny was the first vital feminist reader of Cooper: I think that Baym underestimates Elizabeth's strength. I do not find Elizabeth shallow or "profoundly uninteresting" ("Women," 699). That she should collide at all with the masculine paternal principle, and so spectacularly, is more than interesting.

Thomas writes that the "heart and head" approach makes personal an issue that is not personal at all—the partiality of the laws: "Impartial interpretation (and even administration) of partial laws does not produce impartial justice" (*Cross-Examinations*, 43). I do not believe that Cooper was "displacing" historical conflicts by "'eternal' personal ones"; rather he reports the conventional displacement and embarrasses it through Elizabeth.

36. Gramsci's basic position is valuable here (12). If the spontaneous consent of the governed is not forthcoming, he goes on, "coercive power" prevails. That exactly fits the case here—as throughout Indian history. "Good" Indians concede that consent. It need hardly be added that the history of native peoples on this continent demonstrates that even consent will not guarantee *their* property immune under the law from appropriation.

CHAPTER 3

1. That is to say, Cooper dramatizes Natty's gradual alienation, which is underlined in Natty's sense of humiliation in his decline from hunter to *The Prairie*'s trapper. To draw attention to this is not to impose Marxist criteria on the text; Cooper's intellectual ambience provides abundant support for such a reading. Not only was it a commonplace with the romantic poets and novelists, but Emerson was soon to make it both intellectually central and popular in America; Thoreau, Melville, Stowe, Hawthorne, Theodore Parker, and Margaret Fuller unite in placing alienation as the central concern of the century.

2. Cheyfitz's articles make it necessary to ask why anyone should have expected anything else.

3. Quoted in Dekker and McWilliams, *Fenimore Cooper*, 91.

4. W. H. Gardiner's review is the finest example (Dekker and McWilliams, *Fenimore Cooper*, 104–18). For the critics' vocabulary, see Baym (*Novelists*); for romance criteria see Orians ("Romance"), and Rans ("Inaudible Man").

5. See Dorothy Waples's loving tribute to Cooper that illuminates the impact of party politics on Cooper's career with careful scholarship.

6. What is suggested here is that although, as many point out (most notably McWilliams in *Political Justice*), Cooper consciously embraced and understood certain principles, his novels reveal a profound uncertainty about those principles themselves. Robert Ferguson is instructive on the complexities and contradictions of Enlightenment ideas. The section of my chapter 1 on Crèvecoeur suggests in him an unease approaching panic. William Hedges was among the earliest to draw attention to this and its importance.

7. Cheyfitz ("*Tarzan*") sheds light on this pattern of the hospitality shown to settlers and discoverers by those who are to be displaced, in relation to the Indians—and, in effect, to the colonized generally. The most casual reading of Bradford should confirm his view.

He memorably ends his essay by construing the loving action of Kala, Tarzan's ape "mother," as a figure for the way in which the colonizing power "civilizes the other in order to savage her" (357).

8. Although this passage inscribes Natty as a participant in a series of events that represent the "wonderful . . . progress of the American nation," those stages are seen by Natty as a deterioration. While Cooper's intention may be in doubt, the reader familiar with all three novels, now brought to mind as a succession in time by his introduction of 1831 to what was then the opening novel in chronological series, might well be jolted.

9. Kolodny draws attention as well to Magua's reflection on the valor of the white military (*Lay*, 100); the Indians were used in this campaign not as allies but as mercenaries. The assistance rendered is clear, as is the alienation involved for the Indian.

10. Kolodny (*Lay*) offers the most thorough analysis of Cooper's imagery of the violation of nature, as well as pointing to Natty's complicity in the violation of his bride. While I find Kolodny's conclusion on this novel unconvincing and, really, question begging, the serious vigor of her analysis of whatever she addresses commands respect. Anyway, not to accept her conclusion is not at all to suggest that the conflict she addresses is not there and important.

11. Cheyfitz ("Literally White"), in his stimulating remarks on "translation," points out the difficulty, when one argues from legality, of being sure that "legal" is translated—or translatable—and, if it is, that it will be respected in the same way for the Indian as it is for the white, whether it will make a difference for the Indian, whether it will restrain the acquisitions and invasions of the white. The point here is not whether Cooper would find Cheyfitz convincing, but that Cooper willfully gives a highly complicating element an immense influence in the action when the immunities of romance tolerate a simplification. This is an appropriate point at which to draw attention to the work of Francis Jennings, who addresses the historical issues raised in this note comprehensively.

12. The anonymous reviewer of *The United States Literary Gazette* sees Heyward as only romance hero and nothing else (Dekker and McWilliams, *Fenimore Cooper*, 102). Kelly (*Plotting America's Past*) sees Cooper as intentionally opposed to Heyward and his outworn code, as a defective Oliver Effingham toward whom Cooper is ideologically moving; in the assumed historical narrative, Heyward, for all his qualifications, is only a stage on the way to the perfect social white hope that is Oliver. There is a good deal in this, as long as one remembers Oliver at the pigeon shoot. Kelly's desire for this progressive historical narrative, however, obscures somewhat the comprehensiveness of Cooper's delineation of Heyward's faults.

Kelly develops two elements: one downward toward the possibility of fall; the other upward with the possibility of learning, of escaping the past through one connected with the past (*Plotting America's Past*). But Kelly's view of the two parts of *Mohicans* should be contrasted with Slotkin's view of a reversal between the two parts of the book (*The Fatal Environment*, 96). In *The Prairie* it is Middleton who represents that hope, set as he is between Bush, a man of no restraint, and Inez, a creature of no liberty (99).

While one need not quarrel with the notion that Oliver, Heyward, and Middleton are meant, in their respective marriages, to represent a hope for the future, Kelly's desire to satisfy his own imposed narrative (which is not Cooper's) leads him to force matters: he slightly fudges the end of *Mohicans* in order to affirm Heyward's ascendancy—in fact, Natty and the Indians are left to end the book. Similarly, his discontent with Cooper's resolution of *The Prairie* stems from his assumption that Cooper shares his own liking for the schematic. While Kelly's method is supported by excellent—sometimes inspired—readings, he is led to argue Cooper's failure rather than his success in registering the limitations of his American hero, or his refusal to provide a misrepresentation.

13. Heyward always stands ready, like Temple, to offer money. Earlier he has offered money to Natty and is predictably refused. Harvey Birch in *The Spy* is similarly contemptuous of material reward. Virtue, evidently, is its own reward; the refusal reveals a weakness in the powerful and a strength in the powerless.

14. Natty—as well as what he represents—is surely not unequivocal, in this novel especially. This is a critical difficulty only if we insist that Cooper is a simpler novelist than he in fact is. No one questions that Natty is often subjected to idealization, is everywhere, to varying degrees, a model. Kelly suggests that he can be so because he is a man apart from Indian and European criteria (*Plotting America's Past*, 56); he speaks of Natty's "uncoded vision." But Natty's "without a cross" *is* code for "White Christian," and *that* code is scanted. Kelly is not untypical in overprivileging the undeniable tendency in the works to idealization. I am suggesting a critical procedure of lowered expectations, in which the failures, including Natty's, to satisfy the criteria are as important as the idealizations. The reader should consider, in whatever order we take the books, what it means when we set *The Deerslayer*, in which idealization dominates, against any and all of the other works. Certainly, for me, while I can understand and value Kelly's master narrative of ascent, I find, if one must have such a master narrative at all, that Axelrad's one of decline is more in accord with my reading of the text.

Natty has sometimes been seen as reaching a symbolic stature in this novel; Kelly cites and seems willing to agree with Ringe, Porte, and Bewley (*Plotting America's Past*, 103). He stops short of Richard Chase's affirmation of Natty's transcendence. Instead, he finds most major characters in the novel raised a degree or two in abstraction. I agree and would add only that the abstraction is not consistent but is frequently interrupted by rather rude invasions from the real world.

15. There is no shortage of critics aware of the ambivalences of *Mohicans*: Fiedler, Porte, Smith, and Peck (*World*) are among them. Most seek resolutions of the ambivalences, or of the ways in which artistically the opposing forces are controlled. I see the recognition of Cooper's comprehensive registration of the pandemic fractures in his civilized nation in the making—even at the expense of artistic considerations—as of primary importance.

16. The epigraph to chapter 29 clearly indicates Cooper's generic priorities:

The assembly seated, rising o'er the rest,
Achilles thus the king of men address'd.
[Pope, *The Iliad* 2.ll.77–78]

McWilliams ("Red Satan") addresses the question of the epic expectations associated with both the romance and "North America's heroic tribes." He indicates the acute problem surrounding any idealized epic representation: "To depict the Indian as an inhuman savage lusting to scalp white maidens would be historically indefensible and would ultimately diminish the achievement of conquest. . . . But to depict the Indian as an aged stoic hero or a noble savage would implicitly deny the justice of the continuing March of Civilization" (152). Focusing on a literary formulation, McWilliams's essay makes less of the *racial* complication than Cooper does. If, as Kelly argues (*Plotting America's Past*, 83–84), *Mohicans* seen as an American epic makes America a cultural contender, as well as the political one it already was, one must ask why it is so dark, so deeply fissured. The candidates for epic hero are obviously Uncas, Natty, and Heyward; since Uncas and Natty cannot be granted the necessary primacy, is Heyward, even in the second part of the novel, as Kelly would have it, a convincing substitute?

17. Kolodny's analysis (*Lay*) of the rhetoric of this speech should be read by all students of this novel. I am suggesting not autonomic agreement but that it is exemplary in a way too few treatments are of how to treat Cooper's text with respect.

18. Tocqueville is an interesting exception to prevailing Anglo-Saxon attitudes on this subject. For a straightforward exposition of the latter, see Horsman's excellent book *Race and Manifest Destiny*. Cheyfitz ("*Tarzan*") is especially provocative on the importance of racial considerations in the nation's view of itself and its mission.

19. Or, perhaps, as Cheyfitz ("Literally White") would have it, given Heyward's legal reservations, Cooper wishes us to see the difficulty of "translation" of considerations of that sort.

20. When considering Cooper's position on the head/heart controversy, we might be led by this passage to consider how favorably he viewed consistent rationality, and how cautiously we should take the apparent rejection of Elizabeth Temple's viewpoint about her father's law.

21. See Tompkins's brilliant rebuttal of this imputation (*Sensational Designs*, 94–100); she comprehensively rejects the casual undermining of Cooper it achieves even in Cooper's critical supporters, from Spiller to Slotkin and Sundquist.

22. See n. 16 above.

23. Kelly has an excellent passage on the importance of disguise and its relation to the change he emphasizes in Heyward (*Plotting America's Past*, 69).

24. It is noteworthy that this passage aligns honor untranslatably with blood—and by implication Christianity. In such a view a reasonable expectation of a Christianized or civilized Indian is impossible.

25. Cooper's open attacks on white Christian behavior must have seemed radical to those who were so deeply concerned to sustain biblical creation versions of race. Chingachgook's rational and competent non-Christian and Mohegan's lapsed Christian must in their different ways have been disturbing images for those who were busily arguing the racial, religious, intellectual, moral, and cultural superiority of the Caucasian. See Horsman (*Race*, 149) and McWilliams ("Red Satan").

26. Need it be said that Munro's implicit belief in the pure, nonmaterial basis of knighthood is absolute nonsense and that Cooper knew that? The belief is costly to Munro.

27. See Dekker and McWilliams, *Fenimore Cooper*, 80–120.

28. See Dekker and McWilliams, *Fenimore Cooper*, 93, 100, 111. Most critics of *Mohicans* have been fascinated by its complex treatment of racial issues and especially of racial mixture—sometimes at the expense of other equally important matters. Slotkin is interesting on the cross-typing of racial, sexual, and cultural behavior (*The Fatal Environment*, 92). In ascribing to Cora's mixture of blood and gender(!) her "capacity for action and courage," he rather misses the explosive *critical* effect of her exchange on chivalry with Heyward. While Slotkin unfailingly sheds light on the texts he examines, the attention he pays to myth and the relentless psychologizing of the sexual/racial threat represented in Uncas and Cora and of the undeniable desire to suppress it, kill it off, allows him to miss the equally undeniable facts that Cooper is remarkably successful in allowing all this forbidden stuff to rise to the surface and that the text inscribes *both* the explicit suppression (killing) and the celebration of the possibility. I find Baym's forthright view of the way in which "blood" is allowed to overcome considerations of class and manner, character and breeding, very much to my taste ("Women", 74). Cora's threat is placed by Baym in a real world available to consciousness, where exegesis is secondary to circumstance. Cora, it must be added, is a threat also to the codes of both chivalry and romance.

CHAPTER 4

1. That Cooper was aware of these shortcomings we know from Susan Cooper (*Pages*, 157).

2. Brotherston, speaking more generally, alludes to this novel's "sense of cumulative memory" ("*The Prairie*," 167).

I share Brotherston's disapproval of those American critics who have bought the argument of civilization's destined role, although I feel he is less than just to Smith. The purpose of his important article is to show that Cooper, in some sense a maker of America's sense of its own history, with some of which he must have been familiar, sanitizes the actions of Europeans in North America, and that he is willingly complicit in the process of dehistoricizing America's view of itself. If Brotherston is right, then of course the plea that Cooper merely adjusted history for the purposes of his chosen genre would be a weak one.

While Cooper does provide a narrative that valorizes civilization, he does not, as Brotherston suggests, exculpate civilization for its suppressions. I hope this chapter supports my view. Brotherston, in what is a provocative, informative, and historically specific article, is so fixed on judging Cooper that he entirely misses the irony of Cooper's words about Mahtoree's "simple mind's" inability "to embrace the reasons why one people should thus assume a superiority over the possessions of another."

3. There is significant disagreement about how seriously *Notions* should be taken. Axelrad (*History*) is less convinced of its serious significance than is Mc-Williams (*Political Justice*).

4. Fields ("Beyond Definition") endorses Elliott's position. For him the prairie is "a neutral ground" on which is tested the characters' "ability to order their worlds and themselves" (94) in a landscape that offers no defining frame. My difference from such a formulation, which enjoys wide assent, is that it tends to immunize civilization and the moral life from close scrutiny.

5. Smith, *Virgin Land*, 64–76.

6. While I do not wish to specify, one of the consequences of too fully embraced totalizing views is that mistakes are made with the text. Even Slotkin, usually so thorough and careful, is less than that in his treatment of Cooper in *Regeneration through Violence*. Brotherston has Judith rejecting Natty in an article that insists on Cooper's misrepresentation ("*The Prairie*").

7. A recent and honorable example is provided by Fields ("Beyond Definition"). He notes, with McWilliams and so many others, the need the novel recognizes for civil law, pointing out too Middleton's incompetence at reading both people and natural signs—even at the end. He speaks of the "exposing" function of Sioux/Pawnee law and constructs a pattern of primitive versus pseudo-primitive (Bush) versus white civilized law. There is much in that, but Fields seems uncritically to share assumptions of cultural superiority that need not examine whether or not civilized law works well, is immune from primitive vengefulness, is evenhanded, impartial, and untouched by the selfish motives of the powerful. Cooper does not ignore this issue.

8. Fields is very shrewd on Bush's appearance and the way in which the signs he wears lose their conventional meanings ("Beyond Definition," 95–96).

9. Many have commented on the dreary wasteland setting of the novel; Merrill Lewis, Smith, Kolodny, and Motley, who alludes to Beckett and calls it "a nearly abstract wilderness" (*The American Abraham*, 108), are eloquent on this issue. Fields sees it as a place in which definition and judgment are made difficult ("Beyond Definition," 94); he is especially convincing on the prophetic dimension of the scene, as is Cooper.

10. I share with most critics the perception of Natty's complicity. Many see it as tragic irony. Kolodny's brief treatment sees this as vital, and I agree while stressing Natty's guilt less than she does. I am sure that the tragedy and guilt are present, but to allow the emphasis to lie there deflects attention from the typicality and common reality represented.

11. Spiller observes, "Grossman is the first critic to realize fully that Cooper's work was a quest for 'a wholly adequate symbol in which to concentrate his tragic vision.' He found no Dynamos and no Whale, but his intention was none the less noble for its failure" ("Second Thoughts," 185).

It seems to me that the axe is one among several adequate symbols that Cooper developed. But we expect altogether too much of symbols; certainly we did in 1949 when Grossman wrote. Even Adams and Melville establish their symbols contextually, not in isolation. The adequacy of Cooper's axe is established in a powerful set of historically motivated circumstances.

12. As Kolodny (*Lay*) points out, Natty is charged with reason here against Bush's instinct. She finds the combination of the "meek" and the manly in him unsettling. I think it is meant to be; Cooper's sense of its exceptional nature is absolutely evident.

She is most interesting on Cooper's efforts to sustain the possibility, the "promise," of nonviolent entry in the figure of Natty. I would like to see the focus of Cooper criticism shift from Natty and Cooper to the aim of Simms which she cites: to celebrate nature before progress expunges it and to provide the pause for self-evaluation on the part of America's readers of its founding canonical literary text.

13. It should not be supposed that Cooper was ignorant of the facts of the treatment of the Indians in the 1820s which Tocqueville was so soon to address.

14. We should note Bush's appropriation of Natty's language of freedom; it is a kind of Indian language too that Faulkner assumes in the opening strain of *Go Down Moses*.

Fields touches on this element ("Beyond Definition," 95); he mentions "geography" and "human conduct" but strangely overlooks the importance of property. Again I refer the reader to Godden, Swann, Thomas, and Cheyfitz on the issue. McWilliams reminds us that, for all the similarities, Bush's essential difference as a destroyer is maintained (*Political Justice*, 266).

15. When the assumptions of Judge Temple are shared by so many—by Cooper, by many of his characters, and by so many of Cooper's critics who endorse his preference for "civilization" (McWilliams (*Political Justice*), Fields ("Beyond Definition"), and Smith, for example)—the emphasis I place is likely to seem merely tendentious. I therefore remind the reader that my purpose is not to cast a scornful eye on law, religion, and Western civilization but to draw attention to the extent to which Cooper insists on being critical about these basic elements of a society in practice, in detail, and to the effect such criticism has on our understanding of the text.

16. Axelrad's insistence in *History and Utopia* on a transcending divine narrative governing human affairs is always worth taking into account; it would not explain passages like these but it does accommodate them. Slotkin seems to me to simplify the matter by psychologizing it; while we must agree that Cooper's tale in *Mohicans* seems intent on eliminating the issue of racial difference and union, Slotkin eliminates the way in which Cooper deliberately keeps the issue before us and refuses to erase it (*The Fatal Environment*, 97–100).

17. Fields ("Beyond Definition," 106) and Brotherston have interesting reflections on the scope of Natty's geographical journeys.

18. Porte (*The Romance*, 52), extolling Natty as "Cooper's magnificent yearning myth," cites and assents to Pearce's view that Cooper does not condemn civilization as an "evil force." And, of course, he does not do so, but he provides enough for some readers to reach that conclusion and, perhaps, to suspect that Cooper's doubts were not trivial. The problem for Cooper is less, I think, whether civilization is evil or not than it is the certainty that civilization is acquisitive and destructive, and the difference this knowledge must make in the way we view it.

19. See Dekker and McWilliams, *Fenimore Cooper*, 249–261.

20. McWilliams, Bewley, Brooks, Parrington, Grossman, and Kelly, among others, make this point in various ways. Maxwell's discussion is most thorough.

21. This progressive view of civilization's march is the basis of Fields's view of this novel ("Beyond Definition,"), and it does of course work well to account for Bush's return to society. We should also, however, take into account both Cooper's reflections on the flaws of society and Axelrad's arguments for a nonprogressive history of social man.

The real problem for the meliorist view that is shared by so many, Fields and McWilliams among them, is that if one accepts that Cooper's intent was "portraying the virtues of white civilization" (*Fenimore Cooper*, 291), one must then accept the judgment of failure to find a "satisfactory terminus." Cooper's desire is, most would agree, always obvious; equally evident is the relentless presentation of an always problematic irresolution which makes satisfying closures impossible— Cooper never presents one. Kelly's critical search for artistic control in Cooper (*Plotting America's Past*, 33, 71) is subject in my view, for all its incidental revelations, to the same objection. There may be as much artistic control in the projection of a chaotic and historically uncontrollable narrative as there is in a resolved one.

22. Brotherston should be consulted on Cooper's revisions of Indian history.

23. Fields ("Beyond Definition," 104), legitimately emphasizing the moral perils of self-sufficiency, overlooks this aspect of the common understanding Mahtoree and Hard-Heart—and most of Cooper's Indians—share.

I share Kelly's skepticism about the "optimistic conclusion" of the novel, as well as his recognition that "Hard-Heart has sealed his doom by refusing Mahtoree's proffered alliance" (*Plotting America's Past*, 122–23). But this is surely intended, and not the result of Cooper's "historiographic confusion" in the series. Does a fiction need to "compel" our belief in a program? I see no failure here; we are led by the text to recognize the political and historical conflict; it is our doubt, enabled by Cooper, that allows us to see "Hard-Heart's isolation on the plains . . . as wistful" (122).

24. Nina Baym's high evaluation of Ellen Wade as a kind of "new woman" is undoubtedly right ("Women"). I do, however, feel that she undervalues Mabel Dunham and Elizabeth Temple as characters and as moral deciders. It is worth considering at this point, without undue praise for Bush for not beating his wife,

how well he comes off in allowing Ellen freedom to choose; *The Pathfinder* offers a parallel as Natty forces Mabel to decide her own future.

The crossing of class and gender issues addressed here is also touched upon frequently in *The Pathfinder*.

25. This passage represents the nearest Cooper comes to the actualization of his social vision; the indirect means of its transmission to the reader is therefore of the greatest interest. No more direct, observable version is ever offered.

26. See Cheyfitz ("*Tarzan*"), especially 342–46.

27. Fields suggests Cooper's lack of faith in human potential: Natty represents "what we cannot be" ("Beyond Definition," 111). Or should it be what we choose not to be? At any rate, what we are not. For Fields, Natty represents not a possibility, lost or future, but a perspective of judgment in a moral landscape that offers few pointers. Thomas's suggestion that Natty is a conservative emblem, a kind of folk hero of democracy placed against "propertied class's distrust of the common man" (*Cross-Examinations*, 28) is an interesting but in the end unconvincing speculation. At any rate, whatever susceptibilities might be protected by such a view, it does nothing to save Natty.

28. Agreement on this is so widespread that it is fair to call it the consensus view.

29. I find withering the implications of the pages here considered and have come close to chiding myself for overarguing the issue. I therefore particularly welcome the reassurance I find in recent work of Clark, Swann, Cheyfitz, and Brotherston.

30. Abiram's crime and its trial do indeed place Bush's tribal structure under great stress. Fields ("Beyond Definition") believes that Ishmael's law must destroy the tribe if it is directed against one of the tribe's own. It seems to me that, as long as it is exercised within the tribe, it protects the tribe. Surely, Tamenund's judgment against Uncas does not weaken the tribe. What is true, of course, is that the trial and Ishmael's invention/discovery of law is part of the ideological dynamic of the work that drives them east again, to society.

Kelly (*Plotting America's Past*, 114), with whose argument with McWilliams I have some sympathy, raises the issue of whether Ishmael can be called just, or the bringer of the civil law to the wilderness (McWilliams, *Political Justice*, 269). It is true that Ishmael does not have to answer for his crimes, but then neither does Judge Temple. If Bush is not better in some legal senses than Temple, as I argue, he is in this respect, surely, no worse.

Slotkin (*The Fatal Environment*, 100) is highly unsatisfactory on this vital episode. It is true that Cooper performs a vanishing trick on the Bushes, but is Bush's spirit broken? Does "clan justice merely reproduce among whites the vengeance law of savagery"? Is Abiram's death sentence any different from what a "civilized" court would have proposed? Is Abiram lynched?

31. Brotherston ("*The Prairie*," 166) is interesting on this passage, as is Overland's study of the text. See also Cheyfitz ("*Tarzan*").

32. See n. 2.

33. Crèvecoeur registers Tocqueville's sense in the Nantucket chapters of *Letters*, though more laconically. Brotherston, commenting on Pearce, is unforgiving:

for him, Cooper's prairie setting allowed him more easily to resolve "the gnawing inconsistencies of a Constitution uniquely framed to defend the basic rights of man, but which, in the case of the Indian, did not prevent his massive physical destruction" ("*The Prairie*," 168).

34. The alienation so fully insisted on by Thoreau, Emerson, Whitman, and the transcendentalists derives from a recognition Cooper shares about the destructive nature of nineteenth-century industrial capitalism. The failure of the personalist remedies offered by transcendentalism led to Theodore Parker's "A Sermon of Merchants" (1846), a near-Marxist tract, and the outraged response condemning its lack of spirituality. The same failure leads to the vitality of naturalism in America, founding itself again on alienation and suggesting predictable political solutions.

CHAPTER 5

1. This is no simple matter. It is fair to say that Cooper, in his nonfictional writing, caught up in an ideology of a destined and racially determined civilization, does not fully face the fact; in these novels—even in this one mutedly—I think he does. If not, then surely it is fair to say that Cooper includes more than enough to enable his readers to face the fact.

William Kelly's underconsulted book *Plotting America's Past* provides an extended discussion of the relationship between the old civilization and the new and the dilemma these novels encapsule on that issue.

Overland's study of the revisions to this novel, taken up and extended by Brotherston, does indicate a deliberate modification of tone in Cooper's registration of the issue of Native American ownership. This in turn would fit with the growing skepticism of Cooper after his return from Europe, so ably charted by McWilliams (*Political Justice*).

2. Slotkin's argument (*The Fatal Environment*, 100) about Cooper's skill at "vanishing" the Indian seems to me a good example of the "magical behaviour" indulged in by mythic critics. While it is not exactly Barthes's balancing act, it does seem to me a remarkable descent into linear narrative that succeeds in evacuating most of what the text of *The Prairie* says.

3. *Knickerbocker Magazine* 6 (August 1835): 152–53 (quoted in Dekker and McWilliams, *Fenimore Cooper*, 177–78).

4. It does not even argue, as others did, the obligation of polite literature to uphold the dominant ideology (see Thomas, *Cross-Examinations*, 2), except insofar as this purely Epicurean view of fiction explicitly forbids political critique.

5. For a fuller treatment of this matter, see Orians ("Romance"), Rans ("Inaudible Man"), and Baym (*Novelists*).

6. See Dekker, Maxwell, Bewley, Parrington, Spiller, and McWilliams. I address this line of criticism in my preface.

7. See R. W. B. Lewis, Fiedler, Fussell, Smith, Slotkin, and Bewley.

8. If it seems hard on Peck to single him out in this way, I would like to say that it

is not personal; much the same might be observed of Fiedler, Porte, Slotkin (*Regeneration through Violence*) and, sometimes, Kolodny (*Lay*). Certainly Kolodny and Slotkin do not dismiss history and politics, and Peck shows more responsiveness to materialist concerns in his 1987 piece for *Columbia Literary History of the United States*, but even there he reinscribes his preference for a Cooper who is at his best when "social issues recede into the background" ("James Fenimore Cooper," 255), making a world "virtually immune to the forces of history" (254). His frankness about his categories and priorities allows me to use him as typical of certain tendencies, the debate over which is central to American and English studies today.

9. Bachelard, *The Poetics of Space*, xxvii, xv; cited by Peck (*World*).

10. It is not part of my purpose to speculate on the possible reasons for this change: the desire to recapture an audience, a disaffection with the political and public matters that had so preoccupied him in the 1830s (although surely the 1830s and 1840s saw no slackening in his didactic and polemical inclination), a desire to render Natty in a more idealized or mythic way, or, as Henry Nash Smith maintains, a search to resolve certain fictional problems that the romance genre had raised for Cooper's republican convictions.

11. See Rans ("Inaudible Man") for the treatment of the Indian in literary theory contemporary with Cooper. Cooper's 1839 view had been earlier expressed by Jared Sparks in 1825 (*North American Review* 20 [1825]: 211).

12. Natty's paradoxical advice to Paul Hover at the end of *The Prairie* clearly encodes the ambiguity addressed here. History's "choice" is dramatized in Mabel's choosing.

13. Given the psychoanalytic preferences of Sundquist and others, it is a little surprising that the figuring forth of an incestuous pattern here has not been pursued. I hesitate to make this point in case someone actually follows it up. Not that psychoanalysis is without its rewards: see Kolodny's reading of Natty's dream of the forest hut (*Lay*, 105–9). Other significant reflections on Natty's dream are to be found in Kelly (*Plotting America's Past*, 153), Noble ("Cooper," 424), and Peck (*World*, 79–80). Certain it is that many have found great psychosexual significance in the Mabel-Natty relationship. Porte (*The Romance*) in his comments on the *Paradise Lost* allusion in chapter 29 probably takes this line about as far as it can (or should) be taken. What is clear is that choices have consequences; whether the fear of the female other is more or less important than the underlying dilemma of civilized progress is a matter for each reader to decide.

14. In the order of composition that is clear enough, but even in the chronological order of Natty's life, we still have *Mohicans* and its massive condemnation to recall.

15. If passages like this are borne in mind as we read Swann, Godden, and Cheyfitz, it will be easier to grasp the validity of the disruptive line they are taking.

16. The question of demagoguery and Cooper's relations with the Whigs and their press are fully explored by both Waples and McWilliams and fully expressed in the Littlepage novels, *Home as Found*, *The Monikins*, and *The Crater*.

17. If the references are few, whatever the reason, they may be sufficient for the attentive reader. The critical point involves not so much the number of references but that any reference—even only one—*must* raise in a reader's mind what has gone before and cannot be erased. That is a condition that Cooper has made, intentionally or not, and he is bound by it.

18. Richard Dilworth Rust, historical introduction to *The Pathfinder*, xiii.

19. As Baym has observed ("Women," 701), *The Pathfinder* has received far less detailed attention than any of the other novels in the series. This probably has something to do with the static, almost abstract character it assumes. It is also the novel in which Natty does least (but talks vastly). I find, however, that it is far closer to the center of all the issues Cooper addresses; it is certainly much more complex than Natty's mistaken move into romantic love. When that issue is fully addressed, it is seen to be very like the others, to be emblematic of the entire set of problems the series addresses.

20. Peck eloquently expresses the view that the late works, and especially *The Deerslayer*, have a timeless quality about them. He is not alone in doing so.

21. It should not be forgotten that while Natty is always seen as a free agent who makes his own choices, he has chosen *employment* in the service of masters. He enters the economic pattern of civilization.

22. One should note here too the association of property with domesticity which is a defining mark of "settlement," of civilization. Natty's use of the word "property" is significant. Elsewhere, he draws a distinction between his property-lessness and his possession of his terrain identical to that of Emerson at the opening of *Nature*. Kelly discusses the wider implications of Mabel's marriage with great conviction (*Plotting America's Past*, 143–44).

23. Smith's reflections on Cooper's search for a hero who would not have the class complications attending the heroes of the first three novels, and Thomas's remarks on Natty as a democratic hero without the shortcomings of a threatening unpropertied underclass should be taken into account here. See n. 27 to chapter 4.

24. My difference with the psychoanalytic approaches addressed elsewhere in these notes comes down to this: they depend too heavily on Natty's dream and the critics' overlay of it. What is overlooked in the process is Natty's conscious awareness of his circumstance and the validity of his understanding.

25. On the epic dimension of Natty, *Mohicans* and *The Deerslayer* are perhaps more important. The issue is discussed fully by Brady, Darnell, Fiedler (*Love*, 188–92), Porte (*The Romance*, 39–41), and Davis.

26. The note struck in this epigraph might make us reflect on Elizabeth's preference for heart over head in *The Pioneers*, and on Temple's and the narrator's preference for head.

27. Susan Cooper, *Pages*, 157.

28. Baym ("Women," 702) says that Mabel is given the "virtues of a man"; she observes, in a sideswipe, that in male constructions "the human virtues are masculine ones." Baym is right on both counts, I think, but I do not think that the generosity of Cooper's construction of Mabel is impaired by that.

The envy and social oppression of the officers' ladies is the result of their dependent position, enthusiastically accepted.

29. Kelly expounds this point very carefully (*Plotting America's Past*, 135). It establishes Dunham's possession of his daughter as exchangeable, marriageable goods (Baym would agree) at man's disposition. What I find surprising is that neither Baym nor Kolodny make anything of Natty's role as father. If, as Baym ("Women") correctly says, Cooper returns in this novel to the theme of the "inadequate father," is not Natty, who assumes the paternal role, the adequate father who allows to Mabel—as Ishmael allows to Ellen Wade—the all-important right to choose for herself? Of course, it would be preferable if men did not have the power to confer or withhold, but, when they do, is it not better to confer? Cooper seems to me to be pointing to that. Railton denies the possibility of Natty as a "good father," constructing him in effect as inflexible and selfish (*Fenimore Cooper*, 219); that view is not sustainable in this episode of the novel. Moral flexibility would be for Natty a dubious virtue.

Perhaps the most interesting aspect of Cooper's procedure here is how unnecessary it is. Dunham could have been rendered as a benign father, mistaken in his actions, tyrannical only insofar as society bestows power on fathers. Cooper goes much further than this. A romance could have been fashioned in which Mabel, so clearly virtuous, marries the equally virtuous Natty. The vital polarizing of the paternal behavior of Dunham and Natty is not needed. It is reasonable to conclude that it was all deliberate and that the patterning of decent paternal behavior in Natty is as intentionally exemplary—for Cooper—as almost everything else that Natty does.

Kelly's attempt to make an Eden of the wilderness and his speculations on Natty as Jehovah (*Plotting America's Past*, 146) seem as farfetched as Porte's attempt to make Mabel a figurative Lilith/Eve (*The Romance*, 27).

30. I am sorry if this gives offense to those who share Peck's very well-developed point of view. I agree with him and Kolodny and others who develop the idea of a regressive Natty that there *is* such a dimension to Natty; the "yearning myth" *does* have great appeal, and Natty *is* presented often as explicitly incarnating and expressing it. But I wish to mark as forcefully as I can a difference with that exclusive view of him which masks the criticism that his exile, departure, and rejection mean. While Cooper does frequently speak of the inevitability of civilization's march, he also penetrates and deconstructs the sentiment and self-serving of the inevitabilists.

CHAPTER 6

1. I suggest that Cooper's readers are entangled in a fictional present in which they must remember what has not happened yet; a similar exercise is available in Leslie Marmon Silko's poetic evocation of "Indian witchery" and her storytelling witch who, in what amounts to a prophecy in the past about a present, says,

Okay
go ahead
laugh if you want to
but as I tell the story
it will begin to happen.
[*Ceremony*, 135]

The subject matter is very close to Cooper's and Tamenund's concerns.

2. This is not in the ordinary sense a "failure"; the inability to "concede" fully is the enabling condition that allows these books to remain problematic. To concede would eliminate the problem and leave open only the route to polemic.

3. Both the "timeless" aura and its allegorical nature are the most obvious and unavoidable aspects of this novel. This passage provides Peck with the title *A World by Itself*, and his is the most persuasive account of this aspect of the work. We should not omit to ask, against the pastoral grain, what happened to the forest chieftains.

4. Notwithstanding Cooper's "poetic" tone at this juncture, this sense of the presence of history locally and over relatively brief time spans is not unfamiliar to anyone who has lived in North America outside the metropolitan centers. It is present today in Iowa, Wyoming, Virginia, and Ontario.

5. Despite the emphasis of this passage on the republic, it stresses equally continuity with the past. This forms the central concern of Kelly's study of these novels. The speed of the process that the passage emphasizes might make the reader who is fully conscious of the destruction that attended the colony's progress impose almost unwittingly a sense of the violence that is as large a feature of this novel as the pastoral so many critics find in it. See Kelly (*Plotting America's Past*, 169), Martin ("Beginnings and Endings"), Peck (*World*), Kolodny (*Lay*, 115), and many others.

6. Harry may be a confused fool—and worse—but there is a sense here in which he is right. See Thomas on the way in which law legitimizes interest, not necessarily or exclusively the right and the just. If Harry is confused he has a justification for being so; his confusion clarifies the criticism of civilization's law this book offers.

McWilliams puts the matter succinctly (*Political Justice*, 281); he sees society's failure, Natty's lack of power to alter it, and the impact that the pervasive violence of a civilization in the making has on Natty's Christian principle. One of the most interesting things about McWilliams's book is the way in which his disinclination to simplify what the text contains comes into conflict with his overrigid systematization of the legal issues.

7. See Swann, Godden, Cheyfitz, Thomas, and McWilliams, all of whom deal with the question of civilization's laws and their partiality from differing perspectives.

8. When Natty speaks in this vein, he lends support to Axelrad's master narrative of decline.

If what I suggest here is true and if it is present in Cooper much earlier, should McWilliams's "reactionary" stage in Cooper's career come as a surprise (*Political Justice*)? Should not Axelrad (*History*) "read back" the later phases of his narrative to *The Spy* and *The Pioneers*?

9. See Peck (*World*), and Kolodny (*Lay*, 112, 115).

10. Tompkins mounts a convincing defense of and qualification of the didactic position in *Sensational Designs*.

11. McWilliams, while fully accepting that society does not practice its own ideals as incarnated in Natty, speaks of those heroes of Cooper like Natty: "Retreating to maintain their own values, or simply to be alone, such men become stoics laced with self-pity, activists with a wide streak of fatalism" (*Political Justice*, 61). To make such a judgment is as much an evasion as to make the withdrawal into the "infantile pre-sexuality" argument. It enables a disregard—or at least a disparagement—of Natty that Cooper nowhere endorses. Kelly argues effectively and at length not merely Natty's mythic, allegorical, idealized development but also Cooper's "failure" to imagine a figure to reconcile "Natty's dispute with civilization" (*Plotting America's Past*, 165). And all that is true, except that it begs the question that Cooper *attempted* to or wanted to imagine such a figure in his fiction. Spengemann provides another example of a critic who assumes Cooper's overriding intention to "resolve" (*The Adventurous Muse*, 114).

It seems to me that Kelly and McWilliams do not fail to see what is in the novels, but rather impose an assumed intention on Cooper. It is truly remarkable how many critics assume an obligation or desire of Cooper to reconcile in the novels. The reconciliations Cooper does fashion are usually seen as unsatisfying: as Kelly correctly says, "The marriages he describes are themselves the product of a mythic consciousness. The plenitude they realize, their reconciliation of freedom and restraint, is a comforting fiction which discharges cultural anxiety and achieves a false note of closure." As he insists, "Cooper's detachment from the myth he creates has gone largely unnoticed" (*Plotting America's Past*, 173). Exactly so, but we must not be tempted to substitute another myth for him and attach him to that. Kelly's implication of artistic intent (and he may well be right) masks what Cooper has done to make the conclusions appear as unsatisfactory as they do. It should also perhaps be added that such marriages do convey significance in important ways that are far from romantic in their concentration of property, power, inheritance, and stability.

12. There is a wide measure of consensus about this novel's presentation of a rite of passage. Kelly raises the issue that occupies many others, including Bewley and Yvor Winters, but maintains, unlike most other critics, that Cooper is detached from the myth into which so many of his sympathetic critics have celebrated his withdrawal (*Plotting America's Past*, 170). He cites, for example, Philbrick's view of *The Deerslayer* as a "retreat from the oppressive reality of the here and now" (*Plotting America's Past*, 175). Kelly suggests that by taking the mythic route so resolutely and thus separating Natty, Cooper disallows the earlier "fantasy" of resolution. I agree about the effect of separation but not that the earlier resolutions

are fantasies. They are that only if one assumes the intention to resolve problems through romance closures. I see no reason to do that.

13. My view of this issue is very different from that of Robert Clark (*History*, 95–109). His provocative book argues that the evident confusion about racial characteristics is clearly racist and even in apparently benign forms like Natty's reveals a racial/social prejudice that legitimizes white power and appropriation. I agree with him entirely on that. However, arguing on biographical, historical, and psychological grounds, Clark insists that Cooper *represses* his white guilt in the matter. That seems to me a serious error. He makes Natty's confusion Cooper's, when in fact it is Cooper who inexorably *reveals* the contradictions, making us aware of civilization's hypocrisy and self-betrayal; Natty too, whatever confusions he may be subject to, is hardly ambiguous or slow to speak plainly on this issue. This chapter—and indeed this book—insists on that above all, and *The Deerslayer* and the series contain, on their surface, all that we need to reach this conclusion. It would be more valid, I think, to see the confusions of principle that Cooper relates and that Natty in some matters embodies as the result of the social fracturing and legitimized violence of civilization about which Clark and I would agree. In any case, it seems to me wide of the mark to suggest that in *The Deerslayer* Cooper is "in literary retreat from the aggression of political life and the contradictions of his own ideological situation" (Clark, *History*, 97). Clark makes no mention of Warley.

14. It is noteworthy that in this passage—virtually a hymn of praise—Cooper gratuitously introduces a generalized, but very precisely expressed, digression on the ubiquity of prejudice. It is perhaps a further indication of how important in this novel racial attitudes, individual and institutionalized, are.

15. The word "indifference" is used also about Harry's response to his own act of murder; it indicates a lack of moral discrimination that unites Judith and Harry. It is entirely at one with her being able to contemplate a union with Natty but undertaking to be, in the end, Warley's mistress.

16. Yet again Cooper implicitly calls in question the facile distinction between heart and head, instinct and reason. He is distrustful not of human reason but only of a false and oversimplifying distinction, or of the arrogance that assumes that truth emerges only from reason.

17. See Brady, and Davis for a full discussion of this issue.

18. Philip Fisher's discussion of this episode is the most convincing I have seen (*Hard Facts*, 63–68). Kelly, too, offers a careful analysis (*Plotting America's Past*, 177–79). Hutter's chest, of course, is a plain invitation to exegesis that few are disposed to decline.

19. I cannot accept Pearce's view that Natty's fate is a "tragic story"; Pearce seems to argue that because it was not intended to "crush such a man as Natty," his fate is endowed with a kind of tragic inevitability ("The Leatherstocking Tales," 527). Civilization was not "an evil force," he says, according to Cooper. While I agree that Cooper does not reject civilization as evil *directly*, insofar as it deliberately acts against its declared principles, civilization is as open to as harsh a

condemnation as Harry and Hutter are. Can it be seriously doubted that civilization clearly does act against its declared principles? Insofar as it does it is indeed
evil. "Westward expansion and progress" bring all sorts of good things; they also
bring evil. Cooper tells us that over and over again.

20. While it is difficult to imagine Cooper as a transcendentalist, this passage
seems like a digest of Emerson's *Nature*. Perhaps it is only Wordsworthian.

21. McWilliams too points to the centrality of scalping in this novel and its
betrayal of Christian principle: "The white Christians have sunk to legalizing
Indian codes of vengeance" (*Political Justice*, 278). Natty's prejudice *might* put it
that way, but I do not think that we should. In fact, Cooper's whole thrust in this is
to suggest not a sinking of whites to the level of reds but rather the exercise of a
peculiarly white civilized vice, as corruptive of Indian as of white. For the Indian,
after all, a scalp may be a battle honor, but for the colony it equals money. What
did the Christians bring with them? Commodity exchange. Life itself may be
commodity. Cooper might not have known what to do about that, but he knew
enough to be disgusted.

22. Cooper's use of Oliver's word "cupidity" in relation to scalping and the
colony's encouragement of it is significant. He returns to the accusation of greed
repeatedly. Here, racism and greed enable one another.

23. Gross and comic as Harry is at this moment, bent on scalping and complaining of the bestiality of his assailants, his insistence that his is a "legal operation" is
as correct as the legality of Doolittle and Jones. If Swann is right, even Judge
Temple used game laws to abridge the rights of others, much to his own advantage.
The sanctity of the law is a difficult doctrine to accept throughout the series.

24. It is tempting to see Judith as a free woman. Baym ("Women") is correct, I
think, in pointing to the constraints that "lack of social position," of being
"unmarriageable," place upon her. Her freedom is limited to being an opportunist
"in a man's world." Cooper, surely, is relentlessly realistic in disposing of her.

25. Obviously, Peck's notion that Judith's imposture is merely a game, part of a
"world of play" (*A World by Itself*, 69), has little appeal for me. It is surprising that
Kelly finds it so compelling. At least, it should be seen that the play—if it is that—
is confirmed by the terrifying reality it plays prologue to.

26. McWilliams sees the last two novels, with their idealization of Natty, as
Cooper's disgusted reaction to the world he found on his return from Europe
(*Political Justice*, 222). However, his conclusion is, "*The Deerslayer* is not so much
'Cooper's idyll' or 'a forest myth' as it is a ghastly bloodbath lightened by glimpses
of powerless virtue. By entering Eden, man corrupts it" (289). McWilliams, for all
his love of system, has a wonderful capacity for unembarrassed inconsistency. The
greatest merit of his excellent book is its willingness to follow where the texts lead.

27. For a fuller examination of the treatment of Indians in white fiction, see
Rans, "Inaudible Man."

WORKS CITED

Adams, Hazard. "Canons." *Critical Inquiry* 14 (1988): 748–64.

Adams, Henry. *A History of the U.S.A. during the Administrations of Jefferson and Madison.* 2 vols. New York: Library of America, 1986.

Ames, Fisher. *The Dangers of American Liberty.* In *Literature of the Early Republic,* edited by Edwin H. Cady, pp. 108–18. New York: Rinehart, 1950.

Ames, Nathaniel. *Almanacks, 1726–1775.* Cleveland: n.p., 1891.

Anderson, Perry. *In the Tracks of Historical Materialism.* Chicago: University of Chicago Press, 1984.

Axelrad, Allan M. *History and Utopia: A Study of the World View of James Fenimore Cooper.* Norwood, Pa.: Norwood Editions, 1978.

———. "The Order of the Leatherstocking Tales: D. H. Lawrence, David Noble, and the Iron Trap of History." *American Literature* 54 (1982): 189–211.

———. "Wish Fulfillment in the Wilderness: D. H. Lawrence and the Leatherstocking Tales." *American Quarterly* 39 (1987): 563–85.

Bachelard, Gaston. *The Poetics of Space.* Boston: Beacon, 1964.

Barthes, Roland. *Mythologies.* London: Paladin, 1973.

Baym, Nina. *Novelists, Readers, and Reviewers: Responses to Fiction in Antebellum America.* Ithaca: Cornell University Press, 1984.

———. "The Women of Cooper's Leatherstocking Tales." *American Quarterly* 23 (1971): 696–709.

Beard, James Franklin. "Cooper and the Revolutionary Mythos." *Early American Literature* 11 (1976): 84–104.

———. Introduction to *The Deerslayer,* by James Fenimore Cooper. New York: Harper, 1960.

Becker, George J., ed. *Documents of Modern Literary Realism.* Princeton: Princeton University Press, 1963.

Bell, Michael Davitt. *The Development of American Romance: The Sacrifice of Relation.* Chicago: University of Chicago Press, 1980.

Bellah, Robert N., Richard Madsen, William M. Sullivan, Ann Swidler, and Steven M. Tipton. *Habits of the Heart.* Berkeley: University of California Press, 1985.

Béranger, Jean F. "The Desire for Communication: Narrator and Narratee in *Letters from an American Farmer*." *Early American Literature* 12 (1977): 73–85.

Bercovitch, Sacvan. *The American Jeremiad*. Madison: University of Wisconsin Press, 1978.

Bewley, Marius. *The Eccentric Design: Form in the Classic American Novel*. London: Chatto and Windus, 1959.

Brady, Charles A. "James Fenimore Cooper: Myth-Maker and Christian Romancer." In *American Classics Reconsidered*, edited by Harold C. Gardiner, S.J., pp. 59–97. New York: Scribner's, 1958.

Brooks, Van Wyck. *The World of Washington Irving*. New York: Dutton, 1944.

Brotherston, Gordon. "*The Prairie* and Cooper's Invention of the West." In *James Fenimore Cooper: New Critical Essays*, edited by Robert Clark, pp. 162–86. London: Vision Press, 1985.

Cady, Edwin H., ed. *Literature of the Early Republic*. New York: Rinehart, 1950.

Chevignard, Bernard. "St. John de Crèvecoeur in the Looking Glass." *Early American Literature* 19 (1984): 173–90.

Cheyfitz, Eric. "Literally White, Figuratively Red: The Frontier of Translation in *The Pioneers*." In *James Fenimore Cooper: New Critical Essays*, edited by Robert Clark, pp. 55–95. London: Vision Press, 1985.

———. "*Tarzan of the Apes*: U.S. Foreign Policy in the Twentieth Century." *American Literary History* 1 (1989): 339–60.

Clark, Robert. *History, Ideology and Myth in American Fiction, 1823–52*. London: Macmillan, 1984.

———, ed. *James Fenimore Cooper: New Critical Essays*. London: Vision Press, 1985.

Cooper, James Fenimore. *The American Democrat* (1838). New York: Vintage, 1956.

———. *Cooper's Novels*. 32 vols. New York: W. A. Townsend, 1859–61.

———. *The Deerslayer*. London: n.p., 1899.

———. *The Deerslayer*. New York: Harper, 1960.

———. *Letters and Journals*. Edited by James F. Beard. 6 vols. Cambridge: Harvard University Press, 1960–68.

———. *Notions of the Americans, Picked Up by a Travelling Bachelor* (1828). New York: Ungar, 1963.

Cooper, Susan Fenimore. *Pages and Pictures from the Writings of James Fenimore Cooper*. New York: W. A. Townsend, 1861.

———. Preface to *The Deerslayer*, by James Fenimore Cooper. London: n.p., 1899.

Crèvecoeur, J. Hector St. John de. *Letters from an American Farmer*. Edited by Albert E. Stone. New York: Penguin Viking, 1981.

Cunningham, Mary E., ed. *James Fenimore Cooper: A Re-Appraisal*. Cooperstown: New York State Historical Association, 1954.

Darnell, Donald. "Uncas as Hero: The Ubi Sunt Formula in *The Last of the Mohicans*." *American Literature* 37 (1965): 259–66.

Davidson, Cathy. *The Revolution and the Word*. New York: Oxford University Press, 1987.

Davis, David Brion. "The Deerslayer, A Democratic Knight of the Wilderness." In *Twelve Original Essays on Great American Novels*, edited by Charles Shapiro, pp. 1–15. Detroit: Wayne State University Press, 1958.

Dekker, George. *James Fenimore Cooper: The Novelist*. London: Routledge, 1967.

Dekker, George, and John P. McWilliams, eds. *Fenimore Cooper: The Critical Heritage*. London: Routledge, 1973.

Dryden, Edgar A. *The Form of American Romance*. Baltimore: Johns Hopkins University Press, 1988.

Dwight, Timothy. "Greenfield Hill." In *The Connecticut Wits*, edited by Vernon L. Parrington, pp. 183–247. New York: Crowell, 1969.

Eliot, T. S. *Four Quartets*. London: Faber, 1959.

Elliott, Emory, ed. *Columbia Literary History of the United States*. New York: Columbia University Press, 1987.

Ferguson, Robert A. *Law and Letters in American Culture*. Cambridge: Harvard University Press, 1984.

Fiedler, Leslie A. *Love and Death in the American Novel*. New York: Criterion, 1960.

Fields, Wayne. "Beyond Definition: A Reading of *The Prairie*." In *James Fenimore Cooper: A Collection of Critical Essays*, edited by Wayne Fields, pp. 93–111. Englewood Cliffs, N.J.: Prentice Hall, 1979.

———, ed. *James Fenimore Cooper: A Collection of Critical Essays*. Englewood Cliffs, N.J.: Prentice Hall, 1979.

Fisher, Philip. *Hard Facts: Setting and Form in the American Novel*. New York: Oxford University Press, 1985.

Franklin, Wayne. *The New World of James Fenimore Cooper*. Chicago: University of Chicago Press, 1982.

Freneau, Philip. *Poems of Freneau*. Edited by Harry Hayden Clark. New York: Harcourt, Brace, 1929.

Fuentes, Carlos. "Prometheus Unbound." In *Radical Perspectives in the Arts*, edited by Lee Baxandall, pp. 142–58. London: Penguin, 1972.

Fussell, Edwin. *Frontier: American Literature and the American West*. Princeton: Princeton University Press, 1965.

Geertz, Clifford. *The Interpretation of Cultures*. New York: Basic Books, 1973.

Gilmore, Michael T. *American Romanticism and the Marketplace*. Chicago: University of Chicago Press, 1985.

Godden, Richard. "Pioneer Properties, or 'What's in a Hut?'" In *James Fenimore Cooper: New Critical Essays*, edited by Robert Clark, pp. 121–43. London: Vision Press, 1985.

Goetzmann, William H. "James Fenimore Cooper: The Prairie." In *Landmarks *of American Writing: Voice of America Forum Lectures*, edited by Hennig Cohen, pp. 75–87. Washington, D.C.: United States Information Service, 1970.

Graff, Gerald. *Professing Literature: An Institutional History.* Chicago: University of Chicago Press, 1987.

Gramsci, Antonio. *Selections from the Prison Notebooks.* Edited and translated by Quentin Hoare and Geoffrey Nowell Smith. New York: International Publishers, 1971.

Green, Martin. *The Great American Adventure.* Boston: Beacon, 1984.

Grossman, James. *James Fenimore Cooper.* New York: Sloan, 1949.

Hedges, William L. "The Myth of the Republic and the Theory of American Literature." *Prospects* 4 (1979): 101–20.

———. "The Old World Yet: Writers and Writing in Post-Revolutionary America." *Early American Literature* 16 (1981): 3–18.

———. "Toward a Theory of American Literature, 1765–1800." *Early American Literature* 4 (1970): 5–14.

Hollinger, David A. "The Canon and Its Keeper." In *In the American Province: Studies in the History and Historiography of Ideas*, pp. 74–91. Bloomington: Indiana University Press, 1985.

Horsman, Reginald. *Race and Manifest Destiny: The Origins of American Racial Anglo-Saxonism.* Cambridge: Harvard University Press, 1981.

Howard, David. "James Fenimore Cooper's Leatherstocking Tales: 'Without a Cross.'" In *Tradition and Tolerance in Nineteenth Century Fiction*, by David Howard, John Lucas, and John Goode, pp. 9–54. London: Routledge, 1966.

Ickstadt, Heinz. "Instructing the American Democrat: Cooper and the Concept of Popular Fiction in Jacksonian America." In *James Fenimore Cooper: New Critical Essays*, edited by Robert Clark, pp. 15–37. London: Vision Press, 1985.

Irving, Washington. *The Sketch Book.* New York: New American Library, 1961.

James, Henry. *The Notebooks of Henry James.* Edited by F. O. Matthiessen and Kenneth B. Murdock. New York: Oxford University Press, 1947.

Jehlen, Myra. "New World Epics." *Salmagundi* 36 (1977): 49–68.

Jennings, Francis. *The Ambiguous Iroquois Empire: The Covenant Chain Confederation of Indian Tribes with English Colonies.* New York: Norton, 1984.

———. *Empire of Fortune: Crowns, Colonies and Tribes in the Seven Years War in America.* New York: Norton, 1988.

———. *The Invasion of America: Indians, Colonialism, and the Cant of Conquest.* Chapel Hill: University of North Carolina Press, 1975.

Kehler, Joel R. "Architectural Dialecticism in Cooper's *The Pioneers*." *Texas Studies in Literature and Language* 18 (1976): 124–34.

Kelly, William P. *Plotting America's Past: Fenimore Cooper and the Leatherstocking Tales.* Carbondale: Southern Illinois University Press, 1983.

Kolodny, Annette. "The Integrity of Memory: Creating a New Literary History of the United States." *American Literature* 57 (1985): 291–300.

———. *The Lay of the Land: Metaphor as Experience and History in American Life and Letters.* Chapel Hill: University of North Carolina Press, 1975.

Kundera, Milan. *The Book of Laughter and Forgetting.* New York: Knopf, 1980.

Lawrence, D. H. *Studies in Classic American Literature.* New York: Anchor, 1953.

Lewis, Merrill. "Lost and Found in the Wilderness: The Desert Metaphor in Cooper's *The Prairie.*" *Western American Literature* 5 (1970): 195–204.

Lewis, R. W. B. *The American Adam: Innocence, Tragedy, and Tradition in the Nineteenth Century.* Chicago: University of Chicago Press, 1955.

Lukács, Georg. *The Historical Novel.* London: Merlin, 1962.

———. *The Theory of the Novel.* Cambridge: MIT Press, 1971.

McWilliams, John P. *Political Justice in a Republic: James Fenimore Cooper's America.* Berkeley: University of California Press, 1972.

———. "Red Satan: Cooper and the American Indian Epic." In *James Fenimore Cooper: New Critical Essays,* edited by Robert Clark, pp. 143–62. London: Vision Press, 1985.

Marcuse, Herbert. *Negations.* Boston: Beacon, 1968.

Martin, Terence. "Beginnings and Endings in the Leatherstocking Tales." *Nineteenth Century Fiction* 33 (1978): 69–87.

———. "From the Ruins of History: *The Last of the Mohicans.*" *Novel* 2 (Spring 1969): 221–29.

Marx, Leo. *The Machine in the Garden.* New York: Oxford University Press, 1964.

———. "Pastoral Ideals and City Troubles." *Journal of General Education* 20 (1969): 251–71.

Maxwell, D. E. S. *American Fiction: The Intellectual Background.* London: Routledge, 1963.

Melville, Herman. *Pierre, or The Ambiguities.* New York: Grove, 1957.

Meyers, Marvin. *The Jacksonian Persuasion.* Stanford: Stanford University Press, 1960.

Michaels, Walter Benn, ed. *The American Renaissance Reconsidered.* Baltimore: Johns Hopkins University Press, 1984.

———. *The Gold Standard and the Logic of Naturalism.* Berkeley: University of California Press, 1987.

Miller, Perry. *The Life of the Mind in America.* New York: Harcourt, Brace, 1965.

———, ed. *The Transcendentalists.* Cambridge: Harvard University Press, 1950.

Mills, Nicolaus. *American and English Fiction in the Nineteenth Century: An Antigenre Critique and Comparison.* Bloomington: Indiana University Press, 1973.

Mitchell, W. J. T., ed. *On Narrative*. Chicago: University of Chicago Press, 1981.

Mohr, James C. "Calculated Disillusionment: Crèvecoeur's *Letters* Reconsidered." *South Atlantic Quarterly* 69 (1970): 354–63.

Moore, Arthur K. *The Frontier Mind*. Lexington: University of Kentucky Press, 1957.

Motley, Warren. *The American Abraham*. New York: Cambridge University Press, 1987.

Nevins, Allan, ed. *The Leatherstocking Saga*. New York: Modern Library, 1966.

Nixon, Rob. "Caribbean and African Appropriations of *The Tempest*." *Critical Inquiry* 13 (1987): 557–78.

Noble, David. "Cooper, Leatherstocking, and the Death of the American Adam." *American Quarterly* 16 (1964): 419–31.

Orians, G. Harrison. "Censure of Fiction in American Romances and Magazines, 1789–1810." *PMLA* 52 (1937): 195–214.

———. "The Romance Ferment after *Waverley*." *American Literature* 3 (1932): 408–31.

Outland, Ethel R. *The "Effingham" Libels on Cooper*. University of Wisconsin Studies in Language and Literature. Madison: University of Wisconsin Press, 1929.

Overland, Orm. *James Fenimore Cooper's "The Prairie."* New York: Humanities Press, 1973.

Paley, Grace. *Later the Same Day*. New York: Farrar Straus Giroux, 1985.

Parker, Theodore. "A Sermon of Merchants." In *Speeches, Addresses and Occasional Sermons*, 1:163–200, 2 vols. Boston: n.p., 1852.

Parrington, Vernon L. *Main Currents in American Thought*. 2 vols. New York: Harcourt, Brace, 1927.

Patterson, Mark R. *Authority, Autonomy, and Representation in American Literature, 1776–1865*. Princeton: Princeton University Press, 1988.

Paul, Jay S. "The Education of Elizabeth Temple." *Studies in the Novel* 9 (1977): 187–93.

Pearce, Roy Harvey. "The Leatherstocking Tales Re-Examined." *South Atlantic Quarterly* 46 (1947): 524–56.

Peck, Daniel. "James Fenimore Cooper and the Writers of the Frontier." In *Columbia Literary History of the United States*, edited by Emory Elliott, pp. 240–67. New York: Columbia University Press, 1987.

———. *A World by Itself: The Pastoral Moment in Cooper's Fiction*. New Haven: Yale University Press 1977.

Philbrick, Thomas. "Cooper's *The Pioneers*: Origins and Structure." *PMLA* 79 (1964): 579–93.

———. *St. John de Crèvecoeur*. New York: Twayne, 1970.

Porte, Joel. *The Romance in America*. Middletown: Wesleyan University Press, 1969.

Porter, Carolyn. *Seeing and Being.* Middletown: Wesleyan University Press, 1981.

Pudaloff, Ross J. "Cooper's Genres and American Problems." *ELH* 50 (1983): 711–27.

Railton, Stephen. *Fenimore Cooper: A Study of His Life and Imagination.* Princeton: Princeton University Press, 1978.

Rans, Geoffrey. "Inaudible Man: The Indian in the Theory and Practice of White Fiction." *Canadian Review of American Studies* 7 (1977): 104–15.

———. "A Prolegomenon to Leatherstocking: The Importance of Crèvecoeur— Breaking the Tablets, Destroying the Text." *Canadian Review of American Studies* 20 (1989): 77–96.

Reising, Russell J. "Reconstructing Parrington." *American Quarterly* 41 (1989): 155–63.

———. *The Unusable Past: Theory and the Study of American Literature.* New York: Methuen, 1986.

Ringe, Donald. *James Fenimore Cooper.* New York: Twayne, 1962.

Rogin, Michael Paul. *Fathers and Children: Andrew Jackson and the Subjugation of the American Indian.* New York: Knopf, 1975.

———. *Subversive Genealogy: The Politics and Art of Herman Melville.* New York: Knopf, 1983.

Ross, John F. *The Social Criticism of Fenimore Cooper.* Berkeley: University of California Press, 1933.

Rucker, Mary E. "Natural, Tribal and Civil Law in Cooper's *The Prairie.*" *Western American Literature* 7 (1972): 215–22.

Said, Edward W. *The World, the Text and the Critic.* Cambridge: Harvard University Press, 1983.

Seltzer, Mark. *Henry James and the Art of Power.* Ithaca: Cornell University Press, 1984.

Showalter, Elaine. *The New Feminist Criticism: Essays on Women, Literature and Theory.* New York: Pantheon, 1985.

Silko, Leslie Marmon. *Ceremony.* New York: Viking, 1977.

Simpson, David. "Literary Critics and 'History.'" *Critical Inquiry* 14 (1988): 721–47.

Slotkin, Richard. *The Fatal Environment: The Myth of the Frontier in the Age of Industrialization, 1800–1890.* Middletown: Wesleyan University Press, 1985.

———. *Regeneration through Violence: The Mythology of the American Frontier, 1600–1860.* Middletown: Wesleyan University Press, 1973.

Slotkin, Richard, and James K. Folson, eds. *So Dreadfull a Judgment: Puritan Responses to King Philip's War.* Middletown: Wesleyan University Press, 1978.

Smith, Henry Nash. *Virgin Land: The American West as Symbol and Myth.* New York: Vintage, 1950.

Spengemann, William C. *The Adventurous Muse: The Poetics of American Fiction, 1789–1900.* New Haven: Yale University Press, 1977.

Spiller, Robert E. *Fenimore Cooper: Critic of His Times.* New York: Russell, 1963.

———. "Second Thoughts on Cooper as a Social Critic." In *James Fenimore Cooper: A Re-Appraisal,* edited by Mary E. Cunningham, pp. 172–90. Cooperstown: New York State Historical Association, 1954.

Stone, Albert E., Jr. "Crèvecoeur's *Letters* and the Beginnings of an American Literature." *Emory University Quarterly* 18 (1962): 197–213.

Sundquist, Eric J. *Home as Found: Authority and Genealogy in Nineteenth Century American Literature.* Baltimore: Johns Hopkins University Press, 1979.

Swann, Charles. "Guns Mean Democracy: *The Pioneers* and the Game Laws." In *James Fenimore Cooper: New Critical Essays,* edited by Robert Clark, pp. 96–120. London: Vision Press, 1985.

Thomas, Brook. *Cross-Examinations of Law and Literature: Cooper, Hawthorne, Stowe and Melville.* New York: Cambridge University Press, 1987.

Tichi, Cecilia. *New World, New Earth: Environmental Reform in American Literature from the Puritans through Whitman.* New Haven: Yale University Press, 1979.

Tocqueville, Alexis de. *Democracy in America.* 2 vols. New York: Knopf, 1953.

Tompkins, Jane. *Sensational Designs: The Cultural Work of American Fiction, 1790–1860.* New York: Oxford University Press, 1985.

Trilling, Lionel. *The Liberal Imagination.* London: Secker, 1951.

Vanderbilt, Kermit. *American Literature and the Academy.* Philadelphia: University of Pennsylvania Press, 1986.

Wallace, James D. *Early Cooper and His Audience.* New York: Columbia University Press, 1986.

Waples, Dorothy. *The Whig Myth of Fenimore Cooper.* New Haven: Yale University Press, 1938.

Wasserstrom, William. "Cooper, Freud, and the Origins of Culture." *The American Imago* 17 (1960): 423–37.

Webb, Igor. *From Custom to Capital.* Ithaca: Cornell University Press, 1981.

White, Hayden. "The Value of Narrativity in the Representation of Reality." In *On Narrative,* edited by W. J. T. Mitchell, pp. 1–23. Chicago: University of Chicago Press, 1981.

Whitman, Walt. *Leaves of Grass.* Comprehensive Reader's Edition. Edited by Harold W. Blodgett and Sculley Bradley. New York: New York University Press, 1965.

Williams, Raymond. *Problems in Materialism and Culture.* London: NLB, 1980.

Winston, Robert P. " 'Strange Order of Things!': The Journey to Chaos in *Letters from an American Farmer.*" *Early American Literature* 19 (1984): 249–68.

Yeazell, Ruth Bernard, ed. *Sex, Politics, and Science in the Nineteenth-Century Novel.* Selected Papers from the English Institute, 1983–84. New series 10. Baltimore: Johns Hopkins University Press, 1985.

INDEX